MW00810177

The Romanian Battlefront
in World War I

MODERN WAR STUDIES

Theodore A. Wilson
General Editor

Raymond A. Callahan
J. Garry Clifford
Jacob W. Kipp
Allan R. Millett
Carol Reardon
Dennis Showalter
David R. Stone
Series Editors

The Romanian Battlefront in World War I

Glenn E. Torrey

 University Press of Kansas

© 2011 by the University Press of Kansas

All rights reserved

Published by the University Press of Kansas (Lawrence, Kansas 66045), which was organized by the Kansas Board of Regents and is operated and funded by Emporia State University, Fort Hays State University, Kansas State University, Pittsburg State University, the University of Kansas, and Wichita State University

Library of Congress Cataloging-in-Publication Data

Torrey, Glenn E.
The Romanian battlefront in World War I / Glenn E. Torrey.
  p. cm. — (Modern war studies)
Includes bibliographical references and index.
ISBN 978-0-7006-1839-2 (cloth : alk. paper)
1. World War, 1914–1918—Campaigns—Romania. 2. Romania—History—1914–1918.
I. Title.
D565.A2T68 2011
940.4'147—dc23
                    2011040826

British Library Cataloguing-in-Publication Data is available.

Printed in the United States of America

10 9 8 7 6 5 4 3 2

The paper used in this publication is recycled and contains 30 percent postconsumer waste. It is acid free and meets the minimum requirements of the American National Standard for Permanence of Paper for Printed Library Materials Z39.48-1992.

Contents

Illustrations

MAPS

PHOTOGRAPHS

TABLES

Preface

As I have pointed out elsewhere, Romania's participation in World War I had a far-reaching impact on all the belligerents. Both the Central Powers and the Allied Coalition diverted substantial military resources to the Romanian Front, to the detriment of operations elsewhere. Moreover, the promises of territorial acquisitions that the Entente Powers reluctantly gave to win their new ally tied their hands in negotiating a peace settlement later.[1] The Romanians, for their part, suffered through a crushing defeat in 1916, a hard-won trial by fire on the battlefield in 1917, and the traumatic impact of the Russian Revolution, which forced them into a disastrous separate peace with the Central Powers. The eventual victory of the Entente allowed them to achieve the war aims for which they fought.

Romanian historians, naturally, have always given prominent attention to the events on the Romanian Front from 1916 to 1918, which were decisive for the creation of modern Romania. During the interwar period, historians of other nations also devoted substantial attention to the subject. Their accounts, like the Romanian ones, be they official histories or independent studies, reflected their particular national perspective in both emphasis and documentation. After World War II, while Romanian historians continued to elaborate on their nation's role in the Great War, other historians gave it scant attention, neglecting 1917 altogether. This was partly the result of lack of interest, but it was also related to the difficulty in accessing Romanian libraries and archives. As the latter situation began to ease slowly beginning in the 1960s, I was able, over the succeeding 30 years, to make a series of extended visits, not only to Romanian archival repositories but also to those of its one-time allies and enemies. Using this documentation, I have already written about a number of specific aspects of the theme of Romania and the belligerents during 1914–1918. In this book, I seek to present a balanced survey of military operations and closely related events on the Romanian Front during 1916–1918 that includes the perspective of the Central Powers as well as that of Romania and its allies. The neglected 1917 campaign is given the attention it deserves.

Although this study draws on some of my earlier writings, it is a new synthesis, covering new topics and incorporating additional archival sources and recent secondary literature. Thus it is not an exhaustive operational history, but I believe it presents sufficient detail and maps to enable readers to understand strategic and tactical decisions and follow their consequences on the battlefield. It also seeks to portray a slice of the human side of the war by reference to published and unpublished personal documents. Because most readers are unlikely to have a detailed knowledge of Romania in this era, I have included background information about the country and its leaders. It is my hope that they, and even some academics whose specialties lie elsewhere, will gain a more complete understanding of this often overlooked chapter in the history of the First World War, one whose influence continues today.

I would like to call the reader's attention to the following. First, for consistency, all dates are given according to the Gregorian calendar in use today, even though Romania and Russia utilized the Julian calendar at that time. Second, while the terms *Entente* and *Allies* are used interchangeably to designate Romania's brothers-in-arms until 1917, the latter designation is used after Russia left the war. Finally, the spelling of place-names in the text, and in the maps where possible, follows the Romanian form with a few exceptions—for example, Bucharest, Wallachia, Moldavia, Transylvania, Danube, Carpathian, and Bessarabia, which are given in the accepted English version.

The research behind this book has been made possible by multiple grants from the International Research and Exchanges Board, the Fulbright Commission, the U.S. Department of Education, the American Philosophical Association, and sabbatical leaves, as well as other support from Emporia State University. In addition, I am indebted to more friends and colleagues than I can acknowledge individually here, but I want to express appreciation for the help and encouragement of Keith Hitchins, Paul

Michelson, Dennis Showalter, Ernest Latham Jr., Dan Dimancescu, Opry
Dragalina Popa, Adrian Pandea, and Jean-Claude Dubois. I owe special
thanks to Jacque Fehr of Emporia State University for her indispensable assistance in guiding this project from my handwritten drafts through the
word processor to the final draft. I also want to express my appreciation
to those at the University Press of Kansas who contributed to bringing this
book to publication, including Karen Hellekson, Larisa Martin, Susan
Schott, and especially editor in chief Michael Briggs. I wish to acknowledge
the contribution, above all, of my wife, Audrey, who shared much of the
research travel with me and patiently supported the long process of writing up the results.

Glenn E. Torrey
Professor of History, Emeritus
Emporia State University

Abbreviations

AA	Archiv des Auswärtigen Amts, Berlin
AC	Army Corps
AD	Archives Diplomatiques, Ministère des Affaires Étrangères, Paris
AMR	Arhivele Militare Române
AOK	Armeeoberkommando (Austro-Hungarian High Command)
AN (Bucharest)	Arhivele Naţionale Istoric Centrale
AS (Rome)	Archivio Storico Diplomatico del Ministero degli Affari Esteri
BA (Bucharest)	Biblioteca Academiei
BA (Koblenz)	Bundesarchiv, Koblenz
BA/MA	Bundesarchiv/Militärarchiv, Freiburg
BCS	Biblioteca Centrală de Stat
BGK	Bulgarian High Command
CD	Cavalry Division
CTT	Comandamentul Trupelor din Transilvania
HHStA	Österreichisches Staatsarchiv, Haus-, Hof-, und Staatsarchiv
CQG	Grande quartier général (French High Command)
ID	Infantry Division
IMPR	*Istoria Militară a Poporului Român*
IR	Infantry Regiment
KA (Munich)	Bayerisches Hauptstaatsarchiv, Kriegsarchiv

KA (Stuttgart)	Württembergisches Hauptstaatsarchiv, Kriegsarchiv
KA (Vienna)	Österreichisches Staatsarchiv, Kriegsarchiv
Kmdo	Kommando (Command)
AMAER	Arhiva Ministerului Afacerilor Externe Române, Bucharest
MB	Mountain Battalion
MCG	Marele Cartier General (Romanian High Command)
MMF	Mission Militaire Française
MMO	*Mărăşti, Mărăşeşti, Oituz: Documente militare*
MSM	Marele Stat Major (Romanian General Staff)
NA	Nachrichten Abteilung
NARA	National Archives and Records Administration, Washington, D.C.
NFA	Neue Feldakten
NO	Nachrichten Offizier
NZ	*Notiţe Zilnice din Război*
OHL	Oberste Heeresleitung (German High Command)
OKM	Oberkommando Mackensen, Bucharest
Ops	Operations
PA	Politisches Archiv
PRO/FO	Public Record Office/Foreign Office, London
RAPRM	*România în anii primul război mondial*
RRM	*România în războiul mondial, 1916–1919*
SHAT	Service historique de l'armée de terre, Vincennes
STAVKA	Supreme Headquarters of the Russian Army at the Front
TOE	Théâtre d'opérations extérieurs
VO	Verbindungs Offizier
WGB/WMB	Württembergisches Gebirgs Bataillon/Württemberg Mountain Battalion

The Romanian Battlefront
in World War I

1

The Road to War, 1914–1916

At 9:00 P.M. on 27 August 1916, Edgar Mavrocordat, the Romanian minister in Vienna, delivered a declaration of war to the Austro-Hungarian Foreign Ministry. Simultaneously, avant guard units of three Romanian armies invaded Hungary at multiple locations along the Carpathian frontier. Romania's action was backed by an alliance with France, Russia, England, and Italy that promised military and diplomatic support for the annexation of the Romanian-inhabited regions of the Dual Monarchy. The decision taken in Bucharest to intervene in the conflict, which meant war with Germany, Bulgaria, and Turkey as well, was a political and military risk. However, it turned out to be the crucial step in the creation of modern Romania. At the end of the war, all or part of the Habsburg regions in question, together with Bessarabia from the fragmenting Russian empire, were joined to the Romanian Old Kingdom. This brought into reality, for a generation at least, the Romanians' dream of a *România Mare* (Greater Romania), the unification of all of their historic lands.

BACKGROUND TO 1914

The modern process of unification had begun in 1859 with the election of Alexandru Cuza as prince of both Moldavia and Wallachia, then still under nominal Ottoman sovereignty. The United Principalities experienced stability and progress under Cuza's strong and able successor, German prince

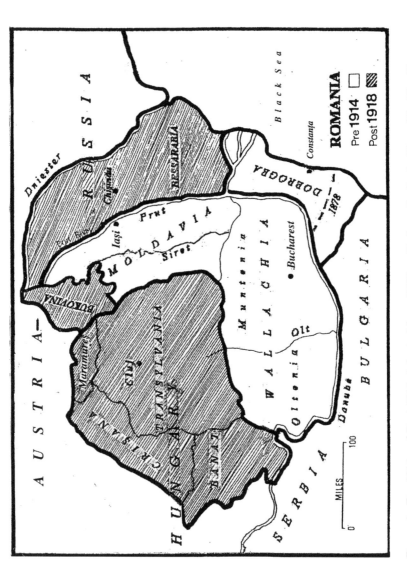

Romania: Pre-1914 and Post-1918. Adapted from William Rodney, *Joe Boyle: King of the Klondike* (Toronto: McGraw Hill-Ryerson, 1974)

Carol (Charles) of Hohenzollern-Sigmaringen, who arrived in 1866. Romania's participation alongside Russia in the war against Turkey (1877–1878) led to the recognition of Romania's independence in 1881, and Carol was proclaimed king. At the same time, in a classic case of ingratitude, Russia, with the approbation of the Congress of Berlin, took from Romania Southern Bessarabia. In return, Romania received Dobrogea, an undeveloped province in which the Romanian public then had little interest.[1]

The loss of Bessarabia exacerbated already existing fear and hatred of Russia and served as a catalyst for Romania's adherence to the Triple Alliance (Germany, Austria-Hungary, and Italy) in 1883. Economic ties and the power of Bismarckian Germany made this connection attractive. The alliance was renewed several times, the last in 1913. Its existence was known only to Carol and a few selected political leaders. Wider disclosure was impossible because of the pro-French sentiments of most of Romania's politicians and the progressive increase in dissatisfaction with Hungary's treatment of its nearly 3,000,000 ethnic Romanians. During the 1890s, intensification of political discrimination and cultural persecution triggered several high-profile protests by Transylvanian Romanians that found a sympathetic response in the Old Regat. As Budapest stubbornly persisted with this program of Magyarization into the twentieth century, it fueled an irredentist current in Romania. Although many politicians and intellectuals sympathized with its aims, no government in Bucharest could support the movement publicly. Romania still needed the German connection, which provided economic advantages and security against Russian designs in the Balkans. It was clear that this required coexistence with Austria-Hungary.[2]

A reevaluation of Romanian foreign policy began after Austria-Hungary's annexation of Bosnia-Herzegovina in 1908 and the advent to power in Bucharest of a cabinet of younger pro-French liberals headed by Ion I. C. Brătianu. It was only during the Balkan wars (1912–1913) that Romanian policy underwent a decisive shift. Bucharest was angered by the failure of Austria to support Romanian interests in this conflict. Ignoring Vienna's advice, Romania invaded Bulgaria in the summer of 1913 when the latter was under attack from Greek and Serbian armies.[3] As compensation for its contribution to defeating the Bulgarians, Romania annexed Southern Dobrogea. This acquisition of 8,000 square kilometers and 300,000 inhabitants, who were almost exclusively Bulgarian and Turkish, was of doubtful practical value. Moreover, the Bulgarians, who charged that the Romanians ruled it with semicolonial abuse, thirsted for revenge.[4] This easy victory and new acquisition bolstered Romanian self-confidence and stimulated dreams of the eventual annexation of Transylvania. By now the alliance with Austria-Hungary had become an anachronism. By the end of 1913, Count Ottokar Czernin, the Habsburg minister in Bucharest, would characterize it—accurately, as it turned out—as "nothing more than a meaningless scrap of paper."[5]

Simultaneously with this alienation from Austria-Hungary, Romania became open to a rapprochement with the Triple Entente. Immediately after the Balkan Wars, the French took the initiative in courting Bucharest and promoting a Russo-Romanian reconciliation. Brătianu, once again premier, was receptive. Even before coming to power in January 1914, he had made it clear that he favored reorienting Romania's foreign policy. Consequently, he arranged secret discussions with Russia that took place under the guise of a social visit of Tsar Nicholas and his entourage to Romania in June 1914. In an unusual act, which seemed to be an acknowledgment of Romanian pretensions, Russian foreign minister Sergei Sazonov accompanied Brătianu on a brief automobile trip across the Hungarian frontier into Transylvania. The reconciliation between Bucharest and St. Petersburg demonstrated that the "old scar of Bessarabia" was easier to forget than the "fresh-flowing wound of Transylvania."[6]

Consequently, when world war broke out a month later, King Carol found it necessary to warn his allies in Berlin and Vienna that it would be impossible for him to mobilize the Romanian army and march with them against Russia because "the question of Romanians in Transylvania has so greatly stirred Romanian public feeling against Hungary." Nevertheless, Carol convened a crown council on 3 August at his summer palace in Sinaia to consider Romania's attitude in the face of the European crisis. With only one exception, this assemblage of cabinet ministers, elder statesmen, parliamentary officers, and party leaders spoke for neutrality. Carol accepted their decision. In the month that followed, as Austro-Hungarian armies retreated before Russian offensives in Galicia and Bukovina, strong agitation developed in Bucharest calling for Romania to join in and give Austria-Hungary the "finishing blow." Carol, ill and depressed over this turn of events, prepared his abdication manifesto. Mercifully, his death on 10 October ended his dilemma. He was succeeded by his 49-year-old nephew, Ferdinand.[7]

King Ferdinand and Queen Marie. From Marie, Queen of Romania, *Ordeal: The Story of My Life* (New York: Charles Scribner's Sons, 1935)

THE DECISION TO INTERVENE

In contrast to his uncle, Ferdinand was not a strong and respected leader at that time. In the popular image of many, he was "poor Fritz," dull, incompetent, and "inclined to alcoholism." In reality, he was intelligent, well educated, and knowledgeable. One on one, he could converse in several languages on botany, art, archeology, theology, or music. But in public or with persons he did not know well, he was socially inept and tongue-tied. He either said nothing or uttered a blend of awkward, meaningless phrases. Critics, including his wife, Marie, believed his problem was not only timidity but a lack of "will and initiative."[8] The queen, charismatic, intense, and decisive, exacerbated her husband's problems, perhaps deliberately, with her dominating personality and verbal intimidation. This earned Ferdinand the reputation of being henpecked.[9] Marie was immensely popular with the Romanian people and united their national aspirations with her own ambitions. Upon the death of Carol, she was eager

Premier Ion I. C. Brătianu.
From Marie, Queen of
Romania, *Ordeal: The Story of
My Life* (New York: Charles
Scribner's Sons, 1935)

to lead them should her husband abdicate his responsibility. As befitting
a granddaughter of both Queen Victoria and Tsar Alexander II, Marie pas-
sionately embraced the Entente cause and helped lead her husband to the
same commitment.[10] Upon his ascent to the throne, Ferdinand declared
that he would be "a good Romanian," acting "exclusively according to
duty and in the interest of the Romanian people." Yet it was not easy for
him, as a German prince, to pursue actively a policy which would almost
inevitably lead to war with his native land.[11] It benefitted both his conscience and his limited skill in statecraft to allow Brătianu a free hand in
conducting the realpolitik that Romania's self-interest required.

The prime minister, an admirer of Caesar Borgia, is alleged to have "read
Machiavelli by night in order to apply him by day." Certainly he was ide-
ally suited for the diplomatic dissimulation necessary to placate the Central Powers while dealing with the Entente over the terms and time of Romania's entry into the war.[12] Described as "one of the most complex

personalities in Romania," Brătianu was an enigma to the mass of Romanians, reserved and distant like a sphinx. In the elite circle of Romanian politics, he was "adored by collaborators, vehemently attacked by adversaries." He was agonizingly slow in making decisions. All possible repercussions were carefully "examined, reexamined, and counter-examined." He once told a *Time* magazine reporter, "I try to put off until tomorrow the mistakes which people tell me I ought to make today."[13] When pressed for a decision, he often made himself unavailable by retreating to Florica, his country estate, or to his bed. Periods of intense work alternated with periods of lethargy. He went to bed early and slept in the afternoon. He spent most of his waking hours in an easy chair or reclining on a sofa. He seldom went to his office, preferring to conduct business from his home. Visitors would often find him with a book in hand; more often than not, its subject was history. Fascinated by historical analogies, he likened Romania's struggle for national unity to that of Italy. The time will come, he told the French minister, Camille Blondel, in November 1912, "when the edifice of Austria-Hungary will be destroyed . . . for this we must be ready . . . to receive our brothers from Transylvania." The advent of war in 1914 convinced Brătianu this time had come. He believed he had a destiny to fulfill a historic role in this process.[14]

King Ferdinand's failure to play an active role in foreign policy allowed Brătianu to exercise a virtual dictatorship. He dealt directly with representatives of the Great Powers in Bucharest, bypassing the Romanian diplomatic service. His minister of foreign affairs was popularly referred to as "the minister foreign to affairs." Brătianu exercised similar control over other areas of Romanian political life through the Liberal Party and a syndicate of relatives and close friends.[15] Brătianu cultivated the support of King Ferdinand and Queen Marie through one of his brothers-in-law, Prince Barbu Știrbey. Although ostensibly only the administrator of the royal domains, Știrbey exercised enormous influence over the royal couple. A rich landowner and successful businessman, he was unusually handsome, socially confident, and "seductive to women." Among the latter was Marie, whose husband lacked all these qualities. In 1907, after a series of infidelities by both her and Ferdinand, Marie found in Știrbey a confidant, lover, and the father of at least one of her children. In a manner not uncommon in Romanian society of that day, Ferdinand not only tolerated this relationship but developed a close friendship with Știrbey. By 1914 Știrbey had become Ferdinand's intimate confidant and personal advisor. A good listener who was sensitive to the monarch's limitations, he would sit and converse with him for hours on end over a cup of coffee or a glass of whiskey. "He is a man with whom I have an understanding," Ferdinand remarked in 1914.[16] Ştirbey, discreet, dedicated, and well aware of the issues the country faced, became Ferdinand's political tutor in 1914–1918. Duca is close to the truth when he asserts that Ştirbey "had an omnipotent influence on the king as well as the queen. . . . He was the true sovereign of Romania." This role was resented by many who saw Ştirbey as an *eminence gris*, the "Romanian Rasputin."[17] Thanks to Ştirbey, there was close cooperation between the crown and Brătianu during the difficult years of neutrality and war.

NEGOTIATING WAR AIMS

With the support of the king and a large Liberal majority in parliament, Brătianu began in 1914 a cautious and calculating process of preparing Romania to participate in the liquidation of Austria-Hungary. His chief domestic problem was a coalition of politicians and intellectuals who, after the opening battles had demonstrated that the Dual Monarchy was weak and that Germany was not invincible, demanded an immediate invasion of Transylvania. Brătianu, well aware of Romania's vulnerable strategic position and military unpreparedness, knew this was a recipe for disaster. As he once expressed to the French minister, he had no intention of going to war until there were "75 chances out of a 100 of winning."[18] Brătianu's chief diplomatic problem was to negotiate an alliance with the Entente guaranteeing Romania's war aims while avoiding a break with the Central Powers. Brătianu, "a first class master of the diplomatic game," concealed his true intentions so successfully that the Entente was in doubt and the Central Powers deluded until the last minute.[19]

Even before Carol died, Brătianu had negotiated neutrality agreements with Italy (23 September) and Russia (1 October). The latter provided that in return for Romania's pledge of benevolent neutrality, Russia would recognize its right to annex those provinces of Austria-Hungary inhabited by Romanians with the right to choose the moment to occupy them. This accord was only a down payment on what Brătianu sought; Russia did not guarantee Romania would acquire this territory, and Britain and France were not party to the agreement. At the beginning of 1915, Britain and France joined Russia in the negotiations, but all were then unwilling to guarantee the high price Brătianu demanded: Bukovina, the Banat, Transylvania, and all or most of Crişana and Maramureş. However, their attitude changed during the summer of 1915. A stalemate with enormous casualties for the British and French armies on the Western Front, the Allied defeat at the Dardanelles, and the disastrous retreat of the Russian army in Poland convinced them that Romania's assistance was now a necessity.[20]

By the beginning of July the Entente Powers expressed a willingness to sign an accord granting, in essence, Romania's full territorial demands in return for its commitment to enter the war within five weeks. However, in light of the recent military success of the Central Powers, Brătianu protested that for Romania to enter the war then would be "suicide." By the end of summer he was unwilling to sign even an agreement with the date of entry left open, lest the compromise of its secrecy provoke a preventive strike by the Central Powers. His cabinet, made aware of his negotiations for the first time, backed Brătianu's decision to abstain.[21] Although no agreement was signed in 1915, Brătianu was morally committed to the Entente and the latter had approved Romania's far-reaching territorial aspirations. When the Allied military situation improved in the summer of 1916, these were the terms on which the negotiations would resume. In the intervening months, Romania found itself in a menacing situation. Bulgaria, having joined the Central Powers (October 1915) and participated in the defeat and occupation of Serbia, had become a dangerous neighbor. The Central Powers used diplomatic pressure and the implication of military action to force Brătianu to draw back and, in addition, sell them the grain and oil they desperately needed.[22]

But in the summer of 1916 another swing in the pendulum of war occurred. The German army failed to capture Verdun, the Allies were assembling a sizable force at Salonika under French general Maurice Sarrail, the British were preparing a grand offensive on the Somme, and the Russians launched an offensive led by General Alexei Brusilov. Beginning in June, Brusilov's forces broke through Austro-Hungarian lines in Galicia and Bukovina and threatened to penetrate into the heart of Hungary itself. There was good reason for Brătianu to fear that the Russian army might occupy Transylvania, that Austria-Hungary might be forced to sue for peace, or that the Entente, exasperated by his procrastination, might decide it no longer needed Romania's assistance. Any one of these scenarios could threaten the achievement of Romania's war aims. Brătianu realized that the time had come to make a commitment. Consequently, on 4 July, Brătianu announced he was ready to sign an alliance. Because the Entente leaders had already conceded Romania's essential territorial demands, they expected a speedy conclusion of political and military conventions. Instead, the negotiations dragged on for five weeks, delaying Romania's entry into the war until 27 August. Toward the end of this interval, the Brusilov Offensive stalled.[23]

FINALIZING THE ALLIANCE

Brătianu had laid down three general conditions for a military convention: that a supply of munitions was assured; that Allied armies on all fronts take the offensive to prevent the diversion of enemy forces against Romania, including the corollary that the position of Russian forces in Bukovina and Galicia "is maintained at least what it is today"; and, finally, "unconditional security" against a Bulgarian attack. The first was satisfied by a British / French pledge that shipments already en route would be expedited through Russia. The French *défensive à outrance* at Verdun, the resurgence of the Italian army on the Piave, the opening of the British offensive on the Somme (4 July), and the success of Brusilov appeared to satisfy points 2 and 3. General Joseph Joffre, chief of the French High Command, assured the Romanians that "Romania could invade . . . and occupy Transylvania without any risk. . . . Austria . . . has not one division available to send into Transylvania." When Brătianu questioned a French military attaché about reports of the formation of a new German army that could be turned against Romania, he was confidently assured "that for eight months the Germans had not been able to create even one new division . . . the formation of a new army was an impossibility."[24]

The Entente leaders, desperately eager for Romania's intervention, were equally misleading about fulfilling Brătianu's condition regarding the Bulgarian threat, which was his greatest concern. Blondel predicted that the Bulgarian army would be "annihilated" by Allied forces at Salonika; French premier Aristide Briand insisted that a Bulgarian attack on Romania was "improbable."[25] Brătianu had reason to be skeptical of these baseless predictions. He therefore sought assurances of an Allied offensive powerful enough to draw off Bulgarian forces from the Romanian frontier as well as the assistance of a strong Russian expeditionary force in Dobrogea. The latter had been counted on by Romanian military planners as far back as November 1914 and had been included in the Romanian war plan. When the final negotiations began in July 1916, Brătianu requested a Russian force of 50,000. He increased this to 200,000 when the French and British insisted that in addition to its main operations directed toward Transylvania, the Romanian army also undertake an offensive against Bulgaria. When the Russians refused to promise more than 50,000, Brătianu threatened not to declare war on Bulgaria at all. This stalemate was broken only after the Romanians agreed to accept the lesser force and the Entente dropped its demand for a Romanian attack or even a declaration of war on Bulgaria.[26]

Brătianu remained highly doubtful of the capability and intentions of the Allied forces at Salonika (AAO). The French represented the AAO as a force of 400,000 men. In reality, it numbered less than 229,000 combatants. The Romanians had evidence of this misrepresentation. The Central Powers supplied reports that questioned Allied troop strength, and dispatches from the Romanian military attachés in Sofia and Athens agreed.[27] His suspicions aroused, Brătianu persisted in interrogating the Allied ministers about Sarrail's forces. He argued they were "not in the condition to defeat the Bulgarians, neither of holding the major portions of them." He also questioned "with much insistence" the intended scope of the operations of the AAO. He indicated that he wanted them not only to draw off Bulgarian forces from the Romanian frontier, but also to push northward with the objective of opening a supply route from Salonika to Bucharest.[28] In reality, Sarrail and his British associate, General George Milne, had made it clear to their governments that they were reluctant "to undertake anything of a serious nature," as the latter put it. Suspecting as much, Brătianu insisted that the AAO not only attack ten days before Romania declared war, but also proposed it be obligated to occupy certain points of Bulgarian territory during this period. The issue was never resolved. The final draft of the military convention ambiguously described Sarrail's mission as *une offensive affirmée,* to begin eight days before Romania declared war. These dates were set for 20 August and 28 August, respectively. The Romanians

interpreted the phrase *offensive affirmée* as at least "a very energetic and prolonged action, if not to break the Bulgarian Front immediately at least to
drive the enemy back and force him to strip the Danube region [of forces]."
The Allies, on the other hand, interpreted it only as "attempting to hold
Bulgarian forces where they are now . . . [not] an attempt to attack with the
object of decisively defeating the Bulgarian forces." Allied leaders were
aware that a serious misunderstanding existed but agreed, albeit with a
twinge of conscience, not to clarify it lest the negotiations be wrecked.[29]

In addition to these contested issues in the military convention, the alliance negotiations were delayed by contention over two related clauses
Brătianu insisted be added to the political convention. One, a no-separate-
peace clause, in effect obligated the Entente to fight until Romania occupied all its territorial desiderata. The other guaranteed Romania equality
with the Allied powers in all discussions and decisions related to the conclusion of peace. The first reflected Brătianu's concern that Austria-Hungary,
dispirited over Romania's entry into the war, might strike a deal with the
Entente to Romania's disfavor. The second, as British minister George Barclay explained to London, reflected Brătianu's concern that Romania's interests might be cast aside in the peace settlement as they had been during his father's premiership after the Russo-Turkish War, "a fear that has
haunted him from childhood." If his conditions on these and other issues
were not met, Brătianu said he would resign, a move that would have
wrecked the negotiations. "That the Romanian claims are ridiculous, I vol-
untarily concede," commented Colonel Maurice Pelle, Joffre's *aide-major* for
the Eastern Front, "but that they merit the rupture of the negotiations, no."
He went on to point out that it was out of the question that in the end the
four Great Powers "would continue the war for Romania alone." Similarly,
on the question of Great Power status, Pelle argued that Romania would
have "influence corresponding to her power" and would "only be paid for
the value of its cooperation."[30] Pelle's arguments overcame Russian resistance, and these reservations were formalized in a secret agreement among
the Entente leaders. They agreed that the annexations promised Romania
would be fulfilled "only in the measure which the general situation would
permit" and that before Romania was admitted to the peace negotiations,
the Allies would come to a prior agreement "on the great decisions." It is
clear that the Allies, especially the Russians, did not feel bound to the letter of the political convention. Viewing Brătianu as a "political usurer" who

was blackmailing them, they were ready, in Vinogradov's words, "to pay him back in his own coin." The capitulation to Romania's demands marked the end of almost two years of diplomatic bargaining. Brătianu's ability "to haggle with a sort of genius" had made the last month especially frustrating for the Allied leaders. It was, in Joffre's words, *"une toile de Penelope."*[31] The desire for Romanian intervention had led them to make promises without fully considering their future impact. Together with other secret agreements, the territorial promises to Romania contained in the political convention virtually eliminated the possibility of Allied separate peace with Austria-Hungary later. It was a major step in an unplanned Allied commitment to the breakup of the multinational empire. These agreements, including the one with Romania, bedeviled the Paris Peace Conference in 1919.

It took several days for all Entente diplomatic and military representatives to receive authorization, so the formal signature of both conventions took place on 17 August at 11 A.M. Obsessed with secrecy and aware that his was "a country of the indiscreet and indiscretion," Brătianu asked the Entente signatories to arrive "by different routes and by foot" at the house of his brother, Vintilă. The premier, after an evasive detour via a friend's house, also arrived by foot. The drafts of the conventions were handwritten to avoid disclosure by typists. After the signing, those present left "furtively one after another."[32] A declaration of war was prepared to be sent to Vienna by courier for delivery on the night of 27–28 August, simultaneously with the advance of the Romanian army across the Austro-Hungarian frontier. A crown council to inform the cabinet and party leaders was set for the morning of 27 August. Mobilization, already under way in preliminary stages, was to be publicly proclaimed that afternoon.[33]

2

The Romanian Army and War Plan

ORGANIZATION, PERSONNEL, AND TACTICS

In August 1916, Romania mobilized 800,000 men, with another 400,000 subject to call, from a population of only 8,000,000. This amounted to 30 percent of the total male population.[1] Some 560,000 formed the operational army and 440,000 of these the combat forces. Of 336 battalions, 146 were active duty, 120 reserve, and the remainder territorial or militia units formed of older men, some as old as 55. The combat forces were organized into 23 divisions of infantry, two divisions and five brigades of cavalry, six mixed brigades, and 329 batteries of artillery. The infantry divisions varied greatly in size, quality, and armaments. Numbers 1 to 10 each had three brigades, two of which were composed of active regiments with younger men and mostly active officers; the third brigade encompassed, for the most part, older reservists. To each division a cavalry squadron was attached, along with some light artillery and support units. The average strength of these divisions, at least according to the rosters, was 640 officers and 27,000 men. Their basic armament was the relatively modern model 1893 Mannlicher rifle. Each battalion had four machine guns. Divisions 11–16 had only two brigades, formed primarily of reservists, and averaged 420 officers and 17,000 men each. They were armed in part with older 1879 Mannlichers and had only one machine gun per battalion. Divisions 17–23 were ad hoc units formed at mobilization or shortly thereafter of older men and battalions taken from various regiments. They were

THE ROMANIAN ARMY AND WAR PLAN   15

armed with the older rifles, and some battalions had no machine guns at all. The cavalry, by its nature, was more elite in personnel and experience but lightly armed and not trained in fighting dismounted, as was cavalry on the Western Front by 1916.[2]

The foot soldiers of the Romanian army were overwhelmingly peasants, 60 percent of whom were unable to read or write. However, they were intensely patriotic and obedient, and they were accustomed to hardship and sacrifice. Enemies and allies alike agreed that they were excellent material with which to build an army.[3] They proved this in 1917 after acquiring equipment, training, and experience comparable to their opponents. But in 1916 even the most experienced had been schooled in pre-1914 methods. They were ignorant of the changes that had come about on the battlefield in 1914–1916.[4] Eighty percent of the men mobilized were reservists. Before 1914, reserve units existed only on paper without cadre, without equipment, and without organization sufficient for concentration. Between 1914 and 1916, enough progress had been made so that virtually all reservists mobilized had at least some military instruction. However, their annual training, carried out for 30 days locally by territorial regiments, was low in caliber, punctuated with liberal home leave. There were even charges that some local commanders further compromised readiness by diverting military funds for their personal use or by operating businesses with their men supplying the labor. General Ioan Dragalina, commander of the 1st Infantry Division (ID), found that "in active regiments, soldiers are generally good, in the others a majority are without military instruction, incompletely equipped, and very poorly organized." "A significant portion of the effectives mobilized," the official Romanian war history concedes, "had no more than summary instruction."[5]

Adequate leadership, which might have compensated in part for the inexperience of the men, was lacking. The creation of many new formations at mobilization led to a critical shortage of cadre. There was only one underofficer for every 87 men. Promotion from the ranks was difficult because of widespread illiteracy. In contrast, excellently prepared underofficers characterized the German army. The Romanian army was top heavy, with 145 generals (55 active and 99 reserve), but with only 220 majors, 30 percent of them reserve, to command 366 battalions. During the early weeks of the war, as officers suffered disproportionately high casualties, captains, even lieutenants, commanded battalions. For 1,701 companies (300 men each) there were only 820 captains, again 30 percent reservists. For 7,800 platoons (and companies without a captain) there were only 6,700 lieutenants, of whom 75 percent were reserve.[6] Because education was the primary qualification, most officers were lycée graduates, teachers, lawyers, engineers, and intellectuals, but with few qualifications for leadership. In his first-line division, General Dragalina found that "every second company is commanded by a reserve officer without military preparation." German prewar assessments of the Romanian officer corps concluded accurately that "its battlefield training was not adequate for the exigencies of war." Although many officers would develop through training and the ordeal of battle into able leaders, the comments of the Romanian official history stand here also. "If we take into account that the preparation of reserve officers . . . was poor, we reach the conclusion that the army mobilized in 1916, above all the infantry, was weak in leadership."[7]

Many of the higher commanders were similarly unprepared for the type of war they would face. A number of them had received advanced military training abroad, particularly in France. A few had begun their careers in the Austro-Hungarian army.[8] They were well read in military classics; not a few had authored books on strategy and tactics or had served as professors in the military schools, and some had been elected to the Romanian Academy.[9] However, many spent too much of their time in Bucharest enmeshed in the social and political life of the capital. They were prominent at the hippodrome, the elite Jockey Club, and in political parties. These connections, unfortunately, were often determinative, as was seniority, in promotion and command assignments, to the detriment of the careers of younger able professionals.[10] In field operations, the Romanian tradition of close centralized control by higher command handicapped subordinate commanders. With their liberty of action curtailed and their suggestions often rejected, the latter were paralyzed and their initiative killed. Difficulties encountered in the campaign of 1913 against the Bulgarians had spotlighted leadership and command problems, but reforms had only begun by 1916. However, it should also be pointed out that many Romanian commanders, although lacking the battlefield experience of their enemies in 1916, gained it through defeat and became effective leaders in 1917. The latter included some who had failed and lost their commands in 1916.[11]

Romanian tactics reflected the views prevailing in Western Europe in 1914, especially the French emphasis on frontal assault and *offensive à out-*

rance. The use of terrain, maneuver, and envelopment was neglected. Defense was viewed negatively, as unnatural. An attack followed successive stages: introduction of an avant guard, positioning of the forces, attack with masses of infantry, execution of the final assault with the bayonet, and finally penetration of the cavalry into the depth of the enemy defense.[12] There was only partial awareness of the changes that were occurring in tactics on the Western Front. Several Romanian military attachés abroad appear to have been particularly ineffective in their reporting. It is alleged that some of the reports of the attaché in Paris, for example, were written by his pharmacist and his wife. The latter featured gossip from feminine circles around the government and High Command.[13] There was recognition of the newer weaponry, especially heavy artillery and machine guns, but its impact was underestimated. Little attention was given to massing artillery fire and its coordination with the infantry. General Alexandru Iarca, who served as inspector general and an influential advisor to the Romanian High Command, had written before the war that the contribution of artillery was not decisive. Its role was only to "prepare the way for the bayonet." In the place of firepower, Romanian military theorists emphasized human valor, epitomized in frontal assault by the infantry and its corollary, the saber charge of the cavalry. "The moral energy of an army," insisted General Ioan Popovici, "is equal to one half of its material force." Romanian commanders were accustomed to old shibboleths: "We attack with the breasts of our soldiers" under "the banner of the flag" and "the sound of the trumpet." German and Austrian soldiers were surprised when the Romanians announced their attacks with "loud cries, trumpet blasts, and other noise."[14]

MATERIAL RESOURCES

The Romanian army entered the war poorly armed when compared with its opponents. Economic crises and budget priorities kept prewar per capita spending on the military the lowest in Europe, below even Greece, Serbia, and Bulgaria. The Balkan Wars of 1912–1913 and especially the outbreak of the European war in 1914 had been the catalyst for an effort to augment and update Romania's armaments. Alas, the Central Powers, the traditional supplier, refused to sell to a potential enemy, and the Entente hesitated to do so until Romania made a commitment. Some modern French 8mm Lebel rifles began to arrive in August 1916 to replace the older Mannlichers, but this introduced the problem of incompatible ammunition.[15] More crucial was the shortage of machine guns. German regiments possessed 18 to 24 heavy machine guns plus three automatic rifles per company. Romanian active regiments had only four to six machine guns, reserve regiments four at most, and many territorial and militia battalions none. The Romanian infantry possessed no automatic rifles. French machine guns, which began arriving as the war opened, had to be temporarily withdrawn from service. As Colonel Romulus Scărișoreanu discovered, the operators in his brigade were "completely uninstructed," and even the officer in charge "did not have the most elemental knowledge of the equipment nor the principles of its use in fighting." The same could be said of grenades. One million arrived from France just after the war began, but personnel could not be trained in their use until 1917.[16]

The Romanian army was similarly deficient in artillery. Each brigade possessed six small-caliber (55mm, 57mm) cannon salvaged from abandoned prewar fortifications. They lacked firepower; soldiers derided them as popguns. Of 368 batteries of field artillery, only 180 (75mm, 105mm) were relatively modern, rapid firing, and reliable. Surprisingly, for a country with 600 kilometers of Carpathian frontier, the Romanian army had no mountain troops and only two modern and six outmoded batteries of mountain artillery. Their well-equipped opponents included the German Alpine Corps, the Württemberg Mountain Battalion, and several Austrian mountain brigades.[17] The Romanian army possessed little heavy artillery and could purchase none during neutrality. The creation of a few batteries by improvising carriages for ancient cannon removed from abandoned fortifications proved to be of little help. Even counting its obsolete guns, Romanian units could at best count on only 50 percent of the field artillery and 30 percent of the heavy artillery possessed by their opponents. Repeatedly, enemy guns, especially the heavy-caliber ones, were able to silence Romanian artillery and devastate the infantry. Lack of support from their own artillery was the repeated complaint of captured Romanian soldiers; George Protopopescu's conclusion that when compared to the firepower of its enemies "the Romanian army was practically disarmed" is exaggerated only in degree.[18]

Support services were characterized by improvisation. Modern communications equipment was limited. There were radio-telex stations for the High Command, for each field army, and for each cavalry division. For command purposes, use was often made of civilian telephone–telegraph lines and couriers, both of which were unreliable. Reports and orders to and from the field were habitually late, in some cases causing operations to fail. Larger echelons, regiment and above, had field telephone equipment, but cable was limited. None was available to spot artillery fire or to coordinate it with the infantry. The Germans, in contrast, had an extensive communications network, including field telephones on the company level.[19]

Romania's rail network provided the primary means of transporting men and supplies. It was superior to the Bulgarian net but could not match the Hungarian system. Romanian north–south lines were adequate, with four crossing into Hungary. However, there was only one east–west line for lateral transfer of troops. Furthermore, all lines converged on Bucharest, creating a horrendous bottleneck that resulted in crucial delays in the transfer of troops. For staff travel 1,500 private autos were requisitioned. The Romanian army possessed only 150 trucks. Field transport of supplies relied upon 50,000 wagons, many of them requisitioned peasant *căruțe* (carts), some driven by panic-prone civilians. Surprisingly, this improvised system was generally successful in providing food and ammunition to men in the field. This was in contrast to the 1913 campaign, when large numbers of soldiers nearly starved.[20] As a whole, the soldiers had adequate summer clothing but lacked winter gear. As new recruits were added at mobilization, shortages developed. Colonel Scărișoreanu found some of his men wearing *opinci*, homemade peasant shoes that disintegrated in march. Romanian gray-green uniforms were similar in appearance to those of the Austro-Hungarian army—so similar that German commanders were admonished to use binoculars and coordinate movements with their Austro-Hungarian counterparts to avoid "shooting our friends."[21] The medical service was provided with 42 hospital trains and 900 ambulances. Many of the latter were requisitioned private vehicles whose owners were exempt from military service if they drove them. Gas masks were available for approximately 50 percent of the operational army. Although rumors surfaced, there is no hard evidence that poison gas was used in 1916 on the Romanian Front, as it was in 1917.[22]

AUXILIARY ARMS

Supporting the field army were the Romanian navy and the Romanian aviation corps. The latter was in its infancy in August 1916, having been founded only a year previously. It possessed 44 aircraft, but only 30 were operable when war was declared. All were old French models, slow and suitable for observation only. They were unarmed, although some air crews carried rifles or pistols. It was a force ridiculous in number and quality when compared to the enemy's. Austria-Hungary mobilized 65 to 70 aircraft on the Transylvanian Front; the Germans had 180 based in Bulgaria, augmented by two zeppelins. The latter were poised for bombing Bucharest in shuttle runs back and forth from Razgrad to Timişoara. Each of the four Romanian armies possessed a squadron of aircraft, together with an observation balloon. The fragile and defective Romanian aircraft completed a few missions in 1916 but failed to give the army eyes in the sky at crucial junctures of the operations. Little reconnaissance was gained from the balloons. One did ascend on the front of the 1st Army but yielded "unsatisfactory results because the officer observer did not have a good pair of binoculars."[23]

The Romanian navy, lacking warships for the open sea, confined its operations to the Danube river. Its forces there were divided into a flotilla division and an underwater defense division. The former was composed of four monitors and numerous smaller craft. Because of vulnerability to shore artillery, it operated only on the lower reaches of the river, where both banks were under Romanian control. For the same reason the Austro-Hungarian flotilla (eight monitors plus many smaller craft) restricted its operations to the upper course of the Danube. The two flotillas never directly engaged in combat. Both had the mission of assisting offensive and defensive land operations along the river.[24] The Romanian underwater defense division encompassed shore batteries, barrages, torpedoes, and mines. Its primary mission was to impede the operation of enemy warships on the Danube. Unfortunately, this section was poorly prepared in 1916. Shore installations and barrages were uncompleted. Its domestically produced mines were notoriously defective, "more dangerous to us than our enemies," a Romanian officer confessed. Moreover, its commander considered his division a personal fief, acting independently and sometimes in opposition to the admiral commanding the Danube division. There was also bitter rivalry and no clear lines of authority between the latter and other Romanian admirals at the Ministry of War and the naval arsenal at Galaţi. All sought to control the navy. No wonder a French naval attaché, arriving after war began, reported a command "anarchy" best described as a "comic caricature" of the chaos in the Ottoman military.[25]

The Romanian army mobilized in August 1916 was large in numbers but weak in training, experience, leadership, and equipment, especially fire-power at all levels. Too many men were mobilized, diluting the resources available. Unfortunately, this army was called on to carry out a plan of operations that exceeded its capabilities.

THE WAR PLAN: HYPOTHESIS Z

Until 1914, Romania's military planning had been based on the alliance with the Central Powers and presupposed Russia as the principal enemy. The military convention with the Central Powers, renewed in December 1912 when Habsburg chief of staff Conrad von Hötzendorf visited Bucharest, called for the Romanian army to advance over the Prut toward Kiev in the event of an armed conflict between Vienna and St. Petersburg.[26] However, in the aftermath of the Balkan Wars, the Romanian General Staff began to consider seriously the option of a war against Austria-Hungary. A short time before the crown council of August 1914, Brătianu ordered the prepa-ration of such a plan of operations. During the uncertainty of the July cri-sis, the General Staff labored feverishly to update existing plans for war against Russia while at the same time developing a strategy for an attack on Austria-Hungary. The latter became the exclusive focus of strategic planning after the death of King Carol. Meetings between Brătianu and military leaders in November 1914 and January 1915, amid indications that Bulgaria would join the Central Powers, determined a strategy in which the Romanian army would remain on the defensive on its southern fron-tier in order to maximize the forces that could take part in the invasion of Transylvania.[27] Bulgaria's alliance with the Central Powers (September 1915) confirmed a war on two fronts whose total length was twice that of the French front and barely shorter than the Russian.

During 1915–1916, a plan of operations, designated Hypothesis B, evolved through a series of variants, although its basic objective remained

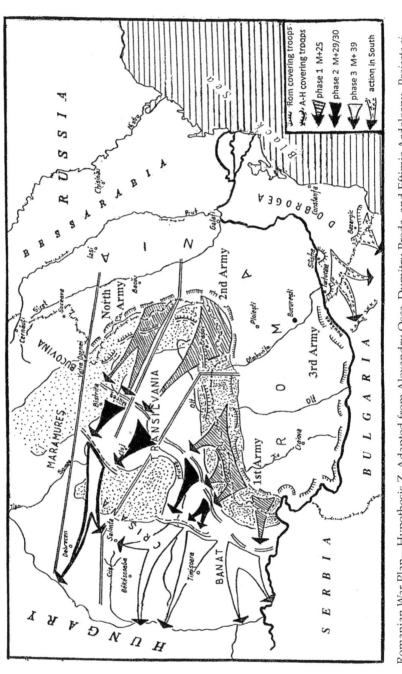

Romanian War Plan—Hypothesis Z. Adapted from Alexandru Oşca, Dumitru Preda, and Eftimie Ardeleanu, *Proiecte şi planuri de operaţii ale marelui stat major pîna în anul 1916* (Bucharest: Arhivele Militare Române, 1992)

the same: "the conquest of territory inhabited by Romanians who today belong to the Austro-Hungary Monarchy." Up to 80 percent of the operational army would undertake an offense northwest across the Carpathians with only defensive operations on the secondary (southern) front. Hypothesis B had a superficial resemblance to Count Alfred von Schlieffen's plan for solving Germany's problem of a two-front war. In contrast to the Schlieffen Plan, which allowed the surrender of territory on Germany's secondary (eastern) front, Hypothesis B planned to maintain Romania's southern frontier inviolate. To make matters worse, during the negotiation of the military convention with the Entente, a provision was added for an offensive against Bulgaria. This contradicted a fundamental premise of all preliminary versions. In effect, then, the Romanian war plan committed the army not only to a war on two fronts, but also to offensives on two fronts.[28]

The final version of the Romanian war plan, fittingly called Hypothesis Z, was completed early in August 1916 and distributed to commanders in sealed envelopes, to be opened only on the day war was declared. Three armies (1st, 2nd, North) comprising 65 percent of all operational forces (369,159) were committed to the immediate occupation of Transylvania. It estimated, correctly, that they would be opposed by no more than 100,000 Habsburg defenders capable of offering little initial resistance. Simultaneously with the delivery of a declaration of war in Vienna, covering forces would penetrate the Carpathians at multiple points. After concentration of the remaining forces (M+17), these armies would advance in three stages: first to the Mureş river (M+25), which would shorten the front from 950 to 300 kilometers, provide a defensible line, and assure good railroad facilities; second, continuing the advance north and west to Cluj and Deva, and the Apuseni mountains (M+29/30); and third, penetrating the Hungarian plain, reaching to the Oradea–Debrecen zone (M+39). This timetable, based on days of march without taking into account possible enemy resistance, was unrealistic. The mission of the 3rd Army in the south was secondary to that of the Transylvanian armies: to "give liberty of action" to operations in the north by repulsing Bulgarian attacks and "defending the national territory." Its 142,523 men, 25 percent of the total of the operational army, were widely dispersed: one division along the upper Danube, one division each at Turtucaia and Silistra, and one division plus a brigade in eastern Dobrogea. Additionally, the general reserve of the Romanian army (51,165), which was stationed in the vicinity of Bucharest, could be used in the-south. Hypothesis Z estimated that the 105,000 to 120,000 German–Bulgarian forces in northern Bulgaria would launch a "brusque" offensive as well as carry out "demonstrations," including fake crossings, along the Danube. Operations of the 3rd Army were intended to develop in two phases. The first was purely defensive. The second, beginning after the Russian expeditionary force had entered the line (M+10), was offensive aimed at destroying enemy forces in northeast Bulgaria, occupying the zone Rusé–Varna.[29]

Most commentators recognize that the general features of Hypothesis Z were dictated by Romania's difficult strategic position and the political necessity of occupying Transylvania. However, it has been severely criticized in several details.[30] Most often mentioned in regard to the Transylvanian Front is the contradiction between the slow (25 day) advance on a broad front to the Mureş river and the absolute necessity of exploiting quickly the enemy's initial weakness before he brought in reinforcements. Critics suggest it would have been better to group Romanian striking power on the enemy's flanks for an aggressive enveloping operation. Questions have also been raised about the absence in Hypothesis Z of any estimate, even a guess, of how the enemy might react or of the reinforcements he might send. Was it believable that Germany would allow the Romanian army to march into the heart of Hungary without sending help, even at the expense of other fronts? Although the cooperation of a Russian force operating out of Bukovina in the invasion of Transylvania was assumed, no details of joint operations were spelled out. As we will see, the Russians had little inclination to cooperate with the Romanians, and the Romanians in turn were reluctant to have the Russians enter the province, fearing a repetition of 1877–1878.

The provisions of Hypothesis Z for the Southern Front have also drawn criticism. As in the north, its estimate of existing enemy forces on the frontier was realistic but again failed to anticipate reinforcements. It was assumed that "the majority of Bulgarian forces would be drawn toward Salonika" and consequently that "the Central Powers and Turkey will not be able to send additional aid into eastern Bulgaria." This assumption became suspect when reports began reaching Bucharest in late July and early August of Ottoman divisions assembling at Adrianople or actually in transport into Bulgaria. The Romanians assumed, according to the British military attaché, that these Turks would be directed against the Allied army at

Salonika. Another target of criticism has been the provision of Hypothesis Z to commit two divisions, almost two-thirds of all Romanian forces in Dobrogea, to the fortresses of Turtucaia and Silistra, where they would be isolated and vulnerable. It has been suggested that moving these divisions to the east and using them in conjunction with the other Russo-Romanian forces would have been more effective. In the case of enemy pressure mandating retreat, all forces could have been withdrawn, while counterattacking, to the narrow waist of Dobrogea. There, more defensible positions could have been prepared along the Cernavoda–Constanța railroad. If necessary, even the entire region of Dobrogea could have been evacuated, holding only the left bank of the Danube. Such an elastic defense in the south could have bought time and economized resources to the benefit of the Northern Front. However, there were strong political objections to the surrender of any national territory.[31]

THE GENERAL STAFF

An evaluation of the Romanian army in August 1916 must include a critical look at those who were in charge during its period of preparation in 1914–1916.[32] Brătianu, who held the portfolio of war, concerned himself primarily with the political implications of preparing for war. He left the military details to the Romanian General Staff, called the Marele Stat Major (MSM). It had been created in 1882 but did not function continuously until 1907. Even thereafter, it lacked professionalism and was plagued with problems. Royal favoritism, politics, and intense personal rivalries among leading generals influenced its composition and decisions. When war began in 1914, it was poorly equipped to provide effective leadership in preparing the army for its eventual intervention. The titular chief of the General Staff, General Vasile Zottu, lacked initiative, had little respect in the army, and was generally recognized as "manifestly unfit" for the position. Moreover, he was later accused of having accepted subsidies from German agents. Because many Romanian politicians and some generals did likewise, from one group of belligerents or another, this does not necessarily prove he was treasonous, only venial. Zottu signed all the directives in 1914–1916, but he seems to have contributed little except to tarnish the image of the army.[33] The de facto head of the Romanian General Staff

in 1914–1916 was the secretary-general of the Ministry of War, General Dumitru Iliescu. A close friend and political loyalist of Brătianu, he was unpopular among higher officers and many politicians. He was also suspected of corruption and had a public image of personal moral behavior
that was scandalous even for Romania. The French military attaché, a
friend and classmate from L'école polytechnique in Paris, admitted that
Iliescu was "worthless as a leader of the army." Nevertheless, Brătianu relied on him heavily for military advice, including the negotiation of the
terms of the military convention. Iliescu, reputedly an administrator, supervised the army's preparations for war, especially efforts to purchase
abroad and improvise at home in order to make up the army's monumental deficiencies. He appears to have been involved only in a general way in
preparing the Romanian war plan.[34] The vice chief of staff in 1914–1916,
General Constantin Christescu, was widely recognized as one of Romania's
most competent generals, an authority on strategy and tactics. He was popular in the army and, having been secretary-general of the Ministry of War
in 1910–1912, was expected to be named chief of staff in 1914 instead of
Zottu. He was most certainly a key figure in military planning before and
after 1914, but his specific influence on Hypothesis Z is difficult to determine. It is alleged that he later sought to have his name removed from
drafts he had annotated.[35]

    As might be expected, the operations bureau of the General Staff played
a central role in the development of Hypothesis Z. Its chief was Lieutenant
Colonel Ioan Răşcanu, whose name appears on every version of a war plan
presented during 1914–1916. He was known as the mover on the General
Staff, intelligent, and, in the words of an Austrian intelligence evaluation,
"very capable, lives only for service." An improviser, he "quickly found
temporary solutions to any problem."[36] Unfortunately this improvisation,
though often necessary, was a characteristic weakness of the Romanian
army. Another key figure in the bureau of operations was Major Radu R.
Rosetti, another of Bratiănu's brothers-in-law. As director (manager) in
1914–1916, he supervised the work of the bureau, including drafting the
evolving versions of the war plan and, in the summer of 1916, the additional details of mobilization and concentration of the field armies. Rosetti's
relationship with Brătianu, with whom he was in constant contact, under-
scores his influence.[37]

    There is little evidence that the General Staff sought or welcomed out-

Romanian Generals: 1. Crăiniceanu, 2. Popovici, 3. Averescu, 4. Iliescu, 5. Zottu, 6. Georgescu, 7. Prezan. From *The Times History of the War* (London: The Times, 1917–1919)

side input from Romania's leading military figures in their preparation of the army for war. Alexandru Averescu, who was widely considered to be the nation's foremost general, is a case in question. He had entered the army as a private and rose through the ranks in the War for Independence (1877–1878). After being commissioned, he attended the Italian War Academy in Torino, where he also found a wife. His outstanding ability won him an ascending series of important posts: director of the Romanian War Academy (1894), military attaché in Berlin (1895–1897), minister of war (1907–1909), and chief of staff of the army (1913). He was extremely popular with Romanian soldiers and the public, but as a man of strong opinions and an acerbic tongue, he was unpopular with some higher officers. Austrian intelligence described him accurately as "vain and presumptuous" but "one of the most capable [of Romania's] highest leaders."[38] Averescu had clashed with Brătianu in 1907–1909 while serving as his minister of war and with Crown Prince Ferdinand while serving as chief of the General Staff during the Second Balkan war. When Brătianu came to power at the end of 1913, Averescu resigned the latter post and was exiled to the command of the I Army Corps at Craiova. During 1914–1916, he nourished his resentment toward the prime minister and the king, convinced they intended to prevent him from exercising a role in the coming war that was commensurate with his ability. He also had an especially hostile relationship with Iliescu, for whom he had nothing but contempt.[39] Consequently, Averescu was given little opportunity to influence the preparation of the Romanian army for war. A chance meeting with Brătianu on a train in March 1915 gave him an excuse to submit his own plan for operations in Transylvania. It differed little from the conceptions then being developed by the General Staff. When a new "Instructions for Mobilization" was issued in April 1915, he submitted a critique. As a follow-up several months later, he was invited to meet with both Brătianu and Ferdinand, but he found them unreceptive to his suggestion that the planned mobilization of 23 divisions be reduced to 15. This, Averescu argued, corresponded more closely to the nation's resources—a judgment that was validated in the course of the 1916 campaign.[40]

While admitting the shortcomings of the Romanian army and its plan of war, it should be emphasized that the General Staff was dealt a very difficult hand of cards. Modern Romania, scarcely 50 years old, had little military experience or tradition. The army had proved to be embarrassingly weak and disorganized in the campaign of 1913. It is unreasonable to expect that it could have been elevated to the standards of its enemies by 1916, especially because they now had two years of battlefield experience. Likewise, rectifying the army's deficiencies in armaments was well-nigh impossible for a nation that had meager domestic production facilities and to whom the belligerents refused to sell. Even when it came to devising a war plan, the basic strategy was dictated by the exigencies of a two-front war and by political, not military, considerations. The evacuation of Dobrogea and the establishment of a strong defensive line along the Danube could not even be considered. This would have been acceptable neither to the Allies nor to the Romanian public. Conversely, adopting a defensive stance in the Carpathians while attacking south in hopes of linking up with the Allied forces at Salonika was also impossible. "Public opinion had been molded for the invasion of Transylvania," as Professor Nicolae Iorga aptly expressed it; "no one could have been able to impose another direction on the Romanian flag."[41] Even if one of these options had been adopted, there is no reason to believe that it would have been more successful than Hypothesis Z. Given the failure of the Brusilov Offensive, the impotence of the Allied army at Salonika, and the deficiencies of the Romanian army, a defeat in the campaign of 1916 was predictable.

3

On the Eve of War

THE CENTRAL POWERS: MISCALCULATING ROMANIA'S ENTRY

The Central Powers were not unaware that the Romanian government was preparing to intervene. Austrian cryptographers had cracked the Italian diplomatic cipher and since April had provided a record of Brătianu's negotiations with the Entente. These intercepted radiograms, which were shared with the German leaders, revealed the terms of both the political and military conventions as they evolved. One message intercepted on 30 July mentioned 14 August as the date when Romania would be obligated to enter the war. This evidence inspired General Conrad von Hötzendorf, head of the Austrian High Command (AOK), to propose a surprise attack on Romania as soon as it was verified that Romania had signed an alliance.[1] General Erich von Falkenhayn, chief of the German High Command (OHL), pointed out that this was impractical because no forces were in readiness to carry out an attack. Furthermore, doubts were raised regarding the intercepts. Count Ottokar Czernin, the Austro-Hungarian minister in Bucharest, insisted he had proof that the radiograms had been intentionally falsified to mislead the Central Powers. This view gained credence at OHL, especially after the time frame mentioned passed and Romania remained quiet.[2]

However, the testimony of the radiograms that Romania was preparing to attack Austria-Hungary was supported by extensive military intelligence. Reports of German attachés from Bucharest listed many measures indicating that the mobilization of the Romanian army was at hand: no officer furloughs after 4 August and no more harvest furloughs (20 July); requisition of horses, wagons, and autos "imminent" (3 August); more reserves called in (5 August); Russian troops assembling in Bessarabia and Russian wide-gauge rail lines extended into Moldavia (5, 9 August).[3] Colonel Hans von Hammerstein accurately described the Romanian army on 11 August as "slowly arriving on war footing and grouping its power for operations, offense with two-thirds against Transylvania, defense with one-third against Bulgaria. . . . At the present tempo it can be ready for the advance against Transylvania at the end of August." The intelligence section of AOK gathered more detail on what it called Romania's "gradual, systematic preparation and grouping of the army for intervention." A telltale sign of another genre, among many, was the attempt of the Banca Românească, controlled by the Brătianu family, to dump German marks on foreign financial markets.[4]

However, the picture presented by Austro-German intelligence was clouded by the dispatches of Czernin and the German minister in Bucharest, Baron Hilmar von dem Bussche. They were convinced that Brătianu was bent on war, but they believed that Hohenzollern king Ferdinand would ultimately block his policy. "I am still convinced the king does not plan an attack on us," Czernin wrote on 9 August. Bussche's "impression" as late as 23 August was that Ferdinand "will not go against us."[5] Both assumed, erroneously, that the monarch's ethnic and family loyalties would, in the end, triumph over his commitment to achieving Romania's war aims and the attendant glory for himself. It was their hope that Ferdinand would replace Brătianu with a government composed of Conservative Germanophiles led by the elder statesman Titu Maiorescu. Even Hammerstein came to adopt this point of view: "A Germanophile cabinet is the most likely option now," he wrote to Falkenhayn on 21 August. Prince Ştirbey, who Czernin naively believed "was on our side," was the chief instrument fostering this miscalculation of Ferdinand's intentions, and the king played his role skillfully. "Our governments," General Seeckt lamented to his wife, "maintained that Brătianu was a man of honor and the King a Hohenzollern." But, he added, "Who were the dumbbells? We soldiers, who[se] daily reports told us [that] those mobilization preparations unconditionally pointed to war."[6]

Consequently, in spite of the intercepts and other intelligence, an unwarranted hope regarding Romania reigned at OHL. The Bulgarian liaison there reported in mid-August that Kaiser Wilhelm did not believe in a break with Romania and that Falkenhayn was "optimistic." Doubts about the reliability of the continuing flow of Austrian intercepts persisted. On 18 August, Falkenhayn told German chancellor Theobald von Bethmann Hollweg that he suspected they were "colored," implying Austrian exaggeration for the purpose of extorting reinforcements. On the same day, the general said he "saw no imminent danger" and two days later judged the situation "not unconditionally unfavorable." He explained later: "I thought that the entry into war [of Romania], if it would happen even this year, must take place after bringing in the harvest, that is, toward the end of September."[7] Given this mind-set at OHL, the news of the Romanian declaration of war, which reached Pless at 10:30 P.M. on 27 August, hit like a "bombshell." Falkenhayn at first refused to believe it. The kaiser, who was informed during his nightly game of skat, "lost his composure completely" and pronounced the war "definitely lost." Falkenhayn's miscalculation of the timing of Romania's intervention came at a critical time in his struggle to retain his command. He had just weathered an attempt by his critics to unseat him and had been reaffirmed by the kaiser. But his misreading of the Romanian situation undermined his standing, and the monarch gave in to his enemies, replacing him with the team of Field Marshal Paul von Hindenburg and General Erich Ludendorff. Under the domination of the latter, Germany embarked on a reckless policy of total war, which would have both immediate and far-reaching consequences for Germany and the world.[8]

STRATEGY OF THE CENTRAL POWERS

Although Falkenhayn miscalculated the timing of Romania's intervention, he had not neglected to prepare for it. In June, he encouraged the Bulgarians to strengthen their 3rd Army on Romania's southern frontier and explored the possibility of augmenting it with Turkish troops. The latter step was premature for Sofia at that time.[9] Von Hötzendorf, whose country was most threatened, had no illusions that Romania would intervene, and soon. On 18 July he visited Falkenhayn in Berlin and proposed that as soon as Romania declared war, the Central Powers should immediately carry out

German–Bulgarian higher command. From left: Field Marshal August von
Mackensen, Bulgarian chief of staff Nikola Jhekov, Colonel Gerhard Tappen,
General Hans von Seeckt, Prince Boris, General Erich von Falkenhayn. From
Album de la grande guerre (Berlin: Stikle, 1915–1918)

an assault crossing of the Danube and march on Bucharest. For this purpose, he offered the Austrian bridging train, which had been used against
Serbia in 1915. Because, in the event of war, Romania could close the
Danube Iron Gates, he had already cached it on the Bulgarian shore of the
river. On 29 July, von Hötzendorf and Falkenhayn met with the operational
chief of the Bulgarian army, General Nikola Zhekov, at OHL. On 3 August,
they met in Budapest with Turkish war minister Enver Pasha, who agreed
to provide Turkish troops. From these meetings, a threefold strategy
emerged: first, a holding operation in Transylvania by Austro-German
forces until reinforcements could be made available from other fronts; second, an immediate offensive on Romania's southern frontier by the Bul-

garian 3rd Army reinforced by German and Turkish troops; and third, a subsequent crossing of the Danube.[10]

This strategy conceded that a Romanian invasion of Transylvania could not be prevented. A year earlier, General Anton Goldbach, charged with the defense of the province, had reported that only delaying tactics, including "guerrilla warfare," were possible before making a stand on the Mureş river. "We can bring no power worthy of the name to the border," von Hötzendorf repeated on 20 July 1916, "only frontier guards augmented by gendarmes. . . . An effective resistance on the border is out of the question."[11] With heavy fighting continuing on other fronts and their armies living hand to mouth with reserves, AOK and OHL were reluctant to send extensive reinforcements until Romania actually declared war. Late in July, 12 battalions of *Landsturm* (militia) arrived to supplement frontier gendarmes. At the beginning of August, three Habsburg divisions, battered from fighting on the Eastern Front, were en route to Transylvania for reconstruction. Of these, the Hungarian 51st ID "made a very painful impression" and required complete reorganization and refitting. In the 71st ID, the Szekler 82nd Infantry Regiment (IR) was also "pressingly in need of rehabilitation." It was hoped the reconstruction of these exhausted units would be completed before Romania attacked. OHL promised to send four or five German infantry divisions and one or two cavalry divisions when these could be spared from other fronts, but in any case only after Romania actually entered the war. A new command structure, the Austro-Hungarian 1st Army, was created to organize the defense of Transylvania. On 14 August, General Arthur Arz von Straussenburg assumed command of the 1st Army and the responsibility for defending the province. He was well acquainted with the land he would defend. The son of a Lutheran pastor in Sibiu, he had served as a young officer at several military posts along the Romanian border. Arz's task was a daunting one. His initial force immediately available to defend a frontier of 600 kilometers totaled only 15 "very weakened" battalions, four Hungarian cavalry regiments, and 13 artillery batteries.[12]

MACKENSEN AND ROMANIA'S SOFT UNDERBELLY

While giving ground in Transylvania, the Austro-German command was determined to pursue aggressively the attack on Romania's southern fron-

Field Marshal August von Mackensen, General Arthur Arz von Straussenburg, General Erich von Falkenhayn. From Ernst Kabisch, *Der Rumänienkrieg, 1916* (Berlin: Vorhut-Verlag Otto Schlegel, 1938)

tier. Although the operation would be carried out primarily by Bulgarian troops, Zhekov and King Ferdinand of Bulgaria agreed that it be led by Field Marshal August von Mackensen, then commander of the armies of the Central Powers in Macedonia. He was an obvious choice. The conqueror of Serbia, "whose name was worth an army," provoked respect among the Bulgarians and apprehension among the Romanians. To accentuate the latter, news of Mackensen's appointment was made known in Bucharest.[13] At the beginning of August, the field marshal visited the Danube to inspect sites for a river crossing. Like von Hötzendorf, he believed such an operation would be more effective in supporting the Transylvania Front than an attack to the east in Dobrogea. However, the Bulgarians had less interest in crossing the Danube and marching on Bucharest than in conquering Dobrogea and reclaiming the territory taken from them in 1913. Their aims fit in with Falkenhayn's strategy. He rightly believed that the power available initially would be insufficient for a river crossing. It must be preceded by a prior advance into Dobrogea, which could provide flank protection and gain time for the preparation and assembly of an adequate force for the Danube operation.[14]

Falkenhayn made this clear to Mackensen, along with the fact that he needed to rely on resources in the Balkans for the operation. At hand, near the frontier or in northern Bulgaria were the three and a half divisions of the Bulgarian 3rd Army, the German Kaufmann Detachment consisting of half of the 101st ID with some miscellaneous units along the Danube, and the Austrian bridging train, together with the Danube flotilla. Two Turkish divisions were assembling at Adrianople, but their contribution was problematic. They were weak, 2,000 to 3,000 men each, and although the Bulgarian government did grant transit permission on 18 August, it would be more than two weeks before they would arrive at the Romanian Front. Mackensen's only other source was his forces on the Macedonian Front. Evidence that Sarrail was planning an attack prior to Romanian intervention convinced the German command to preempt this with an offensive designed to shorten and consolidate this front. Then Bulgarian forces with some German troops and artillery could be sent north to Romania.[15]

Because the German 11th Army in the center faced French forces "heavily superior" in artillery, the German command wanted the Bulgarian 1st and 2nd Armies, which enjoyed more favorable conditions on the flanks, to carry out the Macedonian offensive. The Bulgarians were eager to attack in Macedonia because it offered the prospect of realizing their longtime goal of occupying the Greek cities of Seres, Drama, and Kavalla. Mackensen met with Zhekov and Crown Prince Boris on 13 August at Kyustendil, the location of the Bulgarian High Command (BGK), to arrange command relations and to stabilize operational plans. Agreement was reached that the Bulgarian 1st Army would attack Sarrail's left flank, the 2nd Army his right. The German 11th Army would remain on the defensive. Colonel Richard Hentsch, chief of staff at Mackensen's headquarters (OKM), reported that the field marshal also used the meeting to promote the Romanian operation "energetically," arguing it could "no longer be delayed" because Romania "mobilizes against us." He pointed out that a majority of Romanian power would be concentrated against Transylvania with "merely the V Corps and one or two reserve divisions against Bulgaria." He admitted that their reinforcement with a Russian expeditionary force was "very probable." The prospect of fighting against the army that had liberated Bulgaria from Turkey in 1877 was a sensitive issue for many Bulgarians. However, Mackensen stressed that this was an opportunity to strike the Romanians during mobilization and "grievously" disrupt their preparations. German and Bulgarian forces freed up by the Salonika offensive and sent north would include the remainder of the German 101st ID, a German regiment to strengthen the Bulgarian 12th ID, a brigade from the Bulgarian 6th ID (2nd Army), and a Bulgarian cavalry division. This would increase the strength of the 3rd Army to five infantry divisions and one cavalry division. "This, rightly employed," Mackensen concluded, "would be sufficient for success." According to Hentsch, Zhekov and Boris "indicated they understood this but yet hesitated to make a decision." Their reluctance reflected the desire of the government in Sofia to avoid a premature break with Romania. In fact, some Bulgarian military and political leaders were opposed to attacking Romania at all, and a few were even open to a deal with the Entente for a separate peace.[16]

The Bulgarian offensive in Macedonia began on 17 August. It came at an inopportune time for the Allied forces. They outnumbered their enemies but were beset with health, supply, and command problems. The latter centered around differing British and French conceptions of their obligation to support Romania's entry with an attack eight days prior, as required by the military convention. The British were reluctant to undertake military action until Romania actually declared war, and then only "to do their best to hold the Bulgarian forces where they now are." The French felt committed to an operation closer to Brătianu's intention of an offensive that would force the Bulgarians to withdraw troops from the Romanian frontier. This difference prevented the commander of the British forces from cooperating fully with Sarrail's proposed plan of operations. Sarrail's preparations were also hindered by uncertainty and delay in the alliance negotiations. The signature of the military convention on 17 August left him only three days until the Allied forces were obligated to attack. More importantly, the offensive of the Bulgarian armies, which opened on that very day, was an immediate success—a "brilliant stroke," according to Cyril Falls. Sarrail's forces fell back rapidly. In a little over a week, Florina, Vodina, Seres, and Kavala had been occupied by the Bulgarians. Then resistance stiffened. But Mackensen was satisfied. The battle line had been shortened, Sarrail thrown back on his heels, and the Allied offensive delayed until it was too late to help Romania. The first train of Bulgarian troops left for the Romanian Front on the evening of 22 August. Mackensen and his staff would follow them north in a few days.[17]

Henceforth, operations on Romania's southern frontier became the chief priority of OKM. The planning of the offensive was in the able hands of Colonel Hentsch. With the Danube crossing postponed, he proposed that as soon as Romania declared war, the offensive should be opened with a quick strike in western Dobrogea aimed at the cities of Turtucaia and Silis-tra. This advance would bring about a shortening of the front, "which is pressingly necessary because otherwise the Bulgarian forces would not be able to hold against the attack of the Romanians and . . . the expected Ser-bian and Russian reinforcements." Falkenhayn was somewhat skeptical, stressing that it should only be complementary to a more general advance in Dobrogea.[18] No one foresaw that the capture of Turtucaia in the opening days of the fighting would cause panic in Bucharest and chaos in the Ro-manian High Command. This vigorous and quick response of the Central Powers to the declaration of war would far exceed the calculations of the Romanians and the assurances of their allies.

In retrospect, while the Austro-German miscalculation of the date of Ro-mania's intervention cost Falkenhayn his command, it had little influence on the response of the Central Powers to the Romanian threat. Preparations had not been neglected. A more immediate response, including an ultima-tum or preventive attack, was impossible. Bulgarian participation, a sine qua non for either, remained in doubt until Romania actually declared war. In Transylvania, where time was needed to gather forces, the Austro-German command had already decided to surrender territory rather than defend on the frontier. General Wilhelm Groener, an influential staff chief at OHL, even stressed the positive advantage of allowing the Romanian armies to penetrate Transylvania. Then they could be cut off and destroyed, not just chased back across the frontier.[19]

ROMANIA

The ten days that elapsed between the signing of the alliance on 17 August and the declaration of war were stressful ones for Brătianu, who, in the last analysis, was responsible for the decision to intervene. True to character, his personal internal debate continued. On an evening automobile ride with his closest cabinet advisor, he soliloquized, "I believe I have thought of everything, that I have foreseen all, that I have left nothing to chance. I seek constantly to see what would have escaped me." To his son, Gheorghe, he admitted his doubts, that all might not go well and Romania might be defeated. Reports of the fighting in Macedonia gave substance to these doubts. Dispatches of the Romanian military attaché in Sofia brought immediate word of the Bulgarian success and Sarrail's impotence.[20] The premier was "very disturbed" because these negative reports continued and were accompanied by evidence of Bulgarian troops moving toward the Romanian frontier. The Bulgarian minister in Bucharest added to the concern by boasting privately that they would invade and occupy the capital in five days.[21] Brătianu repeatedly expressed his dismay to the Entente powers over Sarrail's inaction and expressed regret that he had not made Romania's entry dependent on Sarrail achieving specific goals. He took steps to avoid provoking Bulgaria and suggested that the Entente sound out Sofia regarding a separate peace. He had no illusions about the prospect of winning Bulgaria, and the Entente was unwilling to try, "at least until after Romania takes the field."[22] Despite this unfavorable turn of events, Brătianu maintained his resolve to go to war and publicly announced on 26 August that a crown council would meet the next day.

THE CROWN COUNCIL AND ATTITUDES TOWARD WAR

The men that assembled in the ornate, large dining room of Cotroceni Palace in Bucharest on Sunday, 27 August, included many of the same political leaders who had been summoned to the crown council two years before. However, this time the purpose was different. Then, King Carol had sought advice in making a decision; now, King Ferdinand sought support for a decision already made. With uncharacteristic confidence and lucidity, the monarch explained the emotional conflict he had experienced between his German heritage and his duty as a Romanian king. He pleaded for the support of all present in his decision to go to war in pursuit of the national ideal. Brătianu's lengthy exposition of the terms of the alliance and the rationale for entering the war met with the approval of the majority, composed of Liberals and Conservative-Democrats. The Conservative minority who demurred argued that it was perilous to make a commitment because the war was yet undecided. The meeting continued for almost two hours as the king and Brătianu attempted to change the attitude of the Conservatives and gain their approval. In closing, Brătianu spoke again at length. He admitted the possibility that defeat might lie ahead. But, as with the case of Italy's war with Austria in 1859, he argued, defeats can be steps to victory. He said he was ready to take complete responsibility for advising the king to "draw the sword." Ferdinand concluded the discussion by affirming his belief that entering the war to realize the national ideal was the only solution that corresponded to the true interests of the country. He ended the meeting with another appeal for support and the rally cry, "Gentlemen, Forward with God." He left the room in tears. Shortly after the meeting, the sovereign summoned Alexandru Marghiloman, took him by both hands, and asked him to join a coalition government. The Conservative Party leader refused but added: "If things do not go well, it is in the interests of the Crown to have me in reserve."[23] This was prophetic of the role Marghiloman would play in 1918 when he agreed to head the government after Romania was forced to make a separate peace with the Central Powers. Late that evening, as the Romanian minister delivered the declaration of war in Vienna, the invasion of Hungary began.

News of the crown council's decision unleashed an emotional outburst of patriotism. Crowds had begun to gather on the principal streets of the capital, even before the crown council convened, eagerly awaiting its announcement. "After lunch the great news came," remembered historian Constantin Kirițescu, "spontaneously evoking from thousands of breasts that old Romanian hymn, 'Romanians Awake!' For hours, we lingered about the center in an indescribable spiritual excitement." To another, the atmosphere was like "an inferno." When King Ferdinand and Queen Marie appeared in an open vehicle, there was "an explosion of affection and fidelity for the dynasty; the car could hardly move. The queen was radiant." Christian Rakovskii, the antiwar Socialist leader, en route to police headquarters to be arrested, observed crowds marching along the Calea Victoriei and patrons in outdoor restaurants all singing the popular military anthem, "La arme," some with orchestral accompaniment.[24] That evening, armchair strategists drew crowds in the cafés and on the streets with their explications of what lay ahead. Many public figures, including Constantin Stere, a leading opponent of the war, appeared on the streets in uniform as pseudo-officers. "Since Stere was made a colonel," satirized Professor Nicolae Iorga, "I should be a general." As troop trains departed for the frontier, well-wishers decorated them with flowers and sang in unison with the soldiers. Some wagons were festooned with placards, "On to Budapest."[25] These scenes were reminiscent of the mass hysteria that gripped Berlin in August 1914.

Outside the capital, there were similar outbursts of patriotism. In

Râmnicu-Vâlcea, church bells and trumpet fanfare sounded forth as local reservists mobilized in the city square. A priest blessed them and then delivered an inflamed speech. At the village of Broşteni, the entire population turned out to cheer, sing, and dance as the 16th Infantry Regiment passed through en route to Transylvania. The local schoolmaster, though well beyond military age, begged to be given a gun and enrolled in the unit. In a more restrained celebration, General Ioan Dragalina and Colonel Traian Moşoiu, both former Habsburg officers, silently embraced when their command received orders to invade Hungary in pursuit of the Romanian dream. In Dobrogea, troops sang patriotic war songs long into the night. Most Romanians, both civilian and military, seemed to agree with a young lieutenant who reminded his company that this was "a holy war in which we will settle accounts with our enemies of the centuries."[26]

But in addition to euphoria, concern and even fear were present. In the army, some soldiers were sobered by the realization that war entailed considerable risk for themselves and their country. Lieutenant Sterea Costescu spent the final night of peace preparing his last will and testament; his first sergeant hurried to have his newborn child baptized. Higher officers also had doubts. Colonel Alexandru Sturdza, who, like many, feared the alliance with Russia, received the news of war with a "pained heart." General Alexandru Averescu found reason to be pessimistic as he examined the Romanian war plan with a critical eye.[27] In political circles, a sense of apprehension coexisted alongside patriotic emotions. Senator Vasile Cancicov confessed that he lay awake at night, his feelings alternating between fear and joy. Many Conservative politicians were filled with doubt and concern. Alexandru Marghiloman and Tito Maiorescu steadfastly refused to believe that Germany could be defeated. Russophobes like Petru Carp were certain that a war alongside Russia would lead to Romania's ruination.[28] Brătianu, with sober realism, prompted the press to warn the public that Romanian territory might be lost and civilian casualties might result from air attack. He was prophetic. Twenty-four hours after the declaration of war, the German zeppelin Z-101 crossed the Danube from Bulgaria and appeared over Bucharest. Illumined by Romanian searchlights, it transfixed spectators as it drifted over the city. Its bombs caused little damage, but they served as a warning of what was to come. Precautionary measures were taken. Some prominent citizens, including the bold advocate of war Take Ionescu, moved into the Athenee Hotel, one of the few reinforced con-

crete structures in the city. Rudimentary air raid procedures were implemented: church bells, prompted by the patriarchal church, sounded the
alarm; policemen echoed it with whistles. A blackout in the capital was prescribed, and all landlords were ordered to provide a tank of water, a
hatchet, a pitchfork, and a ladder to combat fire.[29]

MOBILIZATION AND CONCENTRATION

The mobilization and concentration of the Romanian army was accomplished quickly and relatively smoothly. This was possible because the majority of the troops were already mobilized when the decree was posted at
midnight, 27/28 August. Unannounced during the preceding month, the
3rd Army in the south had been completely mobilized. The remainder of
the standing army had been augmented by contingents of reserves called
up for regular summer training. Most importantly, unusually large covering forces had already been sent to the frontiers. The latter process, begun
during Romania's armed neutrality, had accelerated during the summer of
1916. On 27 August, 20 covering groups totaling 200,000 men, more than
a third of the operating army, were on or near the frontier. This early deployment eased the demands on the struggling Romanian rail net, reduc-
ing requirements by 30 percent. On the other hand, there were serious
problems resulting from committing so many units to the covering forces.
Although some battalions found themselves located in the vicinity of the
point of assembly of their parent division at mobilization, many were far
away. To avoid massive transfers to unify divisions, these battalions were
ordered to join whatever division was concentrating nearby. As a result,
some first-line battalions were co-opted into reserve divisions and conversely some territorial and militia battalions into first-line divisions. This
seriously modified the order of battle and weakened the homogeneity of
several divisions.[30]

Another serious problem at mobilization and concentration was that of
staff and command assignments. Military politics and Brătianu's obsession
with secrecy meant that even the most senior commanders did not learn
of, let alone assume, their commands until the eve of war. General Mihai
Aslan was informed in mid-August that he would command the 3rd Army,
but he was not allowed to inspect it or assume command until the day war

was declared. Brătianu called Averescu in only two days before hostilities began to inform him that he would command the 2nd Army. In addition, with the exception of General Constantin Prezan (North Army), all the army and corps commanders were strangers to the regions and/or the units to which they were assigned. General Ioan Culcer, who assumed command of the 1st Army, had been without direct contact with troops for more than three years while serving as a subinspector of the army. General Grigore Crăiniceanu, who took over the 2nd Army a few days into the war, was a Brătianu loyalist who had spent the years 1914–1916 as political editor of *Universul,* a large Bucharest daily. The commanders of the six army corps were assigned in a similar fashion as the army commanders. Their suitability in directing combat operations has been questioned; none was an infantry officer; five were engineers, the other an artillerist. All were informed at the last minute of their assignments and operational orders. As Gheorghe Dabija has pointed out, Romanian commanders were as surprised as the enemy at the declaration of war.[31]

Upon the proclamation of mobilization, the Romanian General Staff (MSM) was divided into two sections, sedentary and operational. The former, retaining the designation MSM, remained in Bucharest to handle administrative tasks. It was headed by a vice chief of staff, General Dumitru Stratilescu. The latter, designated the Marele Cartier General (MCG), directed military operations. It was relocated on the night of 27 August to Periş, a small village 35 kilometers north of the capital. Here, it was reasoned, there would be isolation from "noise, intrigue and indiscretions."[32] Quarters were provided by the buildings of the Administration of the Royal Domains. The king, who assumed the title of commander in chief, took up residence at his nearby estate. MCG possessed radiotelegraph links with the field armies, with its representative at the Russian High Command (STAVKA) and with its liaison officer attached to the Russian expeditionary force in Dobrogea. General Zottu, now fatally ill, remained in Bucharest as chief of staff in name only. Brătianu ignited controversy by choosing the poorly regarded Iliescu to be vice chief of staff to the king and de facto generalissimo, over the more highly regarded Averescu or Christescu. Even more illogical was the appointment of Christescu as chief of staff of Averescu's 2nd Army rather than as Iliescu's subchief of staff at MCG. This violated the traditional Romanian practice of bracketing a competent assistant with a weak chief and left MCG without a competent senior officer.[33]

In the absence of an able commander or subchief, the direction of the army devolved on the Operations Bureau, where Colonel Rășcanu remained in charge. Although recognized for his ability as staff officer, doubts were expressed about his ability to "lead everything." Second in influence only to Rășcanu at MCG was Major Rosetti, who continued as director of the bureau. He was known as the workhorse at MCG. He was the first to arrive just after 4:30 A.M. and the last to leave around midnight. He read all incoming messages and assigned work to the operational staff. He presented operations orders to Rășcanu and Iliescu for signature and prepared reports for the king. He handled most of the communications with the field commanders. His telephone manners, often brusque and peremptory, angered some. He was especially anathema to Averescu, who believed that Rosetti had been involved in preventing him from being named chief of staff. Rosetti also functioned as a liaison at MCG for Brătianu. It was he, not the king, Iliescu, or Rășcanu, who had a direct telephone line to the premier's office in Bucharest. Rosetti was in daily contact with his brother-in-law, who closely monitored developments at MCG and, as we shall see later, intervened directly in several major decisions. For the first week of the war, MCG, not the commanders of the four armies, had direct control of field operations.[34] It would become evident in the campaign of 1916 that the Romanian High Command, as a whole, lacked effective leadership, was indecisive, and was driven by political considerations. However, it is necessary to emphasize that it faced an all but impossible task of conducting a two-front war against superior enemies led by several of Germany's most competent field commanders.

4
The Invasion of Transylvania

On 26 August the chiefs of staff of the army corps poised to invade Transylvania were called to Bucharest and given orders to send covering forces across the Austro-Hungarian frontier at 9:00 P.M. the following day. Early the next day, under the pretext of an exercise, a trial run was made to determine travel time from concentration points to the border. After the crown council that afternoon, the four army commanders were ordered to open their envelopes containing copies of Hypothesis Z. This elaborate scheme to maintain secrecy was successful. At all points of penetration, enemy defenders were taken by surprise; only a few offered resistance. Progress of the covering forces was so rapid and extensive that on 2 September MCG instructed them to continue their advance beyond original objectives. With the prospect of gaining sufficient space beyond the Carpathians, the commanders of the North, 1st, and 2nd Armies were ordered to transfer the concentration of the remainder of their units into Transylvania. Unfortunately, the ease of the initial advance evoked popular expectations of a triumphal march analogous to the 1913 invasion of Bulgaria.[1]

THE NORTH ARMY

The North Army, which attacked along the Eastern Carpathians on a front of 260 kilometers from Vatra Dornei to Oituz, was commanded by General

Romanian infantry crossing the Carpathians, 28 August 1916. Muzeul Militar Naţional

Constantin Prezan. He was a military engineer without general staff experience. This, and his longtime service as adjutant to Prince (now King)
Ferdinand, led to a public image as a "salon general," "elegant but of no
particular reputation."[2] Prezan relied heavily on his brilliant but arrogant
34-year-old operations officer, Captain Ion Antonescu, the future marshal
and head of state (1940–1944).[3] The operations of the North Army, which
was composed of three and a half infantry and one and a half cavalry divisions, unfolded in three stages beginning on the night of 27–28 August.
In the first, six covering groups quickly seized control of the most important Carpathian passes on its front: Bistriţa, Bistricioara, Bicaz, Ghimes, Uz,
and Oituz (north to south). At Bistriţa and Uz there were serious clashes,
but elsewhere, only token resistance was offered from Habsburg border
guards and elements of an Austrian *Landsturm* ID, which was spread thinly
over the entire front. On 30 August, Prezan could report: "Enemy frag-
mented in isolated and disorganized units, beaten all along the front, in retreat followed by our columns."[4]

   An anticipated supporting offensive by the Russian 9th Army to the
north failed to materialize. There had been no joint planning before the

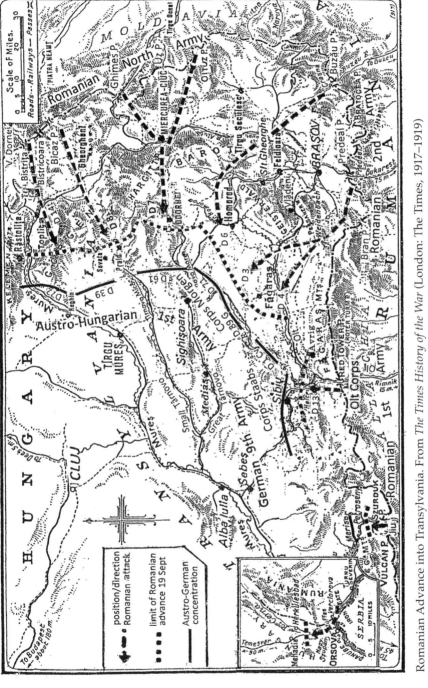

Romanian Advance into Transylvania. From *The Times History of the War* (London: The Times, 1917–1919)

General Constantin
Prezan, commander,
North Army. From
Petre Otu, *Mareşalul
Constantin Prezan.
Vocaţia datoriei*
(Bucharest: Editura
Militară, 2008)

opening of hostilities, but on 30 August a Russian liaison officer appeared at the headquarters of the North Army with a plan for coordinated action to envelop the left wing of the Austrian 1st Army. The Russian brought with him communication equipment for direct contact with his own headquarters, and Prezan was eager for a joint operation. However, MCG, because of other priorities and traditional mistrust of the Russians, did not seize this opportunity. On 31 August, the Russians did begin a limited independent operation, but after encountering rugged terrain and enemy counterattacks, they abandoned their attack pending the arrival of reinforcements. Later on, there were some restricted operations of the 9th Army, but despite repeated Romanian pleas, the Russian High Command (STAVKA) insisted that heavy fighting in Galicia would not allow it to give substantial support to the Romanian invasion of Transylvania. Nevertheless, on their own, in three days Romanian covering forces secured a concentration zone eight to 13 kilometers wide running north–south through the regions of Borsec, Gheorgeni, Miercurea Ciuc, and Târgu Secuiesc. A pause ensued during the first week in September as the main forces of the 14th, 8th, and 7th IDs were assembled and reconnaissance units probed the sub-Carpathian mountains to the west.[5]

The North Army began the second stage of its offensive under Prezan's order of 6 September to "gain control of those heights which border the valleys of the upper Mureş and Târnava [rivers]." During the next ten days, Romanian columns penetrated the Gurghiu, Harghita, and Baraolt ranges and reached the edge of the Hungarian plain. The 14th ID occupied Topliţa and advanced to Rastoliţa on the Mureş; the 8th ID overran Gheorgheni and reached the upper course of the Small Târnava river near Praid; the 7th ID secured Miercurea Ciuc and continued on to the Great Târnava river near Odorhei. The 2nd CD advanced southwest to establish contact with the Romanian 2nd Army.[6] The defending Austrian 61st ID could do little other than give more ground. It had arrived from Galicia exhausted and depleted, then filled out "with elements poorly prepared and without experience." Totaling barely 6,000 men, spread over a defensive front of 90 kilometers, it was outnumbered 6 to 1. On 6 September, fearing that he would be enveloped on both flanks, its commander had ordered his forces to retreat 20 kilometers without fighting. The Austro-German Command was concerned. Archduke Karl complained to AOK that this retreat placed the right wing of his 7th Army to the north in a precarious situation and called for action to stop the advance of the Romanian forces into the Mureş valley. Ludendorff had already sounded the alarm, pointing out the great importance of the rail line paralleling the Mureş, essential for the transport of reinforcements and sustaining military operations. The enemy advance must be stopped, he insisted, on the intervening defensive line of the Târnava "at any price." AOK responded with a belated attempt to strengthen weak, primitive prewar fortifications with more barbed wire. But von Hötzendorf admitted that a successful delaying action by the 61st ID was "no longer possible." If the Romanian advance continued, he predicted, it could force the retreat of the 71st ID, which defended the southeastern sector of the Transylvanian Front.[7]

However, the pause in the advance of the North Army between 30 August and 6 September proved to be a godsend to the Austro-German command as they scrambled to assemble reinforcements. The first units scheduled to arrive, the Bavarian 10th ID, the Hungarian 39th ID, and an

Austrian *Landsturm* brigade, were still en route to Bistriţa, Târgu Mureş, and Reghin. On 8 September, German general Curt von Morgen with his I Reserve Corps staff arrived at Târgu Mureş to take command of the northwest sector of the Transylvanian Front. He was determined to oppose the enemy with a "stubborn resistance accompanied by an offensive blow." Morgen immediately rallied local formations and a few early arrivals to confront the advancing Romanians. All along the front, these ad hoc attempts failed, and the defenders continued to fall back. Morgen then proposed to use additional forces still in transit, which now included the Alpine Corps, to launch a major offensive designed to administer a decisive defeat on the North Army. He suggested two options. The first was an attack on the right wing of the Romanian 14th ID northwest of Topliţa. The second was to attack up the Târnava valleys and break through the center of the North Army. Arz gave his approval to the second option, but Ludendorff viewed the hesitant and confused advance of the 1st and 2nd Romanian Armies to the south as a more promising target. The new quartermaster general at OHL insisted that Morgen remain on the defensive in the northeast. To the offensive-minded Morgen, this meant an active defense. Consequently, he moved quickly to confront the Romanians with those forces allotted him. Prezan noted on 11 September that "the resistance put up by the enemy becomes stronger in the upper Mureş and Olt valleys."[8]

During this second stage of its offensive, the North Army penetrated an average of 50 to 70 kilometers into Hungarian territory and shortened its front by 100 kilometers. It had occupied the important cities of Topliţa, Gheorgheni, Miercurea Ciuc, Odorhei, and Târgu Secuiesc. Then, unexpectedly, a terse order arrived from MCG: "Situation becoming serious on the Southern Front as a result of the fall of Turtucaia and the reinforcements received by the enemy; general offensive in Transylvania to be postponed until new orders." On 11 September, Prezan informed his commanders and ordered them to fortify the terrain already conquered with multiple lines of defense. During this last stage of the offensive of the North Army, most units remained in place and undertook only local operations designed to improve defensive positions. However, over the next week ending on 19 September, there were several additional offensive operations. The 14th ID was instructed to advance to the northwest into the Căliman mountains in cooperation with the Russian 9th Army. The 2nd CD was ordered to move southwest to the line Homorod–Agostin to close the gap to the 2nd Army.[9] Except for these actions, the front of the North Army remained essentially stable for the next month.

Prezan, and by inference Antonescu, have been praised for the "competence and energy" with which they conducted the opening campaign of the North Army. But there has also been criticism, especially for the failure to press ahead faster during the first week of the war while the enemy remained most vulnerable.[10] But without a strong supporting offensive of the Russian 9th Army in the north and a successful advance of the other two Romanian Armies in Transylvania, to have penetrated farther into Hungary could have been perilous. Had the North Army advanced alone beyond defensible mountain positions onto the Hungarian plain, it would have faced the prospect of being caught between the Austrian 7th Army on its right and a powerful new German 9th Army under formation on its left.

THE 2ND ARMY

The 2nd Army, composed of four infantry and one cavalry divisions, attacked along the curve of the Carpathians on a front of 230 kilometers. General Alexandru Averescu, appointed to command it, was incensed about not being named instead as head of MCG, a position to which he believed his ability and experience entitled him. On 28 August, he requested an audience with the king and sought a reversal of the decision, but was rebuffed. Ironically, a few days later, Ferdinand would be forced to turn to Averescu to reverse a disastrous course of events on the Southern Front.[11] Like the North Army, the 2nd Army encountered little initial resistance as it seized the most important passes on its front, including Timiş (Predeal), Törzburg (Bran), Bratocea, and Buzău. At Predeal, Romanian covering forces burst in on the Hungarian customs post as the duty officer was reading a newspaper. At a nearby barracks, 20 border guards surrendered in their nightclothes. Several Hungarian officials were killed or wounded in a brief armed confrontation. In the mountains to the west, a handful of Romanian soldiers engaged Hungarian border guards in conversation, then opened fire before continuing on. The absence of any army formations and the general lack of readiness on the frontier was, in part, a deliberate choice of Hungarian officials. They feared that the civilian population might panic prematurely if army units manned customs posts and telephone and telegraph offices before a declaration of war.[12]

Austro-Hungarian resistance to the 2nd Army was led by General Anton Goldbach, who had directed defensive preparations in Transylvania since 1915. He had at his disposal a melange of units comprising the Austrian 71st ID, recently re-formed but rated "completely unprepared." Leading the defense of the Braşov basin was the 82nd Infantry Regiment, composed largely of Szeklers whose ancestral homeland to the north lay in the path of the Romanian advance. Detachments of the 82nd IR offered brief, spirited resistance just north of the Predeal and Bran passes, but then, in keeping with Austro-German strategy of giving ground in the face of the overwhelming superiority of the Romanians, they retreated. This allowed advance units of the Romanian 4th ID to enter Braşov, an important center of Romanian population and culture, on 29 August.[13] The capture of Braşov opened vital road and rail connections across the Carpathians and beyond.

After crossing the Carpathians, the next objective of the 2nd Army was to reach the line Făgăraş–Homorod defined by the Olt and Homorod rivers. The 3rd ID and 4th ID on the left wing advanced north from Bran and Predeal, and the 5th ID and 6th ID on the right wing advanced northwest from the Bratocea and Buzău passes. Despite little enemy resistance, their progress, unlike the forces of the North Army, was slow. Four days of steady marching were required to reach their concentration areas situated on a line from Vlădeni to Feldioara. There were also unfortunate distractions. On 6 September, MCG ordered the 5th ID transferred to the south to shore up the deteriorating situation there. It was replaced by the 22nd ID, an ad hoc formation that was being created from units taken from other divisions. Then, on 7 September, Averescu was transferred to the command of all Russo-Romanian forces in Dobrogea. Unfortunately, instead of elevating Christescu to replace Averescu, MCG sent him to the south also and gave command of the 2nd Army to the incompetent Grigore Crăiniceanu. Although the 2nd Army was included in the general order of 8 September suspending the Transylvania offense, MCG instructed Crăiniceanu on the 11th to continue on to the Olt and Homorod rivers.[14]

The Austrian 71st ID was expected, according to Romanian intelligence, to take a stand in "permanent positions" 20 kilometers northwest of Braşov.

This proved to be false. Goldbach had decided to withdraw his main forces back over the Olt and leave only a rearguard on the edge of the intervening Geisterwald forest. Consequently, the Romanian columns reached the Olt–Homorod line on 14 September with little opposition. An assault crossing of the rivers was ordered for the next day. At dawn, units of the 4th, 3rd, and 6th IDs (south to north) crossed, often wading because the retreating enemy had destroyed many of the bridges. Some of the heaviest fighting occurred in the vicinity of Făgăraş. Approximately 1,000 Romanian casualties were offset by an equal number of Austrian prisoners and pride in occupying a city of great historic interest. Another lively battle took place in the hilly country near the confluence of the Olt and Homorod, where the Romanians were checked briefly. However, the expectation that the enemy would take a stand in fortified positions on the opposite bank was not fulfilled. Goldbach had decided to pull his forces back again to ensure the security of Sighişoara and to marshal his forces for a counterattack. His position was strengthened when Austrian 1st CD and the newly formed Cavalry Corps of Count Eberhard von Schmettow moved into the gap between the 71st ID and the Austrian 51st ID located to the west near Sibiu. In their offensive, which continued through 17 September, Romanian columns advanced ten to 15 kilometers beyond the Olt and Homorod rivers virtually free of contact with the enemy.[15]

Meanwhile, MCG had made the questionable decision to weaken the Transylvanian Front in order to provide forces for a major offensive on the Southern Front. On 18 September, the 22nd ID and the 21st ID (the 2nd Army reserve) were entrained for Dobrogea. In addition, the main forces of the 3rd, 4th, and 6th IDs were ordered to pull back across the Olt and Homorod, leaving only a security line on the other side. Now the continuing task of the 2nd Army was to fortify its positions and to establish a solid front with the North Army and with the I Army Corps of the 1st Army to the west. The latter, which had invaded Transylvania through the Olt pass, was stalled before Sibiu and was about to become the focal point of a powerful Austro-German counteroffensive. A dangerous gap of 40 kilometers existed between the left wing of the 2nd Army, located 15 kilometers southwest of Făgăraş, and the right wing of the Ist Army Corps at Arvig. The only contact was via daily patrols in the area south of the Olt. Schmettow's cavalry, which operated to the north of the river, posed the threat of severing this connection and isolating the two armies. However, like the North

Army, the 2nd Army had made impressive initial gains, penetrating 70 to 100 kilometers into Transylvania and shortening its front by 100 kilometers. But the halt of the offensive before reaching the Mureş and the transfer of three of its divisions to the south left the 2nd Army in a vulnerable position for a counteroffensive by enemy forces, which were arriving in Transylvania in a constant stream.[16]

THE 1ST ARMY

The Romanian 1st Army formed the left wing of the Southern Carpathian Front. With five divisions, it was responsible for a 260-kilometer segment from the Argeş river west to the Danube. The 1st Army was commanded by General Ion Culcer, a highly regarded military theorist but an unsuitable field commander whose lack of energy and pessimism "demoralized all that were in subordination to him." To be fair, it should be pointed out that Culcer's command was a difficult one. His forces were divided into three battle groups named after the rivers they followed through Carpathian passes into Transylvania: the Cerna, the Jiu, and the Olt (west to east). These battle groups were awkwardly separated from one another by 60 to 100 kilometers of mountainous terrain that lacked lateral means of communication.[17] This dangerous isolation could be overcome only if they succeeded in advancing far enough into Transylvania to form a common front on the Mureş river with the other Romanian armies.

The Cerna Group was led by the commander of the 1st ID, General Ioan Dragalina. He was, in contrast to Culcer, an unusually energetic and able leader whose enthusiasm was contagious.[18] He wasted no time in crossing the frontier along the Danube and then advancing up the Cerna valley. After being held up briefly by fire from Austro-Hungarian Danube monitors, the Romanians captured in quick succession the Cerna heights (1 September), the historic Danube Island of Ada Kaleh (3 September), and the key Danube port city of Orşova (4 September). Having achieved the initial goals assigned by Hypothesis Z and under the restraint of Culcer, Dragalina went over to the defensive. Because the enemy forces were too weak to attack, the Cerna sector remained quiet for several weeks.[19] On this sector, as elsewhere on the Transylvanian Front, personal dramas were played out as Romanian and enemy soldiers faced each other in combat. Colonel

Alexandru Sturdza, who commanded a regiment in the Cerna Group, evaluated his feelings about fighting against the German Army, in which he had served a long internship early in his career. "I have no qualms vis-a-vis my former masters and teachers," he wrote his mother, "I will shoot at my old friends with *sangfroid*." For others, it was more heart wrenching. A German officer wept over the body of a Romanian officer killed in battle when he recognized him as a former schoolmate. Colonel Traian Moşoiu was deeply moved when he discovered that a fallen Habsburg soldier was a Romanian brother.[20]

Almost 100 kilometers to the east of the Cerna, the Jiu Battle Group of the 1st Army advanced into Transylvania over the Surduk and Vulcan passes. It was composed of two brigades soon combined as the 11th Infantry Division. Its objective was the valley of the Mureş river. The leading detachment reached the outskirts of the Hungarian coal mining center of Petroşeni on 29 August. A hastily assembled group of defenders consisting of a brigade of militia and three battalions of miners quickly retreated. The next day municipal authorities invited the Romanian forces to occupy the city.[21] The advance of the Jiu Group posed a significant threat to the defense of Transylvania. The mines of Petroşeni fueled Hungarian trains, and the Haţeg basin to the north contained a rail line vital to the arrival of reinforcements. When a counterattack on 8 September by a small force failed to stop the Romanians, significant reinforcements, including portions of both the German 187th ID and the Alpine Corps, were dispatched. But before the latter arrived, the Jiu Group halted its advance. In light of developments on the Southern Front, MCG was in the process of restricting offensive operations here as elsewhere. The cautious Culcer, reflecting on the dangerous separation of his battle groups, feared that if the Jiu Group advanced farther, it might be cut off. Consequently, he ordered it to halt at Merişor, 15 kilometers north of Petroşeni, and redirect its energies to fortifying the approach to the Jiu defiles. During the remainder of September, the Jiu sector was characterized by alternating attacks and counterattacks by the contending forces in which control of Petroşeni changed hands several times. It came to hand-to-hand fighting before the Austro-German forces were firmly in control of the city and the heights at the entrance to the pass. The Romanians retained control of the pass itself along the line of the old frontier.[22]

The third battle group of the 1st Army, the I Army Corps (Olt Corps), invaded Transylvania another 60 kilometers to the east, where the Olt river cut a passage through the Carpathians. The defile was named Turnu Roşu (Rotenturm, Red Tower) after a crumbling but still massive remnant of a medieval fortress at its northern end, colored, legend tells us, by the blood of Turkish invaders. Its good road and a railway gave it special strategic value. By their own admission, Austro-Hungarian defenders were poorly prepared. Ignoring earlier signs of Romania's intentions, fortifications were begun only when Romanian intervention became obvious. An attempt was made to intimidate the Romanians by parading a handful of German troops along the frontier. This stratagem may have contributed to the exaggerated Romanian estimate of the forces facing them, which in turn led them to advance with hesitation and extreme prudence.[23]

The Olt Corps was the largest battle group of the 1st Army, with two divisions, the 13th and 23rd IDs. After securing the exit from the pass, its mission was to occupy the Sibiu basin immediately to the north. Together with the Jiu Group, it was to serve as a pivot for the advance of the North and 2nd Armies into the heart of Transylvania. As elsewhere, the attack of the Olt Corps was unexpected. At 11:00 P.M. on 27 August, according to the report of an Austro-Hungarian border official, a "Romanian underofficer came toward us and said he wanted to test the Great Boundary Door to see if it shut properly. . . . We were suddenly shot at on the railroad and roadway." One Romanian column advanced relatively rapidly, overtaking and capturing an Austro-Hungarian armored train, much to the delight of its peasant soldiers. However, another column panicked in its first encounter with enemy fire and retreated seven kilometers back onto Romanian territory. It recovered the next day and continued its advance. By the end of the fourth day, the Olt Corps had occupied the entire plain south of Sibiu. The Hungarian 51st ID, the nearest significant enemy force, depleted and incompletely assembled, retreated to the heights north of the city.[24]

Having no desire to subject this important center of German culture to the ordeal of street fighting, Austro-Hungarian authorities ordered military and governmental personnel, but not civilians, to evacuate. On 1 September, a delegation from Sibiu, a German businessman and a Romanian lawyer, approached the leading Romanian column carrying a Red Cross flag. They offered to hand over the city "in order to prevent anarchy." The Romanian commander, Colonel Traian Moşoiu, hesitated to enter the city without permission from higher authority. Although such permission was granted, it was not acted on, thanks to a grotesque chain of mistakes, mis-understandings, and indecision at every level of the Romanian command structure. Poor communication and faulty intelligence played a part. Re-peated errors in deciphering messages added hours, if not days, to the decision-making process.[25] In the end, the city was not occupied even though its "garrison" comprised only 300 men engaged in evacuating sup-plies. General Matei Castriş, commander of the 23rd ID, allegedly delayed advancing because he wanted to prepare his triumphal entry. The always cautious Culcer thought entering the city too risky until the arrival of new forces. The Romanian field commanders were still vacillating on 7 Sep-tember when MCG decided to restrict operations in Transylvania. The Austro-German military was amazed that for almost a week the Romani-ans stood passive before a prize that had been conceded to them. Occupa-tion of the city would have given a moral lift to the Romanian army and populace; it would have hindered the assembly of new enemy forces; and it would have provided a strong position from which to continue the of-fensive. On the other hand, to have occupied the city, the Olt Corps would have been exposed to greater danger when the Central Powers seized the initiative soon after.[26]

THE REACTION OF THE POPULATION

The Romanian invasion of Transylvania touched off panic among the Hun-garian population. For the latter, the appearance of Romanians evoked memories of their intervention in 1848–1849 and fears of retribution for decades of Magyar domination.[27] The Saxon population, whose historical relations with their Romanian neighbors had been more benign, generally reacted more calmly than the Hungarian. But one Romanian military re-port stated that the "spirit of the German population is very hostile." At Cisnădie (Heltau), Colonel Moşoiu felt it necessary to reassure Saxon citi-zens "gripped by panic" that Romanians had not come to "kill or plun-der."[28] The Hungarian administration exacerbated the uncertainty and chaos that accompanied the Romanian invasion by ordering local bureau-crats to evacuate immediately, taking with them state records and valu-ables. Irresponsible local Hungarian military authorities proposed the burning of one village and, in Sibiu, the destruction of the train station, bridges, and warehouses. Fortunately these proposals were not carried out. But within 24 hours, local government and public services ceased. Braşov was plunged into darkness. In Sibiu, utilities failed, transportation broke down, food was scarce, and hospitals were crippled for lack of doctors.[29]

Habsburg military authorities opposed the evacuation of civilians but were helpless to prevent them from fleeing as word of the Romanian advance spread. The exodus reached epidemic proportions. To the arriving German Alpine Corps, it seemed as if "the greatest part" of the population had fled. Gathering what they could, many civilians headed for the railway station first, but few were able to board trains. In valleys nearest the frontier, refugees fled on foot with bundles around their necks. "In endless columns the refugees, grouped together by village, filled all the roads."[30] The more fortunate utilized wagons drawn by oxen, horses, or water buffaloes. Contemporary estimates number the fugitives in the hundreds of thousands, 100,000 in the vicinity of Sighişoara alone—"unequaled in the history of war" was the way Arz von Straussenburg described it. Up to half a million animals added to the confusion as peasants were ordered to drive their livestock deeper into Transylvania. Included were sheep and cattle commandeered from Romanian peasants. However, German intelligence reported that the herders, primarily Romanian, cunningly drove most of the cattle into the forest or toward Romania in order to deny them to the Hungarians. The refugees, upon reaching rear areas, often spread exaggerated reports of Romanian hostility, plundering, and even violence. Most such accusations, as German and Austrian sources affirm, proved groundless upon investigation. Among the instances of plundering that occurred, Hungarians, even the military, were sometimes guilty. Some Romanian civilians did occupy houses vacated by Hungarians and enjoy what they left behind.[31]

Despite Hungarian fears, the transition to Romanian rule was relatively calm. In Braşov, after the flight of the mayor and other officials, the deputy mayor, a German, and the few remaining officials cooperated in submitting the city to Romanian military rule. Habsburg functionaries were quickly replaced by Romanian ones. Other changes reflected the pledge of the military commander that Romanian control was forever: Romanian replaced Hungarian as the official language, Romanian emblems replaced Habsburg insignia, and portraits of King Ferdinand replaced those of Emperor Franz Josef. The usual decrees of military occupation followed: a curfew, restrictions on assembly, press control, confiscation of firearms, and the death penalty for espionage. There were no mass expulsions, although orders were issued for 40 "Hungarian and German notables" to be sent to a village outside of Braşov. According to Romanian army guidelines, property of the Hungarian state was to be confiscated "under all circumstances." The property of Romanian institutions was to "remain unmolested." The property of German and Hungarian citizens was not to be "confiscated but sequestered and utilized by the state." The same principle was to be applied to the property of churches and parochial schools other than Romanian Orthodox or Uniate.[32]

In contrast to the distress caused the Hungarians and Saxons, the arrival of the Romanian army, as might be expected, touched off wild jubilation among Transylvanian Romanians. As the 6th Infantry Regiment entered Braşov, it was greeted with tears, flowers, and vigorous hurrahs. A crowd escorted the commander and his troops to the Romanian Orthodox Church for religious ceremonies, speeches, and the singing of the Romanian national anthem. A headline in the *Gazeta Transilvaniei* in Romanian tricolors welcomed them: *"Bine aţi venit!"* (Welcome). "Brother liberators have arrived," it continued, "The hour has struck. . . . Forward with God for King and country." For most Romanians, it was a dream come true. "I felt like singing and dancing," recalled the internationally respected Transylvanian Romanian philologist, Sextil Puşcariu. Reports of the reception of Romanian troops called forth joy and tears in Bucharest as well. Elsewhere along the Carpathians, in smaller Romanian villages, the welcome was less elaborate but equally heartfelt. At Veşteni and other communities in the Olt valley, the population dressed in holiday costumes and carried flowers. Their priests, historically the conscience of Romanian nationalism in Transylvania, blessed the liberators with cross and gospel. At Săcel as well as Răşinari, men and women danced the hora with Romanian officers and men, "a dance for the reunion that was long awaited . . . the fulfillment of a dream," one participant recalled. At Şercaia, in addition to flowers, the women and girls stuffed the soldiers' backpacks with bread and bacon. Men from many villages helped the soldiers with military construction, acted as guides, and provided intelligence on the enemy. Father Motes, the rector of the Uniate school in Răşinari, "offered his services to the Romanian army on arrival" and performed "espionage services," according to Austrian intelligence sources.[33]

The identification of Transylvanians with the Romanian cause exacerbated the concern of the Habsburg military about the loyalty of its almost 500,000 ethnic Romanian soldiers. Already, following mobilization in 1914, a significant number, including reserve officers, had fled across the Carpathians to avoid fighting for Austria-Hungary. Some joined the Romanian army. After the declaration of war in August 1916, the Romanian general staff issued a direct appeal for others to desert: "Today your place is not in the Austro-Hungarian Army. Leave its ranks and come under the Romanian flag without delay." AOK quickly took steps to transfer sedentary, predominately Romanian reserve units out of Transylvania. Desertions increased immediately and continued as the war progressed, especially on the Russian Front, where most Transylvanian Romanian combat units served. A few weeks into the war, von Hötzendorf reported several cases involving Romanian officers, adding with a trace of bewilderment: "Almost all of these officers deserting had been decorated at the front since the outbreak of war." He issued orders to watch all Romanian reserve officers and aspirant officers. Even the fidelity of career officers, historically loyal to Kaiser Franz Josef, who was viewed as their protector against Hungarian discrimination, was undermined, even more so after the death of the monarch on 21 November. Among rank-and-file soldiers, strict control of information and the brevity of the Romanian success left confusion about developments on the battlefield. Open expression of sympathy for the Romanian cause was risky. But there was much private rejoicing at the news of the invasion and consequently much grief over the reverses that followed. Thereafter soldiers assumed an attitude of "undeclared resistance" to the Habsburg war effort.[34]

5

The War Opens on the Dobrogean Front

As planned, the Central Powers answered the invasion of Transylvania with an attack on Romania's southern frontier. Mackensen moved his headquarters to Tūrnovo in northern Bulgaria on 31 August and met with General Stefan Toshev, commander of the Bulgarian 3rd Army. They agreed on the plan of action authored by Colonel Hentsch: harassing the Romanians all along the frontier, but with the emphasis on a powerful assault on the fortress of Turtucaia.[1] Despite points of tension, a workable relationship developed between Mackensen's command (OKM) and the 3rd Army. The Germans respected Toshev for his honesty and incorruptibility, traits they seldom found in the Balkans. However, like other Bulgarian commanders, he sometimes resisted Mackensen's operational directives. To ensure these were promptly followed, the Germans invoked the royal authority of the 22-year-old crown prince, Boris, who resided at the 3rd Army headquarters, serving as translator and intermediary. With few exceptions, he insisted on the implementation of Mackensen's plans. Understandably, the Germans considered Boris "the soul of the 3rd Army."[2]

THE OPPOSING FORCES

The Bulgarian 3rd Army initially comprised two and a half infantry divisions, one cavalry division, and two small but vital German detachments. The Bulgarian 4th ID was concentrated southwest of Turtucaia, the Bul-

General Stefan Toshev, commander, Bulgarian 3rd Army. From Ernst Kabisch, *Der Rumänienkrieg, 1916* (Berlin: Vorhut-Verlag Otto Schlegel, 1938)

garian 1st ID southeast of Turtucaia, and half of the 6th ID in the east near Bazargic. In addition, the 1st Cavalry Division stood near the midpoint of the Dobrogean frontier, ready to move either to the east or to the west. One German detachment was appended to the 4th ID, and another was placed near the Black Sea coast. The 3rd Army had been stationed in northern Bulgaria during the 1915–1916 campaign against Serbia; hence, it had little edge in battle experience over the Romanians it faced. However, it did have other advantages. By taking the offensive, it was able to choose the point of attack and concentrate its forces. Also, the German alliance had brought important technology: aircraft, communications, transportation, machine guns, and above all, heavy artillery. With it came German tutelage, which was often resented.[3] Other assets were psychological. The morale of the troops was elevated by the prospect of a "holy war" to reconquer former national territory. In addition, the large Bulgarian population in southern Dobrogea could be counted on to render enthusiastic support.[4]

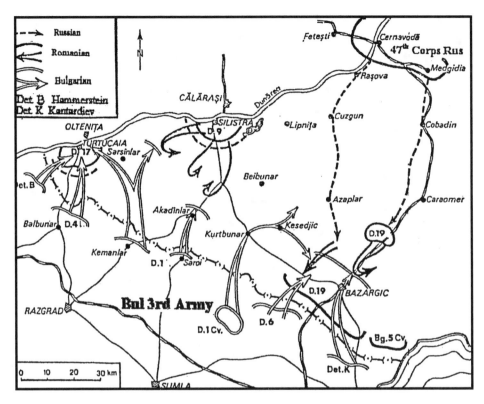

The War Opens in Dobrogea. Adapted from Ion Cupşa, *Armata română în campaniile din anii, 1916–1917* (Bucharest: Editura Militară, 1967)

Defending Dobrogea was the Eastern Battle Group of the Romanian 3rd Army. It was responsible for protecting a frontier that stretched 150 kilometers from the Danube to the Black Sea, across a grassy steppe with a few rolling hills but no natural obstacles. In accordance with the priorities of Hypothesis Z, only three infantry divisions and one cavalry brigade were allocated for Dobrogea: the 17th ID garrisoned at Turtucaia, the 9th ID at Silistra, and the 19th ID with a cavalry brigade in eastern Dobrogea near Bazargic. The secondary status allotted to the south was reflected in the quality of personnel and equipment. Of 54 battalions of infantry, only ten were of top quality, 20 were reserve, 19 were of the fourth (lowest) category, and five were militia. "The battalions of the fourth category and those of the militia would really not be of help in a bloody battle but are an element of panic," was General Averescu's assessment. Many were armed with out-dated 1878 Mannlicher rifles; there were few machine guns. The most crit-ical weakness was inadequate artillery, especially heavy calibers. Roman-ian artillery was unable to answer the barrages of the enemy, which devastated the ranks and morale of the Romanian infantry. The morale of the men was undermined also by the psychology of the war in southern Do-brogea. In contrast to their comrades liberating Transylvania, they were de-fending a recently acquired territory inhabited primarily by non-Romanians, many of whom were hostile. Romanian soldiers were intimidated by the perception that the enemy was better equipped, passionate, and cruel in bat-tle. The latter image was reinforced by the presence in Dobrogea of the fear-some *comitadji*, Bulgarian irregulars who, it was believed, "took no prison-ers, neither male nor female, neither young nor old." The mere cry, "The Bulgarians are coming!" was sometimes enough to precipitate panic.[5]

The Romanian forces in Dobrogea were augmented by a Russian expe-ditionary corps promised in the military convention. Instead of the 50,000 the Romanians expected, it numbered no more than 30,000 on arrival.[6] It was composed of an undermanned Cossack cavalry division, an exhausted Russian infantry division, and an untried Serb division recruited from among Austro-Hungarian prisoners of war.[7] Nevertheless, the Russian force, designated the XLVII Corps, arrived promptly on Romanian soil on 28 August by ship via the Danube and by foot via a pontoon bridge over the Danube at Isaccea. Although they were received with a traditional Or-thodox welcome of bread and salt, the Romanians soon had reason to com-plain about their conduct. The Cossacks lived up to their reputation for ma-rauding by devastating a number of restaurants and estates. The Russians proceeded, as a British observer put it, to "drink all the liquor they can get their hands on." The Serbs, on the other hand, got on well with the Roma-nians.[8] The tension between the Russians and the Romanians was exacer-bated by the commander of the XLVII Corps, General Andrei Zaionchkov-skii. He had tried strenuously to avoid the command and considered it a cross to be borne or a punishment for some misdeed he had committed. Zaionchkovskii had a reputation in the Russian command for a "spiteful wit," a lack of initiative, and a preference for retreat, all of which he man-ifested in Romania. To make the Romanian army fight a modern war, he quipped, was like asking a donkey to dance a minuet. He refused to sub-

General Andrei Zaionchkovskii.
From *The Times History of the War*
(London: The Times, 1917–1918)

mit to the direction of the Romanian command, explaining to Russian chief
of staff Mikhail Alekseev that he did not intend to pull Romanian chestnuts
out of the fire. He was opposed to sending the XLVII Corps so far afield,
and his objective seems to have been to withdraw it back to Russian territory as soon as possible.[9] Relations between Zaionchkovskii and the Romanians did not bode well for the Dobrogean campaign.

All Romanian forces in the Dobrogea were under the direction of 3rd
Army commander General Mihail Aslan. Slim, dapper, and quick-witted,
Aslan was considered by some as "one of the best-prepared commanders"
in the Romanian army. Others dismissed him as a dilettante who neglected
his duties for the card tables at the Jockey Club. Appointed to his command
on the eve of war, he had no opportunity for input on the disposition of his
forces or the strategy he was to pursue.[10] This strategy—rigidly defending the national frontier—was epitomized by the fortress of Turtucaia.

TURTUCAIA

Originally a Roman camp and subsequently a Turkish fortress, Turtucaia was situated at the extreme western point of Dobrogea. Bulgarians described it as a "spike into the heart of Bulgarian territory." As an anchor of the Romanian defensive system in Dobrogea, Turtucaia had been intensively fortified in 1913–1916 with the aid of Belgian military engineers. These defenses, as yet unfinished in 1916, consisted of three concentric lines of defense, anchored on the Danube. The primary line of defense was on the heights overlooking the city, incorporating 15 centers of resistance, or forts about two kilometers apart. These forts were linked by a system of shallow trenches and protected by barbed wire obstacles. Although the latter were ten to 15 meters wide, they were not continuous, and they were so low "a small dog could jump over it." Four kilometers behind the primary line of resistance stood a primitive secondary line whose value was extremely limited. For command purposes, the entire defensive system was divided into three sectors: I (west), II (south), and III (east), each with its own local commander. Most of the artillery the garrison possessed was in the primary line. Guns of light caliber (37mm, 53mm) predominated. Those of heavier caliber were obsolete, immobile, or incapable of firing toward the flank or rear. However, the fortress gained some firepower from Romanian Danube monitors that controlled this stretch of river.[11] Unfortunately, the defensive philosophy implemented at Turtucaia ignored the lessons learned on other battlefields in 1914–1916: the vulnerability of fixed fortifications without a supporting mobile force, the indispensability of heavy artillery, and the danger of concentrating all resources on a single line of defense. Another fundamental weakness of fortress Turtucaia was its location: exposed at the western tip of Dobrogea, far from Russo-Romanian forces farther east and without a secure connection with the Romanian heartland. Although linked to Oltenița, across the Danube, by a submerged telephone cable and an array of small boats, it had no bridge. While its less important sister fortress downstream at Silistra enjoyed a pontoon connection, Turtucaia remained a "bridgehead without a bridge."[12]

But, as Mackensen concluded later, Turtucaia's weakness was not primarily its fortifications but rather its Romanian defenders, especially their leadership. The commander of the fortress and of the 17th ID was General

Constantin Teodorescu. He had received his advanced military education at the War Academy in Vienna and had earned a reputation as a military geographer before being assigned in 1915 to oversee the construction of Turtucaia's fortifications. Although events would demonstrate that he was an ineffective leader, it must be pointed out that Teodorescu's repeated requests for better resources, especially heavier artillery and better means of intelligence, remained unfulfilled. Intelligence and communication in general were so inefficient Teodorescu first learned of the Bulgarian declaration of war through public rumor.[13] The 17th ID, which encompassed the majority of Turtucaia's defenders, had been newly organized with two reserve and two regular regiments. Like the Romanian army as a whole, it had been diluted by incorporating many raw recruits. Its cadre was especially inadequate. Reserve officers with only minimal training predominated. The skill level of the soldiers they led was similarly low. Morale was poor; they felt insecure and isolated.[14]

The attacking force at Turtucaia was composed of the Bulgarian 4th ID, one brigade of the Bulgarian 1st ID, and a detachment of four German battalions commanded by Major von Hammerstein. The attack commander was General Pantalei Kiselov (1863–1927), a hero of the Bulgarian–Serbian war of 1885, who had received specialized staff training in France, which undoubtedly influenced his preference for frontal assault.[15] Kiselov had only a 1.4-to-1 overall numerical superiority, but by concentrating his forces on the main area of attack (Sector II south), he achieved a local advantage of 2.25 to 1. Kiselov's forces enjoyed other important advantages over the Romanians, including excellent intelligence gained with the assistance of local inhabitants. However, the most important advantage Kiselov possessed was the especially high morale of his troops, some of whom were natives of the region who had emigrated after 1913. They had vowed to return Turtucaia to the motherland. For them, "the hour of reckoning" had come.[16]

While Bulgarian forces were staging for the assault on Turtucaia, local encounters occurred in eastern Dobrogea along the Bulgarian frontier. On 30 August, a band of *comitadji* infiltrated the city of Bazargic, devastating property and causing the municipal authorities and Romanian citizens to flee in terror. On 3 September, Balcic, on the coast, had the same experience. As the Romanian garrison fled, "the Bulgarian population, full of joy, raised the Bulgarian flag everywhere."[17] The response of General Nicolae

Arghirescu, commander of the Romanian 19th ID, was erratic. Initially, he sent troops to reoccupy Bazargic, but he almost immediately ordered them to withdraw, citing the need to await the advance of Zaionchkovskii's forces before engaging the enemy. This decision appears wise in light of the disasters that lay ahead, but his superiors, erroneously informed that the battle at Turtucaia was going well, ordered Bazargic reoccupied. On 4 September, after a long, tiring march, units of the 19th ID reached the suburbs, where they were held up by heavy artillery fire and Bulgarian infantry. Although retaking Bazargic was more a strategic and tactical liability than a necessity, a major assault was ordered for 5 September. It was assisted by an advance contingent of Russians, but the attack was poorly organized and unsupported by artillery. It was beaten back with heavy losses.[18] Arghirescu then appeared at the front, ordered a new retreat, jumped in his car, and headed to the rear. His men, exhausted and demoralized after marching up to 60 kilometers in two days, fell back, some of them in disorder. To add to the confusion, Zaionchkovskii, who had been appointed to the overall command in Dobrogea, ordered a new attempt to take Bazargic on 6 September. This was in turn followed by yet another order to retreat. As the 19th ID marched back once again, a young Romanian lieutenant overheard two brigade commanders express their "bewilderment" over "orders and counterorders, now attack then retreat." He concluded that Arghirescu was "completely disoriented" and that the Romanian command, in general, was trying to "learn war on our backs."[19]

In contrast to this confused maneuvering was the aggressive action of the Bulgarian 1st Cavalry Division, commanded by General Ivan Kolev, a seasoned veteran of the Serbian and Macedonian campaigns. On 2 September he surprised two Romanian infantry battalions moving without reconnaissance near Kurtbunar northwest of Bazargic. The Romanians fled in panic, leaving behind 100 dead and 165 as prisoners. The next day, not far away, Kolev attacked the Romanian 6th Mixed Brigade, which was also retreating without proper security. Over 650 Romanians were killed and 728 captured; the remainder fled in disorder. "The confusion was indescribable," a Romanian officer recalled. "In deafening noise troops ran desperately across fields while wagons, two or three abreast, jammed the roads racing at the full speed of the horses." Equipment, including irreplaceable artillery, was abandoned.[20] These early encounters in eastern Dobrogea inflated the morale of the Bulgarians. Premier Vasile Radoslavov "gleefully" boasted to the Austrian minister in Sofia that the Romanians could not withstand "Bulgarian troops filled with fanatical hatred toward them."[21] These Romanian defeats were but an indication of what was to come.

THE ATTACK ON TURTUCAIA BEGINS (2–4 SEPTEMBER)

On the morning of 2 September, German–Bulgarian forces crossed the frontier and approached Turtucaia's advanced defensive outposts. In Sector II (south), where the main assault was focused, units of the 4th ID easily overran the Romanian positions. In Sector III (east), Romanian forces withdrew even before being attacked. Only in Sector I (west) did the attackers meet significant resistance. Here, Hammerstein's Germans advanced quite easily at first, thanks to their intimidating "automobile" cannon. However, later in the day, the Germans were halted by artillery fire, primarily from Romanian Danube monitors. Overall, by the evening of this first day, the defenders of Turtucaia had retreated to their primary line of defense. The Bulgarians were amazed at Romanian passivity. Already on the evening of 3 September Teodorescu's telegrams to MCG and to 3rd Army headquarters showed his alarm at the magnitude of the enemy attack and indicated that he was inclined to evacuate.[22]

The Romanian chain of command, however, refused to recognize the seriousness of the threat to Turtucaia. Prime Minister Brătianu, when informed of the attack, is said to have retorted: "It is a simple demonstration. . . . There they [Bulgarians] have only a brigade while General Teodorescu has a division." The initial response from MCG was simply to decree that Turtucaia "must resist to the end." Attempts were undertaken to send Teodorescu additional troops from reserves in and around Bucharest. However, the first contingent was unable to board troop trains because the railroad stations were blocked by the general congestion and confusion accompanying mobilization. To overcome such problems, motor vehicles were pressed into service, including private automobiles and taxicabs requisitioned off the streets of Bucharest.[23] Unfortunately for the Romanians, the analogy with the Battle of the Marne ended there. The next two days (3–4 September) were relatively quiet as the Bulgarians moved up their infantry and artillery for the main assault. This delay gave the Romanian command an option of initiating a timely evacuation eastward to consolidate all Russo-Romanian forces in Dobrogea in a more defensible position, the prevailing opinion at Romanian 3rd Army headquarters. But MCG was adamant: "Turtucaia must not fall, the garrison must resist to the last man because fresh troops will come to help. This is the Sovereign Order of His Majesty the King."[24]

The possibility of a flank attack from Russo-Romanian forces elsewhere in Dobrogea did concern German and Bulgarian commanders. However, as we have seen, the 19th Romanian ID in the east was hardly in a position to help, and Zaionchkovskii was pursuing his own agenda, the recapture of Bazargic. On 4 September, he ignored an urgent appeal to send all available units on a forced march toward Turtucaia. In Zaionchkovskii's defense, it should be pointed out that even by forced march, it would have been impossible to cover the 100 kilometers to Turtucaia before it surrendered.[25] The only realistic possibility of relief for Turtucaia was the Romanian 9th ID garrisoned at Silistra. On 4 September, General Ion Basarabescu, its commandant, was ordered to send an "offensive reconnaissance" in battalion strength toward the southwest. Upon meeting the first enemy resistance, it panicked and retreated in disorder back to Silistra. A new, larger expedition departed on 5 September. But the next day, when its advance guard came under fire from enemy cavalry and artillery, the entire column began to retreat. Triggered by cries of "the Bulgarians are coming" and "flee from the Bulgarian cavalry," panic soon engulfed the expedition. Infantrymen threw down their weapons and fled, becoming entangled with the artillery. Cannoneers deserted their guns, mounted draft animals, and galloped to the rear. Supply and medical wagons, many of them driven by locals of Bulgarian or Turkish descent, joined the melee. Basarabescu, who accompanied the expedition, sped back to Silistra in his automobile.[26]

THE FALL OF TURTUCAIA (5–6 SEPTEMBER)

Meanwhile, on the morning of 5 September, Kiselov launched his final assault on Turtucaia. In Sector II (south), the Bulgarian soldiers advanced with "burning zeal"; two regiments charged singing, "O Dobrogea, you are our earthly paradise." The Romanians, for the most part, began to abandon immediately what was their only true line of defense. One local retreat triggered another. Too much of the withdrawal was carried out in panic

THE WAR OPENS ON THE DOBROGEAN FRONT   71

and disorder. Major Ulrich von Henning, the German liaison officer, later observed rows of dead Romanian soldiers, lying facing Turtucaia, shot in the back as they fled.[27] Reserves sent to the front quickly scattered when confronted with artillery fire. Here and there Romanian units did fight well. The 79th Infantry Regiment, despite suffering appalling losses that left it with only 400 effectives, re-formed and counterattacked. In some cases, Romanian gun crews resisted fiercely and were subdued only in bloody hand-to-hand combat. Proof that not a few Romanians fought well can be found in Bulgarian casualty figures, which reached 50 percent in some units fighting in Sector II. However, in Sector III (east), the First Brigade of the 1st Bulgarian ID advanced easily northward toward the Danube. At 6:30 P.M., they reached the eastern heights overlooking the river, completing the isolation of Turtucaia. By nightfall on 5 September, the Romanians had surrendered 13 of 15 forts and retreated to a last, primitive line of resistance. Colonel Gerhard Tappen, Mackensen's new chief of staff, who arrived that evening for a personal inspection, was surprised and pleased.[28]

During the night of 5–6 September, confusion and desperation reigned on the Romanian side of the battle line. Only two forts of the primary line of defense remained in the defender's possession. Virtually all artillery had been lost. In almost all units, effectives had been reduced by 50 percent. Many soldiers had already retreated to the banks of the Danube and were seeking to escape to the other side. Yet MCG still clung to the hope that more reinforcements or a relief expedition from the east could save Turtucaia. It maintained its edict that the garrison must fight to the last man. Reinforcements taken from reserves near Bucharest, which had come in driblets earlier, finally arrived in large numbers during the day and evening of 5 September. Rushed to Turtucaia before completing mobilization and concentration, these units arrived without their support sections. They were flung into battle hit or miss, without orders and without purpose. Under these conditions, reinforcements contributed little to the defense of Turtucaia. Many arrived only in time to be captured.[29]

While the Romanians were in turmoil, Kiselov issued an order to his troops to attack at dawn, "to smash the enemy and throw him into the Danube." At 4:30 A.M., his artillery unleashed a "hurricane of shells," followed by the advance of the infantry at 6:00 A.M. Romanian defenders began to give ground almost immediately. Bulgarian soldiers, sensing final victory, unsheathed their bayonets and rushed forward to a roar of hurrahs. Teodorescu immediately ordered a counterattack and urged his men to resist "at any price until the arrival of assistance." Despite the heroic action of some units, the Romanian counterattack failed. Thereafter, the defenders offered no serious resistance as the Bulgarians overran Turtucaia's last line of defense and penetrated the suburbs of the city. Demoralized and in the grip of panic, Romanian soldiers fled back toward its center. At 11:00 A.M., Teodorescu telephoned MCG: "The situation is desperate; no hope of aid from Division 9 [Silistra]. Orders requested." The response he received was not to capitulate, but that "in no case is the general staff of the fortress to fall prisoner." At 1:40 P.M., Teodorescu arrived at the dock in an automobile and boarded a boat for the other side of the river, as MCG had ordered.[30]

The last hours of 6 September at Turtucaia were filled with chaos and tragedy. Confused, without adequate leadership, and terrorized at the prospect of falling into the hands of the Bulgarians, the majority of Romanian soldiers were dominated by one thought: escape. Those who tried to follow the coast toward Silistra were beaten back by enemy artillery and attacked by Bulgarian *comitadji* and local citizens. The majority surged toward the docks, seeking a boat to safety. So fierce was the fight to board the few available boats that many became overloaded and sank, drowning their occupants. Some soldiers threw themselves into the water and attempted to swim, clinging to pieces of wood for flotation. Very few succeeded in conquering the 800 meters of fast-moving water to reach the opposite bank.[31] As Bulgarian soldiers penetrated the city, cries of Romanian soldiers rose from all quarters: "We surrender," "Throw down arms," "We surrender." "Pieces of white cloth, napkins, and handkerchiefs waved over many heads." At 4:30 P.M. Colonel Nicolae Mărăşescu, the ranking officer remaining, sent a note in German to Kiselov: "I surrender without conditions all my officers, troops and munitions." His proposal was accepted an hour later. Because only 3,500 Romanians had been able to escape, 480 officers and more than 25,000 men entered into two years of harsh captivity.[32]

Blame for the disaster at Turtucaia was heaped initially on Teodorescu, Basarabescu, and Aslan. All three were removed from their commands within 48 hours. But in retrospect, it is clear that the magnitude of the disaster resulted from the refusal of MCG to order a strategic withdrawal. This decision was based not on military but political considerations, especially the impact that the evacuation of Turtucaia would have on public morale. This inflexibility, which ensured the loss of the garrison as well as the city, greatly increased the negative impact of the defeat on the Romanian populace, the government, and the army.

THE CONSEQUENCES OF TURTUCAIA

The capture of Turtucaia energized the Central Powers. Bulgarian soldiers were "beside themselves with joy," more self-confident and committed to the war by this "Cannae victory." There was great jubilation in Sofia. Students frolicked in the streets, and Romanian prisoners were paraded before the populace. Premier Radoslavov planned to taunt Romanian diplomats before they departed by marching captured officers in front of their embassy, but he gave up the idea after the Austrian minister objected.[33] News of the capture of Turtucaia brought relief and joy to Austro-German leaders also. "Long live the Fieldmarshal [Mackensen]," exclaimed General Seeckt. Kaiser Wilhelm, recovered from the depression caused by Romania's entry, celebrated with a champagne party for the Bulgarian representative at OHL. The plan of the Austro-German leaders to undermine the advance of Romanian armies in Transylvania with an attack in Dobrogea was succeeding more quickly than they had dared hope. Their analyses, based on these opening encounters in Dobrogea, concluded that the condition of the Romanian army was "very poor," its leadership "very insecure," and that its troops, lacking combat experience, would "fall into disorder" when attacked energetically by artillery and machine guns. Using this strategy, Mackensen was confident that "much could be accomplished" by his numerically inferior forces elsewhere in Dobrogea.[34]

The fall of Turtucaia had a devastating impact on the Romanians. A "wave of consternation" swept over their leaders. Longtime advocates of intervention wept like children. Opponents of the war said "I told you so" and began to think of a separate peace. For Brătianu, who had engineered Romania's belligerency, it was a dark hour of the soul. Deeply depressed, he wept with his head in his hands at a cabinet meeting. His only catharsis was to heap reproach on Romania's allies, especially French general Maurice Sarrail, for failing to aid Romania by aggressively attacking Bulgaria from Salonika. The general population learned of the surrender of

Turtucaia late on 7 September. Coming in the midst of rejoicing over the advance in Transylvania, it hit "like a thunderbolt." Panic swept over Bucharest. Visions of Bulgarians crossing the Danube and marching on the city were on many minds. Citizens of means began to desert the capital for Moldavia or even Russia.[35] Perhaps the one positive result of the catastrophe of Turtucaia for the public was that it replaced dreams of an easy victory with the realization that the war, if it could be won, would be long and bloody. Most importantly, the surrender of Turtucaia and the reaction to it in Bucharest also unnerved the Romanian High Command. It was an embarrassing tactical defeat but in itself of little strategic importance. Yet on the day after the city surrendered, MCG began to curtail the advance in the north and transfer troops to the south. Soon it was decided to halt the northern offensive altogether and send a majority of the Romanian army to the south in an attempt to regain the initiative there. This shift in forces ended in a failed attempt to invade Bulgaria across the Danube and at the same time opened the door for an Austro-German counteroffensive in Transylvania.

6
The Flămânda Maneuver

At noon on 6 September, as the fall of Turtucaia became certain, MCG had ordered the transfer of two additional divisions to the south, one each from the 1st and 2nd Armies. This was the first step in a process that ended in the total abandonment of the original war plan. Under the pressure of the "wave of terror which seized government circles and Bucharest in general," the king sought advice from outside MCG. He summoned Averescu and two older reserve generals to Periş on 7 September. Averescu strongly advocated halting the advance in the north and grouping a powerful force in the south to take the offensive against the Bulgarians. This, he argued, would quiet fears in Bucharest and restore morale in the army. The king responded by appointing Averescu to replace Aslan as commander of the 3rd Army. The next day orders went out for the northern armies to "suspend for the time being" their offensive in Transylvania. Over the next few days additional transfers from north to south began.[1]

THE RISE OF AVERESCU

During the month that followed, Averescu's influence over Romanian military operations increased, much to the satisfaction of his admirers. Crowds in Bucharest cheered as he traveled to his new command. "Averescu cannot be defeated" was on the lips of many. Political supporters proclaimed him Romania's "only hope" and wanted him to take over all military op-

General Alexandru Averescu. From Petre Otu, *Mareşalul Alexandru Averescu. Militarul, omul politic, legenda* (Bucharest: Editura Militară, 2005)

erations. In two memoranda presented to the king on 10 September, Averescu elaborated on his plan for meeting the crisis. Arguing that with its limited resources the Romanian army could not conduct offensive operations on two fronts, he proposed to go over to the defensive in the north, where the Carpathians offered the best possibility of holding the enemy. Then, in the south, his reinforced 3rd Army would go on the offensive against Bulgaria. This, he contended, would end the threat to Bucharest, increase the likelihood of attracting more Russian reinforcements, and possibly lead to a linkup with Allied armies attacking north from Salonika.[2] Averescu's exposition of the advantages of defense in the north and offense in the south had merit. If this strategy had been adopted before the war began, the campaign of 1916 might have developed quite differently. However, to undertake such a radical switch in the war plan now—a proverbial changing of horses midstream—was disastrous, as subsequent events proved.

Coincidentally with the presentation of Averescu's recommendations, Romania's allies weighed in with similar views. On 7 September, Alekseev suggested, in light of the reverse at Turtucaia, a "temporary change of the plan of operations," "taking forces from the 1st, 2nd, and 4th [North] armies to stabilize the situation in the south." "There is no reason to fear what may happen if, temporarily, the offensive in Transylvania stops. There is no threat to Romania from this quarter." This advice was repeated more insistently in the days that followed. The French and British staff chiefs, Joffre and Robertson, echoed Alekseev's counsel, although their military attachés in Bucharest disagreed.[3] Meanwhile, MCG, in the name of the king, solicited the views of General Prezan. In a detailed memorandum dated 12 September, Prezan proposed the reinforcement of the 3rd Army in the south, but "with one or two divisions at most," in order to mount a "vigorous but limited offensive" to extend the front in Dobrogea and protect the capital. In contrast to Averescu, he insisted strongly that the offensive in Transylvania be pursued "energetically" in order to reach the Mureş river, which would shorten the front and allow the creation of reserves. Prezan's advice was probably the better response to Romania's impossible situation, but like Averescu's, it failed to anticipate the speed and power with which the enemy would respond with counterattacks in both north and south. Prezan's realism moved him, in a personal audience with the king, to advocate also that the nation's base of operations be shifted from Bucharest to Moldavia as a hedge against a possible enemy invasion of Wallachia. Brătianu, who was present at this audience, dismissed the recommendation. "It was impossible," he insisted, to evacuate the government because of the "panic it would produce."[4]

Faced with contradictory advice, the king acted on Prezan's suggestion that commanders of all field armies also be consulted. Consequently, Culcer, Prezan, and Averescu were assembled at Periş on the morning of 15

September. Crăiniceanu (2nd Army) was detained by operations on his front. Iliescu and Brătianu also attended. The king opened the meeting by reading telegrams from Alekseev and Joffre urging a temporary shift in emphasis from north to south. He then asked for opinions from those assembled. The session quickly evolved into a sharp confrontation between Prezan and Averescu. When Averescu began his presentation by calling for a reorganization of the army, Prezan interrupted him, pointing out that this was not germane to the king's question. When Prezan reviewed the arguments of his memorandum, Averescu, as he wrote later, found them "theoretical" and "soporific." He then captured the initiative by interjecting: "Given the force necessary, I would know what must be done." "What, general?" Brătianu eagerly asked. "I would cross the Danube and fall on the rear of Mackensen," Averescu replied. Prezan labeled such an operation "dangerous," maintaining that it would denude the primary (northern) front. "This is your opinion not mine," Averescu retorted. Brătianu then ushered Averescu aside for a private meeting with him and the king; Prezan, ignored, left for the front.[5] As a result of the meeting, which continued as a "council à trois," Averescu was appointed to command a new Army Group South and ordered "to pass to the offensive against the Bulgarian–German army in Dobrogea with the aim of destroying it." He was to be reinforced with four additional divisions, of which three were to be taken from the north. At the same time, orders went out to the armies in Transylvania to remain on the defensive, in the positions they then occupied.[6] This decision to abort the offensive in Transylvania definitively and to embark on a major offensive in the south was based on political, not military, reasons: recovery of lost territory, avenging the humiliation of Turtucaia, and raising the nation's morale. It was the final step in a failure of nerve that began with the enemy conquest of Turtucaia.

RETREAT IN DOBROGEA

While preparations were being made for Averescu's operation, the Dobrogean Front was rapidly contracting. Two days after the fall of Turtucaia, MCG ordered the Romanian 9th ID to withdraw from Silistra and move eastward along the Danube to join up with Zaionchkovskii's forces, now designated "the Army of Dobrogea." At the same time, the latter was instructed to withdraw to the pre-1913 Romanian frontier. Consequently, by 13 September the Dobrogean Front had been reduced from 150 to 100 kilometers, encompassing an arc from Lake Oltina on the Danube to Mangalia on the Black Sea. This line did not hold long. The 9th ID panicked and retreated east along the Danube when attacked by a German brigade commanded by Colonel Johann Bode that used armored cars and heavy artillery. In the center, Serbian and Russian divisions also gave ground, but more slowly, and at heavy cost to the enemy. Along the Black Sea, Bulgarian cavalry and bicyclists penetrated Russo-Romanian positions and captured Caraomer. In the face of this enemy success, Zaionchkovskii ordered another general retreat of 30 kilometers on 14 September to a line of Raşova–Cocargea–Cobadin–Topraisar–Tuzla, the latter only 18 kilometers south of the key port city of Constanta.[7] This last retreat entailed the evacuation of towns such as Mangalia with substantial Romanian populations. It was a traumatic experience for the civilians; old men, children, and women, not a few with infants, fled the advancing Bulgarians, abandoning their possessions along the road. Men of the 9th ID, some native to the region, urged them on and helped by carrying small children. Morale was low among the soldiers, ill from diarrhea and exhausted by the marches and countermarches of the past two weeks. Some threw away their backpacks and abandoned weapons, including precious machine guns. The Bulgarian reoccupation of Southern Dobrogea was accompanied by reports of atrocities on both sides.[8]

Mackensen was eager to exploit the Russo-Romanian retreat with an immediate general offensive to inflict a decisive defeat. Until this was attained, his own projected assault across the Danube would be delayed, and with it "relief for our Transylvanian front." However, the Bulgarians, already in possession of the territory lost in 1913 and more, were slow to move. They "would now rather rest on their laurels," Mackensen concluded. Major Henning, the German liaison, attributed Bulgarian lethargy to a desire to stop and collect booty: "a stolen cow for them is what a flag is to us."[9] Certainly the incentive for the Bulgarians to attack had declined once their primary war aim had been achieved. But there is also a basis to Toshev's contention that a general offensive would have been risky because Bulgarian losses and enemy reinforcements had left his 3rd Army outnumbered. Romanian infantry divisions 2nd, 5th, and 15th had arrived, and the 12th ID and the Russian 115th ID were debarking. Toshev's reinforcements at this time were limited to the Turkish 15th Anatolian ID and the 25th Arabian ID.[10] Moreover, the Turks were not fully battle ready. According to Mackensen, they arrived "half-trained" without "uniforms, weapons [and] horses." Most of their lower-ranking officers could not read or write; only verbal orders could be used below battalion level. On the other hand, Mackensen would soon praise their courage and was "astonished" at how quickly they learned. Even the hypercritical Henning later admitted that the 15th ID "as a whole . . . fought well"; but at the same time, he dismissed the 25th ID as "cowardly. . . . Many times . . . the division would simply flee because of a single cannon shot." It proved necessary to intersperse them with the 15th ID or Bulgarian troops. Dissatisfaction with both the Bulgarians and the Turks caused Mackensen to lament, "If I only had German troops! . . . A kingdom for a German division." Despite German pressure, Toshev refused to commit to a general offensive and even considered a limited retreat. The usually successful appeal to Crown Prince Boris was to no avail. Bulgarian troops, he replied, "are brave in attack but if bad times come, they run to Sofia and God cannot stop them."[11]

Consequently, during the last part of September, the Dobrogean Front saw no major offensive. However, there were several local attacks and counterattacks by both belligerents in the strength of one or two divisions that were violent and bloody. For example, on 19 September near Cocargea, an attack by the Bulgarian 4th ID was repulsed in heavy fighting by the Serb volunteers in cooperation with Russian and Romanian troops. The Bulgarians suffered over 2,500 casualties in the battle, which lasted three days. The Romanian losses approached 30 percent of the effectives involved. Serb losses were even heavier, totaling 3,940 dead, wounded, and missing. The division had to be withdrawn from the line temporarily. However, its battlefield performance had gained it respect. "The best the enemy had," Henning would insist, "were the Serbs, despite their heavy losses."[12] On 21 September, Zaionchkovskii ordered the battle-weary Romanian 19th ID to attack south of Topraisar. This operation, known as the Battle of Mustafa Aci, was a monument to the sacrifice of the poorly equipped Romanians. Attacking over open steppe with virtually no artillery support— a "completely idiotic" move, according to the Germans—the Romanian infantry was torn apart and then pinned to the ground by a hurricane of enemy artillery fire. Morale began to crack. Lieutenant Costescu heard a cry from the company next to his: "Advance no more, you are being made

Turkish infantry on the Romanian Front, 1916. From Ernst Kabisch, *Der Rumänienkrieg, 1916* (Berlin: Vorhut-Verlag Otto Schlegel, 1938)

cannon fodder." He "tried to combat retreat but none would listen." Through the energetic intervention of General Constantin Scărişoreanu, who had replaced the erratic Arghirescu as division commander, order was finally restored. Zaionchkovskii then decided to give up the attack, ordering the division to retreat back to Topraisar. In the two-day Battle of Mustafa Aci, 50 percent of Costescu's company became casualties. Its losses notwithstanding, the 19th ID was called on to participate in a new offensive a fortnight later.[13] During the last week of September the Dobrogean Front remained relatively quiet. The Bulgarians went over to the defensive, and the Russo-Romanian forces prepared for their role in Averescu's plan to "cross the Danube and fall on Mackensen's rear."

PREPARING THE FLĂMÂNDA MANEUVER

On 17 September, two days after the council on strategy at MCG, Averescu reappeared with a comprehensive plan for a two-pronged attack in Do-

brogea: an offensive by a reinforced Army of Dobrogea in the east and a
surprise assault crossing of the Danube south of Bucharest by a new battle group of five divisions. The king approved the plan, and an operational
order was issued the same day. Bowing to Averescu's concern over secrecy,
the king waived an obligation for him to report on the details of the operation. This prevented the staff at MCG from vetting Averescu's plans—a
step that might have corrected some of its faults. Averescu attacked his task
with an energy and organization hitherto lacking on the Southern Front.
He visited Zaionchkovskii at his headquarters at Medgidia several times.
Although he found him to be an "irritable person" who had to be treated
like a "ripe boil," he was able to enlist his cooperation.[14] He also reorganized units in the 3rd Army, modifying its order of battle, and appointed a
commission of experts to prepare the river crossing. After surveying the
banks of the Danube south of Bucharest, the commission decided on a location near the tiny delta village of Flămânda. Its advantages included a
width of the river suitable for a pontoon bridge, easily accessible banks,
and proximity to existing transportation. Its chief disadvantage, a vulnerability to flooding in the event of prolonged rain, was recognized but discounted in light of usually good autumn weather and plans to raise and
improve local roads.[15] This gamble on the weather was the first miscalculation that contributed to the eventual failure of what became known as the
Flămânda Maneuver.

    The second miscalculation was the failure to provide adequate protec-
tion for the pontoon bridge that was to be the lifeline of the operation.
Potential threats were the Austro-Hungarian Danube flotilla and German
aircraft attached to the Bulgarian army. Commander Constantin Niculescu-
Rizea, in charge of naval defense, assumed that the combination of mines,
barricades, and shore artillery, which had heretofore kept the enemy ships
bottled up in the Persina (Beline) channel some 75 kilometers upstream,
would be sufficient protection. The strong Romanian Danube flotilla,
which had been supporting the riverine flank of the Army of Dobrogea
downstream, was not called on to play a role in the Flămânda Maneuver.
This decision was not only the result of underestimating the enemy naval
threat, but also of intense rivalry among Romanian naval officers.
Niculescu-Rizea, together with his superior at MCG, Admiral Constantin
Bălescu, on the one hand, and Admiral Nicolae Negrescu, the commander
of the Danube flotilla, on the other, were engaged in bitter personal and

professional conflict. When Admiral Negrescu asked Averescu if his flotilla were needed, he was assured that Rizea's blockade would be sufficient. Averescu's request for aerial protection elicited a promise from MCG of six aircraft.[16]

In less than two weeks, under the prodding of Averescu and the commission, impressive preparations were completed: ten kilometers of roads constructed; 250 boats and other pontoon materials delivered via railroad and horse cart from the Danube delta; telephone and telegraph lines (some double) installed, along with equipment to lay an underwater cable; and additional heavy shore artillery, mines, and barricades assembled near the crossing point. At the same time, Averescu's Army Group South grew into the largest force assembled under a single Romanian commander during the entire war: 128 battalions of the Army of Dobrogea and 58 of the 3rd Army on the Danube. It represented almost half of the Romanian army mobilized in August and over half of the total troops then in the line.[17] Unfortunately, Romanian intelligence on the enemy in Dobrogea was misleading. It placed the total strength of Mackensen's battle group at only 76 battalions, when in reality it was 105.[18] The assembly of the forces destined to take part in the crossing created difficult problems of logistics and secrecy. Virtually no facilities existed at the point of concentration. The two lead divisions (10th ID and 21st ID) were bivouacked in the wooded areas of the delta between Flămânda and Prundu. The other three infantry divisions and one cavalry division were located in small villages ten to 20 kilometers to the north and west. All the artillery was assembled near Flămânda. The infrastructure for supplying these forces and for the evacuation of the wounded also had to be set up. Much of the construction and assembly was carried out at night to avoid discovery by the enemy.[19] Although there were serious shortcomings in the preparations for the Flămânda Maneuver, it is amazing that so much was accomplished in the 12 days before the attack began, all without being detected by the enemy.

Averescu, whose demeanor and words inspired confidence, gathered his higher commanders for a briefing at Colibași near Flămânda on 29 September. They listened, he recounts, with "religious" attention and expressed "indescribable enthusiasm" for wiping out the humiliation of August. "Faith in victory was general," and Averescu believed that "this spirit dominated the troops." Not everyone shared Averescu's optimism. The commander of one of his infantry divisions was skeptical and reportedly traveled to Bucharest to voice his concerns to political leaders. Alarming news of enemy success in the north in the Battle of Sibiu, which began on 26 September, increased the pressure on Averescu to "liquidate the situation against the Bulgarians" quickly. When Averescu visited MCG on 30 September for final approval, the king and his advisors encouraged him to begin the operation that "very night."[20]

EXECUTING OF THE CROSSING

Consequently, at 10:00 P.M. on 30 September, the 10th Division, which initiated the assault, began marching toward the embarkation points. By 3:00 A.M. its first units began crossing in small boats. They wore summer uniforms and carried only limited ammunition and two days' food in their packs. By 11:30 A.M. the remainder of the 10th ID had been shuttled over, and by 3:00 P.M. most of a second division (the 21st Division) had arrived. The pontoon bridge, the construction of which began at 5:00 A.M., had reached only midstream by noon. This meant that except for the very lightest 53mm guns, all artillery had to await the completion of the bridge that evening. Meeting almost no enemy resistance, the Romanian infantry fanned out, enlarging the bridgehead four to six kilometers in all directions. The nearby Bulgarian villages of Babovo and Rahovo were occupied by 6:00 P.M.[21] The Flămânda crossing came as a complete surprise to the German–Bulgarian command, which had been concentrating its attention on a new offensive in eastern Dobrogea. On 28 September German aircraft had reported "stronger" troop movements, including marching columns directed toward the Danube and even bridging materials near Flămânda. However, Mackensen's command thought that only demonstrations, such as had been carried out earlier, were possible. Toshev and his staff, meeting with Mackensen on 28 September, had expressed concern. Mackensen, according to Toshev, assured him these concentrations were intended to protect Bucharest: "The Romanians think of nothing but Bucharest." He even suggested transferring units from Silistra and Turtucaia to aid the offensive in the east.[22]

The news of the Romanian crossing on 1 October "shook the entire command of the [Bulgarian 3rd] Army." The crown prince feared the loss of Turtucaia, which was only 20 kilometers downstream, and the impact of

Pontoon bridge over the Danube, Flămânda Maneuver, 1 October 1916. From *The Times History of the War* (London: The Times, 1917–1919)

the operation on the political opposition in Sofia. Toshev immediately met with Mackensen, who downplayed the significance of the crossing. Initially he refused to allow troops to be transferred from the east to meet it. At this point it was still not clear to him whether the Romanian landing was a demonstration or an attack in force. His preoccupation was still the pending Bulgarian–German offensive against Zaionchkovskii's Army of Dobrogea. With Averescu's invaders 150 kilometers to the west, the Germans believed they had plenty of time to prepare a response to them should it prove necessary. Mackensen did permit the redirection of some units of the German 217th ID, which was then en route to the Dobrogean Front from Macedonia.[23] Only a few Bulgarian militia were in the immediate vicinity of the crossing site. General Robert Kosch, the German commander at Rusé, 20 kilometers west of the crossing, set out with some small Bulgarian and German detachments, including cadets and staff personnel. However, the only really potent force to resist the Romanians was the German 217th ID, still 48 hours away by train. One of its advance battalions, already in Bazargic, was dispatched by truck toward the bridgehead. No other transfers from the east were considered possible, and Mackensen's request to OHL that the remainder of the German 101st ID be sent from Macedonia was refused. Sarrail's long-expected offensive had forced the Bulgarian army there to retreat. Quite understandably, the situation in Bulgaria was the cause of "grave anxiety" in German Supreme Headquarters at Castle Pless.[24]

Fortunately for the Central Powers, the Flâmânda operation, which had begun so successfully, quickly began to unravel. The pontoon bridge, the lifeline of the crossing, was attacked by German aircraft at midday on 1 October while still under construction. Throughout the afternoon bombs fell on the bridge and on the troops massed at the embarkation area on the north bank. These attacks did not deter courageous Romanian engineers from continuing construction, but it did produce panic among some of the infantry and depressed the morale of others as they waited to cross. General Arthur Văitoianu, the bridgehead commander, called for Romanian aircraft to challenge the German aviators, but none appeared.[25] Enemy air attacks ceased at 5:00 P.M., allowing construction of the bridge to be completed two hours later. But during the night, a powerful thunderstorm occurred. Accompanying wind and waves ripped the bridge apart in three places. Heroic efforts by Romanian engineers throughout the night enabled the bridge to reopen at 6:00 A.M. on 2 October. By now, the downpour had raised the level of the river enough to turn the staging and embarkation areas on the Romanian side into a vast lake. Movement of troops was possible only by boat. The movement of artillery into position to protect the crossing was completely impossible. The rise in the water level of the river also allowed enemy ships to surmount the passive barriers the Romanians had constructed: sunken ships, barrages, and minefields. Romanian incompetence assisted the forces of nature. The mines, designed and fabricated domestically, demonstrated their ineffectiveness. Most did not explode at all. Some of those that did exploded prematurely, killing and wounding ordinance specialists. Nets placed near the bridge to catch enemy floating mines also proved ineffective. Most were simple fishing nets from the Danube delta, and there were only enough of these to protect half the span. Orders to install shore artillery upstream to impede enemy ships had not been carried out.[26] Natural catastrophe combined with human negligence robbed the operation of virtually all of its naval defenses.

The lack of significant German–Bulgarian land forces in the area placed the initial responsibility for impeding crossing in the hands of ships of the Austro-Hungarian Danube flotilla. Anchored 70 kilometers upstream at Belene, it was ordered by General Kosch to proceed downstream at full steam, making every sacrifice necessary to halt the crossing. In addition, floating mines were released from locations closer at hand. Aided by the high water in evading the Romanian passive defenses, the first two Austro-Hungarian warships, relatively small patrol boats, reached the pontoon bridge on the morning of 2 October. Approaching to within 200 meters, they released floating mines and fired on the bridge with small-caliber cannon and machine guns. Although they did not inflict serious damage to the structure, they succeeded in driving Romanian infantry off the bridge. Despite being damaged by Romanian artillery, the gunboats were able to remain until their ammunition was expended. The ensuing respite allowed a number of Romanian artillery batteries to cross. At 10:45 A.M. the larger Austro-Hungarian monitors *Bodrog* and *Körös* arrived and approached to within 1,000 meters. They released mines and used their large-caliber guns to damage the span. However, Romanian artillery prevented them from coming closer and also damaged them sufficiently to force their withdrawal late on the afternoon of 2 October.[27]

However, the most important impact of the air and naval attacks on the bridge was not the physical damage they caused. Romanian casualties were light, and damage to the bridge was repaired relatively quickly. The terrifying novelty of aerial bombardment and the totally unexpected appearance of enemy warships undermined the morale of the troops, raising fear of isolation on the enemy shore. Averescu, who had been promised security for the bridge, now began to doubt the viability of the operation himself. At 11:00 A.M. on 2 October, just after the enemy monitors appeared, he ordered the crossing suspended until measures were taken to prevent air and naval attacks. After giving his chief of staff, General Christescu, a signed operations order authorizing withdrawal, he departed for MCG. There he proposed two solutions: one, to continue the action despite its risks; or two, to suspend operations but maintain a bridgehead on the Bulgarian shore with the intention of resuming the crossing when the security of the bridge was assured. MCG chose the latter. The king gave his approval at 4:00 P.M., and the withdrawal began that night.[28]

Averescu's plan to resume the operation later was completely unrealis-

tic and soon forgotten at MCG. As the Flămânda Maneuver was being
played out, the 1st and 2nd Armies in Transylvania, weakened by the transfers to the south, were retreating under attack from the new 9th German
Army led by General Erich von Falkenhayn. On 3 October, MCG ordered
Averescu to withdraw all his troops and to send two divisions to the north
immediately. Others would follow. As the bridgehead was being evacuated, the Austro-Hungarian flotilla attacked again, rupturing the bridge in
three places. The rescue of the remaining troops was completed by boat.
Ironically, during the night of 2–3 October, Bălescu, the chief of naval operations at MCG, had belatedly radioed Admiral Negrescu asking if his
monitors could come to defend the bridge. The latter was willing but had
155 kilometers to travel (at ten kilometers per hour). The request was
dropped when MCG decided on a definitive withdrawal. Although some
artillery and much support material was lost, Romanian casualties in the
Flămânda operation were relatively light (204 dead, 880 wounded, and 221
missing) because the operation ended before the defenders mounted a substantial ground attack. Mackensen's strategy had been to hem in the
bridgehead and delay its expansion. The first counterattack, planned for 4
October with only the limited troops immediately available, was canceled
when the Romanian withdrawal began.[29]

CONSEQUENCES OF THE FLĂMÂNDA MANEUVER

Like the Battle of Turtucaia, the outcome of the Flămânda Maneuver relieved and energized the Central Powers: "The danger on the Danube was
averted. I could sleep peacefully," Mackensen recorded in his journal. OHL,
which had been "shocked" by news of the Romanian crossing, was now
eager for Mackensen to press his offensive, which had been delayed because of transfers toward Flămânda. The Bulgarians received the news of
the repulse of the Romanians "with great joy" and were reinvigorated to
attack Russo-Romanian forces in eastern Dobrogea.[30] In contrast, the Romanian command was dispirited and confused once again. "Up to now,"
lamented Iliescu's *chef de cabinet*, "all operations undertaken by us have
failed. . . . I hope that with this one our bitter series will end." On the other
hand, there were rumors that Iliescu personally celebrated with champagne over the failure experienced by Averescu, his bête noire. The popu-

lation of Bucharest experienced a roller coaster of emotion during the Flămânda Maneuver. Expectations had been raised as convoys of pontoons and many troop trains passed through, headed south. "All eyes had been turned toward Flămânda . . . and we hoped that from there would come our salvation," Duca remembers. An official communique on 2 October announcing the crossing of the Danube had created great excitement, public singing of "La Arme," and shouts of "Long live Averescu!" At the same time, among some, there was a trace of skepticism: "Will this blow succeed? It is too good to be true." Lack of details in the press of 4 October gave rise to fears, confirmed the next day with the announcement of the withdrawal. Although it was portrayed as merely a "demonstration," everyone recognized it as another major defeat. The impact was especially depressing because it came almost simultaneously with news that the 1st, 2nd, and North Armies had retreated from Transylvania.[31]

How should the Flămânda Maneuver be evaluated? It has been variously described as "imaginative," "ingenious," "beautifully conceived," and "audacious." That an operation of this magnitude could be organized in secret in only 12 days and that Romanian engineers could construct the pontoon bridge under such circumstances is certainly praiseworthy. So is the fact that, in contrast to the battle of Turtucaia, the assault commanders and their men performed with distinction. No less an authority than Oskar Regele concludes that its "prospects . . . were not unfavorable"; if Averescu's forces could have completed the landing, they posed a real threat to Mackensen's forces.[32] Temporarily, yes. But it would not have eliminated a future threat on the Danube, nor could it have established a tie with Salonika without the commitment of massive Russian forces and a powerful Allied offensive. There was no prospect of either. In the perspective of the overall Romanian war effort, it was, as George Protopopescu has put it, "strategic adventurism." But the responsibility is not Averescu's alone. Certainly it was irresponsible of Brătianu and the king to approve such a drastic weakening of the Transylvanian armies on the eve of an offensive by the enemy there. Of the seven additional divisions committed to Averescu's operations in Dobrogea, four from the 1st and 2nd Armies were in transit for almost a month as they shuttled to the south and back again. During this time, they made little or no contribution to the fighting on either front.[33] Ironically, the success of the Flămânda Maneuver could have had more disastrous consequences than did its failure. Had the former been the case, these troops would have been tied down in combat, unable to return north, as they did just in time to help prevent Austro-German forces from storming into Wallachia early in October. Surprisingly, despite the Flămânda fiasco, Averescu's reputation suffered little. His political supporters continued to demand that he be named generalissimo. Colonel Lucianu Ferigo, the Italian military attaché, even appealed to Queen Marie to intervene with the king to this end. "I know he is right," Marie wrote in her diary.[34] This did not occur. On 8 October Averescu was reappointed commander of the 2nd Army, replacing Crăiniceanu, whose one-month tenure had been a disaster.

7
The Austro-German Counteroffensive in Transylvania

On 29 August, the day they replaced Falkenhayn, Hindenburg and Ludendorff met von Hötzendorf at AOK in Teschen. A decision was made to
release troops from other fronts and use all available power in a decisive
attack on Romania. During September, an average of 22 trains per day arrived in Transylvania, bearing the equivalent of a dozen divisions from the
Italian, Russian, and Western Fronts.[1] Among them were experienced
mountain units, including the elite German Alpine Corps[2] from France. For
men coming from the Western Front, it was like entering "another world."
In place of blasted and blood-soaked battlefields, they marveled at virgin
land, "forested hills, rich vineyards, cornfields and succulent green alpine
meadows where cows grazed." The numerous Saxon villages, with German names and voices, reminded them of home. "It could just as well have
been in Thuringia," Falkenhayn remarked of one.[3]

Because the preponderance of these reinforcements were German, the
OHL could insist that the direction of operations be in German hands. Von
Hötzendorf had already agreed to the reorganization of Arz von Staussen-
burg's Austro-Hungarian 1st Army into two battle groups under German
generals Curt von Morgen (I Reserve Corps, north) and Hermann von
Staabs (XXXIX Reserve Corps, south). The creation of a new German 9th
Army on 6 September, which took control of the XXXIX Corps as well as
most subsequent reinforcements, further marginalized the Habsburg role
in the war against Romania. The Austro-Hungarian 1st Army was limited

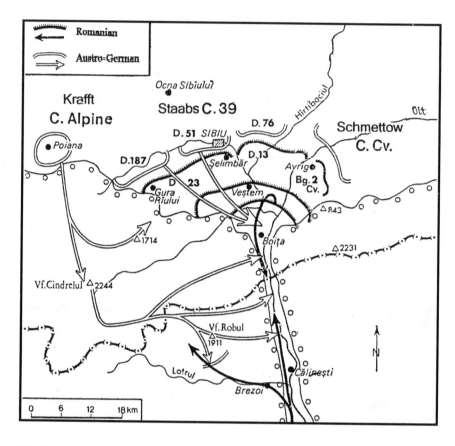

The Battle of Sibiu, 26–29 September. Adapted from Victor Atanasiu, *România în primul război mondial* (Bucharest: Editura Militară, 1979)

essentially to a holding operation in the eastern part of Transylvania.[4] The assumption of command of the 9th Army on 16 September by General Erich von Falkenhayn brought new energy to the operations. He was an excellent military technician and highly motivated. Here was a chance to refurbish his career and gain revenge on the Romanians, whose untimely entry into the war had been the catalyst for his dismissal as head of the OHL. His purpose, he told his army, was "not only to defeat but to destroy" the "disloyal enemy" who had "broken treaties and promises" and "insidiously stabbed us in the back."[5]

THE BATTLE OF SIBIU

Falkenhayn's first target, defined by the OHL, was the Romanian I Army Corps south of Sibiu. The arrest of the Romanian offensive had left it in an extremely vulnerable position, isolated 60 kilometers from other units of the Romanian 1st Army on the Jiu to the west and 50 kilometers from the main forces of the Romanian 2nd Army to the east. For three weeks it had held its position: an arc of 45 kilometers, 18 to 25 kilometers beyond the north exit of the Olt pass. To protect its flanks, it relied on the rugged terrain of the Carpathian Mountains, believed by many to be impassable. Commanded by General Ioan Popovici, the Olt Corps, as it was known, was composed of the 13th ID and 23rd ID, totaling 28 battalions, plus one cavalry brigade of eight squadrons. Both infantry divisions, like many second-line units in the Romanian army, were incompletely organized and contained inadequately trained reservists. With just 19 batteries of artillery (two heavy) and 34 machine guns, the Olt Corps was weak in firepower.[6] Its command was also weak. Like many of his peers, Popovici had an excellent reputation as a military writer and theorist but was unsuited for a field command. He was not an energetic leader, and to make matters worse, when he arrived on 15 September to take over the Olt Corps, its chief of staff fell ill and the commander of the 13th ID declared himself incapable of continuing because of depression. Popovici himself was initially disoriented, with only a vague idea of the enemy forces gathering before him. Two of the three observation planes assigned to the I Corps were inoperable, and the other failed to notice the growing enemy presence.[7] MCG, upon which Popovici relied for intelligence, was equally unaware of the enemy's buildup, believing instead that he was continuing to withdraw troops from the Sibiu area. When Popovici began to gather evidence on the increasing size of the forces facing him, 1st Army Command discounted it. Restrictions by higher command on offensive action limited reconnaissance operations. As a result, advanced units of the German 9th Army were able to assemble near Sibiu undisturbed—a pleasant surprise for Falkenhayn.[8]

Immediately over and against the Olt Corps stood Staab's XXXIX Reserve Corps. It included, in addition to the Hungarian 51st ID, the German 187th ID and 76th ID. It outnumbered the Romanians in battalions 36 versus 28 and enjoyed an overwhelming superiority in firepower: 59 batteries

General Krafft von Delmensingen reports to Archduke Karl near Sibiu. From Albert Reich, *Durch Siebenbürgen und Rumänien* (Munich: A. Reich, 1917)

of artillery (15 heavy) versus 19 (two heavy) and 172 machine guns versus 34. Flanking Staabs to the west were nine battalions of the Alpine Corps commanded by General Konrad Krafft von Dellmensingen. To the east stood the Schmettow Cavalry Corps. The strength of each corresponded to approximately one division.[9] In formulating a plan of attack, Falkenhayn refused to accept the conventional wisdom that the high Carpathians rendered impossible the envelopment of the Olt Corps. He instructed the Alpine Corps to reconnoiter. It reported that the mountains could be penetrated, but without vehicles. Thus encouraged, Falkenhayn ordered Krafft to infiltrate behind the Romanians and seize the Olt pass. This would be the signal for the XXXIX Corps to launch a frontal assault. Schmettow's cavalry was to prevent an escape to the east or the arrival of aid from the Romanian 2nd Army.[10]

On 22 September, six battalions of the Alpine Corps began an arduous climb into the rugged Cibin range of the Carpathians. One detachment, commanded by Lieutenant Colonel Franz Ritter von Epp,[11] marched south and then turned east toward the middle of the pass. Another detachment, led by Major Friedrich Paulus,[12] began working its way around the left flank of the Romanian 23rd ID toward the north end of the defile. Progress became difficult as the route reached heights of more than 2,000 meters. The rocky terrain offered no food for the men or fodder for the few pack animals accompanying them. Most supplies and ammunition were carried on the backs of the soldiers. Several heavy weapons had to be abandoned en route. Upon crossing the frontier, their advance was eased somewhat when they discovered paths recently improved by the Romanians. The secrecy Falkenhayn had hoped for was soon compromised. Late on their second day of march, advanced units exchanged gunfire with a Romanian frontier patrol. Other Romanian intelligence, including telephone reports from local prefects, confirmed the enemy presence. But because precision about numbers was lacking, the Romanian response was slow and inadequate. On 25 September, Popovici sent two detachments, each consisting of one infantry battalion and one cavalry squadron, into separate regions of the mountains. At 1st Army Command, the enemy appearance was considered to be a feint. Concluding that the intruders "could not be too numerous," the 1st Army chief of staff, General Alexandru Lupescu, chided Popovici for overreacting. Only on 25 September, when the enemy columns were nearing the Olt pass, was the threat posed by the Alpine Corps taken seriously.[13]

Neither Romanian detachment was able to prevent the Alpine Corps from reaching the pass on 26 September at three locations (Boiţa, Lunci, and Câineni). Altogether they took control of about three kilometers of its 20-kilometer length. The Germans blew up sections of the railroad, barricaded the highway, and destroyed telephone and telegraph lines, thus cutting the lifeline of the Olt Corps. At Câineni, they were challenged by a small impromptu defense force organized by a Romanian staff officer who happened to be passing through. He recruited a dozen local peasants and filled their pockets with cartridges; with the assistance of two gendarmes, he organized a firing line alongside the road. The Germans, who assumed they faced a much larger force, were detained long enough for Romanian reinforcements to arrive with mortars. After an all-day battle, the intruders retreated into the heights west of the defile. Although here, as at other points, the Alpine Corps did not succeed in blocking the pass permanently, as Falkenhayn had hoped, they were able to interdict traffic with machine gun fire from their commanding positions. Moreover, simply their presence in the rear of the Olt Corps had an unsettling effect on its men and commanders alike.[14]

As the Alpine Corps was nearing the pass, Falkenhayn ordered Staabs's XXXIX Corps to launch a frontal attack on Popovici's main force. The clear, calm, beautiful autumn morning of 26 September was shattered by a massive artillery barrage. Just before midday, assault troops showered the Romanian positions with grenades and surged forward. Their attacks concentrated on the Romanian 23rd ID, especially Colonel Traian Moşoiu's 3rd Infantry Regiment. Previous Romanian timidity and a front realignment the day before had led the Germans to assume that the Romanians would offer only weak resistance. Consequently, when he visited the battle front personally, Falkenhayn was surprised at the "stubborn resistance" his forces encountered. The Romanians answered the initial assault and others later in the day with spirited counterattacks, even in the face of deadly artillery and machine gun fire that they could not match.[15]

Although advances were made on the Romanian flanks on the first day, particularly by Schmettow's cavalry, Falkenhayn was not satisfied. The decisive battle to crush the Romanians had failed to materialize. The prospect of an extended engagement at Sibiu raised serious concerns. The Alpine Corps, deep in the Olt pass with limited men and supplies, could not hold out for long. A Romanian offensive on the Jiu, which began on 25 September, had retaken Petroşeni and threatened the Arad–Deva–Sibiu railroad, the major lifeline of the 9th Army. Also of concern was the probability that the Romanian 2nd Army to the east would march to the aid of the Olt Corps. However, in contrast to the indecisiveness of the Romanian command, Falkenhayn refused to be distracted from his plan of operations. He ordered that "not one man should be sent [to the Jiu] until the operations at Sibiu were terminated." For the second day, he ordered the attack on the Olt Corps pressed "at all costs." Staabs complied. He massed his artillery against the contracting Romanian perimeter and threw in new reserves, including two additional battalions of the Alpine Corps brought in from the Jiu. Nevertheless, according to German testimony, the Romanians "resisted again with bravery." "From early morning until late afternoon they undertook again and again strong counterattacks." This was not true for all of the Olt Corps. Some units of the Romanian 13th ID counterattacked only weakly and then fled. In the afternoon, Paulus's detachment succeeded in circumventing the left wing of the 13th ID, forcing it to retreat. This opened a gap between it and the 23rd ID. The latter was then also forced to retreat. By the end of the second day of the Battle of Sibiu, the Romanian position had been reduced to an arc of 25 kilometers with a depth of nine kilometers. Falkenhayn, viewing the evacuated enemy trenches, was startled to find not only dead and wounded, both civilian and military, but groups of refugees who had fled nearby villages.[16] Despite this marked success on the second day of operations, Falkenhayn still viewed the situation as "not entirely satisfactory." The XXXIX Corps had not "terminated with the enemy," and the exposed position of the Alpine Corps in the Olt pass was "troubling." Falkenhayn was also concerned about the reliability of units of the Austro-Hungarian 1st Army, which protected the left flank of the 9th Army against a possible advance by the Romanian 2nd and North Armies. Still refusing to renounce any modification of the original operations plan, he ordered Staabs to intensify the attack and released to him the last reserves of the 9th Army, which were hurried to the front by truck.[17]

On the third day, 28 September, the Battle of Sibiu turned decisively in favor of the 9th Army. Early that morning, Falkenhayn climbed the high tower of the Lutheran church of Sibiu to view the battle through binoculars. It was obvious that Romanian resistance was diminishing. The 187th ID was advancing rapidly, and the 51st ID and the 76th ID were also progressing well. The Olt Corps was retreating back into an arc now reduced to 12 by seven kilometers. Every corner of the Romanian position now fell under the pounding of German heavy artillery. To this was added unnerving aerial bombardment of staging areas, transportation facilities, depots, and command posts. Exaggerated rumors began to circulate that the pass, the only avenue of escape, had been completely blocked by the enemy. Under these conditions, the will to resist of many members of the Olt Corps, including Popovici himself, began to crumble. Their hope of success had all but vanished. MCG could not help. It had committed all its resources, including two divisions each from the 1st and 2nd Armies, to the impending Flămânda Maneuver. Culcer had unwisely sent what 1st Army reserves remained to operations on the Jiu. Although now in the process of being recalled, they could not reach the Olt in time.[18] Popovici's remaining hope and Falkenhayn's nagging fear were that the 2nd Army would march west to join the Battle of Sibiu.

As early as 23 September, 1st Army Command had requested MCG to extend the left wing of the 2nd Army westward to aid Popovici "if necessary." Crăiniceanu and his staff objected, with reason, that this would dangerously expose their flank. He proposed instead that the entire 2nd Army be shifted westward, with the North Army moved south to maintain coverage of the front. MCG disagreed and on 25 September ordered Crăiniceanu to move only his left wing. It was while this maneuver was in preparation that the assault on the Olt Corps began. One day into the Battle of Sibiu, Popovici warned that action by the 2nd Army was necessary for "the salvation of the critical situation." Culcer agreed. Now finally alarmed, MCG ordered, on 27 September, the maneuver Crăiniceanu had suggested.[19] The 2nd Army began to move westward late that afternoon. However, two days had been lost.

Falkenhayn's concern increased as the 2nd Army advanced toward the left flank of the 9th Army and against the right wing of the Austro-Hungarian 1st Army, whose power of resistance was highly suspect. Only a single Habsburg cavalry brigade bridged a gap of 20 kilometers between the two armies. As Crăiniceanu's forces made contact on 27/28 September, the weak Austro-Hungarian 71st ID began to give way. Even the usually sanguine Morgen feared that a major retreat jeopardizing the 9th Army was inevitable. "Seldom in my life," Falkenhayn recalls regarding the night of 28 September, "have I awaited events with more tension." He insisted to Arz that Austro-Hungarian forces must hold at any price, but he also seconded to him the German 89th ID, commanded by General Friedrich Baron von Lüttwitz. Composed primarily of older "tradesmen from Berlin," the 89th ID responded with a forced march of 30 kilometers to inject a spirit of resistance into their Habsburg allies. The right wing of the Austro-Hungarian 1st Army held.[20]

Falkenhayn's concern about the outcome of the Battle of Sibiu quickly dissipated. On the evening of the 28 September, Popovici conceded defeat and ordered the Olt Corps to retreat into the Olt defile. He had become angry and depressed over the delay of the 2nd Army in coming to his aid. "Its inactivity is inexcusable," he wrote Crăiniceanu on 27 September. In a later message, he compared his predicament to that of King Leonidas at Thermopylae. "When, with certainty, in the course of tomorrow can an attack on the rear of the enemy be expected . . . ? The blood shed by heroic troops that I command cries for revenge." Crăiniceanu replied that his army was advancing by forced march and would reach within 15 kilometers of the Olt Corps by the evening of the 28th. This message, sent by aerial courier, never arrived. Early the next day, Crăiniceanu sent another, announcing that his army was resuming its march at daybreak and would arrive with assistance and munitions. The airplane bearing this dispatch mistakenly landed behind enemy lines.[21] But it was already too late.

RETREAT INTO THE PASS

After waiting all day in vain for aid that never came, Popovici had already begun his retreat into the Olt defile. Throughout the night of 28/29 September a seemingly endless procession of men, animals, and transport struggled southward through the pass. Their ranks included more than 2,000 vehicles: artillery and caissons drawn by horses or oxen, munitions and supply wagons, medical vehicles and more; civilians with their cattle added to the confusion. Officers had difficulty maintaining order among their tired, discouraged, and nervous men. There was no priority of rank; General Popovici and his staff proceeded by foot in the center of the column. Attempts to slip silently by locations where the Alpine Corps lay in ambush failed. The commands and curses of animal drivers alerted the enemy. Suddenly, machine gun fire ricocheted and echoed off the rocky cliffs, unleashing panic among the column. Cries of the victims were drowned out by the bellowing of wounded and frightened animals. Some refugees crossed the Olt in a vain attempt to escape the deadly fire. Most surged forward to escape the rain of fire as quickly as possible. More fortunate were infantry units, which avoided the pass by retreating over mountain paths parallel to the Olt, carrying their wounded in their arms. Along the river, the refugee column was held up for several hours until Romanian artillery could be brought up to force the enemy farther back up into the heights out of machine gun range. Only then could barricades of wagons and dead horses be cleared and the march continued. The Alpine Corps could then only watch helplessly as the Romanians completed their escape. At 2:00 P.M. on 29 September, the head of the convoy reached Câineni at the south end of the pass, which was now securely under Romanian control. They left behind a river littered with overturned wagons, dead animals, and abandoned equipment. The Olt Corps, as MCG admitted, was in "complete disorder." Morale was low.[22] Survivors of the Alpine Corps remind us that it was a "night of sacrifices" for them as well. As Roman-

Alpine Corps monument. Olt Pass, "Das Alpenkorps 26–29 IX 1916." From *Die Grosse Zeit, illustrierte Kriegsgeschichte* (Berlin: Ullstein, n.d. [ca. 1917–1920])

ian relief units arrived, the Germans came under increasingly heavy attack from three sides. Finally, out of grenades and with their ammunition almost exhausted, they withdrew toward the north and reestablished contact with the main force.[23]

Falkenhayn elected not to pursue the Romanians into the pass. Instead, he sealed the north end with the Alpine Corps and turned eastward to confront the Romanian 2nd Army. Although he had won the Battle of Sibiu, he had failed to achieve his original objective: the destruction of the Olt Corps. The Romanians had escaped with the majority of their men and artillery. Nevertheless, they had paid a heavy price, with 3,000 soldiers taken prisoner by the enemy. More importantly, the defeat in the Battle of Sibiu gave the coup de grâce to the superficial optimism that had accompanied the ini-

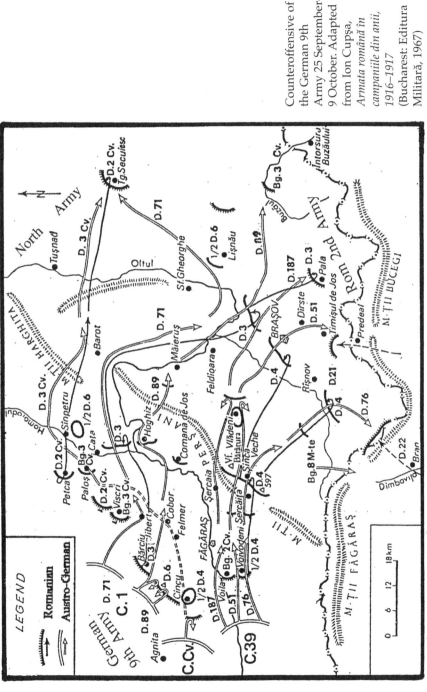

Counteroffensive of
the German 9th
Army 25 September–
9 October. Adapted
from Ion Cupşa,
*Armata română în
campaniile din anii,
1916–1917*
(Bucharest: Editura
Militară, 1967)

tial invasion of Transylvania one month before. Together with the reverses in the south, it discouraged and demoralized the leadership of the army, the government, and the populace. The chief of staff of the 1st Army wept on the telephone. He gave the appearance of a "squeezed dishrag" when he appeared at MCG to report on the defeat. Despite the evidence, some of which is presented above, that responsibility for the Romanian defeat at Sibiu was not Popovici's alone, he was relieved of his command.[24]

FROM SIBIU TO BRAŞOV

Even before the Olt Corps had completed its retreat into the defile, Falken-hayn was preparing to strike quickly eastward against Crăiniceanu's advancing 2nd Army. If the latter were supported by an offensive of the North Army, Arz's weak 1st Army might give way and force the 9th Army to go over to the defensive, for which its resources were totally inadequate. Falkenhayn need not have worried. On 30 September, in light of the defeat at Sibiu and the impending Flămânda Maneuver, MCG ordered its armies in Transylvania to suspend completely all offensive action and hold their current positions. Crăiniceanu went farther. He asked and received permission to retreat.[25]

Falkenhayn planned to deal with the 2nd Army as he had the Olt Corps: a frontal assault by Staabs's XXXIX Corps, supported by Schmettow's cavalry, along both sides of the Olt eastward toward Făgăraş; an attack on the Romanian right wing by Morgen's I Reserve Corps; and an envelopment movement through the Carpathians. The latter had to be postponed for lack of mountain troops. The Alpine Corps, tied down securing the Olt pass, was unavailable, and the Austrian 8th Mountain Brigade was still en route from the Isonzo. Nevertheless, recognizing the danger of delay, Falkenhayn decided to press the attack anyway.[26]

The first serious confrontation occurred northwest of Făgăraş on 2 October, when Morgen's German 89th ID and Hungarian 71st ID ran into a "hornet's nest," a strong counterattack by the Romanian 3rd ID and 6th ID. The 89th ID was thrown back with heavy losses. Morgen was fearful that his forces would be unable to withstand a renewed enemy attack. Much to his relief and Falkenhayn's disbelief, Crăiniceanu failed to follow up this success. Instead, the 2nd Army continued its retreat, surrendering the historically prominent Romanian center of Făgăraş on 3 October. It finally took a stand 25 kilometers to the east at the Perşani Mountains, a range of hills extending north–south perpendicular to the Carpathians. Here the Romanian forces had made elaborate preparations to defend the two main roads leading east toward Braşov. The confrontation, which began on 5 October, is known as the Battle of Geisterwald, after the beautiful, "romantic" forest that covers the western slope of the Perşani mountains.[27] Extensive aerial reconnaissance gave the German field commanders information about the strength and precise location of the Romanian defenders. After intensive preparation throughout the morning by German artillery, Staabs's 76th ID attacked the Romanians head on, while units of the 187th ID and the Hungarian 51st ID attacked their flank and rear. After some initial enemy success, the Romanians counterattacked repeatedly with zeal a German eyewitness admired: "It was a noble sight to see these tightly closed ranks rush forward, recklessly and contemptuous of death despite the fearful countereffects of our artillery and infantry. . . . The direct hits of our howitzers ripped wide holes which were repeatedly closed. Yet our artillery was so heavy, its effect so terrible, that this attack and also two others collapsed completely." Romanian soldiers under the "hailstorm of iron ran helplessly to and fro seeking shelter," noted General Hugo von Elstermann, commander of the 76th ID.[28]

At 2:00 P.M. on 6 October, the Romanian counterattack gave way to retreat, then panic. The latter was initiated by an artillery unit that fled by foot and horse, leaving its infantry in the lurch. Soon the entire front gave way. Columns of soldiers, joined by local refugees, clogged the two roads leading east while German artillery raked these escape routes with deadly fire. The magnitude of the flight meant the Germans took few prisoners; the "heights [of Geisterwald] were covered with the bodies of the dead and wounded [Romanians]." The enemy did not immediately pursue the physically and morally exhausted Romanians because he, too, was exhausted. "If he had been able to exercise the smallest pressure, all was lost," the operations officer of the 2nd Army admitted. Effective resistance by Romanian rearguard detachments also helped prevent a greater disaster. Units of the Romanian 4th ID ambushed a regiment of the 76th ID. A German survivor recalls: "Enemy bullets swept across the road; horses fell, men died and were wounded. . . . Casualties exceeded the total losses of the regiment in all previous battles in the Transylvanian campaign."[29]

The panic at Geisterwald alarmed MCG. Fearing that the flight of the 2nd Army might continue across the Carpathians, officers from its Bureau of Operations were dispatched on 6 October to the Brașov passes to ensure that the fugitives were halted. Commanders were ordered to "take drastic measures against those who propagate panic and those culpable of [criminal] negligence, executing those summarily whatever their rank." The chief medical officer of 2nd Army, Dr. Alexandru Slătineanu, traveled to Periș, allegedly with encouragement and advice of the army's under chief of staff, Lieutenant Colonel Gheorghe Dabija, to tell of the chaos and disorder reigning under Crăiniceanu's command and to demand his removal. Two days later, on 8 October, Averescu, whose Flămânda Maneuver had just been terminated, was named to succeed Crăiniceanu. The end of this operation in the south also brought the return of two infantry divisions (the 21st and 22nd) taken from the 2nd Army three weeks earlier.[30] They arrived too late to reverse the retreat of the 2nd Army but were able to cover its withdrawal into the mountains.

Reports of the transfer of Romanian forces from south to north heightened Falkenhayn's sense of urgency about pressing the attack on the 2nd Army. He hoped to prevent the retreating enemy from reaching the defensible Carpathian passes near Brașov. While the 187th ID and 51st ID advanced directly toward the city, the 76th ID veered south toward the Bran (Törzburg) pass, where it was joined by the recently arrived Austrian 8th Mountain Brigade. Morgen's 89th ID and 71st ID, accompanied by units of Schmettow's cavalry, swung around north and east of the city. By the evening of 7 October, units of the 9th Army had reached the rim of the Brașov basin, formed by the curve of the Carpathians. That same day, German war correspondents joined Austro-German field commanders in the Lutheran church tower at Ghimbav (Weidenbach) to view Brașov, only a few kilometers away. It was a brilliant autumn day, but a cloud of black smoke arose from fires in the railroad station and storage facilities. This led those watching to assume the city was being abandoned. This was true in part. Thanks to a mix-up in orders, some Romanian units had retreated to a line south of the city. New orders to contest the occupation of Brașov required them to attack and reoccupy positions in and around the city already taken over by the enemy. This attempt was costly. A Romanian counterattack north of the city was "smashed with a sinister precision" by the shells of the enemy. During the night of 7–8 October, the Hungarian 51st

Romanians who died defending Braşov, 7–8 October 1916. From Ernst Kabisch, *Der Rumänienkrieg* (Berlin: Verhut-Verlag Otto Schlegel, 1938)

ID was given the opportunity to enter the city first, as recompense for the Romanian conquest. Its commander did not wish to "plunge into a sea of houses" and thus concentrated his heaviest attacks around St. Barthlomew Church and the railroad station. After fierce resistance, a Romanian battalion defending the latter retreated, but a "company of death" fought to the end, leaving a "densely packed line of dead." On the hills of Old Braşov, the Hungarians used bayonet charges to expel the Romanian defenders.[31]

EVACUATION OF TRANSYLVANIA

During the night of 8–9 October, Romanian troops evacuated Braşov and its environs completely. The 21st ID, arriving from Flămânda, provided cover for the retreat back to the entrance of the Predeal pass. Twenty kilometers to the southwest of the city, the Romanian 4th ID was forced to evacuate the village of Bran, the gateway to the Törzburg pass. With the help of the 22nd ID, it was able to draw back into the defile, avoiding encir-

Returning Hungarian troops welcomed in Braşov, 8 October 1916. *Die Grosse Zeit, illustrierte Kriegsgeschichte* (Berlin: Ullstein, n.d. [ca. 1917–1920])

clement by the Austrian 8th Mountain Brigade, which was moving east-ward along the crest of the Carpathians.[32]

At 1:00 A.M. on 9 October, as the 2nd Army was completing its retreat to the frontier, General Alexandru Averescu, accompanied by his longtime *chef de cabinet*, Major Carol Ressel, arrived at the army's headquarters to re-place Crăiniceanu. He found subordinate commanders "literally domi-nated by the sense of fear . . . ready to retreat at the smallest pressure of the enemy." The Operations Bureau "had not even the slightest knowledge about the situation of the troops of the army." Averescu immediately set about to combat the chaos and defeatism in his new command. In this first report to the king, Averescu questioned the plan of MCG to make a stand at the entrance to the passes: "The line ordered . . . cannot be held due to the superiority of enemy artillery and the depressed morale of our troops. Even newly arrived troops are influenced by the disorder and depression they see around them. I am disposed to enter into the defiles in order that the enemy cannot use heavy artillery with such precision." He could offer no guarantees. "All depends on the enemy. If he gives us time to organize positions . . . to reestablish order in the chaos which dominates and to rejuvenate the morale of the troops, then resistance will be possible." In the face of Averescu's irrefutable logic, MCG could do nothing but agree. Within two days, all the divisions of the 2nd Army, like those of the 1st Army, had retreated into the narrow defiles of the Carpathians.[33]

The North Army soon took up similar positions in the Eastern Carpathians. After easy success in the early days of the war, Prezan's progress had been restricted by the decision of MCG to shift emphasis to the south. But like the 2nd Army, the North Army had been ordered to advance again in relief of the Olt Corps at Sibiu. In heavy fighting during 25–28 September, it had pushed the Hungarian 39th ID and 61st ID back a few kilometers toward the west. This posed a potential threat to the left flank of Falkenhayn's 9th Army. The defeat of the Olt Corps and the impending Flămânda Maneuver led MCG to order Prezan on 1 October to halt once more the advance of his forces. He was soon forced to retreat when the withdrawal of the 2nd Army toward Braşov left the left flank of his own forces exposed. An enemy attempt to exploit this through envelopment failed as Prezan conducted a controlled and orderly withdrawal to prepared positions in the eastern Carpathians. By 13 October, he had his army safely ensconced in the mountains, with firm connections to the Russian 9th Army to the north.[34]

Forty days after the Romanian army crossed the Carpathians, it had been expelled from Transylvania. In addition to the military defeat, the related consequences on morale were profound. In Transylvania, the Saxon and Hungarian communities "greeted jubilantly" the German and Austro-Hungarian troops as liberators, shouting hurrah and throwing flowers. They showed their contempt for their Romanian neighbors, who were overwhelmed with anguish.[35] The latter were not overtly hostile toward the returning enemy forces, only silent or sullen. Most shuttered their doors and windows and "wiped away tears in silence." Priests, teachers, and other community leaders, who had prominently supported the Romanian occupation and now expected retribution, experienced an "indescribable panic." Some abandoned their possessions to accompany the Romanian army into exile, among them 100 priests. Typical was the rector of the Uniate school at Răşinari. Upon the arrival of the Romanian army in August, as mentioned earlier, he had volunteered his services and was appointed the local notary. This earned him a place on the Hungarian "wanted" list, men whom Austro-German military units were expected to search for as they invaded Romania. Confessional schools were closed and Romanian notables, mainly priests, were deported from the zone along the frontier. Others were arrested and imprisoned, some for such seemingly innocuous actions as helping the Romanian military authorities choose a new mayor. At the notorious Cluj military tribunal early in 1917, nine Romanians were condemned to death, although the sentences were never carried out.[36]

The retreat of the Romanian armies from Transylvania, coinciding with the failure at Flămânda, touched off a new wave of despair in Bucharest. Although official communiqués had given few details of the defeats on the battlefield, their very vagueness were reasons for concern. There were other unmistakable signs: the transit of troops from north to south and back again; the wounded who flooded Bucharest hospitals; the indiscretions of military personnel. There was an additional cause of public alarm. On 7 October, newspapers reported that objects infected with bacteria had been found on the streets of Bucharest. The basis for this was the unearthing of vials of anthrax in the garden of the German legation the day before. It had been imported a year previously to be used in the event of war to infect horses, thus robbing the Romanian army of its means of transportation. There is no evidence that it was used. Probably the most immediate catalyst for alarming the public, as Brătianu had foreseen, was the sudden appearance of trucks at various government ministries to load documents for evacuation to Moldavia. This touched off a new wave of refugees fleeing the capital. Cabinet ministers set a bad example. The minister of public works sent off his large personal art collection while many citizens were refused permission to send even one piece of luggage. The minister of the interior loaded an entire train with relatives, wine, and food for transport into Moldavia. Even the Entente ministers were caught up in the panic. They burned archives, destroyed ciphers, and prepared to depart for Iaşi, where the invasion from Bucharest was causing chaos.[37]

Regret for having gone to war increased, and there was talk of peace. Austro-German leaders hoped to exploit this. Assuming that "after our victories in Transylvania and their bloody defeats they [the Romanians] no longer have the will to go on," the German Foreign Office took preliminary steps to investigate the possibility of drawing Romania into a separate peace. The former German minister in Bucharest traveled to Copenhagen early in October to contact the Germanophile Romanian minister there. The scenario was to replace the Brătianu government with a Conservative ministry headed by Petru Carp. "To achieve change," the former German chargé in Bucharest advised, "one or more generals must be won." Contemporaneously in Bucharest, a political ally of Carp approached Averescu, who agreed to join a Carp government if it had a mandate for peace. These feelers came to naught. Brătianu, who had recovered his nerve after Turtucaia, remained firmly in control with the support of the king. Both were determined to carry on the fight in Moldavia if necessary.[38]

The Romanians saw a ray of hope in the imminent arrival of a French military mission headed by General Henri Mathias Berthelot, sometime chief of operations for the French army on the Western Front. Brătianu had lost confidence in the Romanian High Command, especially Iliescu, and was prepared to turn over the direction of the war to Berthelot. The latter possessed the tact necessary to respect Romanian amour propre as well as the optimism to bolster their shattered morale. When Berthelot arrived in Periş on 16 October, his first priority was to combat discouragement and defeatism, to "penetrate the spirit of all, general staff and leaders, with the spirit of resistance at any price." "It is necessary to check everywhere the idea of retreat; to defend desperately, at the frontier itself, the national territory." Officers of his Mission Militaire Française (MMF) were sent to major combat units to spread this message. Leaving the leadership at MCG in place, Berthelot assumed the role of military counselor to the king. He exercised his influence through this personal relationship with Ferdinand, who invariably followed his advice. By the end of October, a measure of confidence had been restored that the onset of winter weather and a heroic defensive effort in the Carpathians would delay the enemy invasion long enough for the Allied military efforts on other fronts to relieve the pressure on Romania.[39]

8
Battles on the Frontiers

The failure of the Flămânda Maneuver and the defeat in Transylvania left Romania in a precarious strategic position. Falkenhayn's 9th Army was poised to penetrate the Carpathians, and Mackensen was now free to launch a major offensive in Dobrogea. No help could be expected from Romania's allies. The impact of the Allied army at Salonika on the Romanian Front remained an empty promise. Brief, limited operations in western Macedonia were no help to the Romanians.[1] The French military mission, although a catalyst for the eventual rebuilding of the Romanian army, could provide little in the way of immediate assistance. After six weeks of incessant pleas, it was clear that there would be no substantial Russian help in defending Wallachia. The Romanian army ought not to count on Russian troops in defending its extended frontier, chief of staff Mikhail Alekseev had warned General Berthelot on 12 October when the latter stopped at STAVKA en route to Romania. On a map of Romania Alekseev drew "a large blue line" along the Siret river from Galaţi to the Carpathians. This he termed "the only line of defense." Alekseev repeated the same theme directly to the Romanians, urging them to prepare the evacuation of Wallachia and to build fortifications on the Siret. It became clear that additional Russian troops would be sent only to defend Moldavia as the left wing of the Russian Front. Elsewhere the Romanians would be essentially on their own.[2]

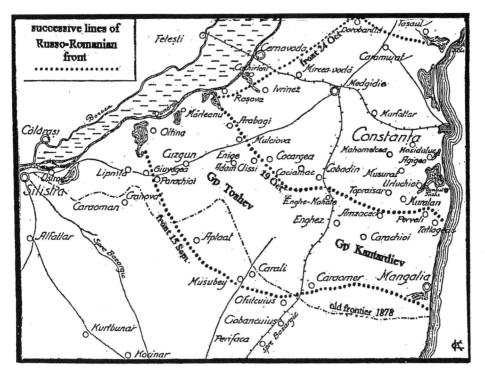

Russo-Romanian Retreat in Dobrogea. Adapted from Constantin Kirițescu, *Istoria războiului pentru întregirea României*, 2nd ed. (Bucharest: Editura Casei Școalelor, 1925)

MACKENSEN'S OFFENSIVE IN DOBROGEA

The ending of Averescu's operations at Flămânda freed up troops and re-moved Bulgarian objections to Mackensen's plans to mount a major attack to inflict a decisive defeat on the Russo-Romanian Army of Dobrogea. Once this was accomplished, troops could be transferred to undertake the long-delayed assault across the Danube southwest of Bucharest. Mackensen's plan of operations divided the front between eastern and western battle groups. Toshev was given more or less a free hand over the latter, com-posed of Bulgarian and Turkish troops. His mission was to hold in place the Romanian and Russian divisions before him while the principal blow was delivered by the eastern battle group. The latter, commanded by Bul-garian general Todor Kantardiev, encompassed three Bulgarian divisions, the German 217th ID, the Bode Brigade, and German heavy artillery. For the first time in the Dobrogean campaign, Mackensen exercised direct command, moving his own headquarters to Bazargic and visiting Kantardiev daily. In his journal he confessed again that he was uncomfortable relying, for the most part, on Bulgarian and Turkish troops: "Fortunate is he who has only German troops to command."[3]

The Army of Dobrogea was in poor condition to meet the enemy attack. No defensive positions had been prepared except a rudimentary firing line. More importantly, Russo-Romanian forces were exhausted from a week of heavy fighting in support of the aborted Danube crossing at Flămânda. On 1 October, they had advanced south from Topraisar toward Amzacea against Bulgarian and Turkish divisions. Progress proved difficult under the battering of enemy artillery. On 3 October, the Romanian 19th ID, attacking with bayonets, threw the Turkish 25th ID into a "complete and disorderly retreat" and captured Amzacea. The Romanians had no time to savor what they called "the beautiful victory" of Amzacea. With the transfer of the Romanian 12th ID and 15th ID to the north before the arrival of the Russian IV Siberian Corps to replace them, it was necessary to evacuate Amzacea and return all Russian–Romanian forces to their original positions. The cost of their sacrificial but ultimately fruitless combat was high. The 19th ID alone suffered 3,195 casualties. For all Russo-Romanian forces in Dobrogea in the period 1–7 October, losses exceeded 11,000.[4] These casualties plus the transfers left a depleted Army of Dobrogea to meet the enemy offensive less than two weeks later. The Bulgarian forces, in contrast, were being continually replenished. Most important was the presence of the German 217th ID. It had a positive impact on their morale. As Mackensen relates, they called repeatedly for "Germanskis. They wanted to see German troops near them."[5]

When the offensive of the 3rd Army opened on 19 October, the progress of the eastern battle group disappointed Mackensen. The Bulgarians, with the exception of Kolev's cavalry, not only hesitated to attack but also held back in pursuit—a common German complaint. The German units enjoyed some initial success, thanks largely to their heavy artillery. Directed by balloons and aircraft, it quickly silenced the Romanian guns and then battered the troops unmercifully. "It was like a man with a club fighting an adversary with a good rifle," a Romanian officer put it. However, a spirited Romanian counterattack and stubborn resistance by the depleted Serbs combined to halt temporarily the advance of the German 217th ID. Henning had nothing but admiration for the "extreme tenacity" of the "remnant" of the Serb division, "our bravest enemy." The Romanian 19th ID, under the inspired leadership of Scărişoreanu, led him to conclude that "the Romanian in October was a completely different enemy than in September."[6]

To the west, the results were quite different. To the surprise of everyone, Toshev's two Turkish divisions ruptured the front of the Russian 61st ID and captured Cocargea. At the same time the Bulgarian 1st ID and 4th ID made advances of five to six kilometers against the Romanian 2nd ID and the Russian 115th ID. Five thousand prisoners were taken, including 2,800 Russians in one day. The only bright spot in the west for Russo-Romanian forces was the strong support they received from the guns of their combined Danube flotillas. Transforming his "holding operation" in the west into an offensive with Mackensen's permission, Toshev proceeded to overwhelm the right and center of the Russo-Romanian Front.[7] At the same time, Kolev's Bulgarian cavalry, attacking along the Black Sea coast, was able to turn the left flank of the Romanian 9th ID. Zaionchkovskii's order, "to hold at any price" pending the arrival of the IV Siberian Corps, was unrealistic. With both flanks turned, the Russo-Romanian forces retreated in what turned into a rout on 20–21 October. The Bulgarians were reported to be burning villages as they advanced. First Topraisar and then Cobadin were occupied; the road to Constanţa was now open. For Mackensen, who surveyed the battlefield from a hilltop, it was the experience of a lifetime: German and Bulgarian troops pursuing the fleeing enemy northward; the port of Constanţa with its white minarets appearing out of the fog and the smoke of burning petroleum tanks; and the Russian fleet hastily sailing out into the Black Sea. "I will never forget the impression of these images," he wrote.[8]

END OF THE DOBROGEAN CAMPAIGN

The Russo-Romanian evacuation of Constanţa on 21 October was accompanied by chaos. Its folly, drama, and tragedy can be grasped by summarizing the graphic reports of the British and French consuls. Panic had gripped the population and administration for several days beforehand. Complaining of a "heart attack," the local prefect had virtually deserted his post, seeking refuge in a small village to the north. Wounded soldiers overflowed existing hospitals and makeshift shelters in schools, hotels, military barracks, and even Constanța's ornate gambling casino. As the enemy drew closer, attempts were made to evacuate them by train before the enemy captured the railroad to Cernavoda. The railroad station became "a vast pile of suffering and bleeding humanity." Enemy airplanes appeared from time to time and dropped bombs, adding to the chaos. Many among the Romanian population fled, leaving in the city mostly citizens of Turkish or Bulgarian descent. On the roads, refugees mingled with soldiers retreating in disorder. Some Romanian soldiers of nationalities native to the region deserted and sought refuge in their homes.[9] General Pavlov's Russian cavalry attempted to hold the enemy south of the city but was thrown back in disorder. Pavlov himself was nearly captured. On 22 October the resident foreign consuls escaped aboard a British steamer amid a hail of enemy shells. Its brave captain came to their rescue after the Russian Black Sea fleet had left them stranded. The latter had done little to support the land forces or destroy more than a token of Constanța's stocks of oil and grain, which the Germans prized.[10]

Despite the fall of Constanța, the Romanians hoped the Cernavoda railroad bridge over the Danube might be held with the help of firepower from Russian and Romanian monitors. As the enemy approached the structure on 25 October, orders went out from MCG to destroy the famous bridge, 750 meters long and 30 meters above the water, the largest in Europe. Romanian engineer Anghel Saligny had been given the painful task of drawing up plans for the destruction of his greatest handiwork. Romanian and even Russian officers on the spot hesitated, considering it a "sacrilege" to bring down this "work of art." Their pain was eased somewhat when the main span withstood the initial detonation, and they had to be satisfied with destroying a connecting span. The Germans refrained from finishing the destruction because it was useful to them but also because of "sentimentality." Mackensen himself went to Cernavoda to walk from one end of the "architectural wonder" to the other.[11]

With the conquest of Constanța, tension mounted within Mackensen's coalition. The Bulgarians were becoming increasingly uneasy about the Turkish presence in Dobrogea. More serious was German–Bulgarian conflict. Topping the list of differences was the German control of the railroads and the administration of Dobrogea, both of which the Bulgarians believed was their prerogative. They responded with passive resistance in the transportation of

troops and supplies—an agonizingly slow process even with their cooperation. The Germans were furious as this delayed preparations for their
planned assault across the Danube. Another point of friction was the division of the spoils of conquest. "The Bulgarians were drawn to rich Constanța,
the Turks to Medgidia, the Holy Medgidia; the Bulgarians must plunder; the
Turks must pray," was the way cynical Henning put it. Bulgarian "aspirations for booty," including the rich stocks of oil and grain remaining at Constanța, caused great difficulties for the Germans, who intended it for themselves. In response to Mackensen's demand, the Bulgarians agreed to the
installation of a German general at Constanța "who will divide the booty
among the allies." Later, general agreement was reached on the division at
a coalition conference in Sofia.[12] Meanwhile, individual Bulgarian looters
were audacious. A cause célèbre was the theft of the bronze statue of the
Roman poet Ovid that stood before the Constanța city hall. Mackensen was
particularly incensed. He had German troops promptly apprehend the
thieves and return Ovid to his pedestal. Later, when the Germans used their
control of the railroads to prevent shipping valuables such as pianos back
home, the Bulgarians "smashed them to pieces" to deny them to their allies.[13]

After the capture of Constanța and the railroad to Cernovoda, Mackensen's "thoughts turned from Dobrogea to Bucharest." He ordered the
withdrawal of the German 217th ID, the Bulgarian 1st ID, and German
heavy artillery to prepare for the long-delayed crossing of the Danube. Toshev refused at first to accept the weakening of his army, especially the
transfer of the 1st ID. He insisted that the forces remaining were not sufficient to complete the conquest of Dobrogea. The Austrian liaison reported
"great resentment" at OKM over Toshev's insubordination: "The Bulgarian 3rd Army does what it wishes and holds itself only partly under commands given [by Mackensen]." The transfer was eventually enforced with
the intervention of Bulgarian tsar Ferdinand. Toshev was soon sent to the
Macedonian Front. The remainder of the 3rd Army, led by Kolev's cavalry,
was given the task of continuing the advance north toward the Danube
delta. But, after the transfer of forces to the west, this advance slowed and
then halted for over a month near Babadag, 90 kilometers north of Constanța. The Bulgarians no longer faced Romanian divisions. All of these had
"lost fighting capacity" and were withdrawn, along with the Serbian Volunteer Division. The line was then held exclusively by Russian forces.
Zaionchkovskii, on whom the Romanians placed the majority of blame for

their defeat on the Southern Front, was sacked on 29 October on the demand of King Ferdinand. He was replaced by General Vladimir Sakharov.[14]

The Romanian attempt during the first two months of the war to defend Dobrogea was a costly affair. Independent of the brief Flămânda Maneuver, where over half of the Romanian army was committed, the Dobrogean campaign eventually involved eight Russian and seven Romanian divisions. Because it was for the most part a war of position, attack, and counterattack, losses were heavy. Although exact casualty figures do not exist, those for Russo-Romanian forces most likely exceeded 75,000. The Central Powers took 37,600 prisoners in Dobrogea between 1 September and 25 October. The Serbian Volunteer Division alone suffered 8,331 casualties, 50 percent of its effectives, between 6 September and 25 October. Although similar figures do not exist for Russian and Romanian divisions, the percentages must have been comparable. The extent of losses is indicated by the fact that it was necessary to combine four Romanian divisions (2, 5, 9, 19) into two, designated the 2nd/5th ID and the 9th/19th ID, after they were withdrawn from Dobrogea.[15]

FALKENHAYN AND THE CARPATHIAN PASSES

The rugged, forested Carpathians appeared to offer a highly defensible barrier to invasion, particularly in winter. But as Frederick II once remarked, "Where a goat can pass, a soldier can pass also."[16] Moreover, these mountains were traversed by more than 15 passes; on five of these, the enemy would mount major offensives. With only 13 divisions to cover 700 kilometers of frontier and not knowing where the enemy would focus his attack, the Romanians had to spread their forces while their opponents were free to concentrate. Liaison between the three northern armies was poor to nonexistent, and inadequate intelligence left them with little accurate information about the enemy before them. Furthermore, many of the Romanian divisions were weak. Several of the best had suffered cruelly in recent weeks. Others were far below normal strength or diluted with a flood of what was known as two- or three-day militia: new levies with minimal training. Reinforcements were arriving without command or support sections. With the exception of one division in Prezan's North Army, no reserves existed. Although total Austro-German forces remained numerically inferior, they were overwhelmingly superior in experience, leadership, and, as always, weaponry. Prewar neglect of fixed defenses in the Carpathians left little for the northern armies to fall back on. Orders finally went out 5 October "to organize solidly with fortifications and obstacles" the high points of the passes. A few positions were hurriedly prepared, but there was a general feeling that "the enemy could rupture with relative ease this thin cordon."[17]

The Austro-German leaders faced problems of their own as they prepared to attack across the Carpathians. Needs on other fronts and the approach of winter dictated a quick conclusion of the campaign. Furthermore, there was disagreement over how to go about it. OHL and AOK wanted to give priority to penetrating the Eastern Carpathian passes into Moldavia; Falkenhayn favored a quick strike into Wallachia. OHL anticipated opening the door for Schmettow's cavalry to operate in the Siret valley, interdicting road and rail communications, hindering the arrival of Russian reinforcements, and isolating Wallachia. Falkenhayn disagreed. Although he favored securing these passes against an enemy attack on the rear of his 9th Army, he doubted that Moldavia could be penetrated with only the infantry and cavalry available: "Without artillery, engineers and auxiliary troops, the undertaking was without a chance [of success]." He also questioned the diversion of resources needed in the southern Carpathians. Falkenhayn's discord with OHL and AOK increased when they subordinated the 9th Army to the Front Command of Archduke Karl, whose chief of staff, German General Hans von Seeckt, he personally mistrusted.[18]

Nevertheless, at the insistence of his superiors, Falkenhayn ordered an attack eastward toward Târgu Ocna. While the Austro-Hungarian 1st Army engaged the right wing of Prezan's North Army, units of the 9th Army became involved in a series of bitter and bloody frontier clashes with the Romanian left wing. The most significant occurred at the Oituz pass, where on 14 October the Austrian 71st ID launched a major offensive and penetrated Romanian territory. Fortunately for the Romanians, their 15th ID, just arrived from Dobrogea, was in position to contest the enemy advance. Its commander, General Eremia Grigorescu, was an energetic leader who inspired his men to resist with fierce determination. To Prezan's worried admonition that enemy success at Oituz would endanger the entire front, Grigorescu replied with a phrase that became legendary: "The enemy will not pass here." An officer of the MMF who visited Oituz in the midst of the fighting had high praise for Grigorescu's division: "Morale is excel-

General Falkenhayn (right center) at the front. From WikimediaCommons.org, Falkenhayn and his staff of the 9th Army during the Romanian Campaign

lent . . . commanders are full of confidence . . . no thought of retreat." After making good on his boast, Grigorescu went over to the offensive on 21 October and threw the enemy back to the frontier. The fighting was heavy, with mounting casualties on both sides. Thereupon the OHL and AOK gave up their hope of penetrating Moldavia.[19]

His judgment vindicated, Falkenhayn was free to transfer Schmettow and his cavalry, which had remained on the sidelines awaiting a breakthrough, to operations in the southern Carpathians.[20] Disagreement then arose over a strategy for piercing the southern Carpathians. Von Hötzendorf and the Front Command of Archduke Karl favored concentrating on the Braşov passes (Predeal, Bran). The German OHL initially agreed that this would be the best route for reaching Bucharest and cutting Romania in two. Again, Falkenhayn dissented. He argued, with good reason, that the long, narrow nature of these rugged passes would favor a "tenacious" defense. He also pointed to their poor rail connections with his concentration points for men

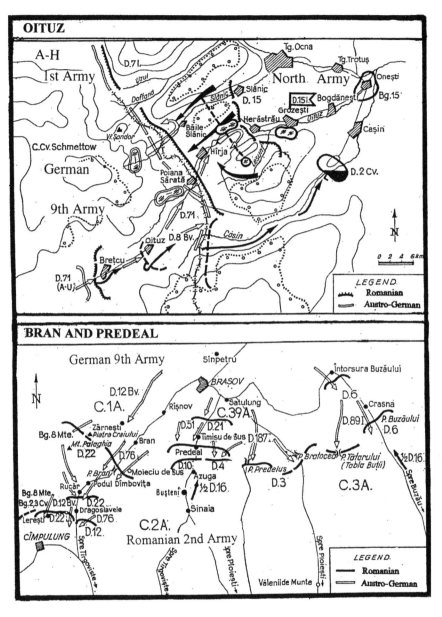

Battles in the Carpathian Passes. Adapted from Victor Atanasiu, *România în primul război mondial* (Bucharest: Editura Militară, 1979)

and supplies at Sibiu and Sighişoara. He was supported in this last point by the German army railroad chief, the influential General Wilhelm Groener. Falkenhayn's preference was to test all the passes, especially the Jiu, which offered the shortest route through the mountains. Seeckt, meeting with him at Braşov on 15 October, tried to resolve differences but failed. Falkenhayn then bypassed the Front Command and appealed directly to von Hötzendorf and Ludendorff. When the latter endorsed Falkenhayn's plan, von Hötzendorf agreed, but only on the condition that the attack on the Braşov passes "must not suffer."[21] Falkenhayn was now free to probe, and penetrate if possible, the four main southern passes: Predeal, Bran, Olt, and Jiu.

THE PREDEAL AND BRAN PASSES

The Predeal pass, with a paved highway and a major railroad, was the best and most frequently used modern avenue of communication across the Carpathians. On the other hand, its narrow defile was overshadowed at many points by rocky promontories that gave a strong advantage to the Romanian defenders. The latter were led by the 21st ID, composed of reservists and commanded by a reserve general, which had just arrived from Flămânda. It was supported by portions of the 10th ID. The attack was mounted by Staabs's XXXIX Corps, led by the Hungarian 51st ID and forces from the German 187th ID. Both units were understrength but were assisted by ten batteries of heavy artillery, including guns of 210mm and 305mm caliber. The first stage of the battle centered on the town of Predeal, which lay astride the frontier. For several days, beginning on 14 October, it was subjected to continuous bombardment. The railroad station, a center of Romanian resistance, was virtually destroyed, as were many of the sumptuous summer homes of the Bucharest elite. Reportedly, enemy gunners singled out those of politicians such as Brătianu who were responsible for the declaration of war.[22] For more than a week, the defenders repelled repeated assaults of enemy infantry. On 23 October, the station was captured, and after two days of house-to-house fighting, so was the remainder of the city. Averescu then allowed his commanders to make a two-stage retreat deeper into the pass, first to Azuga and then on 31 October to a highly defensible position just north of Buşteni. The 21st ID, reduced by incessant combat to only 2,400 exhausted men, was replaced in the line by the 4th ID. It defended fiercely and even counterattacked against repeated assaults by Staabs's forces. As the Austrian official history puts it, "The bloody game of attack and counterattack . . . led to no change in the situation." In the course of two months, the attackers advanced only ten kilometers into the pass.[23] Although the Romanian position remained precarious, the Predeal pass was not finally breached until December, when the Carpathian Front collapsed elsewhere.

The Bran pass, to the west of the Predeal, had been an important medieval avenue of commerce guarded by a castle of the Teutonic knights. Although equally long as Predeal (50 kilometers), it was not as uniformly rugged. The heartland of Wallachia was easily accessible from its southern exit at Câmpulung. If it were penetrated, the neighboring Predeal and Olt passes would be outflanked. Bran, like Predeal, fell under the command of Averescu's 2nd Army. It was defended by the 22nd ID, one of those Romanian units that had seen little combat; they had spent the preceding month riding the rails between north and south. The attacking force was Morgen's I Reserve Corps. Its plan of operations involved a frontal assault by the German 76th ID and a flanking maneuver by the Austrian 8th MB over primitive mountain paths west of the defile. When the enemy offensive began on 12 October, the Romanian defenders gave ground only slowly in the defile where they controlled the dominating heights. However, they were taken by surprise on their flank by the Austrians. To avoid being enveloped, the Romanians evacuated Rucăr on 14 October.[24] Despite strong Romanian resistance, Morgen's forces, now reinforced by the Bavarian 12th ID, continued to advance, occupying Dragoslavele on 16 October. The Romanian 22nd ID was then forced to retreat to new positions only eight kilometers north of Câmpulung. Fortunately, the threat of envelopment from the 8th MB decreased. The Austrians ran short of supplies when bad weather denied them pack animals. Every movement of man or beast became difficult as rain, fog, and then snow with bitter cold set in. Many of the troops and animals were incapacitated by frostbite and other illness. Nevertheless, the situation of the Romanian forces on the lower terrain north of Câmpulung remained serious. Averescu, alarmed at the possibility of an enemy breakthrough, dispatched the 12th ID, which was just returning from Dobrogea. Its arrival on 19 October did little more than compensate for the losses suffered by the 22nd ID in ten days of heavy fighting. Several battalions of the latter had lost 75 percent of their effectives.[25]

During the last days of October, Morgen's forces continued to press the attack. On the night of 22–23 October Câmpulung itself came under artillery bombardment. Some of the local population fled in panic. Others, including women, assisted the Romanian troops with food or guided them on their march. Upon learning that the local commanders were discouraged and defeatist, Averescu made a personal visit and worked out with them a plan for a counterattack. This offensive, which was launched on 27 October, succeeded in forcing the Austrian 8th MB to retreat. This in turn compromised the position of the Bavarian 12th ID, forcing it to begin a temporary withdrawal. In the stalemate that continued throughout November, the fighting at Câmpulung duplicated the deadly pattern at Predeal: attack followed by counterattack. "The Morgen Corps," relates the Austrian official history, "stood on the high points which surround Câmpulung on the northwest, west and east. It lacked, however, the power to break the resistance of its foes' brave defense." When Falkenhayn refused his request for more troops, Morgen proposed to break off the fighting and pull back into the pass. Instead, he was ordered to keep up the pressure while attempts were made to penetrate the Carpathians elsewhere.[26] Only when this happened and its defenders were outflanked was Câmpulung occupied (29 November) and the Bran pass open to the invader. Averescu's leadership in directing the tenacious defense of the Predeal and Bran passes has won widespread praise. However, it was carried out in the context of his ongoing conflict with MCG, a "war" as Otu terms it. Although the differences were about operational issues, they were also personal: Averescu's contempt for Iliescu and Brătianu's anger about the general's involvement with opposition political figures. Soon after his arrival in mid-October, Berthelot joined the ranks of Averescu's critics.[27]

THE OLT PASS

The Olt defile was an attractive avenue of invasion. A railroad as well as a good highway followed the course of the river. After a narrow northern section, the defile broadened, providing access also to the Argeş valley, another important portal to the heartland of Wallachia. Falkenhayn insisted that the Alpine Corps attack on the Olt, rejecting Krafft's preference to work the passes south of Braşov. Two Austrian mountain brigades (the 2nd and

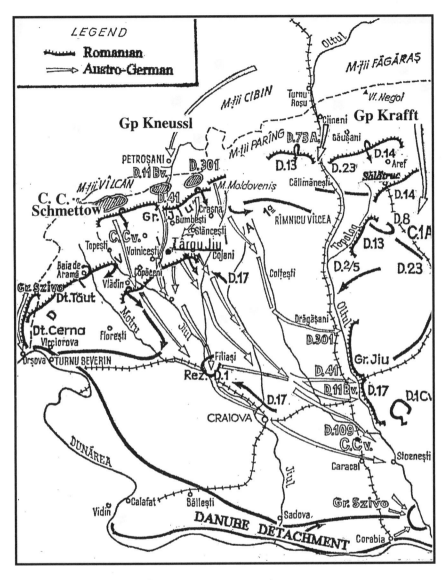

Romanian Retreat on the Olt and the Jiu. Adapted from Alexandru Niculescu, *Luptele de la Jiu* (Bucharest: Editura Militară, 1976)

10th) were added to his command for the operation. Krafft's task was to in-filtrate and envelop the Romanians via the mountains and small parallel valleys to the east and west of the Olt. To undertake a campaign in the high Carpathians so late in the season would be a gamble, as he noted in his journal: "We must have much luck."[28]

Opposing the Krafft group was the Olt Corps. Its 13th ID and 23rd ID were characterized by combined battalions cobbled together from dis-parate companies that had survived the Battle of Sibiu. It totaled 33 bat-talions, which outnumbered the 20 of the enemy. None were mountain units, whereas Krafft's total included 14 battalions of experienced alpinists. Romanian inferiority was even greater when it came to firepower. The Olt Corps had only three batteries of mountain artillery to their opponent's 12 and had few machine guns. The one bright spot was the new commander of the corps, General David Praporgescu, an energetic and inspiring leader. Upon assuming command he told his men, "No one has the right to take a step back, no one will be allowed to waver. . . . We will triumph or die for the glory of the fatherland." This challenge proved to be a premonition of his own fate. On 13 October, two weeks into his command, Praporgescu was killed by enemy artillery while inspecting the front.[29]

Three days after the death of Praporgescu, the Austro-German forces began their offensive on the Olt. Their veteran units quickly made progress on both Romanian flanks, especially to the east. Here the lead columns fol-lowing the Topolog valley advanced 30 kilometers in two days. Meeting little resistance, they were able to penetrate as far south as Sălătruc, near the end of the pass. From here they were in a position to outflank the de-fenders of the Olt and reach the Argeş river. The possibility of a quick end to the Romanian campaign caused a feeling of "euphoria" to sweep over some in the Alpine Corps.[30] The Romanians also viewed the situation as critical; an enemy breakthrough appeared imminent. An inquiry to MCG for reinforcements brought the only reply it could send: "Not one man, not one horse." Consequently, several existing units were grouped together in two large detachments led by Colonel Henri Cihoski and Colonel Traian Moşoiu. They attacked the enemy from two directions and in a three-day battle, 22–24 October, forced them to retreat north of Sălătruc "in great dis-order," leaving several hundred dead, wounded, or prisoners. "One Bavar-ian battalion," Cihoski exalted, "was not able to fire a cartridge, fleeing at the first round fired into its rear." The Battle of Sălătruc temporarily relieved the threat to the right flank and the rear of the Olt Corps. But in the center, the 23rd ID gave ground in heavy fighting with the Alpine Corps. By the end of the month, this division was exhausted and reduced to only 125 officers and 6,000 men. The retreat of the 23rd ID forced the 13th ID west of the river to fall back also.[31]

Fortunately, the onset of winter weather came to the aid of the Romanians in the Olt pass. Fog in the valleys provided cover from the enemy's devastating artillery fire. On 17 October, snow had begun to fall in the higher elevations. Within a few days it turned into a blizzard, with accumulations up to a meter and a half. Visibility was zero, and the temperature plummeted. Mountain paths were transformed into glaciers. Pack animals were useless, so the Germans requisitioned from the civilian population "the last man and woman capable of work." The weather not only hindered operations for Krafft's forces but also made them miserable, as full winter gear was not available. Supplies of all sorts ran short, including food. Except for meat from dying horses, some units were dependent on food taken from Romanians, even bread from the bodies of dead soldiers. Without shelter, and wet and cold, the Alpine Corps "lay in miserable holes they dug themselves."[32] In response, Krafft tried to push south quickly to reach warmer climes but failed. By the end of October, the advance of his forces slowed, and they were drawn into the deadly cycle of attack and counterattack with the Romanians. The latter continued to give ground slowly, suffering many casualties. But as Falkenhayn admitted, "Weeks of heavy fighting had consumed the strength of the Alpine Corps" also.[33] The Romanians bent but did not break. The Olt pass remained closed to the enemy as November began.

During the few days of relative inaction that began November, both sides brought up reinforcements. The German 216th ID and the Austrian 73rd ID joined Krafft's forces while the Olt Corps was augmented by the 14th ID. The latter did little more than compensate for the exhausted 23rd ID, which had retired 50 percent of its effectives. Those that remained were largely "completely untrained" soldiers or survivors from decimated units, which once again were cobbled together into makeshift battalions. The Romanians were therefore ill-prepared when Krafft launched a new offensive on 10 November. In the Olt valley an armored train bombarded the Romanians, but as Krafft noted in his journal, it created "more noise than damage."[34] The main effort of the attackers was concentrated east of the Olt in the di-

rection of Curtea d'Argeş. On the first day the Romanians were able to repulse the enemy in most sectors, but on succeeding days they gave ground.
Some units panicked and fled under fire. Commanders were ordered to
place military police behind the lines to shoot those who left their positions.
However, most Romanian units resisted, even if in retreat.[35] This crisis on
the Olt, plus a contemporary enemy advance on the Jiu, caused the commander of the 1st Army to suffer a nervous breakdown. General Nicolae
Petala, who had succeeded Praporgescu only eight days before, had exhib-
ited signs of emotional instability earlier in Dobrogea. Now, overcome by
the stress of his greater responsibility and unable to sleep for some time,
he reached a state of "complete demoralization." He told Queen Marie later
from a bed in a Bucharest hospital that he had become so confused he no
longer knew where his troops were. An officer of Berthelot's mission, sent
to investigate, persuaded Petala to request a medical leave, and he was replaced by General Dumitru Stratilescu. "We will see if he is better than the
other one," Prince Carol noted in his journal, "Our generals break down one
after another, be it incompetence, be it nerves."[36]

On 18 November, Austro-German forces renewed their attack on the Olt.
On the testimony of their enemies, the Romanians resisted with determination and counterattacked frequently, sometimes to the accompaniment
of loud shouts of hurrah and bugle calls. They did not shrink from hand-
to-hand combat. But overpowered and outflanked by enemy infiltration,
its powers of resistance ebbing, the Olt Corps continued to give ground
during the last half of November. It was no rout; artillery and wounded
were evacuated, and tunnels and bridges were destroyed. Many of the
fiercest battles were for the control of the heights as German and Austrian
mountain detachments, including those led by Epp and Paulus, assaulted
peak after peak. The defenders held each until driven off and then resumed
their defense on the next. Any success, Falkenhayn acknowledged, "was
accomplished by the most difficult fight. The Romanians resisted with desperation. Each mountain had to be taken by assault. And even if through
this process we captured abundant booty and substantial prisoners, it was
necessary to pay serious sacrifices in exchange for our advance."[37]

As November progressed, the Olt Corps was hard-pressed to man the
front. In the first two weeks, over 5,800 men and officers had fallen prisoner. The trend continued. On 16 November, 1,800 additional Romanians
were captured, on the seventeenth 2,000, and on the eighteenth 2,800. The

Romanian prisoners captured on the Olt. From Martin Breitenacher, *Das Alpenkorps, 1914–1918* (Berlin: Vorhut-Verlag Otto Schlegel, 1939)

14th ID, which had arrived only recently at 12,000 strong, was already reduced to 42 officers and 2,974 men. An assessment by one Romanian detachment commander was characteristic of many: "The value of the troops as well as the officers is very inferior with low morale. . . . The infantry is composed of remnants of battalions . . . , a great part from service personnel and those lost from various units of the division which we found on the route of retreat." It was amazing to the enemy that the Romanian troops, "beaten many times, fatigued, inexperienced in trench warfare and vulnerable to artillery fire, have . . . also fought bravely and tenaciously at many points." This stubborn resistance by what remained of the three divisions of the Olt Corps and reinforcements in the form of the 8th ID, which arrived on 19 November, made it possible to stymie the advance of Krafft's forces through the pass until the end of the month. Only after the successful enemy penetration of the neighboring Jiu pass outflanked the Olt did the Romanians give up its defense.[38]

THE FIRST BATTLE OF THE JIU

The last and ultimately successful assault on Romania's Carpathian defenses occurred on the Jiu. This defile was Falkenhayn's preference because
it was the shortest and offered the best prospect for surprise. Here the Romanians were most vulnerable. Reduced enemy action on this front for
most of October and the need of troops elsewhere had led MCG to diminish by eight battalions the 11th ID, which defended the Jiu. Two battalions
transferred in from the 1st ID on the Cerna were insufficient replacements.
The 11th ID was not only undermanned but tired, having been at the front
continuously since the war began. Against the "Jiu Group" was ranged an
enemy force commanded by Bavarian general Paul Ritter von Kneussl. It
was composed of the Austrian 144th Infantry Brigade, the Bavarian 11th
ID, the German 301st ID, the German 6th Cavalry Division (CD), and two
German bicycle battalions. Still en route were the German 7th CD and the
elite Württemberg Mountain Battalion (WMB). The Romanians had little
idea of what they faced. As a division commander reported later, "The enemies before us, according to our intelligence, were a German division and
some cavalry, but we did not know of the troops behind them to help."[39]

Kneussl launched his attack on 23 October against both the Surduc and
Vulcan branches of the Jiu pass. Lacking mountain units initially, he used
regular infantry and dismounted cavalry to attack the heights above the
defiles. He was pessimistic beforehand because snow had recently fallen
and these units had no mountain equipment: hiking boots, warm clothing,
or pack animals. On the morning of the attack, clear autumn weather prevailed. Immediately Kneussl's huge superiority manifested itself. Several
peaks were taken, and on the lower terrain German artillery transformed
the battlefield into a "hell" of explosions that left the "ground littered with
dead and wounded." Local withdrawals by some Romanian units turned
into a disorderly flight south toward Târgu Jiu. Soon the entire 11th ID was
in retreat. To the plea of its commander for reinforcements came the answer
that none were available; he must face the attack with what he had. The
next day his superior, 1st Army commander General Ion Culcer, asked
MCG for permission to make a general retreat. The answer from Periș,
where the newly arrived Berthelot was preaching resistance at any price,
was to replace Culcer with General Ioan Dragalina. He was ordered to stop
all talk of retreat, ceding only step by step with continuous counterattacks.

Dragalina, who took over on 24 October, was even more unyielding with his men: "Troops which cannot advance are to die on the spot while commanders who give an order of retreat will . . . be courtmartialed."[40]

Terming the situation "serious but not desperate," Dragalina ordered immediate counterattacks on the center and flanks of the enemy. Before his plans were realized, tragedy struck. On the second day of his command, while touring an advanced position on the Jiu Front, his road came under enemy fire. Without hesitation, the audacious general ordered his driver to speed through the danger zone. A hail of bullets raked the vehicle. Although all others in his party escaped injury, Dragalina was severely wounded in his right arm. He was evacuated to a hospital in Bucharest, where the arm was amputated. A blood infection set in, and within two weeks he was dead.[41] In the space of only 12 days, the Romanian army had lost Praporgescu and Dragalina, two of its most dynamic and inspiring field commanders.

The loss of Dragalina seemed to portend the collapse of the Romanian defense on the Jiu. Local counterattacks failed, and Romanian forces continued in a full retreat. One battalion surrendered without firing a shot; occupation of prepared positions was neglected. Kneussl's forces gained control of the entire crest of the mountains and reached the forest line on the southern slope. Advance units were only five kilometers from Târgu Jiu. One column even reached the bridge on its outskirts. Only a few militia guarded the city, but townspeople joined them, barricading the streets and fortifying houses near the bridge. Old men, youth, and even women took up arms. They helped delay the Germans from crossing the bridge until Romanian infantry arrived to drive them off. But by the morning of 27 October it appeared as if Kneussl's forces were on the verge of a breakthrough onto the Wallachian plain. Falkenhayn summoned Count Schmettow to lead his cavalry in exploiting it. The German conviction that the enemy was defeated was reinforced by prisoners who "made a rather miserable, ragged impression."[42]

The seeming demoralization in the ranks of Romanian forces in the field had been matched by the confusion in the entire command structure that followed the death of Dragalina. For several days of transition there had been no unified command on the Jiu. Finally, leadership by committee emerged when commanders of the largest units met on the evening of 26 October. They decided to implement immediately Dragalina's plans for a

General Ioan Dragalina,
commander, 1st Army.
Collection of Opry Popa

counterattack before the enemy consolidated his hold on the plain of Târgu
Jiu. Their troops were energized for an assault as word spread of Dragalina's *Heldentod*. On the morning of 27 October a heavy rain fell as Romanian forces attacked the center and flanks of the enemy. Infiltration and
envelopment tactics were successful as Kneussl's forces, not yet consolidated, were isolated in small groups along a front of 20 kilometers running
from southwest to northeast. Although not everywhere successful, the Romanians gradually forced Kneussl's forces to fall back into the mountains
north of Târgu Jiu.[43] Weakened by a struggle, not only against the Romanians but against the rain, snow, and bad roads that cut off their supply,
German resistance suddenly collapsed, and Kneussl's forces began a "full
retreat." Bowing to this stunning reversal of events, Kneussl then authorized a general pullback into the forest and, if necessary, even to the frontier
itself. This retreat, in Falkenhayn's words, "was carried out with hardships
which can hardly be described. . . . The roads were, in many places, icy,

washed away, collapsed or destroyed by flood. Even the retreat of horses was hardly possible; for guns and vehicles it was an impossibility. They had to be destroyed or pushed into ravines." First Lieutenant Erwin Rommel, of the WMB, just then moving up to the front, described one retreating unit of the Bavarian 11th ID he encountered: "Their nerves appeared to be pretty well frayed. . . . A majority of their comrades had been killed in close fighting with the Romanians. . . . They described the Romanians as wild and dangerous adversaries."[44] The severe weather and exhausting combat took their toll on everyone. On 31 October both sides suspended operations. Losses in this first Battle of the Jiu were high. Romanian totals do not exist, but the enemy counted 2,200 prisoners. Austro-German casualties exceeded 3,600. In addition, much equipment was lost, including artillery that the Romanians, already equipped with German-made guns, put to good use. For Kneussl's forces it was, as Seeckt admitted, "a serious defeat." Although the invaders on the Jiu had failed to penetrate Wallachia, they still controlled the heights and most of the pass.[45]

THE SECOND BATTLE OF THE JIU

While the Romanians were accepting congratulations for their victory, Falkenhayn was preparing to attack again quickly before the full onset of winter eliminated all hope of success. Not wishing a repeat of the October defeat, he greatly augmented Kneussl's original battle group with the German 7th CD, 41st ID, and 109th ID, as well as the WMB. This new attack force, designated the LIV Corps under the command of General Victor Kühne, boasted 40 infantry battalions and 52 cavalry squadrons. This dwarfed the Romanian Jiu Group, which totaled only 18 battalions, a mélange of detachments soon to be designated the 1st ID. In order to conceal his intentions on the Jiu, Falkenhayn made several ostentatious personal visits to the Braşov passes. The Romanian High Command was deceived, assuming the enemy would not attack again on the Jiu so soon after his recent defeat. Consequently it had withdrawn the 11th ID for reorganization and had not arranged its immediate replacement, despite reports of the presence of new enemy units. The 17th ID was tardily assigned to the defense of the Jiu on 14 November, but its arrival was delayed even longer by a train derailment. MCG was counting on its armies to hold the

German prisoners captured on the Jiu. From Constantin Kirițescu, *Istoria războiului pentru întregierea României,* 2nd ed. (Bucharest: Editura Casei Şcoalelor, 1925)

enemy for eight days in the hope that the long-promised offensive of the Russian 9th Army in conjunction with the North Army would divert the attention of the enemy. This was a false hope.[46]

In the meantime, Kühne opened a coordinated attack in the Jiu pass on 11 November. While the German infantry and artillery pounded at Romanian positions in the defile, the WMB was ordered to undertake a flanking maneuver in the heights to the west. Rommel, already displaying the bold initiative and drive that became his trademark, led his company as it penetrated the extremely rugged terrain to reach the saddle of the mountains. Even surviving at elevations of 2,000 to 2,500 meters in bad weather, let alone fighting, was a supreme test for the WMB. Drenched from constant rain and unable to start fires, many of the men became ill. Food had to be obtained by foraging; the capture of a Romanian cow brought joy to all. Exposure to the elements ceased only when a village was reached and the Romanian inhabitants were expelled from their houses. At Vălari Curpenel on 12 November, a fierce Romanian counterattack pinned down Rommel's unit throughout the day and into the night. Wave after wave of Romanians charged, only to be beaten back by superior firepower, especially from German heavy machine guns. The next morning, as he counted hundreds of dead Romanians on the battlefield, Rommel marveled at how they "attacked repeatedly" and persisted against his deadly firepower. Other members of the WMB also praised their enemies for "bravery and tenacity" but emphasized how they were "mowed down by our annihilating fire."[47]

While the WMB penetrated the heights, German forces in the center attacked directly toward Târgu Jiu. For two days the Romanians held them at Bumbeşti, withstanding a devastating artillery bombardment and repeated infantry attacks involving grenades and machine guns. But on 12 November, Romanian resistance collapsed. The forces of Kühne were now in complete control of the road through the pass. Immediately he prepared to send the mass of his infantry, artillery, and the two cavalry divisions of Count Schmettow onto the plain surrounding Târgu Jiu. The city was occupied on 15 November with only brief resistance from a few Romanian militia. Many of the civilians had fled out of fear for the German "barbarians," who helped themselves to their homes and livestock. Members of the WMB, describing Wallachia as "truly a land where milk and honey flows," enjoyed comfortable quarters and ate "chicken soup almost daily."[48]

The Germans did not tarry long in Târgu Jiu. General Seeckt, who visited the city the day after its capture, advocated a quick thrust to the south and east before snow made the roads impassable. Kühne agreed and ordered his troops to press on. He was surprised when the Romanian command decided to make a stand on the heights just south of Târgu Jiu.[49] Still unaware of their enemy's massive superiority, the Romanians planned to resist with the 1st ID reinforced by the 17th ID, part of which was still en route. In addition, detachments from the Olt and Cerna were to attack the enemy flanks. In a two-day battle on 16–17 November, the Romanian Front was ruptured and Schmettow's cavalry dashed onto the Wallachian plain. The Romanians, fighting desperately to defend their homeland, suffered catastrophic losses. In one regiment three-fourths of its men lay on the battlefield, dead or wounded, while the remainder were taken prisoner. The 1st ID was reduced to 1,800 men and the 17th ID to 2,000. What remained of the Jiu Group retreated "in great disorder." With the enemy victory on the Jiu, the entire Romanian defense of the southern Carpathians was compromised.[50]

9
The Battle for Wallachia

After rupturing Romania's Carpathian barrier at Târgu Jiu, Austro-German forces, led by Schmettow's cavalry, raced south into the heart of Oltenia.[1] The infantry followed close behind, slowed only by frightened refugees and their oxcarts, which had to be pushed off the roads. The Romanian command vetoed resistance in and around Craiova "so as not to expose it to useless bombardment." Romania's second largest city was occupied on 21 November. Kühne delighted his men with a day of rest and permission to sightsee. They marveled at Craiova's "millionaire palaces," a striking contrast with the poverty they had seen in smaller Romanian towns.[2]

The rapid enemy advance into Oltenia cut the Romanian 1st ID in two, isolating the Cerna detachment and other units along the Danube. Consequently the 1st Army command ordered them to retreat eastward in a forced march. When word of this reached MCG, Berthelot, upset that this would open the Danube to the enemy, "reacted in a violent manner." "In the name of the Entente," he declared to the king, "I ask that the Cerna Detachment resist on the spot." Immediately MCG ordered this unit and others along the Danube "to resist to the end." If capture became imminent, they were "to throw all artillery into the Danube" and "fight as partisans." Resist they did, attacked from all sides not only by Austro-German forces but also by Bulgarian *comitadji* dressed in sheepskins who crossed the

Danube looking for booty. After a "two-week calvary," the remnant that survived surrendered. Four regiments, some 10,000 soldiers, were sacrificed, including four of Romania's better senior commanders who were badly needed elsewhere.[3]

The penetration of strong enemy forces into western Wallachia triggered a debate over strategy at MCG. The Russian liaison, General Mikhail Beliaev, advocated a planned withdrawal eastward to conserve the structure and resources of the Romanian army. To Berthelot this sounded suspiciously like Alekseev's earlier advice that Wallachia be abandoned. He proposed instead that the Romanians launch a major counteroffensive on the Olt river, the only major natural barrier west of Bucharest. If successful, this rebuff and the onset of winter weather might delay the enemy advance long enough to allow time for the arrival of Russian reinforcements and the impact of Allied offenses elsewhere. Berthelot's views prevailed, not only because of his enormous influence over the king, but because most Romanians were not yet resigned to surrender so much of their homeland, including its capital, without a major battle.[4]

Consequently, plans were made for the creation of a special "mass of maneuver" to counterattack on the Olt. General Prezan was called from his command of the North Army to lead this operation. He arrived in Periş on 23 November accompanied by Captain Antonescu. Given command of an army group that included the 1st Army, Prezan left that evening for his new headquarters at Piteşti with Antonescu and Berthelot's chief of staff, Colonel Victor Pétin. By the time they arrived the next morning, they learned of two events that made an Olt maneuver impossible. On the day before, Schmettow's cavalry, advancing southeast from Craiova, had reached the Olt at Stoeneşti and captured a bridge that the Romanians had tried but failed to destroy.[5] The 6th CD soon crossed and continued eastward, followed by the German 109th ID. Schmettow's 7th CD proceeded north along the east bank to outflank the Romanian defenders and cover the crossing of three more infantry divisions at Slatina and Drăgăşani. The Olt barrier no longer existed. But more importantly, also on 23 November, a German–Bulgarian–Turkish force had carried out an assault crossing of the Danube at Sistov-Zimnicea, 35 kilometers east of the Olt.[6]

THE CROSSING OF THE DANUBE

In contrast to the impulsive and hastily mounted Romanian operation at Flămânda, the Sistov-Zimnicea crossing was meticulously planned and flawlessly executed. The site was well chosen, 100 kilometers southwest of Bucharest—not too far for a quick strike on the capital, yet not too close to Romanian reserves quartered there. At this point the river was relatively narrow (1,000 meters) and the current slow. The channel contained many small islands behind which men and equipment could be concealed. Among these was the bridging train that von Hötzendorf had cached there before the war began. The most serious drawback of this site was its history as a Danube crossing, most recently during the Russo-Turkish war of 1877–1878, when the Russian army erected a pontoon bridge there.[7] Would the Romanians remember? Since the outbreak of war, preliminary preparations had been carried out under the leadership of the designated assault commander, German general Robert Kosch. Bulgarian railroads were upgraded, new hard-surface roads built, and bridges strengthened to facilitate the assembly of men and heavy artillery. Great care was taken to camouflage these improvements. Kosch's LII Corps was composed of five divisions: the German 217th ID, the Bulgarian 1st ID and 12th ID, a mixed cavalry division under German general Karl von der Goltz, and the Turkish 26th ID. They were supported by 64 artillery batteries emphasizing heavy calibers, the guns of the Austro-Hungarian Danube flotilla, and 36 German and Austro-Hungarian aircraft.[8] The initial target date, late October, had to be postponed several times, first because of temporary reverses in the Dobrogean campaign, then because of difficulties in transporting troops and artillery. In addition to the poor condition of their railroads, the Bulgarians were reluctant to divert their forces from Dobrogea, where their war aims were centered, to an invasion of western Romania, where they had little interest. Their "passive resistance" was not overcome until Mackensen prompted the personal intervention of Tsar Ferdinand.[9]

The Romanian Danube Defense Group was ill-prepared to offer serious resistance to the landing. Made up of the 18th ID, composed primarily of militia plus three brigades of cavalry, it was divided into three almost equal detachments spread along 210 kilometers of the river. The battalions along the 56-kilometer sector where Zimnicea was located were especially weak, "insufficiently trained, poorly organized and poorly led, with outmoded weapons . . . , the majority without a single machine gun." Only two battalions were reasonably close to Zimnicea.[10] Intelligence failures prevented the Romanian command from marshaling forces in anticipation of the landing. Distracted by crises on other fronts and misled by enemy ruses, including artillery bombardments and at least one false landing elsewhere, the Romanian High Command was caught completely unawares. Indications had been missed: reports of troop movements near Sistov; the appearance of a large number of boats, including Austro-Hungarian monitors on the river; reports from Romanian shore posts of unusual noise from the Bulgarian side; increased enemy activity opposite Zimnicea. In addition, English aviators, flying over Bulgaria from Salonika, reported an enemy column, 25 kilometers long, moving westward in Dobrogea. No conclusions were drawn and no precautions taken.[11]

A heavy seasonal fog over the Danube concealed Kosch's forces as they assembled and boarded a variety of boats on the night of 22 November. The crossing began the next day at sunrise. The initial landing parties met no resistance, and the well-organized transfer of the five divisions began. Each had approximately 20,000 men, 5,000 horses, and 1,200 wagons and required eight to ten hours to transport. On 23–24 November, two divisions crossed. The only hitch came when Bulgarian soldiers, afraid of water, initially hesitated to get into the boats. They were reassured and soon were crossing to the music of their regimental bands. Zimnicea was occupied at 2:30 P.M., and Mackensen crossed shortly thereafter. From the Romanian customhouse, he sent a telegram to the Kaiser announcing the success of the landing. At 7:30 A.M. on the second day, construction of the pontoon bridge began. It was completed in less than 24 hours, so that on 25 and 26 November the remaining infantry, the cavalry, and the artillery crossed. In contrast to Flămânda, the bridge and crossing at Zimnicea were not threatened by hostile warships or mines.[12]

The small unit of Romanian militia that responded to the initial cry of alarm on 23 November quickly retreated. The first serious Romanian counterattack was carried out early on 24 November by two battalions under the command of French colonel Ernest Mercier. "After a semblance of resistance," his Romanians panicked and fled. Mercier, left alone on the field, was seriously wounded. Despite these early encounters, the Romanian command failed to recognize the magnitude of the threat. A Romanian aerial reconnaissance flight on 25 November reported seeing a bridge but no troops on it or in the vicinity—this on the day when the greater part of the two infantry divisions, cavalry, and artillery passed over it. An operational order of MCG on the same day erroneously concluded, "Weak enemy force has crossed the Danube." Berthelot reflected the confusion existing at MCG: "Some say only one regiment has crossed the river at Zimnicea. . . . Others are more pessimistic: [saying] there are already three divisions north of the Danube." Upset by the failure of air reconnaissance, he sacked the French officer heading joint Romanian–French aerial operations.[13]

A vigorous Romanian response was also hindered by the fact that on the day before the crossing the commander of the Danube Defense Group, General Constantin Christescu, had departed for the North Army to replace Prezan. His successor took over the day after, and even then MCG rejected his proposal to send all available infantry and artillery toward Zimnicea. It chose instead to send the 2nd Cavalry Division from the vicinity of Oltenița, 100 kilometers to the east. The weak and tardy Romanian response was hardly a nuisance to Kosch as he completed his transit and concentration.[14] The German 217th ID spearheaded the attack, moving northeast toward Bucharest. Goltz's cavalry pushed north toward Alexandria, its patrols making contact with Schmettow's 6th CD on 27 November. The Bulgarian 1st ID, marching east along the Danube, occupied Giurgiu the same day. They were joined by additional Bulgarian forces, which crossed the river there and began constructing another pontoon bridge.[15] Mackensen's forces were now only 60 kilometers from the Romanian capital.

QUESTIONS OF STRATEGY

The crossing of the Olt and the Danube raised important questions of strategy for both the German and Romanian commands. Falkenhayn, judging from the rapid and disorderly enemy retreat from Târgu Jiu, did not believe that the Romanian army was capable of making a stand west of Bucharest. His intention was to send Kühne's forces northeast toward Ploieşti, leaving to Mackensen the occupation of the capital. His objective was to reach the Siret river before the arrival of winter and Russian reinforcements. Falkenhayn's superiors, not convinced the Romanians would retreat so readily, disagreed. Seeckt wanted to split Kühne's forces, the left wing turning north to join with Krafft and the right wing moving south-

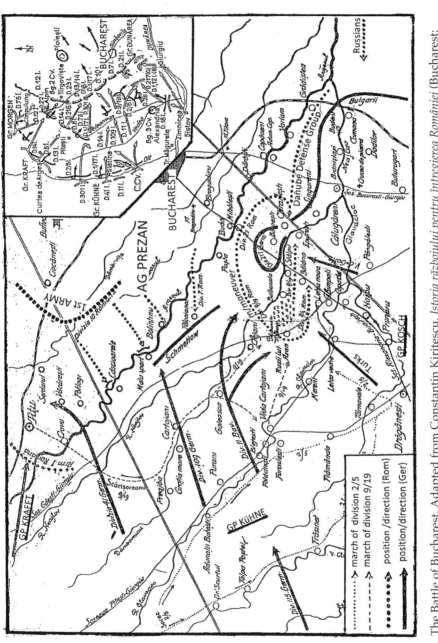

The Battle of Bucharest. Adapted from Constantin Kirițescu, *Istoria războiului pentru întregierea României* (Bucharest: Institut de arte grafice, 1922), and Victor Atanasiu, *România în primul război mondial* (Bucharest: Editura Militară, 1979)

east toward Bucharest and Kosch's Danube Army. OHL preferred a conservative strategy of advancing on a broad front. These differences, exacerbated by long-standing personal antagonisms, led to a flurry of heated
telephone and telegraph communications. Falkenhayn considered the intervention of Seeckt and OHL an infringement on his command authority.
He stated that he would accept Seeckt's wishes only if ordered to do so by
OHL. In the end, the latter accepted Falkenhayn's position in essence, and
in an attempt to bring unity to the Romanian campaign, transferred the 9th
Army from Seeckt's command to that of Mackensen.[16]

For the Romanian command, the simultaneous enemy crossing of the
Olt and the Danube created a much more critical strategic problem. "In-
stantly," Berthelot recorded, "all plans of maneuver on the Olt fall through.
A general retreat of all units of the 1st Army is ordered. One will attempt
to defend Bucharest by grouping all available forces on the Argeş river to
the west of the capital." But, as he added in a report to Paris, "We do not
have sufficient forces for a line of 150 kilometers from the Danube to the
mountains. One solution: a war of movement, actions on the heads of the
German columns."[17] When Prezan and Antonescu returned to MCG from
Piteşti on 26 November, they had a specific plan for such action. It pointed
out that a gap, covered only by Schmettow's cavalry, existed between
Kühne's forces on the middle Olt and those of Kosch on the Danube.
Prezan proposed to counterattack using the mass of maneuver being assembled for the now impossible counteroffensive on the Olt: first to "fall
with power on the flank of Mackensen" and "throw him into the Danube,"
and then to turn north against Falkenhayn's 9th Army.[18] Prezan's plan, according to Duca, "was discussed in detail with all competent authorities at
MCG, with Berthelot, with the oracles of the French mission. All placed
great hope in it." Voices of critics were not heard. Duca, to whom "the
hopes of the military appeared ridiculous," kept quiet. Averescu, whose
opinion was not solicited, considered it "a battle lost from the beginning."[19]
In retrospect, one would have to agree. At the time, most Romanian leaders, and their French advisors as well, were still unwilling to surrender the
capital without a major battle. Underlying their decision to risk a counteroffensive from an extremely unfavorable strategic position were incor-
rect assumptions regarding the strength of the enemy, the capabilities of
the Romanian army, and the probability of Russian assistance.

Romanian intelligence, which had failed miserably in recognizing signs of an impending crossing, was equally deficient in assessing the size and composition of the enemy forces that the mass of maneuver would be facing. The German 217th ID was identified only on 27 November, the Bulgarian 1st ID on 29 November, and the Goltz cavalry division on 1 December. It was 2 December, as the battle was virtually over, before the Romanians recognized that the invading force was composed of five divisions. Romanian intelligence about Kühne's forces on the Olt was more accurate but failed to include the German 301st ID, one of Schmettow's cavalry divisions, and the 9th Army reserve (two divisions and one brigade).[20] Conversely, Prezan overestimated the capacity of his mass of maneuver to carry out the complicated operation he envisioned. He had at his disposal only four divisions, the 2nd/5th ID, the 9th/19th ID, the 21st ID, and the 2nd CD. As their designation indicates, the first two were hasty amalgams of divisions decimated in the Dobrogean campaign. Division 21 had just been reconstituted after sustaining heavy losses in the Prahova valley. A single company of 150 might contain men from five or more regiments. Filler troops were often completely untrained. After debriefing Romanian officers taken prisoner, German intelligence evaluations concluded that such reconstructed units, "indiscriminately thrown together," were of "little value" and exercised a detrimental influence on the discipline and fighting ability of the army. Even homogenous units were suffering from fatigue and depression resulting from weeks of fighting and defeat. Although men in the mass of maneuver obediently marched to the attack, the expectation that they could defeat an enemy superior in firepower, morale, and leadership was an "inexplicable illusion."[21]

Underlying the Romanian decision to counterattack was the expectation that their Russian ally would ultimately live up to repeated promises of vigorous offensive action by the 9th Army in the Carpathians and Sakharov's Army of Dobrogea. There was even hope for direct intervention in Wallachia. Was this realistic? For almost three months, insistent, even desperate, appeals to the Russians for assistance had proved futile. "They did not actually refuse but stalled [and] gave promises," remembers General Coandă, the Romanian liaison at STAVKA. Despite this record of inaction, Romanian leaders, and their French allies as well, could not bring themselves to believe that the Russians would stand by and see Romania defeated. On the eve of the counteroffensive, MCG maintained hope for offensives by the Russian 9th Army and Army of Dobrogea. Although

STAVKA avoided a commitment to intervene directly on the Wallachian Front, a Russian army corps was ordered to move westward along the Danube. Coandă, however, repeated on 25 November a warning he had voiced several times before: "I believe . . . that for the present we have nothing to rely on than ourselves."[22]

Berthelot had approved Prezan's plan with a word of caution: "Yes but on the condition of making haste and attacking energetically." This proved to be impossible. The three attack divisions were separated from one another by 40 to 78 kilometers and were up to 60 kilometers from the intended point of attack. Long marches would mean critical delays and exhausted troops. The concentration and direction of these forces was exacerbated by inadequate communication. Prezan's battle group possessed no telex or Hughes apparatus, as it was then called, and only a limited amount of cable for field telephones. Existing civilian telephone lines were often cut by Schmettow's cavalry or otherwise failed. The dispatch of information by courier was slow and equally unreliable. Aerial intelligence was lacking. The net result was that Prezan had a limited and dated idea of what was going on on the battlefield. His field commanders habitually received orders that no longer corresponded to the current situation—or they received no orders at all. To make matters worse, during the Battle of Bucharest, MCG virtually abdicated its role in supervising operations and coordinating the mass of maneuver with the other Romanian armies.[23]

THE BATTLE FOR BUCHAREST

Prezan's operations order of 27 November set the attack date two days later. Division 21 started out immediately from its reserve position near Bucharest, moving southwest along the national highway toward Alexandria. It was impeded by a column of refugees, described by 19-year-old Lieutenant Emilian Ionescu as "a living river of men in panic and thirsty, starving animals against which the regiment had to navigate upstream." The division entered the line on 28 November, replacing the 18th ID, which had been routed by the German 217th ID after its accompanying cavalry had been virtually annihilated in a foolish saber charge. On 29–30 November, the 21st ID confronted the enemy alone while the other two attack divisions were still en route. It was battered by German artillery that "turned our positions into dust," Ionescu remembered. The division was immediately forced to retreat back across the Neajlov river. The 9th/19th ID, located near Titu and next in proximity to Kosch's forces, began to march to the south early on 28 November. At 2:00 P.M. the next day, it was held up by artillery and rifle fire from von der Goltz's cavalry. The Romanian 2nd CD had failed to provide cover because it was without orders, wasting time in march and countermarch. Division 9/19 continued south but delayed closing with the enemy because Division 2/5 had not arrived.[24]

Division 2/5, engaged with the enemy east of the Olt, had the longest march to the point of attack. The commander, General Alexandru Socec, was alerted on 27 November but received orders only at 7:30 P.M. the next day. These gave no details about the operation but required his unit to be at Drăgăneşti, 80 kilometers away, the next evening. The men began to move south at 9:00 P.M. in two columns about 12 kilometers apart. After 24 hours of hard marching under harassment from Schmettow's cavalry, they covered much of the distance to their attack point. Exhausted, clothed in torn and dirty uniforms, and burdened by their wounded, the men were in no condition for offensive action. With the 2nd/5th ID unable to meet his timetable, Prezan postponed the attack of the mass of maneuver until 30 November. Meanwhile Socec's 9th/19th ID continued to march south, attacked again by Goltz's riders and then by Schmettow's, fighting both off and taking prisoners. Once again Prezan postponed the attack, this time until 1 December. While Divisions 2/5 and 9/19 were en route, Division 21, under heavy attack by the German 217th ID, had been forced to retreat again, this time behind the Argeş river.[25]

Finally, on 1 December, the 2nd/5th ID and the 9th/19th ID arrived on the flank of Kosch's forces. The Romanians were not able to attack until late in the day, in part because new orders from Prezan were late and complicated by a missing cipher. During the late afternoon and evening they drove off Goltz's covering cavalry and attacked the left flank and rear of the German 217th ID. A heavy engagement near Bălăria began at 6:00 P.M. and continued most of the night and the next day (2 December). German casualties were heavy, including 2,000 prisoners. Its regiments were reduced to 800, 500, and 300 men, respectively. The 217th ID was forced to draw back from the Argeş and form a compact defense against the concentric attack of the three Romanian divisions. The position of the 217th ID became "extremely critical." If its resistance was broken, the connection of Kosch's other divisions to the bridges would be endangered. Alarmed at this prospect, Mackensen sent two appeals to Falkenhayn for the diversion of some of Kühne's forces south to render assistance. AOK called this the "high point" of the crisis of the Danube Army.[26]

Exaggerated reports of the early success of the mass of maneuver spread throughout the Romanian military. "The enemy flees in disorder toward the Danube, having the retreat to the bridge cut off," General Stratilescu informed his 1st Army commanders. Unfortunately, Prezan and his staff participated in this unjustified optimism. In an order thrown from an airplane, they commanded the attack be continued on 3 December "without interruption." In an annex, Prezan added, "The general situation absolutely demands that the action must be terminated in the shortest possible time . . . , in a definitive manner in the course of the day of 3 December." This, together with the preliminary evacuation of MCG from Periş eastward to Buzău, indicates Romanian apprehension that the Battle of Bucharest might be lost.[27]

Falkenhayn's skepticism regarding a Romanian counterattack west of Bucharest had led him to disregard Mackensen's initial calls to reinforce Kosch's forces. However, on the afternoon of 1 December, two Romanian staff officers were captured in an automobile lost behind German lines on the upper Argeş. In their possession were documents that revealed the essence of Prezan's plan.[28] Thus enlightened, Falkenhayn ordered Kühne's right wing to turn and attack the mass of maneuver. The Bavarian 11th ID immediately began a forced march to the south. The intercepted documents also revealed to Falkenhayn that the movement of the 2nd/5th ID and 9th/19th ID to the south had opened a gap in the Romanian Front. He ordered Kühne's remaining divisions to exploit this gap by advancing quickly to the Argeş in order to cut the retreat route of the Romanian forces. In addition, the Turkish 26th ID, which had been held back, was brought up.[29]

Early on 3 December, the Orthodox Sunday, the mass of maneuver prepared to resume its offensive as Prezan had ordered. Officers visited their troops in the early dawn, encouraging them for the attack. They were all unaware that the Bavarian 11th ID, approaching from the north, was virtually upon them. The Romanian 2nd CD and 7th ID (in reserve), charged with covering the rear, remained inexplicably inactive. About midmorning, the 2nd/5th ID was suddenly attacked on three sides by the Bavarians, the Turks, Goltz's cavalry, and the regrouped 217th ID. The Romanians held their ground until about 1:00 P.M. Then they fell victim to the exhaustion and demoralization resulting from a week of constant marching and fighting that had already reduced their ranks by almost half. Hit by a "rain of projectiles" that caused "the ground to tremble," they began to give way all along the line. Unable to control his troops, Socec ordered a general retreat. His headquarters, already bombed the day before, was now turned into an "inferno" by enemy artillery. By his own account, one must conclude that he himself suffered a failure of nerve. He moved his command post to the rear precipitately and conspicuously, exacerbating the panic developing among his troops. The next day, the obviously shaken Socec continued his retirement all the way to the environs of Bucharest. His behavior, although open to other interpretations, caused him to be court-martialed for deserting his troops.[30]

The flight of Division 2/5 forced the neighboring 9th/19th ID to retreat also. Soon disorder and panic reigned in both divisions as they retreated toward Bucharest with the enemy only 300 to 400 meters behind. At times, Romanian and German soldiers jostled with refugees as they raced to reach the Neajlov river. Finding the bridge on the national highway under fire and jammed with vehicles and cadavers of men and animals, the Romanians attempted to ford the icy waters of the river. Many perished in the process. Those who succeeded continued their flight back across the Argeş river, halting only at Brăgădiru, 13 kilometers west of Bucharest. Division 2/5 now numbered only 2,500 of the 10,000 that had started the march south five days earlier. Division 9/19 counted 5,000 survivors. Both divisions had lost virtually all of their artillery. On the evening of 3 December, Prezan ordered the mass of maneuver to withdraw to the vicinity of Bucharest. This was nothing more than an acknowledgment of the retreat that had already taken place.[31]

Although Prezan's plan for a counteroffensive contained the seeds of its own failure, as was mentioned earlier, it is necessary to point out that the anticipated Russian supporting offensives failed to materialize. In the eastern Carpathians, the Russian 9th Army, together with the Romanian North Army, was committed to take the offensive against the Austro-Hungarian 1st Army. The Russians, after much vacillation, began an attack on 28 November against enemy positions along the Trotuş river guarding the important Ghimes pass into Transylvania. Gains were not great, one to nine kilometers, but caused sufficient concern for Seeckt to call for substantial

German reinforcements. The Russian offensive could have created serious problems for the Austro-German Command if it had been diligently pursued. Instead, it continued with decreasing intensity for only ten days. It failed to penetrate the front or to cause diversion of German forces from the 9th Army in Wallachia.[32] A simultaneous offensive of the Romanian North Army created even less of a problem for the enemy. Ordered by MCG to launch an attack coordinated with the Russians, General Constantin Christescu objected that his forces were much too weak and lacked the necessary artillery for offensive action. His two principal subordinates, Eremia Grigorescu (15th ID) and Alexandru Sturdza (7th Mixed Brigade) agreed. MCG rejected Christescu's objections and reaffirmed the order for an offensive. Consequently Grigorescu's division launched several attacks between 30 November and 2 December that, in the words of the enemy commander, were "deep, organized," but that "failed amid huge bloody losses." Sturdza, who was already deeply disaffected with Romania's leaders, was prepared to disobey the order. In the end he succeeded in stalling the initiation of action by his brigade until the order to attack was rescinded. Thereafter, the Russian and Romanian forces in the northern Carpathians conducted only small-scale operations.[33]

Likewise, there was little help in the Battle of Bucharest from the Russian forces remaining in Dobrogea, even though they enjoyed a marked numerical superiority as a result of the withdrawal of German and Bulgarian forces for the Sistov–Zimnicea crossing. An offensive ordered by Sakharov on 24 November achieved little and was abandoned two days later. Similarly, no effective aid materialized from the Russian IV European Corps, which had been positioned along the Danube east of Bucharest. Upon news of the enemy crossing, Coandă had presented at STAVKA, in the name of King Ferdinand, a request that the IV Corps march west to reinforce the Danube Defense Group. STAVKA refused at first, but after Coandă's appeal directly to the tsar, it reversed itself and promised to send two divisions (30th ID, 40th ID). The first contingent, a brigade, reached the Argeş river south of Bucharest on 1 December. Mackensen was seriously concerned when he received reports of Russian troops on the flank of the Bulgarian division there. He need not have worried. The Russians remained totally inactive on 2 December, a critical day for the mass of maneuver. They attacked about noon the next day but "without much vigor," then joined the Romanians in retreat. Mackensen's command considered Russian inaction "chiefly to be thanked that the [Danube] army, despite the difficult position of the left flank, could hold the ground won."[34]

THE RETREAT OF THE 1ST ARMY

While the mass of maneuver was engaging Mackensen's forces, the Romanian 1st Army to the north was retreating under a concentric attack from Falkenhayn's 9th Army. The diversion of Divisions 2/5 and 9/19 to exploit a gap between the forces of Kühne and Kosch had in turn created a gap of 60 kilometers in the Romanian Front. This allowed Schmettow's cavalry, followed by infantry, to penetrate eastward with little resistance. Fearing that this advance would envelop the right wing of the 1st Army, Prezan ordered it to make a 25-kilometer retreat on 27 November. This meant surrendering the strong defensive positions north of Curtea d'Argeş, which had stymied Group Krafft for weeks. Once begun, the Romanian retreat could not be arrested. After occupying Curtea d'Argeş without opposition, Krafft's right wing moved southeast toward Piteşti while the Alpine Corps advanced east over the Carpathian foothills. This disappointed some of Krafft's men who had hoped for easier fighting on the Romanian plain after weeks of mountain combat. They responded with determination. Braving cold rain, impassable roads, and swollen rivers, they covered up to 30 kilometers a day. Their advance outflanked the Romanian II Army Corps (2nd Army), which had held Morgen's I Reserve Corps at Câmpulung since October. On 27 November, Averescu ordered it to retreat, and the Germans occupied the evacuated city at 10:00 A.M. on 29 November.[35]

Both Krafft and Morgen now turned east toward the Prahova valley to seize the Romanian "oil belt," stretching from Târgovişte to Ploieşti, and to envelop the remainder of Averescu's 2nd Army, which was still holding the Predeal pass. Northwest of Târgovişte, Morgen's forces advanced rapidly, inflicting enormous casualties on the retreating Romanians. On 30 November alone, they captured 3,000 Romanian soldiers, some of them disguised in civilian clothing; others disappeared into the obscurity of their home villages. A counterattack by a Romanian cavalry regiment was shot down by a German bicycle company. When Morgen ordered Târgovişte taken by storm on 3 December, the defenders, he relates, offered "determined resistance and could only be thrown back in bayonet fighting."[36] The city was finally occupied at 2:30 P.M.

To the southwest of Târgovişte, the Romanian 14th ID attempted to halt the advance of Krafft's 216th ID. But its counterattacks failed, and the commander reported pathetically on 30 November, "It is no longer possible to resist anywhere. The troops flee in disorder. . . . The headquarters of the division is threatened by enemy cavalry. Please send orders urgently what must be done." The next day, as the division continued to retreat behind the Argeş, some of its units were captured in their entirety. Division 13, brought up from the reserve, counterattacked under its energetic commander, Colonel Henri Cihoski, but was unable to reestablish the situation. Thereupon the two divisions were combined as Division 13/14 under Cihoski. Together they numbered no more than 4,000 men. Unfortunately, on 2 December, the first day of his new command, Cihoski was gravely wounded, as was French colonel Georges Dubois, who commanded one regiment. The division was thrown into disorder in full retreat to the east.[37]

To the south of Morgen and Krafft, Kühne's LIV Corps was also advancing rapidly. The Romanian 1st/17th ID stood before it virtually alone after the mass of maneuver was sent to the south. The only available reserve (10th ID) was just emerging from reconstruction at Ploieşti and was still 45 kilometers away. On 30 November–1 December, the 1st/17th ID was able to repel strong attacks by the German 301st ID and even recapture some position previously lost, but at a price. In his after-action report, the commander warned that the continued combat ability of his men was questionable: after three months of continuous fighting, only "a handful of regular officers remain" to lead the "fragments" of his division. His orders to hold the east bank of the Argeş "until the last man" were impossible to carry out. Enemy patrols had already reached the bridge at Ioneşti. Most of the division was able to ford the river at another spot but had to abandon much of its artillery. On the other side, "all the roads were filled with enemy patrols." The neighboring 8th ID was in a state of disintegration itself. "Enveloped on both sides," the commander of its 69th Infantry Battalion reported, "the men, in the highest degree of indiscipline, have retreated in disorder and could be held back neither through officers nor through gunfire." On 2 December, a German battalion overran the division headquarters, capturing the division staff and archives, the commander alone escaping "miraculously."[38]

Once the Argeş was surrendered, the Romanian retreat accelerated and chaos increased. Enemy patrols were operating far to the rear of large bodies of Romanian troops. The I Corps commander was stunned when a German armored car shelled his headquarters in Găeşti. All roads leading east were jammed with retreating troops, convoys, and carts of refugees. Division 10, which finally arrived as reinforcement, fled in disorder when it first met the enemy. Its commander confessed that he was "completely disoriented and no longer had control of his troops." The personal account of Captain A.-S. Ionescu captures the atmosphere of the eastward flight of the 1st Army: "Through many more districts, Olt, Argeş, Ilfov, Teleorman, Dâmboviţa, and Prahova, it followed a very depressing course with forced marches, little rest, insecurity, indecision, contradictory orders and a totally disorganized retreat without even a battle, without resistance."[39] By 4–5 December, the front approximated the line of the Bucharest–Ploieşti–Sinaia railroad. Averescu's forces holding Staabs's XXXIX Corps in the Predeal pass, now outflanked, were forced to pivot to the southeast, surrendering the Prahova line also.

OCCUPATION OF BUCHAREST AND THE OIL FIELDS

The Romanian command had failed to anticipate the magnitude of either the disintegration of the mass of maneuver or the precipitate retreat of the 1st Army. Prezan, to whom control of both had been delegated, had kept it poorly informed. On 4 December, MCG decided to resume direction of the field operations. During initial discussions in the Operations Bureau on what to do next, French colonel Pétin arrogantly demanded "in the interests of the Entente" that a new battle be undertaken near Ploieşti and Bucharest. A Romanian colleague protested: "Our army would be irreparably destroyed." Berthelot wisely agreed that Romanian troops could not sustain a new effort. He suggested a course of action that was adopted by the king in his 5 December briefing. It called for a general retreat 100 kilometers eastward to the line Râmnicu Sărat–Vizirul, where Russian forces were assembling and preparing defensive positions. Fixed stages for the withdrawal were specified, but "if the enemy attacks, then a general battle will be avoided and the retreat continued step by step."[40]

The king's order ensured that Bucharest would not become the target of the heavy artillery, which Mackensen had brought up to pound it into submission. Responding to his ultimatum of 5 December threatening to do just that, municipal officials, flanked by the American and Dutch ministers, met with German parliamentarians outside the city, assuring them that the city was undefended. This was confirmed during the night by German cavalry and bicycle patrols. On the afternoon of 6 December, Mackensen, to whom OHL had assigned the honor of accepting the surrender, arrived in an open automobile. In the suburbs, the inhabitants watched "apathetically." In the center, he was surprised to see the shops open and coffee houses filled. "Instead of cannon and rifle fire, hurrahs and flowers," Mackensen noted. He received the official surrender of the city before a crowd composed primarily of members of the German and Austrian colonies. For the field marshal the experience of 6 December was enormously satisfying. It was his 67th birthday. For some Bucharestians, the entry of the Germans involved a "night of insomnia and moral terror"; it appeared as if "God had turned his face from us."[41]

The transition to the enemy occupation authority was well ordered.[42] The German troops, under threat of court-martial if they plundered or caused unnecessary destruction, satisfied their desire for booty primarily in meeting their need for clothes and shoes. They characterized their reception by Romanians as "polite if not friendly." The Turks were not so well received, and the Bulgarians less so.[43] Mackensen restricted access to the city for their forces, except in token numbers, to prevent pillaging. However, Bulgarian troops stationed along the Danube and *comitadji* found opportunity to indulge their addiction to plundering. They despoiled Giurgiu, Oltenița, and Călărași, burning buildings and making off with huge quantities of livestock, grain, and valuables. A German hussar regiment was detailed "to impede Bulgarians that steal animals and other booty in order to send them across the Danube." The Austrian Danube flotilla was also assigned to hinder shipments over the river. The Bulgarian demand for a larger share of the spoils of war, which threatened German and Austrian requisitions, continued to cause much tension within the occupying coalition—so much so that Colonel Hentsch concluded that it

Mackensen in Bucharest. Biblioteca Academiei

would have been wiser to have left the Bulgarian 1st ID in eastern Dobrogea and used instead a second Turkish division in the river crossing.[44]

Also on 6 December, German troops entered Ploieşti. The Alpine Corps
bivouacked in the suburbs while the Bavarian 12th ID occupied the city
center. "The population received us with flowers," a unit history recounts,
"crying with enthusiasm, Hurrah Germany." "They certainly could not
have been Romanians," a Romanian comments, implying, not implausibly,
that the crowd represented disaffected minorities.[45] Ploieşti, the center of
Romania's oil industry, had special priority for the fuel-starved Central
Powers. Denying them access to its petroleum resources was an equally
high priority for the Allied leaders. When the Romanian government
indicated a reluctance to destroy the facilities of their greatest economic
asset, the British government despatched Lieutenant Colonel John Norton-
Griffiths to see that the job was done. Norton-Griffiths, a British engineer
who had distinguished himself in mining operations on the Western Front,

Destruction of Romanian oil district. From J. Weis, *Mit einer bayerischen Infantrie-Division durch Rumänien* (Munich: Verlag Jos. C. Huber, 1917)

arrived in Bucharest on 18 November. Finding little cooperation from the Romanian authorities, he recruited a team of British officials and engineers, commissioned on the spot, to lead a whirlwind campaign of wrecking oil wells and firing petroleum stocks. Energetic, relentless, and often arrogant, Norton-Griffiths led his team, which also included Romanians, from one oil field to another. He ignored the vacillating Romanian Oil Commission and cowed local authorities with his intimidating personality. If opposed, he pulled his revolver and thundered, "I don't speak your language." Beginning at Târgoviște on 26 November, Norton-Griffiths and his team worked eastward, operating at times behind the lines of the advancing enemy. Oil derricks and machinery were wrecked, wells plugged, and storage tanks drained, their contents burned. "The troops which approached the petroleum district," a member of the Alpine Corps recalls, "noticed that all the streams, above all the Prahova, were covered by a thick multicolored oil slick and that the entire eastern sky was black from smoke and haze" that extended for 100 kilometers.[46] After the battle lines moved east of the oil districts, Norton-Griffiths turned his efforts to the destruction of grain supplies and factory machinery. This raised strong opposition from the Romanians, who were concerned about feeding their people and preserving their limited industrial infrastructure. Norton-Griffiths' scorched-earth policy was less successful with hard-to-burn grain, but he left a trail of destroyed factories and railroad rolling stock all the way to the Siret river. When the Angel of Destruction, as he came to be known, attempted to continue his campaign of demolition into territory not in immediate danger of occupation, Berthelot felt compelled to ask the British military attaché to "moderate the destructive ardor of Norton-Griffiths."[47]

10
Retreat to Moldavia

THE COLLAPSE OF THE ROMANIAN ARMY

After the Battle of Bucharest, Falkenhayn was determined to destroy completely the fighting capability of the Romanian army with a vigorous and relentless pursuit to the east. His goal was to reach the Siret river and the ramparts of Moldavia before winter weather and the arrival of Russian reinforcements made offensive operations impossible. Refusing to be diverted from this objective, he dismissed fears of OHL about a possible flank attack from south of Bucharest, and he warned Schmettow and Kühne not to be "seduced" by the attraction of the capital. While Kosch's forces, seriously weakened in the Battle of Bucharest, were regrouping, Falkenhayn ordered Krafft and Morgen to strike quickly northeast toward Buzău and then on to the Siret. Under their aggressive advance, Romanian forces found it impossible to carry out, as MCG intended, a controlled retreat, "step by step." The "enemy gave no respite, he followed closely with a bayonet in the back."[1]

The progress of the 9th Army was slowed less by the Romanians than by incessant rain, impassable roads, destroyed bridges, and exhausted men and horses. Although some Romanian rearguard units put up "stubborn resistance," as Falkenhayn acknowledged, those who did were "almost annihilated."[2] Other units, including battalions, regiments, brigades, and even divisions, found themselves isolated in the chaos of retreat and were forced to capitulate. On 6 December, 25 kilometers north of Bucharest, the

German 41st ID enveloped a large segment of the Romanian 10th ID (1st Army). Among the 3,000 prisoners were the division staff and the commanding general, Constantin Costescu, taken while they were dining at the castle of Tâncăbeşti. The meal, begun by the Romanians, was continued with the "guests," with whom Costescu discussed the tactical situation in German.[3] On the same day, near Câmpina, the 4th ID (2nd Army) was surrounded and its headquarters captured. Leaderless, subordinate units tried but failed to fight their way out. The next day the entire division, except for a handful of men, capitulated through mediation of a Romanian Orthodox chaplain who, cross in hand, walked into the enemy lines. A Bosnian Orthodox believer in the Austrian 8th Mountain Brigade, recognizing a priest, knelt, kissed his cross, and then arranged a peaceful surrender. Numbering more than 10,000, this was the largest unit to surrender since Turtucaia. MCG reacted in disbelief, demanding of Averescu, "What has become of Division 4 . . . and what sanctions are proposed against the traitors?"[4]

In the period 23 November–7 December, Krafft's forces alone captured 23,000 Romanian soldiers. Between 1 and 8 December, the total for the 9th Army was 60,000. Many of the Romanian divisions that escaped capture in their entirety were now mere "phantoms." Divisions 12, 22, and 23 numbered no more than 1,000 men each. Divisions 8, 10, 11, 13/14, and 1/17 had lost up to one-third of their effectives.[5] Prezan's 1st Army was in the most advanced state of decomposition. "Fugitives and strays fill the roads in all directions," he complained. On 7 December he had only a vague knowledge of the situation of half of his divisions; he had also lost contact completely with the 2nd Army. The latter was in slightly better condition. Averescu, with his usual foresight, had worked out a detailed plan of retreat so that the units on his right wing in the Carpathians were able to maintain a measure of cohesion. Elsewhere, in addition to the surrender of the 4th ID, divisions 12, 16, and 22 fell into disorganized retreat. As Averescu admitted to MCG, they "had lost all capacity to fight. . . . Even the simple appearance of a[n enemy] patrol produces a disordered retreat. The level of discipline has reached an alarming state. Extreme measures of repression no longer have an effect." The crisis facing the Romanian command was compounded by the tendency of General Eris Khan Aliev, commander of the Russian IV Corps holding the line south of Bucharest, to retreat, thereby exposing the left flank of the 1st Army.[6]

A failed attempt on 9–11 December to hold the enemy on the Cricov

Romanians in full retreat toward Moldavia. Sketch by A. Reich. From Albert
Reich, *Durch Siebenbürgen und Rumänien* (Munich: A. Reich, 1917)

river 30 kilometers east of Ploieşti convinced MCG that delaying action was
impossible. It was decided to retreat directly to the Râmnicu-Sărat line and
to ask the Russians to take over most of the front. There was an air of helplessness and a reference to Russian self-interest in the Romanian appeal:
"Our troops are very tired and will not be in condition to hold . . . against
the German troops . . . better equipped . . . and with very high morale. . . .
The situation is critical and it concerns not only our fate but also the fate of
the entire war for Russia."[7] All Romanian divisions on the Wallachian Front
were to be withdrawn from the line, with the exception of five deemed the
best. The Danube Defense Group, the North Army, and the 1st Army were
to be dissolved. Only the 2nd Army would remain, with Averescu retaining command. It would be composed of the Râmnic Group (Divisions 1,
3, and 6 in line, and 7 and 12 in reserve) holding a small segment of the
front north of Râmnicu-Sărat and the Oituz-Vrancea Group, the residual of

the North Army (15th ID, 7th Mixed Brigade), holding the crest of the eastern Carpathians. Of these seven units, only the 12th ID and the 7th Mixed Brigade were near full strength; the others counted one quarter to one half of their normal complement.[8]

REORGANIZATION OF THE RUSSO-ROMANIAN COMMAND

In response to the collapse of the Romanian army, the Russians agreed to take over the front from Râmnicu-Sărat south to the Danube. Their previous indifference and lethargy in the face of repeated and frantic Romanian appeals for assistance had disappeared. With the fall of Bucharest and the rapid advance of strong Austro-German forces eastward, Moldavia now became the southern flank of the Russian Front. STAVKA had no choice but to send massive reinforcements. Many Romanians interpreted the tardiness of Russian aid as deliberate, the result of Alekseev's conviction, first verbalized to Berthelot in October, that the Siret line was "the best line of defense." The Russian buildup began with the reinforcement of Aliev's IV Corps with several units of the Russian Army of Dobrogea stationed on the left (north) bank of the Danube. Joined later by additional Russian forces evacuated from Dobrogea, they were subsequently organized as the Russian 6th Army under Aliev's command. In addition, more than a dozen Russian infantry and cavalry divisions were converging on the defensive line under preparation at Râmnicu-Sărat. These would be organized as the Russian 4th Army under the command of General Aleksandr Ragoza. To the north, three Russian cavalry corps arrived to back up the Romanian 2nd Army. In the Bukovina, the Russian 9th Army under General P. A. Letschitskii assumed responsibility for a large segment of Moldavia's Carpathian frontier. At the end of December more than 30 Russian divisions were committed to Romania in one way or another.[9]

Quite understandably, in return for such massive aid, the Russians insisted on a predominant role in directing operations. STAVKA preferred to have the Romanian army simply incorporated into the Russian command structure. The Romanians, historically fearful of Russian domination, insisted on complete independence for their army and staff. They were aided by the goodwill of Emperor Nicholas, a cousin to Queen Marie. In deference to the amour propre of King Ferdinand, he decreed that all Russian troops on Romanian soil would remain under the king's nominal command. STAVKA had reservations, but after some tense negotiations had to be satisfied with placing Russian general V. V. Sakharov as Ferdinand's chief of staff. Additionally, STAVKA insisted that Berthelot, their bête noire, be banished from operations and restricted to training and reorganizing the Romanian army. In practice, the new "Romanian Front Command" functioned rather well. Sakharov, tactful and restrained in the exercise of his position, limited his immediate authority to the Russian forces. Berthelot, in turn, exercised his influence more discreetly.[10]

The Romanian command itself was also reorganized. On 14 December, Ferdinand called Iliescu aside after the daily briefing at MCG. Citing "the great dissatisfaction which exists in the public and the political parties," he announced that Prezan was replacing him as chief of staff. Iliescu's request that he remain as assistant chief of staff or be given a field command was refused. Instead he was exiled to a liaison post in Paris.[11] Prezan's selection might appear strange in light of his unsuccessful leadership in the Battle of Bucharest. Averescu, the most logical candidate, was unacceptable to those who made the decision: Brătianu, Ferdinand, and Berthelot. Prezan, on the other hand, enjoyed a history with Brătianu dating from their school days in Paris, a relationship with the king, the blessing of Berthelot, "the only soldier here who is truly capable," as well as the active support of Queen Marie. Passed over once again for the post he had long coveted, Averescu took Prezan's appointment as a personal affront and disparaged the latter's suitability for the position. Although Prezan lacked the popularity and stature of Averescu among both soldiers and civilians, he had the character and personality suitable for leading the Romanian army through its rehabilitation and its trial by fire in the crucial battles of 1917. He proved to be a more suitable choice than the vain, contentious, and politically ambitious Averescu.[12]

THE BATTLE OF RÂMNICU-SĂRAT

By mid-December the speed of the Romanian retreat had exceeded the ability of the 9th Army to exploit it. "Gradually," Morgen notes, "the Romanians disappeared completely from the field." Russian cavalry, the advanced units of the reinforcements pledged for Romania, launched an occasional counterattack, but they also were bent on retreat. However, Falkenhayn decided his men were too exhausted, physically and mentally, to continue the pursuit uninterrupted. Discipline was declining and had to be monitored. Commanders were concerned about the impact the German peace initiative (12 December) might have on the offensive spirit of their men. Falkenhayn had already proclaimed one day of rest on 8 December, and on 16 December he halted his forces near Buzău for almost a week of preparation before challenging the enemy at Râmnicu-Sărat. After a month of pursuit across Wallachia, German infantry were in need of rest, clothing, and munitions. Schmettow's horses were weak from lack of fodder and needed to be reshoed. During the pause, railroad battalions labored to reopen a direct line through the Carpathians to Transylvania. Engineering companies worked to improve roads on which caissons and supply wagons were sinking to their axles. Bridges, in whose destruction "the Russians are masters," were repaired using hundreds of prisoners who carried planks and rock to shore up sandy and marshy approaches.[13]

This respite allowed Russo-Romanian forces to consolidate the new line of resistance, which was anchored in the Carpathians and the hills west of Râmnicu-Sărat. Falkenhayn, after viewing aerial photographs, considered it quite strong because of the natural terrain, an opinion with which Berthelot and his French officers agreed. The Germans had a healthy respect for Russian cavalry and infantry, which were now arriving daily, delayed only by the overtaxed Romanian rail net. Sakharov promised to hold the Râmnicu line as long as possible. Berthelot appealed to his pride, reminding him that nearby stood a statue of the famous Russian general Aleksandr Suvorov commemorating his victory over the Turks on 22 September 1789, for which history gave him the appellation *Rymnikii*.[14]

Falkenhayn's plan of attack called for Kosch and Kühne to apply pressure along the Danube, for Morgen to attack Râmnicu-Sărat directly, and for Krafft to outflank it over the mountains to the northwest. For the latter, who now commanded all Austro-German mountain units, progress was slow and difficult. Russian and Romanian soldiers "defended their positions with great bitterness" and sometimes even forced their enemies back in counterattacks. Forced from one peak, they resumed their resistance on the next. German participants had a painful memory of this December *Weihnachtsschlacht*. Some Christmas trees were improvised and carols sung, but "the Christmas season," Martin Breitenacher recalls, "was

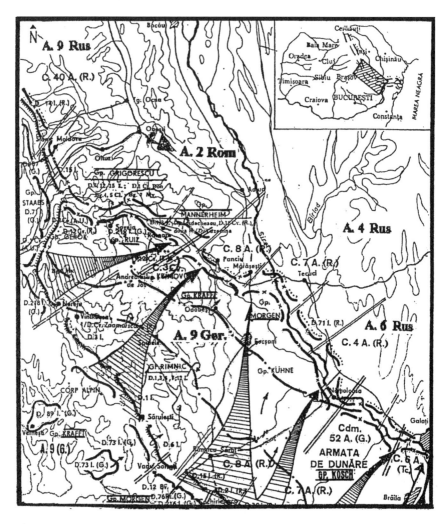

The Battles of Râmnicu-Sărat, Focşani, and Vrancea, December 1916–1917.
Adapted from Victor Atanasiu et al., *România în anii primului război mondial*
(Bucharest: Editura Militară, 1987)

celebrated by the troops of the Alpine Corps in the wretched huts of poor
mountain people, partly on sentinel duty, partly on patrol, partly in battle
with enemy units in the snow." "We spent Christmas eve deep in the
mountains under the most miserable conditions," Erwin Rommel agreed.
For four days, a sequence of attack and counterattack continued as Krafft's

forces worked their way across the mountains to a commanding position north of Râmnicu-Sărat.[15]

Meanwhile, Morgen's I Reserve Corps was assaulting Râmnicu-Sărat directly along the railroad from the southwest. On 26 December, after several days of artillery preparation and infiltration of advanced positions, the Bavarian 12th ID stormed a key height on the outskirts of the city. Control of the hill changed hands twice amid heavy bayonet fighting before the Russian defenders retreated. The next day, amid strong enemy counterattacks, the 76th ID penetrated the city center, and the Russians began withdrawing to the northeast toward Focșani. Morgen counted 6,000 prisoners, mostly Russians. Between 22 and 27 December the total for the 9th Army was 10,000. The evacuation of Râmnicu-Sărat by the Russian 4th Army induced Aliev's 6th Army to the south to retreat back to the Siret. Also simultaneously, Russian forces in the Dobrogea began to withdraw across the Danube. This subsequently led to the surrender of Brăila and its important port facilities. The right (west) bank of the lower Siret was now completely under enemy control.[16]

The Russian abandonment of the Râmnicu-Sărat line, including the Danube delta, was disillusioning to the Romanians and raised doubts that their ally intended to defend even Moldavia. "[We have] hope only in God that he may sustain us," wrote a Romanian officer early in January, "because we who have fought by the side of them are not able to have much hope in the help of the Russians." Berthelot blamed Sakharov's timidity and belittled the Russian army: even if "they compare to the Austrians, they do not hold a candle in regard to the Germans and Bulgarians." His fear, he wrote to his family, was that "a day will come when they will abandon the Siret for the Pruth line and Romania will suffer the same fate as Serbia."[17] In reality, there was no immediate danger of the enemy attempting to cross the Siret. As Falkenhayn explained to OHL, facing only the Romanian army he could have achieved this "with great probability." However, "the situation has changed with the appearance of powerful Russian units." Even if a bridgehead across the river were established, it would have difficulty surviving in winter "without cantonments, communications and combustibles in this country, so poor and systematically devastated by the Russians." OHL agreed but insisted that Focșani be conquered. Falkenhayn had reservations. His troops were physically and morally depleted. His commanders doubted or opposed continuation of field operations. On the other hand, Falkenhayn recognized that the renunciation of the Focşani would be "a bad ending to the most brilliant campaign of the 9th Army." In order to motivate his men to fight on, he instructed his division commanders to spread the word that an offensive to take Focşani would be the last.[18]

THE BATTLE OF FOCŞANI

Focşani, the communications portal between Wallachia and Moldavia, lay astride the historic route of Russian incursions into the Balkans. To defend against such an invasion, which they feared before 1914, the Romanians had fortified the city as the anchor of a defense line from the Carpathians to the Danube. Between 1888 and 1893, Focşani was ringed with 15 armored forts, based on the design of the German Maximilian Schumann, equipped with 150mm cannon. Because Russia was the anticipated enemy, these emplacements faced north, east, and south but not west—from which the present enemy approached. Twenty-five kilometers south of Focşani, less complex fortifications were also installed at Nămoloasa on the Siret. Between 1914 and 1916, when Romania was fashioning an alliance with Russia, the guns from both were removed and converted into mobile artillery for use elsewhere.[19]

Falkenhayn's strategy at Focşani was similar to that he had used at Râmnicu-Sărat. Kühne's LIV Corps would attack the Russian 6th Army south of Focşani in the vicinity of the Nămoloasa bridgehead. Morgen's I Reserve Corps would attack the city and the troops of the Russian 4th Army defending it. Group Krafft had the crucial role: outflank Focşani by capturing the Carpathian heights to the north. There the Romanian "Group Râmnic" supported by a Cossack division held the line. German participants Breitenacher and Rommel give vivid and detailed accounts of this winter mountain combat. Moving up from the battle of Râmnicu-Sărat, their units marched for hour after hour in rain and snow "over high ridges and through steep ravines," where "no house, no human beings are to be seen." The use of pack animals was out of the question, so the men were burdened with heavy machine guns and ammunition. In the extreme cold, their guns often froze and had to be thawed with alcohol. In between battles, the firing mechanisms were kept warm with blankets. Bivouacking at night, the exhausted men simply sank down into the deep snow. On New Year's Eve, when a primitive Romanian village was spotted, the men "began a true competitive race for the best quarters." In addition to struggling with the weather and terrain, the Alpine Corps was opposed by Romanian defenders who "fought with desperate effort and great bitterness on every peak and ridge." Gains were made slowly, often at the point of a bayonet.[20]

The key battle was over control of Mt. Odobeşti, a 1,000-meter peak that overlooked the Putna valley 13 kilometers northwest of Focşani. Its capture would compromise the defense of the city. In the battle, which began on 4 January, infantry from both the Alpine Corps and the Württemberg Mountain Battalion were ordered to occupy the peak. The heights of Mt. Odobeşti were defended by units of the Romanian 3rd ID and 12th ID. The rugged and forested terrain prevented the use of artillery. Frontal assault up the slopes would have been costly. Thus a plan of infiltration and envelopment was developed. A friendly competition to reach the top first developed between units of the Alpine Corps (ascending the south slope) and the WMB (ascending from the west). Erwin Rommel commanded one WMB detachment, Lieutenant Lieb another. True to his later reputation, Rommel led aggressively, even audaciously, always in the forefront of battle. When in doubt about the enemy, he always attacked. On the other hand, Rommel prepared meticulously, reconnoitering the terrain and the enemy carefully before each operation. A network of field telephones, which the Romanians lacked, enabled detachments of the WMB to coordinate their advance. Here as elsewhere, the Romanian defenders, handicapped by heavy losses among its experienced officers, were often caught off guard and unable to organize effective resistance. As an after-battle report of the WMB observed, "The Romanian leadership appears to have been rather purposeless. Regarding the troops, one has the impression that they wander about in difficult mountain and forested terrain without definite tasks and commands and without contact with one another."[21]

On the southern slopes, the Alpine Corps encountered stronger resistance. In contrast to the patterns of flight and surrender Rommel describes, Martin Breitenacher describes slow progress in "bitter, close combat" with the Romanians that involved the use of the bayonet. One Romanian battalion fought "hand to hand" for an hour and a half before being subdued, leaving 170 men dead and wounded and its commander a prisoner. The Alpine unit reached the highest ridge, "where the outlines of the city and fortress Focşani was visible," ten kilometers away. At approximately the same time the Württembergers also arrived at the top, a situation that led to a postwar controversy over the bragging rights for the capture of Mt. Odobeşti. That night the two detachments of the WMB took shelter in the Tarniţa monastery on the mountain's eastern slope. Their comfort was short-lived. The Alpine Corps arrived soon after, and because their commander outranked Rommel and Lieb, the Württembergers had to move to earthen huts nearby, where they "spent a miserable and bitterly cold night."[22]

Early the next morning, 7 January, Rommel received permission to advance down the north slopes of Mt. Odobeşti toward the town of Găgeşti and the Putna river. While leading a lightly armed squad approaching the village, Rommel suddenly came upon "a large number of Romanians. . . . We advanced toward the enemy ordering him to surrender by shouting and waving handkerchiefs. . . . I was secretly worried about the outcome. . . . Finally we came up to them and had them disarm. I told them a cock and bull story about the end of the war." But in another encounter, the Romanians "took aim and a hail of lead whistled past" before fog enabled Rommel to escape. When Rommel's detachment reached Găgeşti, the entire garrison of 360 men surrendered without firing a shot. The mayor then offered Rommel the key to the city, along with a gift of 300 loaves of bread, several slaughtered cattle, and a number of casks of wine. After a comfortable night in warm and dry quarters, Rommel's detachment dug in around the village, expecting a Russo-Romanian counterattack, but none came.[23]

Mt. Odobeşti was the key to the defense of the Putna valley. When it passed into the hands of the enemy, Averescu immediately ordered Russo-Romanian detachments from the Vrancea region to the north to reoccupy it. This was impossible, however, because Austro-German forces were on the offensive all along the front. Consequently, on the evening of 7 January, Russo-Romanian forces began a general retreat across the Putna. German patrols that probed the east bank were repulsed. They reported that the high banks and enemy artillery made an assault crossing impossible, at least immediately. The capture of the commanding heights of Mt. Odobeşti also guaranteed success for 9th Army's advance on Focşani. This had been delayed when the Russians repulsed an attempt by Kühne's LIV Corps on 4 January to conquer Năneşti on the Nămoloasa bridgehead, a foothold the former had retained west of the Siret on a sharp horseshoe in the course of the river. In a counterattack that followed, the Austrian 144th Brigade retreated, allowing the enemy to penetrate the German 41st ID. Heavy artillery was lost, and Falkenhayn considered the situation "very critical"; Morgen was ordered to delay his attack on Focşani. Other German units were quickly repositioned to meet the threat. Concern vanished when an intercepted Russian radiogram revealed that the enemy did not intend to exploit his success at Năneşti. Falkenhayn then gave Morgen the green light for a direct assault on the city on 7 January. There was bitter house-to-house fighting in the suburbs, but outflanked by Krafft's forces on the Putna, the Russians abandoned Focşani on the night of 7–8 January. The next day Morgen's forces pushed forward to the juncture of the Putna and the Siret.[24]

Falkenhayn was satisfied with having reached the Siret–Putna line. OHL, however, still harbored the idea of crossing the Putna valley in order to use its road to link the 9th Army and the Austro-Hungarian 1st Army and to bring Romanian communications in the mid-Siret valley under German artillery fire. Falkenhayn argued that the exhaustion of his men and the onset of winter made further operations impossible, especially since several of his key units were scheduled for transfer to other fronts. Also, the appearance of cholera in the region put German troops at risk. In a compromise, OHL agreed that the Putna not be crossed while Falkenhayn agreed that Kühne's forces would try again to conquer Năneşti. This was accomplished on 19 January, but a portion of the Nămoloasa bridgehead still remained in Russian hands. The 9th Army went over to the defensive until the summer of 1917.[25]

OITUZ-VRANCEA

While the 9th Army was attacking Râmnicu-Sărat and Focşani, the Austro-Hungarian 1st Army carried out a supporting operation to the north in the Oituz-Vrancea region, where its right wing adjoined Group Krafft. Its aim was to penetrate the Trotuş valley and threaten lines of communication between the Russian 9th Army in Bukovina and Russo-Romanian forces on the Siret. The operation, under the command of Württemberg general Friedrich von Gerok, featured only two Austro-Hungarian divisions (71st

ID, 1st CD). Others were deemed too weak for offensive action. The German 187th ID and 218th ID bolstered the attack force. Gerok enjoyed marked superiority in numbers and artillery, but among his opponents were the best units remaining in the Romanian army: the 15th ID, commanded by the energetic Grigorescu, and the well-trained and fresh, though largely untested, 7th Mixed Brigade of Colonel Sturdza. The latter was grouped with the Russian 12th CD under the command of the Finnish–Russian general Karl Gustav Mannerheim.[26] Grigorescu's division was the primary focus of the initial Austro-German attack, which began on 29 December. For several days it put up "bitter resistance" in defense of Mt. Caşin. After suffering more than 800 casualties, the 15th ID was forced to retreat. Sturdza, reinforced by a brigade of dismounted cavalry, was ordered to mount an attack near Soveja to relieve the pressure on Grigorescu. In what Gerok's command described as "strong counterattacks," Sturdza's forces initially succeeded in driving the enemy back. Then, citing a threat of enemy envelopment, Sturdza ordered a retreat that was later criticized as unjustified. The end result was that by the close of December, Mt. Caşin had been lost and Soveja evacuated. All Russo-Romanian forces defending the Oituz-Vrancea region were now in a slow but general retreat. Cossack cavalry, if we can believe contemporary accounts, took advantage of the withdrawal for acts of pillage and violence in Romanian villages through which they passed.[27]

On 2 January, Grigorescu launched an offensive to retake Mt. Caşin. The Austrian 1st CD absorbed "many strong enemy attacks" but held. Several adjoining heights were reoccupied by the Romanians but then relinquished under heavy counterattacks. Sturdza also went over to the attack against the German 218th ID but was "repulsed easily." Then on 5 January, citing a withdrawal of neighboring Russian troops, he ordered a retreat. This in turn forced Grigorescu's 15th ID to pull back. Averescu was furious and asked Sturdza to explain this "precipitate" and "inexcusable" move. He subsequently took steps to have Sturdza banished from his army.[28] On 6 January, German patrols had penetrated to within 15 kilometers of the Trotuş valley. Thoroughly alarmed, Averescu reported the situation as "very serious" and that he was "without ability to stop the enemy advance." MCG responded by outlining procedures for a retreat to the Trotuş river if necessary. On 10 January, before this could be accomplished, Gerok launched a new attempt to reach the Trotuş. In several days of intense combat involving grenades and bayonets, Grigorescu's division, with support by other Russo-Romanian units, held the attackers to minimal gains. Included, however, was the village of Mărăşti, insignificant then but immortalized later in the fighting of 1917. By mid-January the Austrian 1st Army renounced offensive action for the same reasons as the German 9th Army: winter weather, exhaustion of the troops, and the withdrawal of units for service elsewhere.[29]

The Romanian Front remained essentially stable for the next six months as the Austro-German command gave priority to other fronts and as the Romanians were licking their wounds and rebuilding their shattered army. Units of the former North Army and 1st Army, which had been dissolved, were sent to the rear for reorganization. Only Averescu's 2nd Army remained at the front. Of its six divisions, only one, the 8th, was anywhere near full strength of 12,000 "bayonettes." Several of the others numbered between 2,500 to 5,000 men each. Austrian intelligence determined on 9 February that only 23,000 Romanians were in the line on their front.[30] This front of less than 40 kilometers ran from just west of the Caşin Monastery south to Răcoasa. On its right flank (north), it connected with the Russian 9th Army, which had shifted south to take over much of the former front of the North Army. On the Romanian left flank stood the Russian 4th Army, whose front ran along the Putna to its confluence with the Siret. To the south, the Russian 6th Army defended along the Siret to the Danube and on to the Black Sea.

CONSEQUENCES OF THE ROMANIAN DEFEAT

The collapse of the Romanian army elated the military and political leaders of the Central Powers. On the night Mackensen entered Bucharest, an atmosphere of triumph reigned at OHL. Kaiser Wilhelm toasted the field marshal and proposed a battle cruiser be named after him; the *Mackensen* was launched in 1917.[31] The occupation of Wallachia also raised hope among people of Germany and Austria that access to its rich natural resources would provide significant relief for their crises of food and fuel. Despite the efforts of Norton-Griffiths, vast stocks of grain and petroleum products were captured. To this were added the harvests of 1917–1918 and the results of a crash program to restore the pumping of oil. From December 1916 to October 1917 alone, two million tons of grain and an equal amount of additional foodstuffs were exported from Romania, 90 percent of which was divided about equally between Germany and Austria-Hungary. In addition, local requisitions by occupation troops and authorities allowed them to live off the land. During the same period, 272,000 tons of petroleum products reached the Central Powers, with 90 percent going to Germany. Romanian forests provided additional fuel.[32] Also, the spectacular success against Romania provided diplomats in Berlin and Vienna with an occasion deemed suitable for launching their long-planned peace move (12 December). In contrast, it encouraged OHL to believe that the military situation had changed so significantly that the war could be prosecuted without restriction, not only on land but also with submarines.[33] The Romanian campaign was costly for the Central Powers, even if casualties, which for the Germans alone exceeded 60,000, are excluded. It had required the diversion of 33 infantry (17 German) and eight cavalry divisions (three and a half German) at the expense of operations on other fronts. Because Romania continued to fight on, the Central Powers were forced to retain lesser but significant forces to cover indefinitely a new front of almost 300 kilometers. As Ludendorff admitted later, "Despite our victory over Romania we became weaker in the overall conduct of the war."[34]

The Romanian defeat also had a far-reaching impact on the Entente Powers. To stabilize the front, STAVKA was forced to send, eventually, 36 infantry divisions and 11 cavalry divisions. This amounted to 23 percent and 37 percent, respectively, of Russian forces on the entire front from the Baltic to the Black Sea. Henceforth the Russian army was overextended and incapable of offensive action elsewhere. The Romanian fiasco, as the culmination of a series of blunders and disasters, exacerbated the discontent with the government and its conduct of the war on the eve of the Russian Revolution. Disappointment and anger over the Romanian collapse also led to tension and recrimination among other Entente leaders over who was responsible, and even whether Romania should have been brought in at all. It influenced the sacking of Joffre at French GQG and the overturning of the Briand and Asquith cabinets in Paris and London.[35]

For the Romanians, the defeat of 1916 meant hundreds of thousands of casualties and the loss of two-thirds of their national territory. With it came bewilderment and depression. The dream of a *România Mare* (Greater Romania) was thrown into question. Bulgarian and Austro-Hungarian plans for annexations threatened to replace it with the reality of a *România Mică* (Smaller Romania). Even if its allies won the war, the possibility that they would fulfill the promises contained in the Treaty of 1916 appeared questionable. British foreign secretary Arthur Balfour, terming Romanian conduct of their war "incompetent to the verge of a crime," was ready to scrap the secret treaty with Romania altogether.[36]

11
Reconstructing the Romanian Army: January–June 1917

REORGANIZING THE REMNANTS

"Apart from the divisions in the mountains," Berthelot informed Paris on 13 December, "there is nothing more of the Romanian Army." Ten days later, he added: "Impossible yet to determine how many guns, men, etc. we have . . . we must seek out and reclaim them."[1] The losses proved to be shocking: 163,515 dead, gravely wounded, or disappeared, and 146,600 taken prisoner. Of the 505,000 men and officers of the field armies mobilized in August 1916, only 194,945 (39 percent) reported to their units in Moldavia. Some units had virtually disappeared. "Nothing remains other than wagon drivers and 70 to 80 men coming from the hospital," lamented a company commander of the 54th Infantry Regiment. Even in the 2nd Army, which had the best divisions, some units were severely depleted. "We have only 15 percent of the men mobilized left in our regiment," wrote a young officer at the front.[2] On the other hand, the potential for a formidable military force of about 400,000 still existed, as enemy intelligence recognized. In addition to the 90,000 to 100,000 men in Averescu's 2nd Army, there were 90,000 to 150,000 men of the old 1st Army, up to 100,000 recruits of the 1917–1920 classes who had obeyed the call of the authorities to accompany the retreat from Wallachia, and 50,000 convalescents available.[3]

Except for the divisions of Averescu's 2nd Army, soldiers and recruits were directed to north-central Moldavia for reconstruction. Destination zones, itineraries, and points of provisioning for these movements were

elaborated at MCG in mid-December. But many ad hoc changes were necessary, so final plans were not stabilized until late January. Meanwhile,
chaos and suffering ensued. "Many officers and soldiers . . . wandered aim-
lessly through cities, villages, railroad stations, and roads," MCG complained on 3 January. "It is painful and disgusting to see . . . the enormous
quantities of men which stream through Bacău in search of the units to
which they belong," Averescu noted; "a greater disorder is difficult to
imagine." Some men of Moldavian origin simply went home. Except for
the cavalry, the migration was largely on foot. Many of the soldiers, still
wearing the summer uniforms they were mobilized in, walked up to 300
kilometers "in the midst of a winter of severe cold, snow storms and the
wrath of the heavens." It was particularly hard on the unorganized recruits,
"unfed, especially weak, poorly clothed and shod." Some survived only by
begging.[4]

MCG, with the input of Berthelot and his staff, adopted a new structure
for the Romanian army. The number of infantry divisions was reduced from
23 to 15, "the number which it is possible to rearm," Berthelot explained to
Paris. Division strength was set at "19,000 rationaires with 12,000 rifles." The
top ten divisions were to consist of two brigades of infantry, each with two
regiments, plus two squadrons of cavalry for reconnaissance. Each infantry
regiment would have three battalions, and each battalion three companies
of infantry plus one machine gun company. Companies were reduced in
size from 260 in 1916 to less than 200. Fourth companies in existing battalions, with officers and equipment, were later withdrawn and combined to
create an extra battalion in each regiment. These extra battalions would in
turn be formed into a *régiment de march*, a divisional reserve. The top ten
divisions, organized to fight autonomously, were to include field artillery,
engineers, and service personnel. Independent of the infantry divisions in
the order of battle were two cavalry divisions, a mountain battalion, four
regiments of heavy artillery plus one of mountain artillery, and an aviation
corps. The six divisions of Averescu's 2nd Army (1, 3, 6, 7, 8, 12) were organized into the II and IV corps. Their reconstruction was to be carried out
at and near the front. The remaining nine divisions (2, 4, 5, 9, 10, 11, 13, 14,
15), the future 1st Army, were grouped in four army corps (I, III, V, and VI).
They were to be rehabilitated at separate zones in the hinterland. The cavalry divisions, the heavy artillery, and aviation corps were assigned their
own zones for reconstruction.[5]

The Russian High Command proposed that the reconstruction of all those divisions not in the line be carried out in South Russia, between the Bug and Dniester rivers. STAVKA argued, undeniably, that Moldavia was overcrowded with refugees and a million Russian troops, short on food and fuel, and difficult to supply over the inadequate Russo-Romanian rail net. A concurrent benefit from the Russian point of view was that with the French military mission accompanying the evacuation, Berthelot's influence on the Romanian Front would be ended. Prezan and his staff were initially open to the move and began preliminary studies. However, Berthelot energetically opposed the idea, pointing out the impracticability of marching thousands of soldiers hundreds of miles in winter over miserable roads. More importantly, he correctly stressed, forsaking the homeland for a strange and suspect environment would destroy the morale of the army and lead to mass defections. These arguments, together with the realization that evacuation would diminish the French influence in Romania, rallied strong support for Berthelot's position in Paris. The War Ministry, supported by chief of staff Robert Nivelle, argued that evacuation was "contrary to military honor" and would "ruin the military spirit of the nation." Even after reconstruction commenced in Moldavia, the Russians continued to press the issue, causing much apprehension among Romanian officers. However, with the outbreak of the Russian Revolution and the rise of revolutionary disorder, the idea of evacuation was abandoned.[6]

THE ENVIRONMENT OF RECONSTRUCTION

Reconstruction was carried out, as Berthelot put it, under "great physiological misery." Units sent into the interior in most cases found few facilities existing at their destination. Regiments were quartered in small villages for which they sometimes competed with units of the Russian army. Initially, Romanian soldiers were crowded into the primitive houses of the villagers, many with only one room. Regiment 3, comprising 3,629 men and 39 officers, was quartered at Todirelu with 102 houses. This meant an average of 35 soldiers per house. It was only slightly less crowded for Regiment 19 at Bîrnova, with 200 houses for 4,482 men and officers.[7] Overcrowding in an environment where animals and humans lived in intimate contact and where toilet and bathing facilities were primitive or nonexistent endangered the health of the soldiers. Eventually the men were housed in hastily constructed cabins, but sanitary conditions were slow to improve. In a visit to the V Army Corps near Vaslui in late March, Berthelot described its cantonments as "almost wallowing in filth."[8] Many of the men of the 1st Army still had only the clothing with which they had entered the war. "The men are completely undressed," wrote the commander of Regiment 26 on 26 February; "not one man has a coat, all are clothed in summer blouses, having a sheepskin mantel but nothing underneath." Of 2,300 new recruits in this regiment, 1,000 were completely barefoot; the rest wore deteriorating *opinci*. "From 25 percent to 75 percent are practically bootless," a British military attaché reported after an inspection tour. "What they have are tied together with string and pieces of cloth."[9]

No regular mess had been provided for most of the men during evacuation, and it was meager when it was resumed. Meat was seldom available in adequate quantities. According to one regimental commander, even bread was often insufficient because almost 50 percent was pilfered before arrival. As might be expected, complaints about food were prominent in the debriefings of Romanian prisoners and deserters.[10] Priority in requisitioning from the local economy had been conceded to the Russian forces for the first months of 1917. Unfortunately, the Russians continued to monopolize the available foodstuffs because their intendants offered higher prices to Romanian proprietors. Berthelot saw a vivid contrast between Russian troops "strong, rosy and fat as a pig," and Romanian "skeletons." "It is black misery and almost famine," he wrote after his visit to the V Army Corps. He termed the Russian monopoly deliberate "suppression by nourishment," "a crime against humanity." Berthelot was too harsh. Initially the Russians did show little concern for the Romanian army. However, their need to live off the land was related to a weak Russo-Romanian rail net, which gave priority to the transport of troops and war material.[11] Attempts were made to supplement the nourishment of Romanian troops. Averescu formed a commission to promote the cultivation of vegetables, "especially potatoes," in every possible location, including courtyards and rooftops. One ingenious local commander supplemented the food supply of his regiment by bribing the alcohol-starved custodian of a nearby Russian food depot to trade cattle for liquor and wine.[12]

The privations experienced by the 2nd Army during reconstruction were similar to those of the future 1st Army but were complicated by the necessity of fortifying and manning a front line in mountainous terrain blanketed with heavy snow. "Everything is frozen," wrote one young officer, "the men and horses are outside without shelter." When primitive *abris* were constructed, starving artillery horses ate the branches. French colonel Gabriel Landrot reported that men of the 1st ID and 12th ID were in "great suffering" as a result of cold, the condition of their shoes, and the lack of shirts and pants. General Dumitru Stratilescu, commander of the 12th ID, proposed that "shirts and drawers" be requisitioned from the civilian population. Averescu's wife, Clothilda, organized women in Bacău to sew garments. As with food, such limited, local initiatives helped but little. The situation was slow to be corrected. Austrian intelligence reports as late as April described Romanian soldiers as wearing "completely dilapidated clothes and shoes" or makeshift uniforms of Russian origin. But as Landrot affirmed, "the men bear courageously these miseries" and "are producing a good impression of resistance."[13]

EPIDEMICS

The poorly sheltered, poorly clothed, and poorly fed Romanian soldiers, whether in the interior or at the front, were extremely vulnerable to deadly illness. Already during the first month of the war, cholera, the scourge of the Balkans, had appeared in Dobrogea. It broke out among some 7,000 aliens interned on ships on the Danube under squalid conditions. It spread to the Romanian 5th ID among men who had evaded earlier armywide vaccination. Wisely, the government gave plenary powers to deal with the crisis to Dr. Ioan Cantacuzino, an internationally known epidemiologist. He relocated and quarantined the internees and persuaded MCG to isolate the 5th ID, delaying its proposed transfer until an incubation period had passed. Although some 120 cases developed, the army was spared an epidemic.[14]

A new and more deadly epidemic, exanthematic typhus, for which no vaccine existed, appeared during the winter of 1916–1917. It was accompanied by other debilitating illnesses: typhoid, relapsing fever, dysentery, jaundice, and infectious influenza. Statistics from the I Army Corps (2nd ID, 4th ID, 11th ID) under reconstruction south of Iaşi documenting the course of the epidemic are listed in Table 1. The death total, December

Table 1. *Statistics from the I Army Corps (2nd ID, 4th ID, 11th ID) under reconstruction south of Iași, 1917*

Status	December	January	February	March	April	May	Total
Dead	16	629	4,322	5,500	1,928	765	13,160
Ill	483	8,453	16,547	17,387	9,451	5,643	58,324

through May, was 23 percent of the corps' manpower. In the 2nd ID, it reached 33 percent. These percentages matched or exceeded losses in heavy combat. Statistics do not exist for the Romanian army as a whole, but losses have been estimated at more than 100,000.[15] In some units of the 1st Army, the illness fell proportionately more heavily on the officers. Of 32 officers who sat with Major Rosetti at mess on 8 February when he took command of his regiment, only eight remained to dine with him on 3 April, the evening he himself fell ill. Whether men or officers, reports of mounting numbers of victims had a depressing effect on morale. Colonel Ștefan Holban, commander of the 2nd ID, lamented on 14 March, "A multitude of our brothers have died, while the lives of others hang in the balance. I cried when I read the report of deaths and my heart breaks when I see how the flower of Oltenia perishes day by day." A few days later Holban himself fell ill. The epidemic was less severe in the units of the 2nd Army at the front, which were farther from the apex of the contagion in or near Iași. Nevertheless, the Austro-German command was worried enough to implement preventive measures on its side of the line.[16]

The Romanian medical system was ill prepared to counter the new epidemic. Despite the warning sounded by the brief cholera outbreak and knowledge of the disastrous wave of typhus that had swept over Serbia in 1915–1916, few preparations had been made. The head of the army medical service and the director general of public health, who were in jealous conflict, must be faulted for failing to prepare in advance procedures and facilities for dealing with the problem. Disinfecting stations did not exist; nor did plans for quarantining the ill and the suspect. Larger medical facilities, still crowded with wounded from the campaign of 1916, were overwhelmed when the epidemic hit. Local unit hospitals were more crowded. The hospital of Regiment 10 had only 90 beds for 400 patients; some cantonments had no hospitals at all. At first, the ill were housed with the wounded or convalescent. The consequences were disastrous. Some of the ill were transported to hospitals in the cities, spreading the epidemic among the civilian population. The ill or dying dropped on the street or in the railway stations. Hospitals in Iași became such a "terrifying hell" that some doctors were afraid to enter the wards.[17]

At the end of January, Dr. Cautacuzino was appointed to head all medical services, civilian and military, with virtual dictatorial powers. He initiated aggressive measures of prevention, isolating the sick and quarantining the suspect while improving hygiene and nourishment for the well. Separate cabins for the infected were built outside the cantonments. They were guarded to keep the delirious from wandering away. New latrines, sanitized with lime, were constructed and bathing facilities provided, in some cases with mobile "shower trains."[18] Invaluable assistance in fighting the epidemic was provided by medical personnel from England, Italy, Switzerland, the United States, and, above all, France. From the latter came physicians, surgeons, radiologists, pharmacists, dentists, and even veterinarians, as well as a host of nurses and other health workers. Some were French army doctors of the MMF, but most were civilians recruited in France and paid by the Romanian government. Berthelot appointed Dr. Coullaud as head of a French medical mission to exercise a measure of supervision. On 12 January, it numbered 89 physicians and surgeons; 25 percent were of the MMF. In March Berthelot petitioned Paris for 40 more. Although there were exceptions, most of the French medical workers set an example of dedicated service at the risk of their own lives. Many fell ill. Nineteen French doctors and many more auxiliary workers died. Dr. Pierre Clunet, a brilliant young physician who had previously battled typhus at the Dardanelles and Corfu, became, on his death, the most revered of the "martyrs."[19]

Many Romanian doctors matched their French colleagues in selfless dedication. Dr. Traian Rămurescu became their symbol. Wounded in battle, he insisted on leaving his hospital bed to tend victims of the epidemic before eventually succumbing to the disease himself. At least 180 Romanian doctors died and 200 fell seriously ill. More than 1,000 other health workers were also among the dead.[20] On the other hand, there is ample evidence that more than one Romanian doctor, intimidated by the terrifying epidemic, avoided becoming involved. Shirkers were present in the army medical service. A French liaison officer reported at the height of the crisis that of 60 doctors assigned to the 10th ID, only 36 were present, of whom nine had typhus. The others were absent without cause. At the same time, a French officer with the 4th ID reported that of 68 doctors assigned only 25 were on duty, 43 being absent without cause. "It is necessary, first of all, to make these fugitives return to the division," he concluded. Rosetti's regiment had had no visit by a doctor as late as April.[21] Only with the return of warmer weather and the impact of preventive measures did the epidemic decline during the spring of 1917.

MORALE

Reports gathered by Austrian intelligence confirm the testimony already given that defeat, privation, and epidemics severely tested the morale of Romanian soldiers. As military leaders worked to bolster their spirits, many prominent Romanian personalities stepped up to help. Literary figures such as Mihail Sadoveanu, Octavian Goga, Barbu Delavrancea, and Radu Rosetti wrote regularly for *România*, an army newspaper founded by MCG and aimed specifically at strengthening morale. George Enescu, Romania's virtuoso musician, entertained in army hospitals. On 12 January, for example, he played his *Romanian Rhapsody* in various wards of the military hospital at Dorohoi; then in a larger venue, he gave a two-hour concert on both the violin and piano, on which he was equally adept.[22] Queen Marie made good use of her charisma, tirelessly visiting hospitals, bringing encouragement to the ill and consolation to the dying. Her image as the mother of the wounded was widely acclaimed. When Marie asked one soldier in a hospital ward if he needed anything, he replied that seeing her was enough. He then burst into tears and kissed a signed photograph that she had given him. Prisoners reported that Romanian Orthodox chaplains were active in raising morale at the regimental level. At the end of December, the chief of the religious service of the army had instructed his chaplains that their activity should not be limited "to conducting religious services and comforting the ill and grieving. Priests must be above all sustainers and even shapers of the morale of the army." Concerned local commanders and officers were often the key to improving morale. In his regiment, Rosetti used "two measures not foreseen in military manuals: music and cigarettes. . . . I induced musicians in the regiment, and there were

Behind the lines: Romanian Orthodox chaplain, an Alpine Corps ski fest, and a Romanian hora. From *The Times History of the War* (London: The Times, 1917–1919), Roland Kaltenegger, *Das Deutschen Alpenkorps im Ersten Weltkrieg* (Graz-Stuttgart: Leopold Stocker Verlag, 1995), and the collection of Jean-Claude Dubois, respectively enough, to play in the lanes and open spaces, sing love songs and even dance." A French officer with the 6th ID agreed. "It is easy to influence his [the soldier's] morale: a flute, a violin [and] there is a dance organized. Every evening in the reserve battalion there is music and dance."[23]

While members of the MMF had almost unlimited praise for the devotion of Romanian peasant soldiers, describing them as "courageous, long suffering, submissive, and devoted" if properly motivated and led, at the same time they had doubts about the dedication of some officers. They were especially critical of reserve officers who "lounge in their offices and houses," "disinterested in their duties" and their men. Members of the MMF were frustrated also by officers who delayed joining their units or, once there, absented themselves for frequent visits to Iaşi or other places of diversion. This criticism must be kept in perspective. There were also many reserve officers like Second Lieutenant St. Petrovici, who wrote in March to his former professor acknowledging the hardship and discouragements at the front but adding, "with all that, nothing will impede us from doing our duty under any circumstances and at any price."[24]

A serious threat to morale, especially to that of the officers, was the talk of evacuating all or part of the Romanian army into Russia. The apprehension over evacuation was dramatically illustrated by the desertion of one of Romania's most respected officers, Colonel Alexandru Sturdza, commander designate of the 8th ID. On February 6 he crossed the Austro-German lines, and with enemy support, he issued an appeal for Romanian soldiers to follow his example. Although the Russophobia that motivated Sturdza was widespread, his plan was a miserable failure. There had been some numerically significant desertions in January. Two battalions of the 12th ID had lost 120 to 150 men in a four-day period and had to be withdrawn from the front. However, there is no evidence that Sturdza's action motivated an increased number of Romanian soldiers to desert. In fact, the commander of the German 218th ID, which launched Sturdza's appeal, reported only a few scattered desertions afterward, and these were motivated by poor food or harsh officers. This confirmed Austro-German leaders' skepticism of Sturdza's plan and reinforced their personal distaste for his violation of military honor.[25] Although the Sturdza affair did not seriously affect the Romanian army, reports of it did strengthen temporarily the view among Entente leaders that the Romanian army was unreliable. Berthelot felt obligated to warn Paris not "to conclude from the isolated case of the Sturdza defection that

General Berthelot (center) with some officers of the French military mission. From the collection of Jean-Claude Dubois

Germanophile ideas have overrun the Romanian army, that the latter is ready for defection."[26] The Sturdza affair also demonstrated the depth of Romanian suspicion of Russia, soon to be reinforced by the behavior of revolutionary Russian troops. Fear that revolution might spread into the Romanian army stimulated the government to improve the physical condition and future prospects of its peasant soldiers. King Ferdinand's reaffirmation in May of his earlier promise to carry out land reform is a case in point.[27] More crucial in the upswing in morale were warmer spring weather, the improvement of living conditions, and the amelioration of the epidemics. These factors allowed the instruction process to go forward.

INSTRUCTION

Training had been seriously curtailed and in some cases suspended altogether by the conditions described in detail above. During January, February, and March, reports of French officers were in agreement: "deplorable sanitary state . . . instruction cannot take place"; "instruction has been stopped because of illness." Beginning in April, these reports changed: "instruction revives little by little"; "centers of instruction function normally." The instruction process was inspired and directed by members of the MMF, which by 15 February had grown to 400 officers plus several hundred underofficers and technicians. They were active at all levels, regimental and higher, instructing not only raw recruits but also veterans of the 1916 campaign in the use of new weapons and tactics. The most important centers of instruction were at divisional level, where schools or short courses conducted intensive training in the use of machine guns, automatic rifles, grenades, and communications equipment as well as skills such as scouting, patrolling, fortification, and stretcher bearing. Graduates of these courses returned to their regiments to pass on what they had learned. At higher echelons, special schools trained officers and underofficers in intelligence, communications, logistics, fortifications, and tactics.[28]

Cadre schools were of critical importance. Here privates were turned into corporals, corporals into sergeants, and sergeants into warrant officers. High priority was also given to cadet schools to provide a new generation of young officers for the infantry, cavalry, and artillery. Berthelot made a special point to visit these schools and challenge the cadets "on the necessity of a continuous effort and on their duties as officers, especially paying attention to the needs of their men." Great hope was placed in the graduates of these cadet schools whose enrollment in various classes exceeded 4,000 by mid-April. French officers agreed that they were sorely needed to replace incompetent reserve officers and to fill critical shortages of platoon commanders. As in all training enterprises, members of the French military mission "elaborated the regulations or instructions for combat as well as organizing and conducting the instruction," but with the cooperation of Romanian officers. Administrative command of the schools was vested in Romanians but with a French adjunct who exercised effective control over training and technical matters.[29]

By May, according to reports of French officers, products of all the training programs were beginning to fill the needs of field units. Major Legros with the 2nd Army described recruits arriving at the front as having "very good instruction with an attitude of youth and enthusiasm." "The cadet officers arriving here," he continued, "have made an excellent impression." Colonel Letellier (1st Army) agreed. On 29 May, Berthelot proudly reported

to Paris: "The cadres have been filled out by ardent young officers instructed in our schools by our officers."[30] However, the shortage of field-
grade officers was not so easily corrected. "Majors to command two infantry battalions are lacking," Colonel Sancery (5th ID) had written in
March. "MCG responds that it has no officers available." The same problem was reported as late as May by Colonel Letellier (9th ID): "Of 14 battalions in this division, five are commanded by lieutenants. . . . It is urgent
to provide majors to command these battalions."[31] Reconstruction of the
two cavalry divisions lagged behind that of the infantry, in part because
of their lower priority in current tactics and in part because of the shortage
of mounts. Many had been lost through combat or starvation. Those that
remained were in poor condition, the best going to the artillery. Fodder
continued to be scarce. These issues led to the decision to train many of the
cavalrymen to fight on foot as light infantry, but with the increased firepower of machine guns and automatic rifles. In this role they would dis-
tinguish themselves in the summer offensive.[32]

Ignorant of the tremendous obstacles to be overcome, Colonel Victor
Pétin, chief of staff of the MMF, estimated in January that the reconstruction of the nine divisions of the 1st Army sent into the interior would take
at least three months. On 31 March, Berthelot extended the estimated target date to 15 June. He informed Paris on 14 May that only four would be
ready to take the field along with the six divisions of Averescu's 2nd Army.
Yet he was proud of what had been accomplished: "Ten divisions will be
presented in perfect condition and will make, without doubt, an honorable
figure." Of the remaining five divisions under reconstruction, only one
(10th ID) was ready when the Romanian army opened its summer offensive on 24 July. Three more divisions (11th ID, 15th ID, and 2nd ID) came
on line in August, but with incomplete armament. The 4th ID was partially
organized in November.[33]

Averescu, as was his style, exercised tight control in the reconstruction
of the 2nd Army. The fact that he commanded the only operational units of
the Romanian army gave him power and prestige when compared to the
apparent impotence of the leaders in Iaşi. He could ignore, even defy, MCG
when it suited his purpose. The same spirit of independence characterized
his approach to the instruction of his army. It included the same skills being
taught to the units withdrawn into the interior, and the technical training
was led by members of the MMF. Averescu sought to limit the direct in-

fluence of French officers in other areas. He established a center of instruction at his headquarters in Bacău and followed a format compatible with the mission of his army to maintain and defend the front. Every month, one division from each of his two army corps was withdrawn from the front for a month of training and refitting. Each division at the front kept one regiment behind the lines in reserve, with a rotation of regiments every three weeks. Battalions within regiments were rotated every seven days. In order to hasten and simplify the reconstruction of the 2nd Army, it was decided to arm three of its divisions (6, 7, 8) with existing stocks of the familiar Mannlicher 6.5mm rifle. The other three divisions (1, 2, 12), like all of the 1st Army, were armed with the new French 8mm Lebel.[34] According to traditional dating, two divisions (3, 6) completed reconstruction on 28 February, another two (7, 12) on 29 March, and the remaining two (1, 8) on 5 May. Yet there is reason to question how thorough this process was. On 24 March, Austrian intelligence concluded that the "combat value" of several of the divisions in the 2nd Army "cannot be considered reestablished. They consist of regiments which are poorly clothed and deficiently armed, which through necessity were filled out with men from other greatly exhausted units." A month later, a similar estimate reported that the refitted 12th ID, upon reentering the line, had only 70 to 80 men per company instead of the intended 194. Reports of French liaison officers indicated that it would be summer before the 2nd Army was effectively "reconstructed."[35] Fortunately, the enemy did not mount any significant attacks during the six months of reconstruction. Many of their key units, including the Alpine Corps, had been removed for service on other fronts. The cold weather kept those that remained passive.[36]

REARMAMENT

The process of reconstruction involved virtually the complete rearmament of the Romanian army. Lost in the 1916 campaign included 80 percent of its rifles, 50 percent of its artillery, and 85 percent of its machine guns. By the end of March, shipments of French munitions began to arrive by large quantities. The total received or en route at that time was impressive: 199 airplanes, 300 vehicles, 220,000 rifles, 4,500 automatic rifles, 2,700 machine guns, 80 cannon (75mm), 85 cannon (120mm), 1,945,000 artillery shells,

101,500,000 rifle cartridges, 1,370,000 grenades, 600,000 gas masks. This equipment and what followed by the end of May was sufficient to equip ten divisions. Equipment for the other five envisioned would not be authorized by Paris, despite Berthelot's persistent lobbying, until July, too late to prepare all of them for the summer offensive.[37]

Most of the material had to be shipped via the Arctic Ocean to Arkangel, a route increasingly perilous after the German resumption of unrestricted submarine warfare on 1 February 1917. It still had to travel an additional 2,000 kilometers over the deteriorating Russian rail net to the Romanian frontier. Not only was the movement of Romanian supplies agonizingly slow, but it also had to compete with shipments for the Russian Army. On 28 March, Berthelot wrote, frustrated, "The arrival of material destined for the Romanian army has made hardly any progress . . . absolutely blocked on the railroads and in the Romanian depots organized in Russia." A mixed Allied railroad commission, which included a French advisor, was created in Iaşi to ameliorate the crisis. With the supervision of French officers along the route, the movement of materiel began to improve.[38] However, with the coming of the March Revolution and the consequent disorder in Russia, a crisis of a greater magnitude would develop. Despite these difficulties, by the summer of 1917 the Romanian army had received sufficient stocks to arm its ten first-line divisions to a level comparable to that of German divisions and superior to that of Austro-Hungarian, Bulgarian, and Turkish divisions. Regiments, which had two to six machine guns and no automatic rifles in 1916, now possessed, on average, 24 machine guns and 96 automatic rifles. Romanian divisions now averaged 112 machine guns compared to 81 to 108 for their German counterparts. Heavy artillery, virtually nonexistent in 1916, now numbered 49 batteries.[39] This augmented armament permitted implementation of a new tactical emphasis on firepower similar to that in the West. Instead of naked infantry assaults, artillery, machine guns, and automatic rifles would play a decisive role in Romanian attacks.

AUXILIARY ARMS: NAVAL AND AVIATION

At the beginning of 1917, the Romanian navy reached its nadir. Enemy monitors and shore batteries made it impossible for it to operate on the

Danube except for its lower reaches. Internecine conflict among its officers continued. Morale was low. Under French pressure, a partial reorganization of its chaotic leadership took place, and reforms were instituted under the direction of a French naval mission. "We have frankly taken over the direction and the responsibilities," wrote a French officer, "imposing our solutions, turning topsy-turvy men and practices." For the remainder of the war, the mission of the Romanian navy involved protecting the Romanian and Russian banks of the lower Danube, keeping these reaches of the river closed to enemy traffic, and escorting Russian and Romanian ships on the same waters. In these tasks it worked in cooperation with the Russian navy. By June, the French mission reported to Berthelot that the Danube fleet had been reorganized and reequipped, and its morale restored. It was deemed ready for action. However, this action remained defensive and restricted to the tasks mentioned above.[40]

Romanian military aviation, still in an embryonic state, had contributed little to the campaign of 1916. The impetus for its revitalization came from Berthelot. His interest in air power, particularly its cooperation with infantry and artillery, dated from 1911, when he himself went aloft. In December 1916, with the Romanian army in retreat, he petitioned Paris for resources to "immediately constitute a powerful and swift aviation corresponding to that which the enemy already possesses on this front." Instead of the outmoded models heretofore sent, he requested the newest models—something the French war ministry was hesitant to divert from the Western Front. During 1917, a sizable French air mission arrived consisting of 74 officers, 42 underofficers, and 209 lower ranks. Pilots and observers were represented in all three categories. The remainder of the personnel included mechanics (each pilot came with his own), airframe specialists, and photographic reconnaissance technicians. A school for pilots was established at Botoşani. It was directed, as was the air service as a whole, by a French officer with a Romanian adjunct. The instructors were all experienced aviators from the Western Front. Among them was Bert Hall, the American soldier of fortune, who had been one of the original members of the Lafayette Escadrille.[41] Because the output of the aviation schools was insufficient, French pilots and observers took part with Romanians in mixed aircrews and combat squadrons. These were organized into three aviation groups composed of one fighter and one observation squadron. Each group was assigned to a field army: Group One based at

Inscription: "Luncheon of the Franco-Romanian Farman 5 Aviation Group,"
1/14 June 1917. Biblioteca Academiei

Bacău to the 2nd Army; Group Two based at Tecuci to the Russian 4th
Army; and Group Three based at Galați to the Russian 6th Army. Initially
these groups were commanded by French officers and French pilots undertook the "difficult and delicate" missions. But gradually Romanian pilots assumed a more prominent role and a number distinguished themselves. French aviators were sometimes critical, believing, for example, that
their Romanian colleagues lacked "audacity," that reckless derring-do that
was often found in the air war on the Western Front. However, in the aerial operations in 1917, the mixed Franco-Romanian squadrons were able to
hold their own with the enemy.[42]

FRENCH–ROMANIAN RELATIONSHIPS

Differences in national character and the threat to Romanian amour propre
inherent in the mentoring relationship sometimes resulted in tension and

even serious conflict in French–Romanian relationships. French officers, from Berthelot on down, were disgusted when they encountered—too often, they believed—Romanian officers who were incompetent, indolent, morally corrupt, or cruel toward their men. These attitudes, together with an impatient and critical spirit toward the Romanian way of doing things, were not hidden from their hosts. Already in November 1916, the Romanian censor informed Berthelot that letters of his men posted to France contained remarks "absolutely unkind for the Romanian army and offensive for the population." Berthelot felt it necessary to remind his officers that if their mission were to succeed, they must exercise "tact," "good humor," and "modesty." Vis-à-vis Romanian officers, French advisors were "not to criticize [but] to give reasons for advice." Officers were "to march with the troops and not [ride] in vehicles during moves; in cantonments to be present at delivery of rations, to inspect the preparation of meals, to visit the housing of the troops, to meet with soldiers to show interest, to be an example in all circumstances." Berthelot sent a copy of these instructions to Prezan, who repeated them almost verbatim to Romanian officers. It may have had a positive effect. Several Romanian prisoners told Austrian interrogators that they had not been beaten or had been beaten less "since the arrival of the French officers."[43] Needless to say, the MMF elicited strong feelings of respect and affection among the troops. Many, if not most, Romanian officers also welcomed the mentoring of French officers "because they had much greater experience in modern war than we." "I came to know him well," remarked Lieutenant Costescu of Major de Meru, "I have nothing but praise for him." As Romanian and French officers dined and socialized together, many of them came to understand and appreciate each other better. Even Romanians who were not enamored of their French colleagues at least offered them politesse and cooperation in achieving their common goal.[44]

Serious conflicts did arise. Some resulted from ill-defined spheres of authority, especially in areas of command where career and pride were heavily involved. In May, French colonel Steghens, to whom the king had delegated technical command of Romanian heavy artillery, requested that Prezan suspend the promotion of Lieutenant Colonel Jetianu "because of his unwillingness to execute orders given." At the same time, Berthelot asked for the removal of Colonel Paşalega, commander of artillery of the 2nd ID, who proved to be "absolutely hostile" to the French agenda.[45] On the other hand, as Rosetti points out, "there were some French officers, few in number it is true, who lacked tact. They appeared to consider us as some colonials, maybe not as blacks but as Algerians, Moroccans, and Indochinese." Colonel Pétin, Berthelot's chief of staff, was among those Rosetti mentioned. Others agreed that Pétin was "haughty" and "very arrogant," or as Queen Marie put it, "not known to be a very amiable man." Colonel Antonescu, Prezan's chief of operations, with whom Pétin was in daily contact, did not complain publicly during the war. However, much later, after acknowledging the French "taught us to make war," he added bitterly, "They also humiliated us daily by tactlessness and haughtiness."[46]

Averescu's feud with Berthelot has already been mentioned. However, Averescu did enjoy cordial relations with several senior French technical officers. But he was angered by the role of liaison officers "correcting" Romanian colonels and generals and by "mixing in command affairs." This he termed "immoral because they did not share in the responsibility." He took steps to restrict the involvement of French officers in operational matters. Averescu's resentment was increased when Berthelot requested, and the king approved, revised letters of service for French officers attached to Romanian units officially expanding their role from instruction to areas of command authority. With these letters, Berthelot explained to the king, "French officers can march into the fire on the same footing as their Romanian comrades." Averescu angrily condemned it as a "presumptuous" extension of French domination.[47]

Relations between the MMF and their Romanian hosts were not idyllic. Tension and conflict existed along with respect, affection, and camaraderie. Overshadowing all of these was a commitment to rebuilding the Romanian army. This reconstruction was a cooperative effort, best characterized, perhaps, by one of Argetoianu's felicitous aphorisms: "The French showed us the road but we traveled it." This guidance was not only technical. The presence of the MMF, as Duca said of Berthelot, inspired confidence, "that imponderable factor which from time immemorial has decided the fate of battles."[48] The success of the French–Romanian partnership in reconstructing the Romanian army was dramatically demonstrated in the military operations of the summer of 1917.

12

The Russo-Romanian Offensive: Mărăşti, July 1917

THE PRELUDE: DEVELOPING A PLAN OF OPERATIONS

At the Inter-Allied Conference at Chantilly in November 1916, Russia
agreed to launch a general offensive on the Eastern Front in 1917 to complement offensives planned by England and France in the west. The Russian General Staff decided the main effort would take place in Galicia on
their Southwest Front, where it was hoped that General Brusilov could du-
plicate his spectacular success of 1916. The other three fronts, including the
Romanian, were to conduct supporting operations. The original conception of STAVKA, which then viewed the Romanian army as a liability, envisioned for it a limited role, a holding action on the front of Averescu's 2nd
Army.[1] The Romanians planned a more significant contribution, not only
to hasten the liberation of their homeland, but also to protect their position
in the Allied coalition. In late March, Prezan and Averescu each presented
a plan to King Ferdinand for far-reaching Romanian involvement. Prezan
proposed that a new 1st Army, composed of four to six reconstructed divisions, launch an assault west of the Siret at Nămoloasa in conjunction
with the Russian 6th Army. Simultaneously, the 2nd Army would undertake a secondary offensive through the Oituz pass into Transylvania. In
Averescu's mind, this would be "insane." He proposed that instead of two
armies attacking in different directions, his 2nd Army should be reinforced
and undertake the principal offensive, south toward the Putna river,
Focşani, and eventually Buzău. Although his proposal can be defended on

189

strategic grounds, one is tempted to see Averescu's ego behind it as well. These rival conceptions of the offensive served to exacerbate "old rivalries in the bosom of the Romanian command" once again.[2]

By this time, STAVKA was prepared to welcome an enlarged role for the Romanian army. This volte-face was due, of course, to the impact of the March Revolution. The provisional government, in the name of democratization, had abolished the death penalty, reduced the authority of officers, and instituted soldiers' councils to participate in command decisions. Released from the harsh discipline of the imperial army and agitated by revolutionary rhetoric, an increasing number of Russian soldiers demanded peace, refused to follow orders, and pledged not to take the offensive. Officers and commanders were frustrated and intimidated. When General D. G. Shcherbachev replaced Sakharov as Ferdinand's Russian chief of staff at the end of April, he inspected his armies on the Romanian Front. The tour, he recorded, "inspired serious fear for the future." He agreed with many Russian generals that an offensive was "indispensable to quell the anarchy." Prezan, citing the declining morale of the Russian army, insisted to Berthelot that the offensive begin "as soon as possible." The latter agreed. "The sole means of freeing the Russian army from indiscipline," he told Paris on 14 May, "is to send it into the fire."[3] Shcherbachev met with Alekseev and the other Russian Front commanders at STAVKA in mid-May to discuss the crisis in the army and the summer offensive. From there the group traveled on to Petrograd to seek approval for reversing the democratization of the army and for a general offensive on all fronts. Although the former was rejected, the latter was approved. Alekseev's intention was to begin operations on all fronts simultaneously in order to maximize the impact. However, on 15 June he was replaced by Brusilov. The new impetuous chief of staff decided to open with an offensive on the Southwest Front on 1 July, with the other fronts joining in as local circumstances permitted. The need to complete the reorganization of the Romanian army dictated that operations on its front would come last.[4]

Meanwhile, Shcherbachev had returned to Iaşi with STAVKA's approval for a general plan of operations for the Romanian Front. His chief of staff, General Nikolai Golovin, quickly delineated objectives for the two Romanian and three Russian armies. Operational instructions were sent out on 1 June. The Romanian 1st Army was given the principal offensive role, "to attack and rupture at any price" the front of the German 9th Army west

General Dimitri Shcherbachev,
commander, Romanian front.
From *The Times History of the
War* (London: The Times,
1917–1919)

of the Nămoloasa bridgehead. Advancing toward Râmnicu-Sărat, it would
envelop the enemy rear. The Romanian 2nd Army was assigned a secondary offensive, attacking the right wing of the Austrian 1st Army. Advancing into the upper Putna valley, it would threaten the main avenue of communication between the two enemy armies. The Russian 4th Army,
operating between the two Romanian armies, was instructed to rupture the
enemy front near Ireşti; then, turning south toward Focşani, it was to join
the 1st Army in destroying the enemy forces located between the Siret and
the mountains. The Russian 9th Army in the north and the 6th Army in the
south were committed to local offensive action designed to support and
cover the advance of the other three armies. The offensive was projected to
begin sometime between 12 June and 14 July. As it turned out, delays in
completing preparations pushed the attack date forward to 24 July with the
artillery preparation to begin two days earlier.[5]

Averescu reacted negatively to the operations order of 1 June. Not only
did it generally affirm Prezan's concept over his, but it added insult to injury by transferring two divisions from his command to the control of
MCG. After he had voiced his criticisms to Shcherbachev personally, "a sort

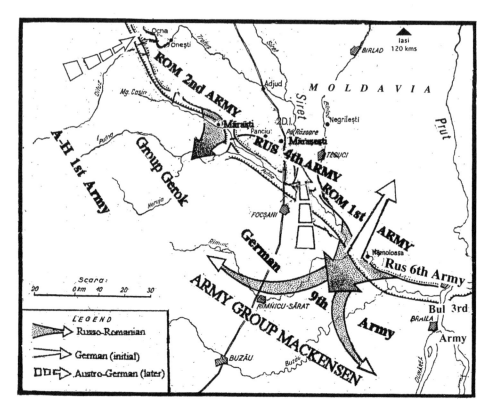

Offensive Plans for 1917. Adapted from Victor Atanasiu, *România în primul război mondial* (Bucharest: Editura Militară, 1979)

of council of war," as Berthelot put it, was held in Iaşi on 12 June to listen to Averescu's objections. After providing a critique of the existing plan, Averescu presented an entirely new one. Instead of a breakthrough at Nă-moloasa, he proposed one in the Vrancea region where the German 9th and Austrian 1st Armies joined. The enemy left wing would be thrown back into Transylvania while the enemy right would be forced south toward Râmnicu-Sărat. Averescu's plan, in essence, was an enveloping maneuver. The unspoken assumption was that he would lead it. The council unani-mously rejected Averescu's proposal. Irrespective of the latter's merits, such a radical change now was impossible. Preparations for the attack at Nămoloasa were too far advanced: the zones of the armies were fixed, en-gineering works begun, much of the artillery moved into place, and the transport of troops under way. The confrontation on 12 June increased Averescu's alienation and left Prezan "embittered" and "disgusted" by the manner in which the former had presented his criticism.[6]

FINAL PREPARATIONS FOR THE OFFENSIVE

During June and early July, Romanian preparations for the offensive accelerated. Furloughs for agricultural work were curtailed, munitions and material stockpiled near the front, and artillery emplaced. On 23 June, the 1st Army passed from "instructional" to "operational" status, and General Christescu officially assumed command, with his headquarters at Tecuci. As Romanian units moved from the interior toward the front, "all the roads of Moldavia between the Prut and the Siret were full of military columns." Many traveled at night to avoid detection by enemy aircraft.[7] On the night of 1–2 July, the 1st Army began assuming responsibility for a portion of the front between the Russian 4th and 6th Armies. The III Army Corps (5th ID, 13th ID, 14th ID) took over a 14-kilometer section centered on the Nă-moloasa bridgehead. The VI Army Corps (9th ID, 1st Cavalry Brigade, Russian 80th ID) assumed control over a 20-kilometer segment to the north on the left bank of the Siret. Nămoloasa was chosen for the point of attack, not only because Russo-Romanian forces held a foothold west of the Siret there, but also because an existing bridge and road would facilitate placing large numbers of troops across the river. To the south the terrain was too marshy, and to the north the eastern bank was high and steep. In the plan of operations developed by Christescu, the III Corps was scheduled to open the offensive on a front of six kilometers. After the enemy front was ruptured, the Cavalry Corps (two divisions) and three divisions of the Russian VII Corps (4th Army) would join in exploiting the advance toward Râmnicu-Sărat. Cooperating units of the Russian 6th Army would push the enemy's right wing southeast toward the Danube.[8] The weaknesses of this plan, and that of the Russo-Romanian offensive as a whole, was first, that it assumed Russian units would fight well, and second, that it took no account of possible enemy reinforcements.

The challenges faced by the 2nd Army differed from those of the 1st Army. Instead of arriving at the front fresh, a number of its units had spent months in the line. "It's absolutely indispensable," a French liaison officer wrote on 28 June of the 3rd ID, "that it go into repose. The officers and men are absolutely exhausted after four months in the forest." A rotation of two-to four-day furloughs was set up in the month before the offensive. An additional challenge was that, in contrast to the open country of the lower Siret, the field of battle for the 2nd Army was the rugged terrain of the sub-Carpathians. It was characterized by forests and high points up to 1,400 meters, separated by many small valleys. During their six-month occupation, the Germans and Austrians had fortified their positions well. Utilizing the high ground, they had constructed 18 centers of resistance with barbed wire, concrete gun emplacements, and shelters against enemy artillery. However, only a primary line had been completed in July. A second line was needed, especially in the south, where the Mărăşti plateau offered a less rugged avenue of attack.[9]

Averescu, given a free hand to develop his own operational plan, divided the front of the 2nd Army into two sectors. The first extended from a juncture with the Russian 9th Army in the shadow of 1,200-meter Măgura Caşin 25 kilometers southeast to Încărcătoara Hill. It was manned by the IV Army Corps (8th ID and half of 6th ID) with the mission to hold in place all enemy forces before it. The second sector, less rugged, continued 12 kilometers southeast to Răcoasa. Here the II Army Corps (1st ID, 3rd ID, half of 6th ID) was scheduled to carry out the principal attack. Cooperating in this opening assault were three divisions of the Russian VIII Army Corps (4th Army), which occupied an additional 13 kilometers of the front from Răcoasa to Ireşti. The initial objective for the II and VIII Corps was to pierce the front and occupy Mt. Momaia and the Mărăşti plateau. If successful, their advance would continue on to occupy the upper Putna valley.[10]

Averescu's preparations were carried out in "his methodical spirit." Perhaps with the experience of the Flămânda Maneuver in mind, he made sure that "almost nothing was left to chance." To facilitate access to the front, a narrow-gauge rail line was constructed and new roads opened. In conferences with his corps and division commanders to explain his plan of operations, Averescu stressed two lessons learned in 1916: the need for close cooperation between artillery and infantry, and that masses of infantry should be sent against enemy lines only after the artillery had breached the defensive positions. For lower officers, he set up minicourses on tactical problems they might encounter. On the eve of the attack, Averescu recorded in his journal a "firm belief in the success of our troops on the front of my army." With it he expressed skepticism about the success in the other sector of the Russo-Romanian offensive: "I do not believe in the destruction of the enemy. I do not believe in reaching Râmnicu-Sărat, above all through the direction of Nămoloasa. To the contrary, I am afraid of a terrible defeat in that sector after an easy initial success." Pessimism about this operation may have also created doubts about the ultimate success of his own attack.[11]

The morale of the Romanian soldiers in the 1st and 2nd Armies as they prepared to attack was strong. The disillusionment and depression of the defeat of 1916 had been overcome, and the naive enthusiasm of 1916 had been replaced by a determined commitment to redeem their homeland. New skills and modern weapons had been acquired. One soldier expressed his delight with the new French helmets and the long bayonets, which he said penetrated "as in butter." But it was new firepower that produced confidence. A French analysis concluded that Romanian divisions in June 1917 had armament "identical to that of infantry divisions on the Western front." In artillery and machine guns they enjoyed equality with their German opponents and superiority over their Austrian ones. In 1916, the infantry had been intimidated by the overwhelming dominance of enemy artillery. Now they could count on strong support from their own guns. A Romanian interrogated by Austrian intelligence reported that his officer had assured him the preattack bombardment would so devastate the enemy that the infantry "could advance with their hands in their pant pockets." The new image of the Romanian army was apparent to Berthelot. After a visit to the front on the eve of the offensive, he pronounced the men "well equipped and well armed, impatient to pass to the attack." In a letter to his sister-in-law, he added: "If the Russians march, one may hope for a nice success."[12]

Berthelot's reservation was well taken. While most Russian soldiers were still ready to defend, for others, an officer in the Russian 9th Army reported, "even the word offensive throws them into a frenzy." Attempts by commanders and representatives of the provisional government to stir up enthusiasm for the attack were largely unsuccessful. Reports by Romanian liaison officers from Russian units on the eve of the offensive were disturbing. Although some Russian regiments voted with a narrow majority to attack, others voted they would not. The most radical attempted to intimidate the willing. Lieutenant Mavrocordat reported on 20 July that the XLVII Corps (6th Army) "sends soldiers almost daily to the 40th ID urging them not . . . to take the offensive. If this division should begin to advance, the soldiers of the XLVII Corps would be obligated to fire on the soldiers of the 40th ID." In both the 4th and 6th Armies, special shock battalions, created to inspire by example, were shouted down and threatened with death. Men in some regiments deserted their positions at the front. Others insisted on access to operational orders before deciding whether to attack. On the eve of the offensive, many Russian officers felt helpless and depressed. "The division commander spoke to me yesterday of the situation with tears in his eyes," reported the Romanian liaison with the Russian division neighboring the Romanian III Army Corps. Enemy intelligence confirmed a widespread aversion to attack.[13]

Apprehension about how the Russian troops on the Romanian Front would respond when the offensive began was reinforced by the arrival of negative reports concerning the Russian offensive on the Southwest Front, where, as Berthelot recorded, "many regiments refuse to march." There Russian forces had enjoyed initial success, breaking through enemy lines at Zloczow (1–3 July) and Stanislau-Kalusz (6–12 July). But heavy losses and the arrival of Austro-German reinforcements from other fronts stalled the Russian advance. On 17 July, enemy forces launched a counteroffensive that broke through the Russian lines. The entire front began to dissolve. News of the Galician disaster triggered a wave of anxiety in Iaşi. "People are depressed, Brătianu the foremost," Berthelot wrote, "I combat this state of mind as much as I can." Even Shcherbachev, a consistent advocate of the offensive, showed signs of wavering. At a council of war on 24 July, Brătianu asked that the offensive be suspended. He was supported by General Coandă, who had just returned from STAVKA with a pessimistic report. But Shcherbachev stood firm with Prezan and the king that the attack go forward.[14]

AUSTRO-GERMAN INTENTIONS

During the spring of 1917, the Central Powers made no specific preparations for major military operations on the Romanian Front. Their priorities had dictated that many important units—the Alpine Corps, the Württemberg Mountain Battalion, Schmettow's Cavalry Corps, and the XXXIX Corps, among others—be transferred to other fronts. Those that remained had suffered through a hard winter. Food and fodder were in short supply. Frostbite incapacitated many who served in the trenches. Illnesses of winter were followed by sicknesses of summer. Training had suffered, and the combat readiness of the troops caused concern. There was another reason to abstain from offensive action. The March Revolution in Petrograd was viewed in Berlin and Vienna as a promising opportunity to eliminate the Eastern Front through a separate peace with Russia. It seemed essential to avoid military operations that might disturb unofficial diplomatic discussions then in progress. Consequently, OHL ordered Mackensen to abstain from "aggressive action on the east front, especially during the Russian holidays." A three-day truce was proclaimed unilaterally by the German and Austrian commands for the Orthodox Easter (14–16 April). Invitations to fraternize were extended to Russian soldiers at many places on the front. Thousands responded enthusiastically, leaving their trenches to trade bread for wine and to drink, sing, and dance with their enemies in the neutral zone. For a few days, the front was like a sieve.[15]

Fearful the revolutionary spirit would infect their own troops, Austro-German leaders soon changed their emphasis from fraternization to pacifism. Detailed guidelines were sent out to intelligence officers for exploiting the war weariness of the Russian soldiers. A Russian-language propaganda newspaper was published at Brăila in many thousands of copies and distributed at the front. Russian-speaking agents operated behind the lines. Intelligence summaries, especially those of the Austrians, who "collected reports with great zeal," described in detail the growth of disorder, disregard of discipline, and pacifism in the ranks of the Russian armies on the Romanian Front. These reports encouraged the Austro-German commands to underestimate the number of soldiers still willing to attack—and especially the much greater number who were still willing to defend. As late as 3 July, Hindenburg concluded that the Russian army could not "attack for a long time in the future."[16] Intelligence information about the Romanian army was similarly misinterpreted. Debriefings of deserters stressed that Romanian troops were "weak," "depressed," "with no desire to attack," or "ready to desert." An Austrian evaluation of 25 June concluded that Romanian morale had "become worse. The earlier war spirit has strongly declined even among the officers." Efforts had been made to distribute pacifist propaganda among Romanian soldiers, including an appeal from the Romanian Orthodox metropolitan, Alexandru Donici, for them to leave the front and return to their homes and families in Wallachia. General Seeckt met with Colonel Sturdza to discuss the latter's efforts in this regard and indicated that he believed propaganda efforts were having an effect on the Romanians. Moreover, Austro-German intelligence estimates on the reconstruction of the Romanian army were inaccurate or, at best, contradictory. An analyst at AOK complained that one report described it as "completely restored" another as "completely disorganized. . . . The truth probably lies somewhere in the middle." This ambivalent attitude continued into early July as AOK still concluded the Romanian army was "hardly battle ready" and without "great intentions to attack." Only local attacks by individual divisions were deemed possible.[17]

However by mid-July, Russo-Romanian preparations for an attack were too obvious to be ignored: construction of additional bridges and jumping-off positions at Nămoloasa; increased traffic in men and matériel on roads; and the appearance of large numbers of Romanian troops near the front. German attempts to gain intelligence became more aggressive. Raiding parties infiltrated to assess the strength of the Romanian forces before them. Deserters specified the Oituz valley, Mărăşti, and the area of Focşani as points where the attack might come. Seeckt noted on 13 July "almost certain signs of an enemy attack against the right flank of the [Austrian] 1st Army." The next day General Friedrich von Gerok, to whose battle group that sector belonged, warned his commanders that an attack was expected and that they must be ready to counterattack. On 15 July, OKM concluded quite accurately that on the front of the German 9th Army, an attack must be expected along a 20-kilometer line from Voineşti north to Nămoloasa.[18]

The German command decided to answer an enemy offensive on the Romanian Front with a counteroffensive, as it had on the Galicia Front. On 24 July, OHL gave Mackensen the mission of repelling the impending enemy offensive and then to "attack the Romanians, especially, and cross the lower Siret." In the best-case scenario, the advance would continue east to the Pruth and then sweep north, collapsing the entire Moldavian Front with the aid of a supporting offensive of the Austro-Hungarian 1st Army. General Johannes von Eben, who had succeeded Falkenhayn as commander of the 9th Army in May, quickly drew up plans for Operation Weisenernte. Like their enemies, the Germans chose Nămoloasa as the point of attack. Once the Siret had been crossed, they planned to establish at least a wide-ranging bridgehead east of the river for the development of future operations.[19] The feasibility of this plan is open to question. Only five divisions of General Morgen's I Reserve Corps were available for the initial attack, barely enough to equal the initial Russo-Romanian attack force. Some German reinforcements were en route, but the Romanians and the Russians also had additional divisions in reserve. Lacking the numerical superiority usually necessary for offensive operations, the German plan appears to have been based on the assumptions that the Russians would offer little resistance and that the Romanians could not hold up under a sustained attack. Both of these assumptions were wrong, as we shall see. Because neither the Russo-Romanian or the German plan for an offensive over the Siret was implemented, the outcome of the anticipated confrontation at Nămoloasa remains a matter of speculation. But the stalemate that developed later at Mărăşeşti would indicate that neither side would have attained their objective.

Conditions similar to those of the 9th Army existed in the Austro-Hungarian 1st Army as it faced the attack of the Romanian 2nd Army and the VIII Corps of the Russian 4th Army. Transfers to other fronts, including 19,000 men to Italy in June, had weakened it considerably. "We had to give somewhat too many for Galicia and beforehand for the Isonzo," Seeckt lamented on 15 July. Additional troops had been released for summer harvest. Given the heavy fighting still continuing in Galicia, OHL was reluctant to grant the request of AOK for the return of divisions sent there earlier. A few miscellaneous units and reserve formations were en route, but the 1st Army was told, in essence, that it would need to rely on its own resources. Ironically, on 21 July the Austrian Front Command, after correctly identifying the right wing of Group Gerok as the point of enemy attack, pronounced it sufficiently strong. A comparison of forces shows how mistaken this was. This sector, under the command of General Eugen Ruiz de Roxas, was defended by the Austrian 8th Mountain Brigade (3,500 Czechs, Poles, Ruthenians, Bosnians, and Albanians); the Austro-Hungarian 1st Cavalry Division (3,200 men, two-thirds dismounted); the German 218th ID (7,400 reserve and *Landwehr* troops); plus another division in reserve. Facing Group Ruiz were four divisions of Averescu's 2nd Army plus the three divisions of the Russian VIII Corps. This gave the attackers a superiority of 2.7 to 1 in infantry and 1.6 to 1 in artillery. This disparity was even greater on the front of the German 218th ID, which was thinly spread over 30 kilometers. At its point of attack on the Mărăşti plateau, the Romanian

3rd ID enjoyed a 4.3-to-1 superiority in infantry as well as a 1.4-to-1 superiority in artillery.[20]

THE BATTLE OF MĂRĂŞTI (24 JULY–1 AUGUST)

Rain and fog on 22 July hindered the direction of artillery fire preparatory to the infantry attack of the Russo-Romanian armies two days later. The weather on the lower Siret was so inclement that Christescu received permission to delay the attack at Nămoloasa by forty-eight hours. To the north, where the weather was less disruptive, Averescu and the Russian 4th Army commander, General Aleksandr Ragoza, decided to go ahead lest a delay exacerbate the unstable morale of the Russian soldiers. Over 200 Romanian guns, supplemented by an equal number of Russians, delivered devastating firepower for two days. German defensive positions, which had been well delineated by aerial photography, were demolished. Enemy counterfire was restricted as the bombardment impeded the resupply of German artillery. During the night of 23–24 July, Mărăşti, the small village that gave its name to the battle, was engulfed in flames. Just before the ground attack began, gas shells were added to the barrage.[21]

THE RUSSO-ROMANIAN BREAKTHROUGH

On the principal attack front, which centered on Mărăşti and vicinity, the Romanian 3rd ID began to advance at 4:00 A.M. From the cover of forested staging areas where they had spent the night, the men moved silently, but not without emotion. Prisoners testified later to Austrian interrogators that they had "great enthusiasm for the attack" and "great determination to reconquer the occupied area." Three regiments on the right (north) attacked enemy strongpoints on Mt. Mărăşti and adjacent hills. Passing quickly through gaps in the barbed wire opened by their artillery, the Romanians were in the enemy trenches by 4:15 A.M. Soon the Germans were in retreat. Warm food on their mess tables indicated the measure of surprise. During the afternoon, the enemy was cleared from the other heights in bloody fighting, which ended in hand-to-hand combat with bayonets. On the left wing of the 3rd ID, three other regiments stormed the village of Mărăşti.

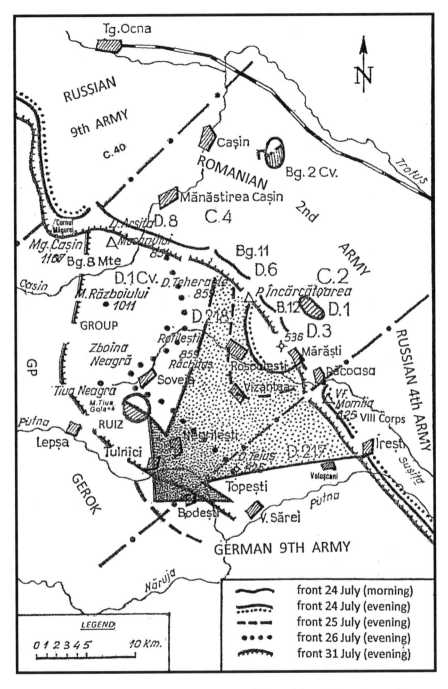

The Battle of Mărăști, 24 July–1 August 1917. Adapted from Victor Atanasiu, *România în primul război mondial* (Bucharest: Editura Militară, 1979)

Reaching the outskirts at 6:30 A.M., the Romanians gained control of the center before noon. In the afternoon, they advanced southwest to Vizantea, where the Germans put up stronger resistance. A direct assault at 4:00 P.M. succeeded, and most of the defenders fell prisoner. By evening, contact had been made with the Russian VIII Corps.[22]

The Russians, "full of revolutionary ardor . . . with great élan," as Shcherbachev put it, duplicated the Romanian success. In the words of an enthusiastic French observer, they "swept away the enemy line between Răcoasa and Ireşti." The 15th ID continued to advance and by evening had occupied Mt. Momaia. The 14th ID and the 3rd Turkestan Division captured Voloşcani. By the end of the first day of the offensive, both the Romanian 3rd ID and the Russian VIII Corps had exceeded their assigned objectives. The German 218th ID had retreated all along the line, often precipitately, abandoning equipment and personal belongings. Its losses on 24 July included 1,500 prisoners and most of its artillery. The success had an exhilarating effect on the morale of the Romanians: "Rarely had they seen German soldiers fleeing in such haste."[23]

Elsewhere on the first day, other divisions of the 2nd Army did not experience the same success. On the center of the front, at Încărcătoarea Hill, the 6th ID attacked in extremely difficult terrain against heavily fortified enemy positions. When the division commander ordered a frontal assault without adequate artillery support, his troops became cannon fodder for the enemy guns. After fierce combat, the first line of trenches was captured but then lost again in a German counterattack. This pattern of attack and counterattack was repeated three times on the afternoon of 24 July, with the Romanians ending essentially where they had begun. At the northern extremity of the front, the Romanian 8th ID, as planned, maintained an active defense confined to artillery fire and infantry patrols. Units of the neighboring Russian 9th Army made a weak attack in the Caşin sector. They were beaten back decisively by the Habsburg 82nd Infantry Regiment, composed of Szeklers defending the frontier of their homeland. As a whole, Russo-Romanian success on the first day of the offensive was truly astonishing. It was also costly. The Romanian II Army Corps reported 2,335 dead, wounded, and missing. A prisoner told Austrian intelligence that on the first day, his regiment had lost 1,200 men, or the equivalent of one of its battalions.[24]

The crisis of the 218th ID, which Gerok reported had "broken in the middle and suffered heavily," continued. On the evening of 24 July, Gerok decided that to save it from "annihilation," a general retreat of the entire Group Ruiz was necessary. He ordered a withdrawal during the night to the Şuşiţa river, which, along with the Putna, formed his priority line of defense. The Austrian 8th MB, whose strong position in the north was not threatened, served as an anchor as Ruiz's forces pivoted to the west. The virtual collapse of the 218th ID sent shock waves through the Austro-German command. Archduke Josef, the front commander, noted that Seeckt, "looking at me through his monocle," remarked "strong is my fear that nothing can be done with this division. . . . It is no longer capable of resistance; the unit has lost its confidence and morale is low." "The events which happened to the 218th ID are inexplicable," AOK wired the archduke, demanding reasons for the defeat. The latter, who well remembered how his front had been stripped of troops for operations elsewhere, concluded that Baden was "out of touch with reality" and simply seeking a "scapegoat." Nevertheless, he appointed a special investigator. His subsequent report blamed not the troops or the commander, but the long 30-kilometer front of the 218th ID, the lack of airplanes for reconnaissance, the Romanian superiority in infantry and artillery, especially the close coordination between the two, and "the use of great quantities of munitions with gas." But Ruiz was sacked and his forces placed under the direct control of Gerok. Ludendorff demanded that AOK, headed since March 1917 by Arz von Straussenburg, take "energetic measures to restore the situation." What few reserves were available within the region were directed toward the Romanian "intrusion," and calls went out to OHL for more assistance. It would be several days before any substantial help could arrive. Meanwhile, Gerok was instructed to limit the enemy advance as much as possible with an elastic defense.[25]

For 25 July, Averescu ordered his commanders to press the attack. The 1st ID, in reserve, entered the front between the 3rd ID and the 6th ID. The German 218th ID continued to retreat faster than the Romanians, struggling to move up their artillery over muddy roads, could follow. When contact with the enemy was lost, the Romanian 2nd Cavalry Brigade and a section of Russian armored cars moved ahead to scout the direction of retreat. With sustained vigor, the Russian VIII Corps advanced along the left flank of the German 9th Army on the Putna. On the center of the front, the 6th ID broke out of the stalemate of the previous day. After two assaults, it forced the left wing of the 218th ID to retreat from Încărcătoarea Hill and neighboring heights. Only in the Caşin region, where the Austrian 8th MB continued to hold its ground against the Romanian 8th ID, did the front remain essentially unchanged.[26]

ABORTING THE OFFENSIVE

The initial success of the offensive generated great enthusiasm in Iaşi. Among the public, some entertained the fantasy that "Averescu had set out for Bucharest . . . and that Mackensen would be enveloped." The rejoicing was short-lived. As Shcherbachev lunched with Prezan at the American Legation on 25 July, he received the famous Kerensky telegram ordering all Russian armies to cease offensive action. Half seriously, Berthelot told Shcherbachev that if he had received such an order, "I would have simply put it in my pocket." "Impossible," the Russian replied. The telegram had arrived en clair, and the soldiers' councils knew its contents before he did. He could do nothing but order his armies to hold their positions. Reluctantly, MCG did the same. The 1st Army, which had not yet begun its attack, was ordered to "remain in position." Averescu was told to hold his army in the positions reached by the evening of 25 July. Both were instructed to group their forces for a possible enemy attack. In a matter of hours, disillusionment had replaced jubilation in Iaşi. "All at once all our hopes of reoccupying Muntenia crumbled," Duca recalled.[27]

Averescu reacted with disbelief and anger to the order suspending the offensive, pointing out that it would leave the enemy in dominating positions all along the front. His response was to order his commanders to advance "uninterruptedly to the Putna," and to do so quickly. Consequently, on 26 July the II Army Corps continued to harass the 218th ID as it fell back toward Soveja with only brief signs of resistance. Some units were surrounded and had to fight through to escape. The disorder of the flight was documented by a trail of overturned carts, dead horses, and abandoned guns, clothes, and documents. The Germans, together with the Austrian 1st CD on their left, continued to pivot toward the west, their left wing still stabilized by the 8th MB in the Caşin heights. The Romanian pursuit slowed as it encountered more rugged terrain and as advanced units waited for the main force to catch up. When impatient commanders launched attacks on high points without artillery support, casualties were high. By the end of action on 26 July, Romanian officers were beginning to think about reaching the Hungarian frontier. "The idea appealed to me," Averescu noted, "to be able to plant a flag on a patch of the soil we wished to conquer, in order to symbolize our national aspirations." The next day Romanian forces occupied Soveja, the support center for the 218th ID. Here many prisoners and much material, including valuable pharmaceutical supplies, fell into Romanian hands. The women and children of this town, "crying for joy," paraded in holiday costumes before their liberators. Old men offered to act as guides in pursuing the Germans. Peasants, who had hibernated in the mountains to save their cattle from German requisition, moved down into the valleys again.[28]

In light of the continuing enemy retreat, MCG gave qualified approval to Averescu's request for sanction to continue his advance: "If [you] believe it possible and necessary, take dispositions on the one hand to advance the right [wing] of the army to Măgura Caşin while on the other [wing] to a general line of resistance to interdict enemy movement through the Putna valley." This permission was intended for limited tactical operations to rectify the front line, not to prejudice the previous order to go on the defensive. Averescu applied it in a manner that prolonged his offensive several days. He laid out a line of advance from the connection with the Russian 9th Army in the north at Măgura Caşin, through the peaks Cornul Măgurei, Zboina Neagra, Tuia Neagra, Tuia Golaşa, and Tulnici, then along the heights on the left bank of the Putna from Negrileşti to Valea Sărei. There it would connect with the Russian VIII Corps.[29] With the exception of Măgura Caşin and Cornul Măgurei on the front of the 8th ID, these goals were reached on 27–28 July. The 6th ID, operating north of Dragosloveni, encountered little resistance from the retreating Austrian 1st CD on 27 July. The next day Gerok ordered the latter to counterattack from the heights of Zboina Neagra with the help of a battalion of the 8th MB. This was repulsed rather easily, and by the evening of 28 July, Zboina Neagra and neighboring heights south to Tuia Neagra were in Romanian hands. The 1st ID, operating south of Dragosloveni, encountered significant resistance from the 218th ID only when it approached its objectives: the peaks south of Tuia Neagra. After artillery softened up the defenders, Romanian infantry stormed the high points late on 27 July in five hours of attack and counterattack. On the next day, both the 6th ID and the 1st ID sent patrols

Austro-Hungarian prisoners taken in Battle of Mărăşti. Museul Militar Naţional

into Hungarian territory along the Lepşa valley. The Austrian command was now thoroughly alarmed; they feared that Gerok could not prevent a Romanian advance into Hungarian territory. The reports of aerial observers describing "strong enemy columns" moving west from Soveja were not encouraging.[30]

AVERESCU CONTINUES TO ATTACK

The 3rd ID, Averescu's left wing, continued to follow the retreating 218th ID back to the Putna. On 27 July, it occupied Baba Maria and Topleşti with the enemy retreating across the river. The southernmost units made contact with the Russian VIII Corps at Valea Sări. They reported that reconnaissance forces provided with artillery had passed to the right bank of the Putna, followed immediately by important elements charged with clearing out the Coza Bârseşti region. Crossing the Putna aroused the ire of MCG, which feared an enemy counterattack and did not want to provoke the German 9th Army. Prezan complained to Averescu that it violated "the latitude allowed the Army" and was "contrary to the interests of the operations order and the wishes of His Majesty the King." "The attacks of MCG have begun again," Averescu wrote in his journal. "It is said that I have gone too far, that I have exceeded orders." He added defiantly, "Not one inch of ground which we have won will be ceded without an imposed order. . . . There, where the local situation will necessitate, we advance to the line imposed by the form of the terrain."[31] Averescu's assertion of operational autonomy called forth "profound indignation" at MCG, where the consolidation of Romania's defensive position was considered imperative. The Austro-German advance in Galicia and Bukovina raised the fear that Moldavia would be enveloped from the north in its entirety. To meet this threat, the Russo-Romanian command was planning a major shift of Russian forces in that direction. The Romanian 1st Army was scheduled to take over much of the front of the Russian 4th Army, whose forces would be sent north. Averescu's 2nd Army would be required to extend its right flank 25 kilometers to the north, relieving Russian forces in the Oituz valley.[32] Moreover, an enemy counteroffensive was in preparation. The Austro-German command was rushing reinforcements to Gerok by truck and train from other sectors of the Eastern Front. Romanian intelligence had noted early arrivals. In addition, OHL and AOK were on the verge of a major shift in strategy. Instead of simply counterattacking on Averescu's line of advance, they would threaten his flanks. The 9th Army would attack from the south on the Putna, and the Austrian 1st Army would attack from the north in the Oituz valley. The Romanians would be forced to evacuate their conquests or be enveloped.[33]

Unaware that Averescu had been ordered to halt, Austro-German leaders feared that Gerok's position would continue to worsen before these new operations could be organized. Their concern was nourished by the offensive action of the Romanian 8th ID to the north, which continued several days after the other divisions had halted. Held up earlier, the division began to move forward on 27 July. The Austrian 8th MB, its flank exposed by the retreat of the 1st CD, withdrew westward from Arşiţa. It took up prepared positions in the range of peaks that straddled the Caşin river: Măgura Caşin and Cornul Măgurei on the north and Mt. Războiul and Mt. Seciul on the south. This terrain was precipitous, forested, and well fortified. Mt. Caşin boasted semipermanent hardened positions and emplaced artillery. These conditions led the 8th ID to plan an enveloping movement

in addition to a frontal assault. The 15th Brigade of Colonel Liciu was ordered to attack the right (southern flank) of the 8th MB while the 16th
Brigade of Colonel Dabija attacked Măgura Caşin head on. Units of the
neighboring Russian XL Corps were under orders to attack from the north.
However, according to the interrogation of Russian prisoners by Austrian
intelligence, representatives of soldiers' councils had already voted against
participating in an attack. Some of the men declared that they would "in
no case attack but would desert." A so-called death battalion that was
scheduled to lead an attack was threatened with death if it advanced. The
Romanians were forewarned of what to expect when the Russians refused
to occupy enemy trenches vacated at Arşiţa.[34]

The offensive of the 8th ID began in force on 29 July. At Mt. Caşin,
Colonel Dabija's brigade was opposed by the Szekler 82nd IR. The latter
unit, fighting to shield its homeland, launched repeated counterattacks that
stymied every attempt of the Romanians to advance. No help came from
the Russians. Their troops, including the death battalion, not only refused
to attack, but also withdrew from some of their positions. South of the
Caşin river, Colonel Liciu's brigade was able to advance. Here the enemy
positions were less fortified, although the terrain presented obstacles. Access to the dominating heights was possible only over narrow mountain
paths impassable for artillery. On 30 July one of Liciu's regiments occupied
the main crest of Mt. Războiul while another continued to the west to occupy Mt. Seciul. However, Măgura Caşin and neighboring peaks remained
firmly in Austrian control.[35] Attempts to occupy these peaks were repeated
on 31 July and again on 1 August. These "senseless" and costly operations
were carried out under Averescu's orders to continue "battles which are
still on course" for the purpose of establishing better defensive positions.
For the commander of the 8th ID this meant, above all, the conquest of
Măgura Caşin. Dabija insists that he warned division commander General
Pătraşcu that an attack would not succeed because of the difficult terrain
and lack of artillery preparations. Nevertheless, his brigade was ordered
to assault the peak with all its power. The well-positioned Szekler defenders, whose commitment matched that of their attackers, used hand
grenades to drive the Romanians back with heavy losses. This battle was
closely followed at AOK, and that evening, Kaiser Karl sent a telegram of
thanks to the 82nd IR. Unwisely, the Romanians repeated the same operation on 1 August with similar results. A personal visit to the battle scene

that day convinced Averescu that Măgura Caşin and nearby Cornul Măgurei could not be conquered without great sacrifices. He ordered the cessation of attacks.[36] The Battle of Mărăşti was over.

CONSEQUENCES OF MĂRĂŞTI

The tangible consequences of the Battle of Mărăşti can be easily summarized. In one week, although handicapped by the cancellation of the complementary operation at Nămoloasa, the Romanian 2nd Army and the Russian VIII Corps recovered some 500 square kilometers of Romanian territory and liberated 30 villages. Three thousand Austro-German troops and at least 60 cannon were captured. The cost of success was high. The most credible source lists the Romanian losses at 1,469 dead, 3,052 wounded, and 367 missing.[37] The intangible consequences of the Battle of Mărăşti were more far-reaching. It was, as Averescu expressed in a personal letter, "the first true victory in the history of the modern Romanian army." It demonstrated that Romanian soldiers, if properly trained and equipped, could fight on a par with their opponents. This success elevated morale and gave confidence to men and officers throughout the army. It was an important precedent for the Battles of Mărăşeşti and Oituz, which would soon follow. For Averescu himself, the Battle of Mărăşti proved to be the apogee of his military career. It augmented his already widespread prestige and popularity, upon which he later built his political career.[38] For the Central Powers, the Battle of Mărăşti had negative consequences beyond the losses suffered. It forced them once again to curtail operations on other fronts in order to send reinforcements to Gerok's shaken forces. More importantly, it led them to launch the inadequately supported and consequently unsuccessful offensives of Mărăşeşti and Oituz.

13

The Austro-German Offensive: Mărăşeşti, August 1917

THE PLANS OF THE CENTRAL POWERS

The success of Russo-Romanian forces in the Battle of Mărăşti prompted the Austrian AOK to appeal to the German OHL on 28 July for the direct intervention of the 9th Army. In a radical change of strategy, Ludendorff ordered Mackensen to postpone his plan to attack east across the Siret and instead advance north up the west side of the river. Here the Russian 4th Army defended a 40-kilometer front running from Bilieşti on the Siret northwest along the Putna river to Ireşti. After breaking through the lightly regarded Russians, Mackensen's force would attack Averescu's left flank. At the same time, to the north, the left wing of Group Gerok would attack Averescu's right flank in the Oituz valley. Once the Romanian 2nd Army had been dealt with, a bridgehead over the Siret would be established in the vicinity of Mărăşeşti–Tecuci. The attack of the 9th Army was set for 6 August, that of Gerok two days later. The first initiated the Battle of Mărăşeşti, the second the Battle of Oituz. Expectations were high. Ludendorff proclaimed to the Reichskanzler's representative that "the conquest of all of Romania was at hand." Negotiations were already under way between OHL and AOK for the division of occupational authority in Moldavia.[1]

Mackensen was favorably inclined to redirecting the offensive of the 9th Army because Averescu's advance also threatened its flank. Among his commanders, however, questions were raised, notably by General Curt von

Morgen, whose I Reserve Corps was designated to open the offensive. The space between the Siret and the Carpathian foothills was restricted and possessed only one good road. It was hardly conducive to the type of open warfare that had proved successful in overrunning Wallachia. In addition, extending the 9th Army to the north would expose it to flanking fire from Romanian artillery across the Siret. Here, in contrast to the area around Nămoloasa, the eastern bank was a formidable obstacle, averaging 40 to 80 meters in height. It provided excellent sites for Romanian guns. The chiefs of staff of Army Group Mackensen, meeting at Râmnicu Sărat on 1 August, noted that the advance of the Romanian 2nd Army had halted, thus weakening the original raison d'être for the change in plans. The meeting characterized "the return to the original idea of OKM of the strike in the area east of the Siret as the most effective attack direction to pursue." Furthermore, a consensus existed at OKM that "no far reaching success" could be expected in the new direction unless Gerok could carry out a powerful supporting operation, about which there was some doubt. On the other hand, a second change in plans would entail unacceptable delay because the 9th Army was already repositioning for the strike to the north. Consequently, the only modification in the final version of the new operational plan was to emphasize a future Siret crossing. The offensive would unfold in two stages: first, an advance north to the line Panciu–Mărăşeşti-Băltăreţu. Then, the attacking force would divide. Four divisions would continue north and northwest against the Romanian 2nd Army and force it to retreat from the mountains. Another five would establish an expansive bridgehead over the Siret in the form of a large arc centered on Tecuci. This presence east of the Siret was intended to protect the flank of the 9th Army as well as to serve as a base for further operations.[2]

Preparations were not fully completed by the 6 August attack date. The German XVIII Corps, which was to join the I Reserve Corps in the attack, was still in the process of organizing. General Karl von Wenninger and his command staff had just arrived at Focşani. Several key elements, including the Alpine Corps, were still en route from other fronts. Nevertheless, Ludendorff insisted the offensive open as scheduled: "There is no need," he telegraphed OKM on 4 August, "to await the arrival of the entire Alpine Corps." The initial assault, therefore, would be restricted to the I Reserve Corps consisting of the German 76th ID, 89th ID, 216th ID, and the Bavarian 12th ID.[3] Opposing them would be the Russian VII Corps (13th ID, 34th

ID, and 71st ID). The VII Corps was already scheduled to be transferred to Bukovina and replaced by divisions of the Romanian 1st Army freed up by the cancellation of its Nămoloasa offensive. However, the Romanian units began to move north only on 5 August and all were still east of the Siret when the German attack began. The evidence indicates the German command failed to anticipate these changes and expected to meet only Russian troops, "lacking discipline, tired of fighting, who would not resist."[4] Conversely, the Russo-Romanian command did not anticipate the German offensive until the very eve of the attack. On 5 August, Romanian aerial observers made an extensive overflight of Focşani and the attack sector, reporting evidence of extensive enemy troop movements. The launching of a German artillery-spotting balloon near the lines of the Russian 34th ID on 5 August delivered a clearer message. "My opinion," the commander of the VII Corps reported to Russian 4th Army headquarters, "is that the German troops prepare an offensive in the sector of the VII Corps." He brought up five battalions from his reserve, but substantial reinforcements would come only with the arrival of Romanian forces after the attack began.[5]

THE INITIAL ATTACK (6–8 AUGUST)

At 4:30 A.M. on 6 August, Morgen opened the Battle of Mărăşeşti with a three-hour artillery barrage that included shells with asphyxiating gas. The following assault by the 76th ID, 12th ID, and part of the 89th ID was concentrated on a ten-kilometer sector of the front between the Siret and the Focşani-Mărăşeşti railroad, which was manned primarily by the Russian 34th ID. Outnumbered and outclassed, the Russians soon evacuated their lines of defense and retreated three kilometers along the railroad and ten kilometers along the Siret. While some Russians, according to German reports, offered "very tough, heavy resistance," others fled in disorder, hiding in wooded areas or escaping over the Siret on a bridge at Ciuşlea. Heavy fire from Romanian artillery on the east bank delayed the pursuing Germans long enough for the Russian commander to fire the bridge. In its retreat, the 34th ID abandoned most of its artillery; gas clouds had killed its draft horses.[6] Morgen reported that over 1,300 Russians were taken prisoner on 6 August. Still there was disappointment at OKM: Siret bridges had

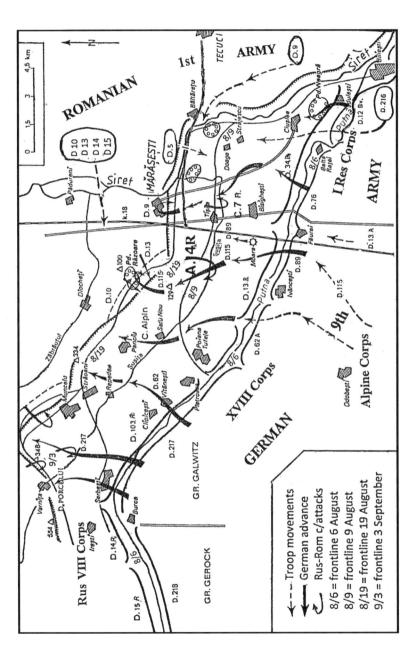

The Battle of Mărăşeşti, 6 August–3 September 1917. Adapted from Ion Cupşa, *Armata română în campaniile, 1916–1917* (Bucharest: Editura Militară, 1967)

not been captured; the front had not been ruptured; and the anticipated line of advance had not been achieved. Romanian firepower from the east bank had proved to be unexpectedly "painful."[7]

Reports of the retreat of the 34th ID provided by Romanian aerial observers created "a state of nervousness and extreme anxiety" among Christescu and his staff at 1st Army headquarters at Tecuci. They hesitated at first to fulfill a frantic Russian request to send the Romanian 5th ID across the river to help because it was not yet fully concentrated. But MCG so ordered, and by the evening of 6 August, one regiment was on the west bank. During the night, another followed. To reach the front, the Romanians had to force their way through crowds of retreating Russians, among whom even the bayonets of Cossack police could not keep order. Despite chaotic conditions of entering battle, the Romanians were able to repulse German attacks that night and stabilize the front temporarily.[8]

On 7 August, Morgen ordered attacks only in the morning and evening to mitigate the suffering of his troops in suffocating August temperatures, which reached 46°C and lasted days on end. "Unbearable heat," wrote a German officer, "and a thirst that could not be satisfied." The acclimatized Romanians shed their tunics and bared their skin to the burning sun. Along the Siret, the 5th ID was subject to violent attacks by both the German 76th ID and the Bavarian 12th ID. The Romanians resisted stubbornly and launched local counterattacks with bayonets. Officers leading the defense fell one by one, including a regimental commander. Lower-ranking officers and a French captain stepped up to rally the troops. At the end of the day, the village of Doaga was in German hands, but the front still had not been ruptured. To the west, along the Focşani–Mărăşeşti railroad, the right flank of the Romanians was endangered as the Russian 34th ID continued to give ground under the attack of the German 89th ID. The German gains were hard won. "The enemy supplies tenacious resistance," the Austrian liaison at OKM reported, "Russians and Romanians made many deeply organized counterattacks."[9]

Early on 7 August, General Aristide Razu, commander of the 5th ID, had called for reinforcements. That evening units of the Romanian 9th ID began to cross the Siret. Operational command over both Romanian divisions and the Russian 34th ID was entrusted to General Eremia Grigorescu, commander of the Romanian VI Corps. Because the impact of the reinforcements was not felt until the next day, the 34th ID and the 5th ID bore the

German command observation post, Battle of Mărăşeşti. Ernst Kabisch, *Der Rumänienkrieg 1916* (Berlin: Vorhut-Verlag Otto Schlegel, 1938)

brunt of the enemy attack on the first two days, as the casualties reveal. Only 3,500 of 15,000 men of the 34th ID now remained in the line. Its commander confessed that his division was "incapable of more fighting and therefore could not be counted on." Casualties for the 5th ID, estimated by a French officer to be "very considerable," were later determined to have exceeded 2,200. The German command admitted that its own losses were "not insignificant," especially in the 76th ID. The failure of the I Reserve Corps to achieve its objectives in two days of heavy fighting led to a modification of the German plan of attack. Morgen was ordered to shift his emphasis away from the Siret toward the north and northwest, aiming at Mărăşeşti and Panciu.[10]

Consequently, on 8 August, the 76th ID and the 89th ID attacked along the Focşani–Mărăşeşti railroad and to the west. The Romanian 5th ID, 9th ID, and the Russian 71st ID, which had arrived to replace the decimated 34th ID, were ordered to hold their positions "at any price." They fought resolutely, aided by Romanian flanking fire from across the Siret, which a

German lieutenant described as "terrible," inflicting "heavy losses." The German attacks continued throughout the day. Although some ground was lost, the front of the 5th ID was stabilized with the help of the first contingent of the 9th ID. The latter took up a position along the railroad with the 5th ID on its left and the 71st ID on its right. The German advance was arrested just short of the line's junction with the Tecuci railroad 3.5 kilometers south of Mărăşeşti. Farther to the west, the Russian 13th ID became involved, staunchly resisting enemy attempts to cross the Putna and advance toward the Şuşiţa river. It was only late in the day that German infantry was able to reach the latter.[11]

OKM was "in no way satisfied" with the results of the first three days of the offensive. More than 3,300 prisoners had been taken and territory averaging six kilometers in depth and 20 kilometers in width had been occupied. These accomplishments "were not able to compensate . . . for very considerable losses" suffered by the I Reserve Corps. More importantly, the expected breakthrough had not been achieved. Despite its shortcomings, the Russian VII Corps had slowed Morgen's initial progress enough to make possible the timely arrival of Romanian forces. Berthelot was not worried by the initial enemy success, because as he wrote his family, "we have in reserve four Romanian divisions." The prospect of the arrival of additional Romanian divisions fueled doubts at OKM about the entire operational plan. General Emile Hell, Mackensen's chief of staff, proposed to OHL that if the attack toward the northwest did not succeed in a few days, one must be content with what had been achieved and regroup to carry out the original plan to cross the Siret at Nămoloasa. Ludendorff peremptorily rejected this and ordered the offensive to the northwest continued with more artillery. "With this artillery fire we will gradually fight through," he insisted.[12]

ATTACK AND COUNTERATTACK (9–11 AUGUST)

Wenninger's XVIII Corps entered the battle on 9 August to press the attack toward the northwest, aiming at Panciu and eventually Muncelu. Because the Alpine Corps was not yet fully assembled, the attack began with the German 115th ID and the Austrian 62nd ID. One regiment of the latter, which included a large number of Czech territorial reserves, had just ar-

rived from the Italian Front "worn out" and "pressingly in need of replacements." After an initial advance, the Austrians ran into a Russian
counterattack that threw them back across the Putna. General Eben confirmed "the disappearance of 2500 men. . . . Probable that they have passed
to the enemy. Otherwise, disappearance is inexplicable. This division has
no combat value." In order to prevent the total collapse of the front of the
62nd ID, advance units of the Alpine Corps were brought up. Until the latter was fully concentrated, the offensive of the XVIII Corps would be delayed. Consequently, for three more days, action remained centered on
Morgen's front, where the cycle of German attacks and Romanian counterattacks continued. West of the Focşani–Mărăşeşti railroad on 9 August,
the German 89th ID forced the Russian 71st ID back over the Şuşiţa and the
main east–west road south of Mărăşeşti. East of the railroad, the 76th ID
and the 216th ID launched repeated assaults on the Romanians. The latter
retreated, but only "step by step," with spirited counterattacks. Only a few
hundred yards of ground changed hands. Casualties were heavy on both
sides. In the Romanian 9th ID, the 34th Regiment counted 586 dead and
wounded, the 36th Regiment 990. Three battalions of the former had to be
reformed as one. The 76th ID and 89th ID, the Austrian liaison at OKM reported, "have been considerably weakened through heavy massed attacks
in which it constantly came to hand-to-hand fighting." OKM shifted the
Bavarian 12th ID from the Siret toward the west to relieve these two divisions.[13]

Morgen continued his attacks on 10 August, forcing the 9th ID and 5th
ID to retreat north of the Tecuci–Mărăşeşti railroad. Shcherbachev's Front
Command in Iaşi responded by ordering a counteroffensive all along the
line. The Russians, attacking west of the Focşani-Mărăşeşti railroad, started
strongly, advancing to occupy their old positions south of the Şuşiţa. They
soon fell back under renewed German pressure. At this point, General
Alexandr Ragoza, commander of the 4th Army, unilaterally canceled the
offensive. General Constantin Scărişoreanu, commander of the Romanian
9th ID, had reported the night before that in view of losses suffered already,
he did not believe that his division also was in condition to attack. Nevertheless, he followed orders from MCG to continue. His 34th Regiment
reached the German lines, but, stalled by barbed wire, it was pummeled by
enemy artillery. Returning to their trenches, the men were ordered to attack again. Small gains were made but, of the 3,020 men of the regiment

General Curt von Morgen,
commander, I Res. Corps. From
The Times History of the War
(London: The Times, 1917–1919)

who entered battle two days before, only four officers and 250 soldiers now remained in the line. Two other regiments incurred serious but lesser losses. The commander of one had the courage to report that "any attempt to advance is useless, slaughtering men in a wasteful manner." General Scărişoreanu agreed and suspended the attack.[14] To the east, the 5th ID suffered a similar fate in an attempt to retake Doaga on 10 August. One regiment advanced to within 200 meters of the perimeter of the village but was then held up by heavy enemy fire. Three assaults were made under a glowing August sun. The Germans answered each with counterattacks of their own. The battle at Doaga ended in a bloody stalemate. French Major Caput, reporting to Berthelot, summed up the fighting of 10 August: "The combat has been very severe, 5000 have been killed and wounded, a true battle." Postwar calculations have established that Romanian casualties alone on 10 August were 4,795, including 1,200 prisoners. Virtually all these losses were suffered by the 5th ID and the 9th ID. The latter's 9th Rifle Regiment was reduced to seven officers and 400 men in the line. For the Romanians, 10 August stands out as one of the bloodiest days of the Battle of Mără-şeşti.[15]

On 11 August, despite the enormous losses of the previous day, Christescu and Ragoza, under pressure from higher command, agreed to resume the offensive. While morning artillery preparation was under way, Ragoza suddenly backed out again. He cited reasons that were believable: "losses suffered, illness of the troops and lack of reserves." The Romanians went ahead anyway, but after negligible gains, they were forced back to their starting positions. Morgen responded to the stillborn enemy offensive with one of his own. He concentrated his pressure on the west side of the Focşani–Mărăşeşti railroad at the juncture of the Romanian 9th ID and the Russian 71st ID. Under attack from the Bavarian 12th ID, the Russians gave way and uncovered the flank of the Romanians. The latter were forced to retreat back toward two key strongpoints, a parquet factory and the railroad station on the outskirts of Mărăşeşti. The 40th Regiment of the 9th ID bore the brunt of the casualties. In the words of Kiriţescu, "Officers and men fell one after another. . . . The enemy captured seven officers and 120 men; the rest remained to crown the field of battle, dead and wounded." Scărişoreanu brought up his last reserves, and the enemy advance was halted.[16] Morgen's forces now stood on the south and southwest perimeter of the city, which was at the mercy of his guns. Yet after almost a week of heavy fighting, the German command had little reason for optimism. Eben reported to Mackensen that the "fighting power" of his forces was "reduced as the result of heavy losses" and that "in order to continue the battle, it is necessary to fill out [the ranks of] the officers and men." But OKM had no new reserves available. In contrast, their enemies, despite horrendous losses—11,724 for the Romanians alone—still had resources on which to draw. As yet, only two Romanian divisions (5th ID, 9th ID) had been involved. Four others (10th ID, 13th ID, 14th ID, 15th ID) were in the process of arriving from the east bank. In addition, the Russian VIII Corps, which had gained German respect in the Battle of Mărăşti, the 124th ID, and the Zamurskaia cavalry division had not yet been involved in the Battle of Mărăşeşti.[17]

PANCIU AND THE RUSSO-ROMANIAN COMMAND
CRISIS (12–14 AUGUST)

Beginning on the evening of 11 August, the intensity of fighting around Mărăşeşti itself lessened for almost a week as only limited offensive action was undertaken by Morgen's "rather exhausted divisions." German prisoners reported that casualties had reduced company strength to 60 to 70 men in the Bavarian 12th ID and to 20 to 30 in some companies of the 89th ID. Grigorescu, whose divisions were equally depleted, rejected pressure from MCG to launch another counteroffensive but ordered all Romanian units "to maintain present positions at any price until new orders."[18] Attention was now focused to the northwest, where Wenninger's XVIII Corps had resumed its advance. On 10 August, the Alpine Corps had crossed the Putna and headed for the Şuşiţa. For many of the men, marching in the shadow of nearby Mt. Odobeşti reminded them of the battles there in 1916 and the cold winter months they had stood guard on the Putna. The Russian 13th ID gave ground before them gradually, confining its resistance to artillery fire and periodic skirmishes. Upon reaching the Şuşiţa, the Russians withdrew to the north side. Although completely dry, the river was a formidable obstacle. It was almost a kilometer wide, and it was under fire from the enemy dug in on its 50-meter-high bank. General Leo Sontag, who now commanded the Alpine Corps, decided to wait for more artillery before attempting an assault crossing.[19]

The delay lasted until 12 August. As the Germans stormed across in waves that afternoon, artillery and machine gun fire turned the rocks of the riverbed into showers of shrapnel. The Russians, stunned by the violence of the attack, withdrew to the nearby village of Satul Nou, where they forced a bloody house-to-house fight. Under heavy pressure, they retreated north into a maze of vineyards. Here the 13th ID organized a counterattack with the assistance of the 15th ID of the Russian VIII Corps, which had just moved up to the front.[20] At 5:00 P.M. a brief but violent thunderstorm interrupted the fighting. Members of the Alpine Corps welcomed the rest and opportunity to collect water in their helmets to slake their burning thirst. After hardly more than an hour, the battle resumed, and the Russians continued their withdrawal. As darkness fell, their retreat accelerated. Dumbrava, Crucea de Jos, and then Panciu were occupied. Before surrendering the last two, the Russians mounted bayonet charges only to be stopped by machine gun fire 100 meters from the German lines. After securing Panciu, the XVIII Corps paused two days before they resumed the advance toward Muncelu and the heights to the north that protected Averescu's 2nd Army.[21] This brief respite was fortunate for the Russo-Romanian leaders because they were then in the midst of a command crisis.

On the night of 11–12 August, MCG informed Christescu that Grigorescu was replacing him as commander of the 1st Army. "For what reason," Berthelot wrote Paris, "I do not know." Elsewhere, he mentioned the "duality of command" between Christescu and Ragoza and their "inability to listen to one another." He also reported dissatisfaction at MCG with the "timidity" of Christescu in sending Romanian divisions across the Siret to counter the German offensive. The first issue, as Berthelot explained, could be traced to a "never well defined" command relationship between the two men. It was exacerbated by Ragoza's insistence on isolating himself at his headquarters in Bârlad, 60 kilometers from Christescu at Tecuci and even farther from the battlefront. He was uncooperative with Christescu's attempts to coordinate operations. He laid the blame for this problem on his colleague in a complaint to the Front Command. Shcherbachev responded by asking Prezan to replace Christescu.[22] MCG had reasons of its own to comply. Already on 9 August, Antonescu, in a tone of a superior addressing a subaltern, had castigated Christescu for "hesitation after hesitation to follow orders" and reestablish the situation after the German attack. He blamed him for the destruction of the 34th ID and the heavy losses of the 5th ID and 9th ID. Christescu's reasoned response was to no avail.

He had lost the confidence of Prezan as well: "Christescu has no faith that we will be able to resist," the latter wrote in a memorandum. Christescu's reassignment to a humiliating post as inspector of recruit centers in Moldavia reinforced a public perception that he had made a serious mistake. But Christescu has his defenders. They justify his caution and suggest he may have been the victim of another manifestation of rivalry within the Romanian command.[23]

Be that as it may, Grigorescu was a superb choice to lead the 1st Army. He was an experienced field commander, which Christescu was not, fa-

General Eremia Grigorescu (center), commander of the Romanian First Army, confers with General Berthelot. From the collection of Jean-Claude Dubois

mous for his "they shall not pass" promise of 1916. By emotive appeals to patriotism and sacrifice, he encouraged a similar spirit of resistance among his troops in August 1917. But the appointment of Grigorescu was accompanied by the ill-advised subordination of the 1st Army to Ragoza's command. It exacerbated rather than solved the command crisis as Ragoza continued his erratic behavior. Early on 13 August, less than 24 hours after assuming command of the battlefront, he ordered a general retreat of Russo-Romanian forces. Alarmed by the enemy occupation of Panciu, he called for sweeping withdrawal northward to the line Ireşti–Diocheti––Pădureni–Siret. For the Romanians, this meant surrendering what they had fought and died to defend, Mărăşeşti and the Băltăreţu bridgehead.[24] Grigorescu delayed implementing Ragoza's order and conferred with Prezan via telex. After prompting from the latter, Grigorescu proposed an alternative to retreat, an attack on the flank and rear of the German XVIII Corps, "freezing their further advance." Later in the afternoon, Shcherbachev, who was present at MCG, spoke with Grigorescu on the telex in the presence of Prezan. His chief concern was that the 1st Army relieve the Russian VII Corps, its three divisions "each having less than 1000 bayonets," and share the front of the VIII Corps. In return for the Romanian troops assuming "the principal effort of future operations," Grigorescu would be appointed to replace Ragoza in command of the entire front. Upon being assured that the 1st Army would be reinforced with "fresh" Romanian divisions, specifically the 10th ID, 13th ID, 14th ID, and 15th ID, Grigorescu agreed to Shcherbachev's conditions. Immediately upon assuming command of the front, Grigorescu revoked Ragoza's order to retreat. The command crisis was over.[25]

FIRST BATTLE OF MUNCELU (14–15 AUGUST)

During the brief lull that coincided with the command crisis, both sides regrouped their forces. Their success at Panciu encouraged the German command to press the attack northeast toward Muncelu. This direct threat to the flank of Averescu's 2nd Army would be a material aid to Gerok's Oituz offensive, which had been stalled by a Romanian counterattack on 13 August. No new reserves were available, but the Austrian 13th ID (half division) and the German 217th ID were shifted to assist the Alpine Corps. Aware of the enemy's intention, and fearful that a wedge would be driven between its two armies, the Romanian command decreed "the enemy advance must be stopped." The introduction of fresh Romanian divisions was speeded up. On the night of 13/14 August the 13th ID took over the front of the Russian VII Corps. The 10th ID marched west to assist the VIII Corps north of Panciu. Forty-eight hours later the 14th ID completed its transfer from the east bank to back up the 5th ID along the Siret. The 15th ID was repositioned to serve as the 1st Army reserve. In addition, MCG ordered Averescu to send a detachment from the 2nd Army to back up the right wing of the VIII Corps near Ireşti.[26]

On 14 August, Wenninger's XVIII Corps resumed its advance on Muncelu by launching an attack on the Russian VIII Corps. The Alpine Corps led the way with the Austro-Hungarian 13th ID on its right and the German 217th ID on its left. Initially, the VIII Corps, well regarded by the Germans because of its success in the Battle of Mărăşti, provided "determined assistance." Its 15th ID even launched several strong counterattacks in some localities, including Văleni, which forced the Germans to go on the defensive. But as Berthelot reported to Paris, "the Russians are unstable. One time they counterattack energetically; at another, the same troops retreat if they are bombarded." True to form, during a German assault supported by a violent artillery barrage, one regiment of the 15th ID soon left its position in disorder, opening a gap in the front. If the latter were not closed, the nearby Romanian 10th ID could have been enveloped. Although his men were tired after six days' marching from east of the Siret, division commander General Henri Cihoski ordered them to intervene immediately. Confronting the Germans by surprise at Hill 334, the 10th Regiment launched a bayonet charge supported by strong Russo-Romanian artillery and aerial bombardment. After a fierce battle, the gap was closed. As the fighting continued on 15 August, Crucea de Sus, Străoanei, and Hill 334 were lost, but the front was not breached. The intensity of this opposition was noted at OHL. "By Străoanei," the Reich Chancellor's representative reported, "the Alpine Corps was repulsed many times by very strong Russo-Romanian attacks." The enemy's success was sufficient to induce panic among support personnel of the Alpine Corps when the rumor spread that Russians had penetrated rear areas. Its source, as determined later, was the unexpected appearance of Russian prisoners, who had been allowed to march into captivity without guard. The combat of 14–15 August produced serious casualties. The 20th Brigade of the Romanian 10th ID counted 693 dead, wounded, and missing. Russian prisoners interrogated by German intelligence estimated their losses at 50 percent in some units. Included among the dead was General L. Pogosky, commander of the 15th ID. At least one battalion of the Alpine Corps "suffered heavily."[27]

On the left wing of the XVIII Corps, the German 217th ID forced the Russian 103rd ID to retreat from Şerbeşti. A Romanian liaison officer with the division reported that a number of Russian soldiers shot themselves in the hand, while others cut links with their command and disbanded. But others fought well. German units reported that before reaching Ireşti, they "met especially strong resistance which could not be broken." Opposition came also from a detachment of the 3rd ID of the 2nd Army, which Averescu had pulled back from the Soveja basin to avoid being enveloped. After two days of intense combat, the advance of the XVIII Corps halted and both sides began to dig in. When the battle for Muncelu began, Mackensen, who had come from Bucharest to observe, had been optimistic about achieving a decisive victory. He was less confident after spending 15 August atop Mt. Odobeşti surveying the course of the fighting. The next day he wrote, "Yesterday we again made almost 4000 prisoners. But thereby the number of enemy will not decrease. The Russians and Romanians always bring up new divisions."[28]

THE CAPTURE OF BĂLTĂREŢU BRIDGEHEAD

While Wenninger's XVIII Corps was attacking to the northwest, Morgen's I Corps made a renewed attempt to occupy the bridgehead on the Siret at Băltăreţu. The Germans hoped thereby to reduce the deadly artillery fire and the threat of a flanking attack from the east bank. The Romanian 5th ID had erected three lines of defense south of the Tecuci–Mărăşeşti railroad. On the afternoon of 14 August, a hurricane of gas and explosive shells fell on the ranks of the defenders. Communications were cut, troops buried in their trenches, barbed wire barriers destroyed, cannon and machine guns smashed. At 7:00 P.M., infantry of the German 216th ID attacked from the south and west. By 8:30 they had crossed the railroad, but strong Romanian rearguard action delayed their advance toward the bridge. The intensity of the enemy assault caused panic in several Romanian units, with some men fleeing across the bridge, others drowning as they attempted to swim the river, still others surrendering prematurely. German losses were light, but the Romanian 5th ID was virtually obliterated: 2,827 dead and wounded, 3,500 taken prisoner. The total of 6,018 dead and wounded over seven days of continuous fighting goes a long way to explain the collapse of this division. The failure of the 216th ID to follow up quickly its initial success provided time for the Romanians to maintain control of the bridge. Impassioned orders went out for men and officers to respond to the crisis with energy and patriotism. Units of the 14th ID replaced the remnants of the 5th ID, which was withdrawn for reconstruction, only its artillery remaining at the front. Romanian engineers blew up the steel rail and road bridge on 15 August. The German advance was stopped at the water. With the western bridgehead in enemy hands, Romanian concern about a river crossing or "diversion" by Morgen's forces remained.[29]

MCG was anxious to answer Morgen's success with a counteroffensive. In a telex conversation on the evening of 15 August, Antonescu asked Grigorescu's chief of staff, Colonel Nicolae Samsonovici, "When could a counteroffensive be opened?" Antonescu unrealistically believed that it could "liquidate in a favorable manner . . . the battle of Mărăşeşti." Then, he argued, divisions could be transferred north to aid the 2nd Army in defeating the enemy in the Oituz valley. When Samsonovici indicated that Grigorescu was inclined to remain on the defensive, Antonescu labeled this "a grave mistake." Later that evening, Prezan continued the discussion with Grigorescu himself. The latter countered the optimism at MCG with pessimistic comments: the 5th ID was now in no condition to fight; the 1st Army had only one division in reserve; the Russian VII Corps with only 3,000 bayonets would require at least a month to reconstitute; the VIII Corps now "no longer had the capacity to fight being composed of only 6000 bayonets . . . men tired and weak who retreat at the first pressure of the enemy." He continued, "I propose that until we reach . . . approximate equilibrium [of forces] . . . to maintain at any price the present front." Prezan attempted to dissuade him. "Although we are exhausted so also is the enemy. . . . If . . . we remain on the defensive nothing is gained. Defense lowers the morale of the troops. . . . Once again I ask you . . . should it not be possible to conduct a counteroffensive with the aim of success?" Grigorescu stood his ground. "In view of the ratio of enemy forces and our forces, I consider that the probability of success is 50 percent. Nevertheless, if you judge otherwise, I will execute the order." Prezan's response demonstrated his confidence in Grigorescu. "My wish is that we reach the Putna. . . . However, unfamiliar with the situation there and unfortunately unable to view it, I leave you the final judge to see if it is possible or not to realize this wish. But what is necessary, absolutely, not to cede more, not at all." Grigorescu's firm assertion of the realities of the battlefield triumphed over the "inexplicable optimism" prevailing at MCG 180 kilometers away. To have acted otherwise could have led to a disaster.[30]

THE TURNING POINT (19 AUGUST)

The failure of the XVIII Corps to occupy Muncelu on its initial attempt led the German command to pause and regroup its forces before resuming the attack. According to the Austrian liaison, OKM was impressed with the "exceptionally strong" Russo-Romanian counterattacks, which "were especially well supported by artillery." He attributed it to the "pronounced superiority" of enemy aircraft, which spotted for their own batteries and also "severely restricted" the employment of German artillery. Before continuing the advance of the XVIII Corps, OKM decided to bring up more heavy artillery and a "new flying unit." This would require several days. In the meantime, Morgen's I Reserve Corps remained the focus of action. Believing an attack by the Romanians along the Siret improbable, OKM decreed that Morgen's primary task now would be to cover the flank of the XVIII Corps by extending his own front to the northwest: "the line Mărăşeşti–Diocheţi must be taken." Simultaneously, Gerok was ordered to attack again at Oituz.[31]

Consequently, on the morning of 19 August, Morgen attacked along a front extending ten kilometers northwest from the southern edge of Mărăşeşti. The assault forces, the German 76th ID, 115th ID, the Bavarian 12th ID, and the Austrian 13th ID were all far from full strength, averaging only 500 men per battalion. Opposing them was the Romanian V Corps composed of the 9th ID, 10th ID, and 13th ID. The last two were fresh and at full strength, but the battle-scarred 9th ID, even though it had undergone some reconstruction, was only at about half strength, some 5,500 men. Defending the town of Mărăşeşti proper, the 9th ID was dug in with two lines of trenches anchored by two large buildings in the suburbs: the parquet factory (south) and the railroad station (west). The two-hour preliminary artillery duel between German and Romanian guns was the heaviest of the Battle of Mărăşeşti. At 9:30 A.M., German infantry was observed advancing through cornfields two meters high. After a fierce battle with grenades and bayonets, the Romanian defenders on the left were forced from the factory and back to their second line of defense on the perimeter of the town. To the west, a retreat by the left wing of the neighboring 13th ID forced the 9th ID to withdraw to its second line of defense, which ran in front of the railroad station. Machine guns mounted in the upper windows of the building inflicted heavy casualties on the attacking Germans. The latter succeeded in occupying some accessory structures, but the station, "defended with a courage born of desperation," remained in Romanian hands, as did the town itself.[32]

The weight of Morgen's attack fell heaviest on the 13th ID, which manned the front from the western outskirts of Mărășești northwest to the Răzoare forest. Its defensive line was incompletely organized but well supported by artillery. Added to 13 Romanian batteries were 12 Russian ones, which had remained after the departure of the VII Corps—a total of 25 batteries for five kilometers of front. Aware of this power, the German infantry was spread out as it attacked: lead patrols at 150-meter intervals, groups of 20 to 50 infantrymen at intervals of 50 meters, then a line of sharpshooters at intervals of five or six meters. "It was necessary for us to pass through a terrible barrage of fire," recorded a soldier in the attacking Bavarian 12th ID. "Not even at Verdun have I seen such terrible artillery fire." The initial German assault overran the first line of Romanian defenders forcing the left wing (Regiment 50) adjoining Mărășești to retreat to the north, endangering the position of the 9th ID at the railroad station. At the center of the 13th ID, the attackers advanced eastward toward Hill 100. Its capture would open the way for the envelopment of Mărășești and much of the 1st Army. The Romanians resisted unto death to hold Hill 100. One battalion of Regiment 51 lost all of its officers, including Captain Grigore Ignat, who, when his gunners fell, manned a machine gun himself. The discovery, after the battle, of his body still clutching the weapon made him one of the most celebrated Romanian heroes of the war.[33]

On the right flank of the 13th ID, the 47th Regiment defended the Răzoare forest, a relatively small wooded area, where it maintained a connection with the neighboring 10th ID. Here portions of three enemy divisions focused their attack. At 9:00 A.M. on 19 August, after an intense bombardment on the Romanian positions, "wave after wave" of enemy infantry attacked. The Romanian right, anchored to the 10th ID and supported by its artillery, held. But on the left, the Germans advanced, hidden by a high cornfield. Colonel Radu Rosetti, commander of the 47th Regiment, ordered his 1st Battalion to counterattack. It responded energetically but was assailed by the enemy from three directions and virtually destroyed. By evening, only one lieutenant and 71 men of the battalion remained. Rosetti himself was gravely wounded. With strong support from the artillery of the 10th ID, the other battalions of the 47th Regiment were

Romanian prisoners
carrying a wounded
comrade. Ernst Kabisch,
Der Rumänienkrieg, 1916
(Berlin: Verhut-Verlag
Otto Schlegel, 1938)

able to prevent an enemy breakthrough. However, by noon, virtually all
the primary positions of the 13th ID had been overrun and the rear areas,
where artillery was sited, threatened.[34]

During the afternoon of 19 August, the situation changed. General
Popescu, the commander of the 13th ID, ordered reserves brought up for
a counterattack on both sides of the German penetration. At the same time,
General Henri Cihoski, the commander of the neighboring 10th ID, took
the initiative and launched a counterattack in support. It broke through the
lines of the Bavarian 12th ID and threatened the position of the neighboring 115th ID. The Germans began to retreat. One regiment of the Romanian 13th ID was able to reoccupy its old positions. Regiment 47 advanced
one kilometer beyond its starting line. The third regiment stabilized its position. The aggressive Cihoski ordered his forces to continue as far as the
Şuşiţa valley; in this region of vineyards and tall cornfields, he warned
them to guard against ambushes. Their enemies, especially the Austrian
13th ID, retreated in great disorder, abandoning weapons en route. Russian
artillerists cheered on their brothers in arms with shouts of "bravo Rumyn-

skii." The advance of the Romanians continued throughout the day, with lead units reaching Dumbrava and Satul Nou. There were false reports that the Germans had even evacuated Panciu. News of the victory sent a wave of enthusiasm throughout the 1st Army, obvious enough to be noted by German intelligence.[35] The fighting on 19 August turned out to be the turning point in the Battle of Mărășești.

WHAT NEXT?

Grigorescu was now concerned that the Romanian advance might get out of control. Late in the afternoon of 19 August, he warned the V Corps "not to venture too far in advance." That night he was more explicit: "Troops will stop their advance and establish control over positions they occupied today before the enemy attack." Grigorescu's caution was motivated by heavy losses and fears of enemy counter operations elsewhere. On 19 August the 13th ID counted 3,264 men and officers dead, wounded, and missing; some of its regiments were reduced to an average of 1,000 men each. The 9th ID, already at half strength, lost 1,361 more. A prisoner reported his company had been reduced from 90 to 100 men to only 16. The 10th ID lost 773, which brought the one-day total for the V Corps to 5,398. Grigorescu was also concerned about reports of new enemy columns advancing on the Focșani–Mărășești road toward the battle front. Additionally, he thought possible a German attempt to force the Siret. He ordered aerial observation to monitor enemy troop movements, and he repositioned Romanian forces on the east bank. Grigorescu's preoccupation with defense raised questions within the Romanian command. Colonel Samsonovici, his chief of staff, was convinced that the enemy had suffered a serious defeat. He proposed to exploit it by utilizing the fresh Romanian 15th ID and the Russian 124th ID, both in reserve, as well as some battalions of the still-organizing 11th ID, to continue the offensive. He also envisioned requesting a diversionary attack by the Russian 6th Army at Nămoloasa. MCG was thinking along the same lines. As Antonescu expressed it in a telex conversation with Samsonovici on 21 August, "We have the impression that an occasion was lost to profit from the success obtained . . . that it was possible to advance the entire front up to the Șușița." With unusual modesty, Antonescu admitted he "could ascertain the facts only approximately from my distance and therefore be in error." Anyway, he insisted, MCG was determined not to "give the enemy time to reorganize and the possibility of concentrating forces in view of a new blow." Meanwhile, the 1st Army should maintain a "strategic defense." As soon as new forces were regrouped, "which I believe will be very soon," he continued, "we will retake the offensive."[36]

The embarrassing and costly failure of the offensive of Morgen's I Reserve Corps on 19 August had a crucial impact on the thinking of the German command. General Eben ordered Morgen to cease his offensive immediately because "facing the weakened German divisions, the Romanians possess a great numerical superiority." A rest and regrouping of his troops, Eben reported to Mackensen, "appears absolutely necessary. . . . The effectives of the infantry have diminished. A continuation of the offensive no longer appears advisable." For Mackensen, however, it was a matter of pride. He wanted the I Reserve Corps to occupy Mărăşeşti and the XVIII Corps to occupy the line Muncelu–Moviliţa "in order not to give Romanian authorities the idea that their local successes . . . had influenced German operations." Hell, his chief of staff, proposed to Ludendorff on 21 August that all the power that could be freed up elsewhere on the Eastern Front be turned against the two Romanian armies. If this blow succeeded, he argued, it would undoubtedly force the Romanians to seek peace. Ludendorff replied that this goal was desirable, but because of heavy fighting on the Western Front and the unfavorable situation regarding reserves, it was impossible to send additional troops to Romania. The conquest of Mărăşeşti was to be renounced, he ordered, and only Muncelu and the heights to the north should be won. Gerok would cooperate by renewing his attack. Should the Romanians evacuate the mountains, then OHL would reconsider if the offensive should be pursued. At OHL there was little confidence that this would happen. Intelligence estimates predicted "additional stubborn resistance must be expected" from the Romanian army, which "has fought well in attack as well as in defense."[37]

Ludendorff eliminated the option of extending the offensive when he informed Mackensen on 24 August that the Alpine Corps and the Austrian 13th ID would be transferred to Italy at the beginning of September. Similar transfers were ordered from Gerok's forces, and his offensive was cancelled. These decisions by the OHL reduced the upcoming Muncelu operation to one of local significance only: the creation of a defensible front for the 9th Army. The decisions handed down from OHL caused much frustration among Austro-German commanders on the Romanian Front, beginning with Mackensen. He realized now that he would not be able to add the conquest of Moldavia to his many laurels. He left the front and returned to Bucharest on 23 August. A few days later, he recorded his disappointment: "Under tactically favorable conditions, a very promising operation could have been made which would have had significant political consequences. It is very regrettable that they make me dependent on events on other battlefields."[38]

THE SECOND BATTLE OF MUNCELU

On 28 August, before the departure of the two divisions for Italy, the 9th Army launched its final offensive. German artillery opened its most intensive bombardment of the campaign with the aim of tying down Romanian forces all along the front while the XVIII Corps assaulted Muncelu. At 7:00 A.M., the Alpine Corps attacked on a sector of only 1.5 kilometers at the juncture of the Russian 14th ID and 124th ID. The first wave was "torn apart" by the hand grenades and machine guns of the Russian defenders. Continued German assaults forced the Russians to retreat, but according to testimony of members of the Alpine Corps, Muncelu was defended fiercely: "House by house, courtyard by courtyard had to be stormed in tough combat." By midmorning, the town was occupied and the Russians were retreating to the north. Two regiments of the 124th ID subsequently left their positions and fled in panic. The retreat continued throughout the day, allowing the Germans to create a bulge in the front five kilometers wide and four kilometers deep. The Russian retreat also left a gap between the Romanian 1st and 2nd Armies. Only the intervention of two regiments of the 3rd ID from the latter prevented a serious rupture. A similar scenario occurred to the west, where the German 216th ID forced the Russians to retreat from Ireşti. Again Averescu was forced to send reserves to close another alarming gap.[39]

On 29 August, units of the Romanian 9th ID, 13th ID, and the Russian 15th ID were brought up to help recover ground lost by the Russians. While the Romanian forces put pressure on the enemy's flank, the Russians attacked straight toward Muncelu. They advanced, Martin Breitenacher of the Alpine Corps tells us, "wave following wave with admirable discipline and precision as on an exercise field." As soon as the Russian ranks came into range, they were torn apart by German riflemen, machine guns, and artillery. Three times that day, the Russian attack was repeated until "the ravines and slopes before the German lines stood full of dead and wounded." Although Muncelu was not retaken, the Russo-Romanian forces were able to regain some of the ground lost the day before. Heavy rain then forced a suspension of the fighting for most of two days. The enemy presence north of Muncelu was considered "an extremely critical situation" by MCG, which still feared a rupture between the 1st Army and the 2nd Army. Grigorescu was ordered to undertake a counteroffensive against the right flank of the German penetration. However, the role of the Russians had now become questionable. The commander of the VIII Corps, in view of previous losses, did not wish to attack. Could the Russians be counted on to hold defensively while the Romanians attacked? This was the question Prezan posed to Grigorescu in a telex conversation on 30 August. Yes, Grigorescu responded, "because a proof of sincerity was made in past battles." Berthelot agreed: "The Russian 15th Division has shown itself until now equal to the task."[40]

Under these conditions, Grigorescu's counteroffensive began on 1 September. The VIII Corps did hold its positions, but things did not go well for the Romanian attack group commanded by General Popescu. Artillery preparation was insufficient, and coordination with the infantry during the battle was poor. The Alpine Corps was entrenched in rough, wooded terrain, well supported by artillery, machine guns, and mortars. Its infantry resisted the Romanian assault step by step. From the perspective of the Alpine Corps, it was a repetition of the slaughter of the Russians two days before, only now it was Romanian soldiers who were being mowed down. The attack was suspended at noon but resumed in the evening. Only a quarter of the lost ground was reconquered. Continuation of the Romanian advance was postponed until 3 September in order to rest and reorganize the troops.[41]

In the first assault on 3 September, the Romanians gained only an average of 300 yards in the attack sectors. A second assault succeeded in reaching the vicinity of Muncelu but got no closer than 50 meters to the enemy's barbed wire on the perimeter of the town. On this day alone, Popescu's group lost 35 officers and 2,700 men dead, wounded, and missing. Among those who died was Lieutenant Ecaterina Teodoroiu, a former nurse whose bravery in defending Târgu Jiu in 1916 had earned her a battlefield commission and the command of an infantry platoon. That night Grigorescu ordered the attack on Muncelu to cease and defensive positions to be organized.[42]

Testimony from the Alpine Corps confirms that German forces were also exhausted and depleted. Long days of heavy fighting in extreme heat had been made unbearable by lack of water. Existing sources in Muncelu had been polluted by artillery shells and dead bodies. Losses had been high. The battles of Panciu and Muncelu had reduced some companies to only 30 to 40 men each. The Leib regiment alone had lost 36 officers and 1,000 men. On 30 August, General Eben had informed Mackensen that continued offensive action would be possible "only if the Alpine Corps would remain a longer time." However, plans to remove it from the front beginning on 4 September remained in effect. Consequently, on 3 September Eben ordered both the I Reserve Corps and the XVIII Corps to cease attacks and fortify the existing front for permanent occupation.[43] The Battle of Mărășești was over.

EVALUATING THE BATTLE OF MĂRĂȘEȘTI

The human cost of the Battle of Mărășești was high. The 9th German Army lost 16,000 dead and wounded. One of these was General Wenninger, killed by an enemy bullet on 8 September. The best available casualty figures for the Romanians place their dead and wounded at over 17,000, with almost 10,000 missing or prisoners. This is comparable to the German losses, with the exception that fewer than 1,000 Germans were taken prisoner. Russian losses were similar to the Romanian losses, as Table 2 shows.[44]

The German command found it difficult to put a positive face on the outcome of the Battle of Mărășești. Eben's public pronouncement that the 9th Army had "achieved almost all assigned objectives" was unconvincing. Morgen's claim of "a local but not a decisive success" was more realistic. Both could point to the heavy losses inflicted on the enemy, including 15,000 prisoners, the retreat of Romanian forces from much of the territory occupied in the Battle of Mărăști, and the fact that Romanian forces were now in no condition to take the offensive. The fact remained, however, that

Table 2. *Romanian and Russian losses in the Battle of Mărăşeşti, 1917*

Status	Officers	Men
Romanian		
Killed	125	5,000
Wounded	367	12,100
Missing	118	9,700
Total	610	26,800
Russian		
Killed	83	7,000
Wounded	400	10,000
Missing	167	8,000
Total	650	25,000

the offensive of the 9th Army was "from the first days a disappointment." The German official history offers several factors to explain this lack of success: the unfavorable terrain, the extreme heat, too many objectives, insufficient artillery, inadequate reserves, but "above all the enemy had been underrated." Eben's final report to Mackensen, even if an apologia, touches on the heart of the matter: "The presuppositions and hopes that the Russians and Romanians would retreat without resistance or allow themselves to be made prisoner were in error. To the contrary the Russo-Romanian armies fought bravely. Each trench, each house, each hill was defended resolutely. . . . Counterattacks were well conducted and most ended in hand to hand fighting."[45] Eben's words remind us that Russian soldiers made an indispensable contribution to the Battle of Mărăşeşti. Although some did flee the field of battle, others fought well. The behavior of the former understandably caused resentment and hostility among the Romanians. Prezan, responding to a complaint by Shcherbachev about overt manifestations of these attitudes, reminded his officers of the heavy price the Russians were paying to help defend Romanian soil. "It is known," he wrote, "that the VII and VIII Corps, alone, lost almost 30,000 killed and wounded . . . proving through this the military value and sincerity with which they cooperated."[46]

Although the Germans also acknowledged the part the Russians played in arresting the offensive of the 9th Army, they reserved their highest praise for the Romanians. In Morgen's understatement, the latter "had become re-spectable opponents. . . . They fought better, were more skillfully led, in-fantry and artillery cooperated [better] than at the beginning of the Ro-manian campaign." Austrian intelligence summaries elaborate these themes: "In attack Romanians show energy and contempt of death," and "the men inspired by intense Romanian patriotic propaganda freely al-lowed themselves to be led into battle." Captured Romanian officers, even the youngest aspirants, were described as "serious militarily, well versed, bear themselves worthily, and exhibit in their conversation much patriot-ism, sense of duty, enthusiasm, and confidence." Another attributed "the extremely stubborn resistance" of the Romanian infantry and "their confi-dence in their power" to the leadership of their officers, the abundance of machine guns, and "strong support" from their "accurate and well-supplied artillery." The Austrian official history sums up the Battle of Mărăşeşti suc-cinctly: "The idea of the German OHL to invade Moldavia over the Siret was wrecked on the resistance of the Romanians."[47]

If the Battle of Mărăşti was as Averescu described it, "the first true vic-tory of the modern Romanian army," the Battle of Mărăşeşti was the most significant victory of that army in World War I, and possibly in all of Ro-manian history. It was a defensive victory that Romanians termed their "lit-tle Verdun." Along with the Battle of Oituz, discussed in the next chapter, it prevented the collapse of the Romanian Front in 1917. During the inter-war period, Mărăşeşti became the symbol of the courage, sacrifice, and achievement of the entire Romanian army in 1917. August 6, the day the battle began, was designated a national holiday, the Day of the Heroes. South of the city, on the road to Focşani where some of the heaviest fight-ing took place, a fortresslike mausoleum was constructed. In the central ro-tunda stands the sarcophagus of General Grigorescu, and surrounding it are crypts containing the remains of more than 6,000 men who died in the battle.[48]

14
The Austro-German Offensive: Oituz, August 1917

ATTACKERS AND DEFENDERS

Two days after the German 9th Army attacked at Mărăşeşti, the left wing of Group Gerok launched its Oituz offensive eastward toward the Trotuş valley. The immediate objective was to outflank and pinch off Averescu's intrusion into the Soveja basin. The Austro-Hungarian command also hoped Gerok's forces could continue on across the Trotuş river. Then, under pressure from the 9th Army and the Austrian 7th Army attacking out of Bukovina, the Romanian army would be crushed and all of Moldavia occupied. Otherwise, Archduke Josef argued, "Romania will revive and cause us much trouble."[1]

When the Oituz operation was first conceived, this sector of the front was defended by the Russian XL Corps. Its record of indiscipline and receptivity to German pacifist propaganda was well known. Characterized by Austrian intelligence as having "little delight in battle," its mood was a major factor in Gerok's choice of a direction of attack. "We expect an enemy retreat," he concluded in his operations order of 3 August. "Be ready to press and follow the enemy, inflicting breakup."[2] Before the operation, code-named Czernowitz, began, the XL Corps was replaced by Romanian troops. Beginning on the night of 1–2 August, the 7th ID, commanded by General Nicolae Rujinsky, took over a ten-kilometer sector of the front from the Doftana river south to the Oituz valley. Two days later, the 6th ID, commanded by General Nicolae Arghirescu, assumed responsibility for an-

237

other ten-kilometer sector from the Oituz valley south to Măgura Cașin. There it connected with the 8th ID, which anchored the connection between the Mărăști and Oituz Fronts. These three divisions, the IV Army Corps commanded by General Gheorghe Văleanu, remained under Averescu's 2nd Army. The 7th ID, entering battle for the first time, was at full strength. The 6th ID, having been heavily engaged in the Battle of Mărăști, was understrength. Both divisions were weak in artillery. They did have the defensive advantage of rugged terrain dominated by peaks of 700 to 1,000 meters linked by steep, forested ridges. On the other hand, the positions inherited from the Russians left much to be desired: shallow trenches, incomplete wire obstacles, and few shelters for troops. Russian and Romanian intelligence failed to detect enemy preparations to attack. On 7 August, the IV Corps actually reported "enemy troops are being reduced."[3] Furthermore, the Oituz sector was weakly manned compared to the remainder of the front, and without significant reserves. Averescu bears responsibility for both. He habitually neglected to maintain reserves, and on 8 August, there were only four battalions for the entire 2nd Army. MCG—his consistent critic on the issue since the war began—ordered him on 7 August to withdraw from the Soveja basin, shorten his front, and form "a powerful reserve." Reluctant to give up the fruit of his victory, Averescu requested and received permission to delay the pull back. This left the majority of the 2nd Army idle on the Mărăști Front, where the exhausted enemy posed no threat, and only two divisions in the northern Oituz sector, where the attack would come. Only four days after Gerok's attack did Averescu order the pullback and the withdrawal of one division into reserve.[4]

Gerok's attack force was the Austrian VIII Corps, commanded by General Siegmund Ritter von Benigni. It was composed of General Béla Sorsich's Hungarian 70th ID (half strength), General Anton Goldbach's Austrian 71st ID, and a diverse formation organized as the German 117th ID under General Paul Seydel. The latter incorporated a number of unrelated units, including the Bavarian 15th Infantry Brigade, several German and Hungarian regiments, and, after its arrival on 9 August from the Western Front, the Württemberg Mountain Battalion (WMB). As soon as the Austrian command realized they would be facing Romanian soldiers, who, they acknowledged "rejoiced in battle," instead of Russians, six dismounted regiments of the Austrian 7th CD and 8th CD were integrated

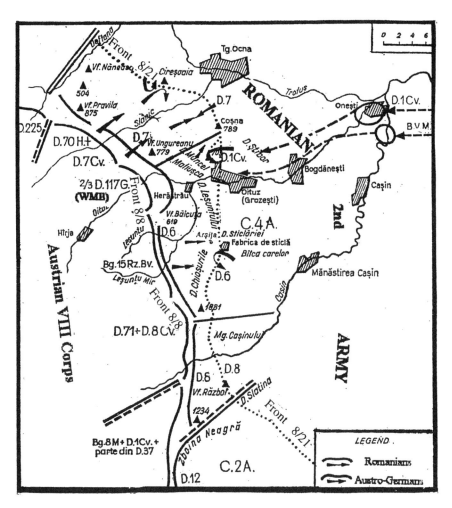

The Battle of Oituz, 8–21 August 1917. Adapted from Victor Atanasiu, *România în primul război mondial* (Bucharest: Editura Militară, 1979)

into the 70th ID and 71st ID. The VIII Corps then totaled 24,300 men with over 200 light and heavy cannon. With two divisions against three, the Romanians were outnumbered 1.6 to 1 in troops and 2.3 to 1 in artillery. At the point of attack, the ratio was higher.[5] Benigni's operational plan called for the 71st ID and the 117th ID to lead the offensive. The former would attack south of the Oituz river in the direction of Oneşti and expel the Romanians from the Leşenţu and Chioşurile crests of hills that extended to

Măgura Caşin. The 117th ID, operating north of the Oituz, was to occupy Mt. Ungureanu and Mt. Coşna en route to the Trotuş river at Târgu Ocna.[6]

THE INITIAL AUSTRIAN ATTACK (8–11 AUGUST)

Archduke Josef and General Seeckt were present at the command post of the 71st ID when it began its attack at 10:00 A.M. on 8 August. The infantry assault was preceded by a concentrated artillery bombardment that pulverized the trenches of the Romanian 6th ID in many places. The right wing of its front was ruptured, the defenders retreating back toward Herăstrău. A Romanian counterattack in the afternoon failed, and contact was lost with its neighboring 7th ID. Farther south, the attackers forced other units of the 6th ID to retreat toward the Leşenţul and Chioşurile ridges. The IV Corps reported to Averescu that the division was "disorganized as the result of heavy losses." Nevertheless, when the fighting ended with darkness, the 71st ID had still not fulfilled Gerok's intention that "on the first day Fabrica de Sticlărie, at least, is to be reached."[7]

Meanwhile, at 11:00 A.M., Austro-German heavy artillery had been turned against the 7th ID north of the Oituz. The assault of the German 117th ID followed at noon. Two Romanian companies that attempted to counterattack were buried in artillery explosions. Their regiment fell back, surrendering the crest of Mt. Ungureanu. Casualties among the Germans who stormed its slopes included Reserve Lieutenant Rudolf Hess. A bullet in his left lung, his third wound of the war, ended his career as an infantryman.[8] The extreme left of the 7th ID, compromised by the retreat of the 6th ID, was forced to pull back toward the village of Grozeşti. Its attempt to aid the latter accomplished nothing. Even contact between the two divisions could not be reestablished until after midnight. Further north, on the right wing of the 7th ID, Sorsich's 70th ID attacked in the direction of Mt. Pravila. It was stopped initially by determined Romanian resistance and accurate artillery fire that inflicted heavy losses. However, in the afternoon, the Hungarians resumed the offensive and succeeded in capturing this important peak. The Romanians retreated two kilometers to the east. At the end of the first day's fighting, the IV Corps had more or less held onto the extremities of its front. The center had sagged back to the east in a wide pocket. The situation was especially perilous on both sides of the

Oituz river. Overall, Gerok was pleased with what the VIII Corps had achieved. He praised his troops and ordered them to continue their attack the next day: "We must give the enemy no rest!"[9]

On 9 August, the VIII Corps and the IV Corps went head to head in attack and counterattack. Benigni ordered the 117th ID to continue its advance north of the Oituz river to occupy Mt. Coşna. The 71st ID was to occupy Fabrica de Sticlărie and continue southeast toward the Caşin river. Averescu, on his part, ordered the IV Corps to launch a counteroffensive to recover the ground lost on the previous day. The Romanians struck first with an attack at sunrise. The 6th ID advanced one kilometer but then fell back under heavy enemy pressure. Despite several attacks as the day proceeded, the division was forced to surrender Mt. Arşiţa and retreat to the western slopes of Mt. Leşenţul and the crests of Mt. Chioşurile. The Szekler 82nd Infantry Regiment led the attack in the vicinity of Fabrica de Sticlărie, where heavy fighting continued until midnight. The Romanian 7th ID, its left flank compromised by the retreat of its neighbor, cancelled its counteroffensive, which had already stalled under the attack of the German 117th ID. The latter had been strengthened both in numbers and in fighting spirit by the arrival of the WMB. According to First Lieutenant Erwin Rommel, the Württembergers, expecting a repetition of the 1916 campaign, were eager to join in the offensive lest they miss out on a breakthrough. Their first task was to clear the southern and eastern slopes of Mt. Ungureanu. Under Rommel's skilled and aggressive leadership, three companies infiltrated along the Oituz valley and drove a wedge behind the leading Romanian echelon. Facing envelopment, the 7th ID evacuated Ungureanu completely on the night of 9–10 August. Rujinsky, the division commander, then ordered a general withdrawal to shorten his front. Averescu, who was at the command post of the IV Corps, did not approve but accepted the fait accompli.[10]

In two days the Austrian VIII Corps had inflicted a serious defeat on the Romanians. The latter's troops were exhausted and had suffered many casualties, including 1,200 prisoners. One told Austrian interrogators that "strict orders to hold positions had resulted in heavy losses. . . . Hardly more than 20 men remained in his company." Gerok's forces had taken important heights, Pravila, Ungureanu, and Arşiţa, which marked the Romanian first line of defense. North of the Oituz the attackers were now threatening those crests which represented the last physical barrier to the Trotuş valley, espe-

Lieutenant Erwin Rommel in 1917.
From Charles Douglas Home, *Rommel*
(New York: Saturday Review Press,
1973)

cially Mt. Cireşoaia and Mt. Coşna. An atmosphere of anxiety reigned at
IV Corps headquarters on the night of 9 August. Reinforcements were desperately needed. Of the handful of battalions available to be rushed to the
front, only the Romanian Mountain Battalion was fit to fight. The others
were incompletely trained and equipped "regiments of march," which included men recently arrived from the hospitals and instructional centers.[11]
Averescu's neglect of the reserves had contributed to a serious crisis.

There was nothing Averescu could do but telephone an appeal to MCG
for help. In a sharply worded response, Prezan rebuked him for failing to
have a reserve "as prescribed in all operational orders" and repeated the
order to create one. However, "given the critical situation," Prezan released
to the 2nd Army the 1st Cavalry Division and the Grăniceri Brigade, both
from the general reserve of MCG. Averescu was admonished to "reestab-

lish at any price and quickly" the situation of the IV Army Corps. In a private conversation with Duca, Prezan complained bitterly that Averescu had advanced at Mărăşti "more than was necessary in order to toot his own horn" and thereby "thinned the front without justification." Prezan was correct in making the last point, but not when he went on to assert that this imbalance had invited the enemy to attack at Oituz. The Austro-German command had decided to attack at Oituz a week before Averescu's troops replaced Russians in that sector. As pointed out above, it was the weakness of the latter that invited the attack.[12]

On 10 August, while reinforcements were en route, the tempo of Gerok's offensive slowed. Benigni ordered the VIII Corps to "stick to the heels" of the Romanians. This proved difficult. His men were weakened by casualties and "very fatigued" by the hot weather and rugged terrain. Moreover, the Romanians now gave ground, in Archduke Josef's words, only "little by little with powerful counterattacks." In the north, Romanians retreated slowly east from Mt. Pravila to the slopes of Mt. Cireşoaia. To the south, the 6th ID held its positions on the Leşenţul ridges and near Fabrica de Sticlărie. In the center, the 117th ID continued to advance eastward from Mt. Ungureanu.[13] The WMB spearheaded the latter advance along the line of ridges that led to Mt. Coşna. Rommel, entrusted with a large portion of the battalion, led the attack utilizing the elements of deception and surprise that later earned him the title of the Desert Fox. After infiltrating men and machine guns to the very edge of the main enemy position during the early morning hours, Rommel launched a surprise attack. The Romanians retreated two kilometers and appeared to be in trouble. Then Colonel Mihail Cezari rallied his 16th Infantry Regiment, and bitter close combat ensued. Rommel, always in the forefront, had two brushes with death that day. "One of my combat orderlies," he recalled, "put a bullet through the head of a Romanian on my left who was aiming at me from a distance of about 15 yards." Later, he was wounded in the arm when suddenly confronted by a group of Romanians. As Rommel and his staff dashed for safety, the French officer accompanying the Romanian unit, in Rommel's words, "kept shouting 'Kill the German dogs' until he took a bullet at close range."[14] The Romanians held their positions for about two hours, but by the end of the day, they were forced back to within 500 meters of the principal peak of Coşna (Hill 789).

AUSTRIAN ADVANCE CONTINUES (11–12 AUGUST)

On 11 August, Gerok's offensive resumed its full intensity. Sorsich's 70th ID continued its advance in two columns to the east at the expense of the 7th ID. After overcoming determined Romanian resistance, one column occupied Mt. Cireşoaia and pushed on toward the Trotuş valley north of Târgu Ocna. A few Romanian units and the command post of the 7th ID retreated to the east bank of the river. The other column, attacking along the Slănic river, reached a point just to the west of Târgu Ocna. The city and its key lines of communication were now under enemy guns. The civilian population began to flee. In scenes reminiscent of 1916, columns of refugees with carts piled high with their possessions filled the roads to the east. On the southern sector of the front, Goldbach's 71st ID was surprised by the vigorous opposition of the Romanian 6th ID as it advanced toward Bâtca Carelor. Gerok's battle summary mentions eight "strong" enemy counterattacks. Benigni even felt it necessary to ask the 117th ID to support the 71st ID by attacking the Romanian flank. Bitter fighting continued near Fabrica de Sticlărie well into the night. The 6th ID made no advance but held its positions.[15]

On 11 August, the 117th ID continued its advance on Coşna, with the WMB again spearheading the attack. Despite his wound, Rommel was asked to lead six companies of the battalion in an assault on the west and northwest slopes. "The new and difficult task was most attractive," he recalls, "so I remained with the outfit." The Romanians had established a ring of outposts to avoid being surprised again. With Rommel directing them personally, four companies of the WMB infiltrated unnoticed through the Romanian perimeter, single file. At noon, while machine guns laid down withering cover fire, Rommel's men stormed through the Romanian defenses and took possession of the first crest. "Everything went with the clock-like precision of a peacetime maneuver," Rommel exulted. Then the Romanians counterattacked, and the battle for control of the summit continued fiercely throughout the day. "Our losses began to mount at an alarming rate," Rommel recalled. Late in the day, the Romanians retreated down the eastern slopes and left the summit of Coşna in enemy hands.[16]

By the evening of 11 August, the situation of the 7th ID was perilous. Its forces had been pushed off the summits of Mt. Cireşoaia and Mt. Coşna. "Troops are reduced to 70/100 men per company and the men are exhausted after four days and four nights of continuous fighting," its command reported. With the Trotuş valley and the entire front of the IV Army Corps endangered, Averescu delivered an emotional charge to the higher officers of the dismounted 1st CD, two battalions of 700 men each, which had just marched 82 kilometers to reinforce the shaken 7th ID. Stopping the enemy "avalanche" depended on them, he said. They must tell their men that they "were destined to fight and to die for the fatherland." At 7:00 P.M., the cavalrymen, described as displaying "undescribable enthusiasm," attacked along the southern and eastern slopes of Mt. Coşna. They were unable to retake Hill 789 but did stop the German advance. Encountering "very strong enemy forces" that "attacked in dense masses from the east," the Bavarian battalions supporting the WMB pulled back with heavy losses. Even the daring Rommel would not consider continuing down Coşna's eastern slopes that day: "We had to be satisfied with the possession of the peak."[17] The crisis of 11 August was the first turning point in the Battle of Oituz.

Early on 12 August, the Bavarians, with Rommel's tired forces playing a secondary role, were ordered to storm Romanian positions east of Coşna. They encountered strong resistance, supported by accurate artillery fire that inflicted heavy losses, including 300 wounded. The aggressive Rommel was inclined to continue on with his detachment, but he was ordered to withdraw half a mile to a ridge on the southwest slope of Coşna. Reports had arrived that enemy forces had broken through the positions of the Hungarian 70th ID north of the Slănic valley, raising the threat of envelopment. For 12 August, Averescu ordered the IV Corps to "maintain present positions" in order to recover from the heavy combat of the preceding day. They were not to engage in major action except "in the case of imperious necessity." The latter occurred when Hungarian 70th ID continued to advance east from Mt. Cireşoaia toward the Trotuş with orders to occupy the river crossings and destroy the railroad. The right wing of the 7th ID, together with the Romanian Mountain Battalion and neighboring Russian forces, met the 70th ID with a counterattack that succeeded in rupturing its front. The Hungarian forces retreated in disorder back to Mt. Cireşoaia and the Slănic valley. The key blow was delivered by the mountain battalion, which captured over 400 enemy soldiers. Instead of the Romanian flank in danger of being turned on 12 August, the flank of the VIII Corps was now threatened. Gerok decreed that the 70th ID must hold "unconditionally" to Mt. Cireşoaia.[18]

THE ROMANIAN COUNTEROFFENSIVE (13 AUGUST)

The success of 12 August encouraged Averescu to order the IV Corps to take the offensive on 13 August and recover its old positions. To bring more energetic leadership to the Oituz Front, he exchanged his corps commanders. General Arthur Văitoianu, who had led the successful Mărăşti offensive, took over the IV Corps, Văleanu replacing him at the II Corps. The right wing of the 7th ID, assisted by five neighboring Russian battalions, continued the advance of the previous day. The weakened Hungarian 70th ID was unable to fulfill Gerok's order to hold, surrendering Mt. Cireşoaia and the exit to the Slănic defile. The Russians, who according to Averescu, had "fought very decisively" the day before, began in the same way. In the afternoon, when the Hungarians counterattacked with the aid of a German battalion, the Russians panicked. They retreated and left a gap of 600 meters in the front. With their flank now uncovered, the Romanians were forced to retreat also, evacuating Mt. Cireşoaia once again.[19]

Elsewhere on 13 August, the remainder of the 7th ID and the entire 1st CD directed their counteroffensive against the German forces on Mt. Coşna. "Thick Romanian columns assaulted from the southeast, northeast, and north," recalls the adjutant of the WMB. "Despite heavy losses, ever more enemy kept coming," adds the battle report of the WMB. "The road and slopes, especially also the ditches, filled with enemy bodies." Rommel adds in graphic and chilling detail a tribute to the tenacity and sacrifice of the Romanian soldiers:

> The enemy repeatedly hurled new forces against our thin lines. . . . The battle raged with undiminished fury . . . into the afternoon. . . . The hostile forces stormed up the bare knoll in a dense mass. . . . [Our] heavy machine guns struck among them and mowed them down like ripe corn. . . . In spite of the heaviest losses, the Romanians continued their attack into the night. . . . When noise of battle died down, we heard the groans and laments of the wounded all along the front.

Rommel admits his own forces "also suffered heavily." He himself "felt very debilitated"; it had been five days since the bandage on his wound was changed or his shoes removed from his swollen feet.[20] The Romanians

ended the day established on the summit of Coşna, but the Germans remained firmly entrenched on its western slopes.

Also on 13 August, south of the Oituz river, the right wing of the 6th ID
made repeated assaults on the 71st ID in the vicinity of Fabrica de Sticlărie.
Although only one assault penetrated his positions, Goldbach feared an envelopment because of the Romanian success on Coşna. He asked VIII
Corps command whether his division should retreat also. Benigni's answer
was to send reinforcements immediately. With this assistance, the Austrians averted a Romanian breakthrough. South of Fabrica de Sticlărie the left
wing of the 6th ID attacked in the vicinity of Mt. Arşiţa with the assistance
of the Romanian Grăniceri Brigade. The latter, a unit of 4,000 former frontier guards, had been hurried by truck and train from Tecuci. After an additional overnight march of 20 kilometers, they reached the front at 5:00
A.M. When ordered to attack immediately, the commander, Colonel Gheorghe Cantecuzino, telephoned 6th ID headquarters, protesting he needed
more time to assemble his troops, allow the arrival of munitions, and reconnoiter his sector. Averescu, who was at the division command post,
ordered Cantecuzino to attack or lose his command and be arrested. Cantecuzino chose to attack. The operation was a disaster. The brigade obediently made repeated assaults against a Croat regiment dug in on higher
ground. They were pinned down for hours before wire obstacles they could
not penetrate. Nevertheless, later in the day, Averescu ordered the ill-con-
ceived attack to continue. Nothing was achieved, and the brigade reported
"colossal losses" totaling 50 percent of the officers and 40 percent of the
men taking part. The unit had to be withdrawn from the front. On 14 August, the entire IV Corps assumed a defensive stance. The Romanian counteroffensive on 13 August recovered only a small percentage of the territory it lost in the days preceding. But it pushed the enemy back from the
edge of the Trotuş valley and reoccupied the key heights that dominated
it. The Austrian VIII Corps had been seriously weakened and time gained
for Averescu to realign the forces of the 2nd Army. The results might have
been more decisive if the operation had been postponed until 14 August
when all participating units would have been better prepared.[21]

The Grăniceri Brigade incident became yet another point of conflict between MCG and Averescu. The latter blamed the tragedy on the "brusk
changes" in the composition of his army orchestrated by MCG, which ne-

cessitated "marches and countermarches which caused them to go against the enemy weakened." Prezan was angered by Averescu's "accusations," which he took as nothing more than a lame excuse to avoid responsibility. He refuted the charges in a blunt and sarcastic 15-page reply penned by Antonescu. The latter had just received a personal letter from a MCG staff officer who was visiting the front. It criticized Averescu's policies and included Colonel Cantecuzino's version of the incident. In addition to blaming Averescu for the brigade's losses, Prezan included a detailed critique of his generalship: his "linear" organization of the front, which "always made it impossible to form reserves"; his delay in shortening the front and withdrawing a division; the introduction of the unprepared regiments of march into battle; and his failure to foresee Gerok's attack. Prezan closed with a sweeping charge that Averescu's failure to create a reserve forced MCG to divert to the 2nd Army units that could have been used for an offensive of the 1st Army: "An occasion was lost to defeat the enemy both at Mărăşeşti and at Oituz."[22] It is probably true that if Averescu had properly distributed his forces, Gerok's offense could have been halted earlier. However, it is improbable that the reserves sent to the 2nd Army could have materially influenced operations of the 1st Army on the Mărăşeşti Front.

A pause occurred in the Battle of Oituz 14–18 August as both sides rested, filled out, and regrouped their forces. It coincided with a similar lull on the Mărăşeşti Front as the German 9th Army prepared for a new offensive and the Russo-Romanian forces experienced the "command crisis." Ragoza's announced intention to retreat on that front moved Averescu to order the II Corps to evacuate the Soveja basin, retreating to a line running from Mt. Slatina in the north to Ireşti in the south. The withdrawal of about ten kilometers occurred on the night of 13–14 August. The work of engineers in blocking roads and destroying bridges did not prevent the German 218th ID from reaching Soveja the next evening. To the north, Austrian units reoccupied Mt. Zboina Neagra and approached Mt. Războiul. In just a few hours, half the gains of the Battle of Mărăşti had been surrendered. At the same time, after a direct order from MCG, Averescu withdrew the 1st ID from the front and established it as a reserve.[23]

GROUP GEROK'S LAST OFFENSIVE (19–22 AUGUST)

Meanwhile, the Austro-German commands agreed to renew their offensives with simultaneous attacks at Oituz and the 9th Army at Mărăşeşti beginning on 19 August. The primary goal of the Austrian VIII Corps was to expel the Romanians once again from Mt. Coşna and to reach the Trotuş in strength. Once this was achieved, Archduke Josef had high hopes that Gerok could cross the river. Then, by continuing on to the Siret, his forces could form a shield to facilitate a river crossing of the 9th Army downstream.[24] For the offensive of 19 August, limited heavy artillery dictated Benigni's strategy. With the support of the big guns, the 70th ID and 71st ID would attack in the morning. The 117th ID would wait until afternoon when the artillery could turn on Coşna. At 7:30 A.M. on 19 August, the 71st ID launched its offensive between Grozeşti and Fabrica de Sticlărie. It succeeded in pushing the 6th ID back until the heavy artillery was shifted to support the 117th ID. At that point, a Romanian counterattack regained some of the ground lost. "The attack did not succeed," explained the battle report of the 71st ID, "because of the stubborn resistance of the enemy." At the opposite end of the front, the 70th ID succeeded in pushing the Romanians and some cooperating Russian forces back to Mt. Cireşoaia and the village of Slănic. There units of the 7th ID and the Romanian Mountain Battalion stopped the Hungarians.[25]

The WMB played a leading role once again in the new attempt to retake the summit of Mt. Coşna. Because of his experience and past success, Rommel was asked to organize its attack. Disregarding his painful wound, he worked around the clock to coordinate artillery in a new attempt to break the front by storm. At 11:00 A.M., German heavy artillery shifted from the south began to shower high explosives on the positions of the Romanian 1st CD. "The 210 mm and 305 mm shells threw earthen geysers into the air and bushes splattered down," Rommel recounts vividly, "Some of their craters could easily accommodate an entire company." By prearrangement, the artillery fire ceased in a small sector. Rommel's forces charged through amid smoke, haze, and a rain of grenades and gunfire, engaging the Romanian defenders in their trenches. Although overwhelmed, the latter fought back. A Romanian cavalry captain killed Rommel's assault leader with a pistol shot to the head. This captain and many other Romanians were taken prisoner amid the shock and confusion of the battle.[26]

To remedy the situation, Văitoianu ordered the 1st CD to "hold at any price where you are" and asked the 7th ID to send assistance. The latter, under heavy attack itself, could not respond. The only option for the 1st CD was to withdraw from the summit of Coşna to secondary positions on the eastern slopes. The retreat turned into a rout with Rommel and his men in close pursuit. "We rushed downhill as fast as our legs could carry us," Rommel recalled. "Many dead and wounded Romanians lay all around us." Four hundred Romanians were taken prisoner that day. While waiting for reserves enabling them to follow up the breakthrough, Rommel's detachment paused on a high point overlooking the Trotuş valley, "within two miles striking distance was Târgu Ocna." Rommel adds, "The town itself was under heavy artillery fire and we could see endless columns of vehicles halted near equally long trains in the station. We could have reached this town in thirty minutes." The reserves he expected never arrived. Furthermore, elsewhere on Coşna, other Romanian units still clung stubbornly to their positions and even counterattacked. It was too risky for Rommel to push on immediately. Disappointed, he resigned himself to wait until the next day to complete the breakthrough.[27]

For the Romanians, it was imperative to stop the German advance. To aid the diminished 1st CD on 20 August, Văitoianu formed a special assault detachment, including one regiment from the 1st Infantry Division, which was now arriving from the south. Additional artillery was added to the detachment, and Colonel Ioan Manolescu, the chief of staff of the IV Corps, took over personal direction of the attack. The assault concentrated on Hill 703 with the intention of outflanking the enemy position on the summit, Hill 789. As Romanian artillery began, it became obvious to Rommel that a major enemy attack was in preparation. "It was high time to shift to defense," he concluded. Digging in quickly, the WMB was in a position to repulse easily the initial Romanian assault. But, as Rommel recalls, "The battle increased hourly in violence and during the day the enemy launched at least 20 assaults against us." Deadly machine gun fire stopped each Romanian attack a kilometer short of the crest of Hill 789. During the night of 20–21 August, the WMB and a Bavarian battalion launched six counterattacks. These were all repulsed. Losses on both sides were heavy. One casualty was Rommel himself. Exhausted from the fighting and with a high fever from his wound, he had been reduced to giving orders lying down. That evening he relinquished his command and left Coşna.[28]

Although 20 August marked the end of the Austro-German offensive at Oituz, the Romanians continued their counteroffensive for two more days with deadly determination. "With all means," reads the battle report of the WMB for 21 August, "the enemy attempts again to reconquer Coşna. Attack now follows attack. Recklessly the Romanians drive against our lines again and again. . . . All the attacks were beaten off mostly in bitter hand to hand fighting. . . . Between the two positions, the bodies of dead Romanians piled up." On 22 August: "The Romanians stormed forward in thick masses over the bodies of their dead and could be driven back only after stubborn close combat. The unit is almost at the end of its power while the enemy always sends fresh troops from Târgu Ocna." These last two days of intense and bloody combat on the Oituz Front resulted in no appreciable change in the front. The latter now ran through Mt. Cireşoaia, Mt. Coşna, the village of Grozeşti, and Mt. Sticlărie, then to Măgura Caşin. Austro-German forces controlled the summits and the Romanians the eastern slopes.[29] As in the Battle of Mărăşeşti, neither side possessed the force to secure a definitive victory. In two weeks of combat (8–22 August), the casualties of the Romanian IV Corps numbered approximately 1,850 dead, 5,000 wounded, and 5,700 missing. Although figures for Austro-German losses are incomplete, the casualties for the 70th ID alone numbered about 1,700. For the WMB, "The battle for Mt. Coşna exacted a terrific toll from the young troops," Rommel lamented, "We had 500 casualties in two weeks and sixty brave mountain soldiers lay in Romanian soil." For these losses, the capture of 1,150 Romanians by the WMB was scant compensation.[30]

EPILOGUE: THE BATTLE OF CIREŞOAIA (9–10 SEPTEMBER)

The Austro-German command gave brief consideration to one more offensive by Gerok in coordination with the final attempt of the 9th Army on 28 August to take Muncelu. This proved impossible. The order of 24 August from OHL, which announced the impending transfer to Italy of the Alpine Corps, included the WMB as well. This, plus the retirement of the 117th ID and the transfer of two regiments of cavalry to the Soveja region, reduced the troop strength of the VIII Corps by one-third. Archduke Josef was alarmed and complained to Mackensen that the Oituz pass was "in peril." Recognition of his enemy's weakness reinforced Averescu's desire to launch a new offensive. As the point of attack, he chose Mt. Cireşoaia. From its heights, enemy guns still had Târgu Ocna under fire, paralyzing communications in the Trotuş valley. Also, if Cireşoaia were retaken, Coşna could be outflanked and a base established for future operations. As early as 21 August, Averescu initiated discussions with Ragoza and Shcherbachev on a joint Russo-Romanian operation. On 1 September, he and Ragoza worked out a plan. Mt. Cireşoaia would be attacked from the north by the Russian 49th ID and from the east and south by the Romanian Mountain Battalion and the recently arrived Romanian 1st ID. The 6th ID and 7th ID were to hold in place the enemy before them, with the latter following the 1st ID if it was able to advance. Originally scheduled for 7 September, the attack was postponed for two days at the insistence of the Russians. King Ferdinand and Averescu were both present at the command post of the IV Corps on 9 September to observe the attack.[31]

Misfortune characterized the execution of the offensive. The night before, a Romanian deserter revealed when and where the attack would take place. Immediately the enemy made adjustments: the neighboring German 225th ID sent reserves to Cireşoaia, the tough Szekler 82nd IR was sent north to Coşna, and the two regiments of cavalry were recalled from the Soveja basin. The loss of secrecy also allowed Austro-German artillery to bombard and shock the Romanian assault troops just before they attacked. More serious and tragic was the inability of Romanian artillery to create openings in the barbed wire defense. Held up before these barriers, the Romanian 1st ID was pummeled with grenades and fire from rifles and machine guns. Little or no advance was made, and losses were tragically heavy. The experience of the cooperating units of the 7th ID was similar. Casualties for the two divisions on the first day exceeded 500. To the north of Cireşoaia, the Russians, led by a "death battalion," made small gains but were soon thrown back, their desire to attack extinguished. To the south of Cireşoaia, the Szeklers and a Bosnian regiment repulsed an attempted Romanian advance on Coşna. Averescu ordered the offensive to continue on 10 September, but Văitoianu wisely added the condition that the infantry attacks would not be renewed until "breaks in the nets [of wire] have actually been made." Consequently, Romanian forces confined their action on 10 September to artillery fire as they wrestled with the problem. On the night of 10–11 September, several parties of engineers from the 1st ID were sent out with wire cutters. They succeeded in opening only one hole of about 20 meters. When the infantry attacked the next morning, the first wave was able to penetrate the gap. But then the men encountered additional barriers and enemy machine guns. Virtually all were either killed or wounded. Succeeding attempts to penetrate were repelled by withering enemy firepower. During the evening, the commander of the 1st ID reported that additional attacks "had no chance of success" unless sufficiently prepared by artillery. Ragoza was of the same mind and ordered the Russian troops to stop their attacks. Averescu then agreed the Romanian attempts should cease also. Thereafter, the only action in the Oituz sector were local attempts to rectify the front. The final attempt to take Cireşoaia was a needless and costly failure. Casualties for the Romanians in two days exceeded 1,200 killed, wounded, or missing.[32]

CONCLUSIONS ON THE BATTLES OF 1917

For the Austro-German command, especially Archduke Josef, the Battle of Oituz was, like Mărăşeşti, a bitter disappointment. It did achieve an advance of two to six kilometers on a front of 18 to 20 kilometers. Included were Mt. Cireşoaia and Mt. Coşna, from which the Trotuş valley was brought under hostile fire. However, enemy artillery was never able to interdict completely the rail and road traffic at Târgu Ocna. The Austrian VIII Corps was now committed to a longer front than previously. Gerok's advance did force Averescu to withdraw from the Soveja basin, but it failed to break the Romanian Front, cross the Trotuş, and outflank Russo-Romanian armies west of the Siret. This potential catastrophe was averted by the determination of the Romanian command to resist at any price and their soldiers to pay that price. Austrian after-battle analyses stressed the "contempt of death" and "steadfastness" demonstrated "repeatedly" by Romanian soldiers in close combat during the Battle of Oituz. Group Gerok's offensive had a chance to succeed only if a breakthrough was achieved in the first two days. The VIII Corps had no reserves for a sustained campaign, and significant reinforcements did not arrive when needed. Combat losses could not be replaced. Key units like the Szekler 82nd IR became "very diminished." Would the outcome of the battle have been different if, as Ludendorff's chief of operations, Major Wilhelm Wetzell, "urgently recommended," the Alpine Corps had been sent originally to the Oituz rather than to the Putna? The German official history says no.[33] However, the success of the smaller Württemberg Mountain Battalion suggests that the Alpine Corps would have been better utilized on the mountainous Oituz Front rather than on the less difficult terrain northwest of Mărăşeşti.

The Austro-German offensives at Mărăşeşti and Oituz, undertaken with high expectations, achieved limited tactical success but were strategic failures. The Russo-Romanian armies were not defeated and Moldavia not occupied. These objectives were not achieved, Austro-German commanders agreed, because of unexpected enemy resistance. They had anticipated encountering either Russian divisions rendered ineffective by revolutionary propaganda or little-regarded Romanian forces. Instead, they met some Russian units with fight left in them and divisions of reconstructed and rearmed Romanians, disciplined and determined to defend their homeland. Miscalculation of their opponents led the Austro-German commands to undertake operations without adequate resources. This jeopardized their chance of success, which was linked to a quick breakthrough. This prospect was further compromised by initiating the offensives before key units had arrived, including the Alpine Corps and the Württemberg Mountain Battalion. After absorbing the initial shock, the Russo-Romanian forces were able to resist on successive lines of defense, which necessitated repeated violent assaults. These exhausted the attackers and created resupply problems for their artillery. Although the Austro-German offensives at Mărăşeşti and Oituz were planned to be complementary, in execution, they had little influence on one another. The same can also be said of the Russo-Romanian defensive effort, even though it was carried out on interior lines with battle fronts less than 50 kilometers apart. Despite mistakes and shortcomings, this effort was sufficient to thwart the enemy intention of breaking the front and knocking Romania out of the war. The latter was accomplished only as the consequences of the Bolshevik Revolution in November were played out. Meanwhile, for over six months, the Central Powers were denied the fruits of victory: access to the granaries of the Ukraine and freedom to carry out massive transfers of troops to other battle fronts. In addition, by attracting and engaging additional enemy troops in the summer of 1917, the Romanians aided their allies who were struggling on the Western and Italian Fronts. The Romanian Front was one of the few bright spots in Entente military operations that year.[34]

While the battles on the Romanian Front in 1917 had important consequences for the Great Powers, it must be admitted that they occupy a small
chapter in their total war effort. However, for the Romanians, these battles were a defining moment in their national experience. An enemy victory would have forced the Romanian government and army to capitulate
or retreat into revolutionary Russia. The political and military consequences of either would have been disastrous. In both cases, Mackensen
had plans to initiate a coup from Bucharest, led by the Conservative Petru
Carp, designed to overturn the dynasty and the constitution, then ally Romania with the Central Powers. "The breakdown of the offensive," the
Austrian diplomatic representative in Bucharest wrote on 29 August, "has
. . . brought the political action of Carp . . . into discredit since the . . . conquest of Moldavia formed not only the intrinsic presupposition for Carp's
program but . . . had been announced as the starting point for its debut."[35]

The admirable performance of the Romanian army also played a crucial
role in persuading the Entente to stand by the promises made in the Treaty
of 1916. After the weak showing of her army in 1916, the Allies were seriously considering dropping support for Romania's war aims. Another defeat might have decided the issue. As it turned out, the heroic and successful performance on the battlefield in 1917 restored Romania's respect
and credibility with the Entente. Moreover, it was this army, proven under
fire at Mărăşti, Mărăşeşti, and Oituz, that later occupied Bessarabia, Bukovina, and Transylvania, thereby creating Greater Romania. The reputation
acquired by her army was a major determinant for Romania's postwar
value to the Allies in their cordon sanitaire against Bolshevism and in the
French alliance system in Eastern Europe.[36]

Less tangible but no less important was the impact that the success of
the army had on the collective mentality of Romanians. Peasant soldiers
"understood that the fate of their country depended on their determination and spirit of sacrifice, that they were a force which must be taken into
account. Returning to their homes, they brought into villages a new spirit
which modified the frame of mind of the entire peasantry." This current
was the catalyst for economic, social, and political change. For Romanians
as a whole, the ability of the army to more than hold its own in 1917,
against foes once held in fear and awe, enhanced their self-image and self-
confidence. "The shame of the 1916 campaign was washed away."[37] During the interwar period, the memory of the battles of Mărăşti, Mărăşeşti,

and Oituz was celebrated, in heroic proportions, in Romanian literature, art, and historical writing. The readable and passionate three-volume history by Constantin Kiriţescu, which vividly portrayed both the agony and ecstasy of the war, captivated and inspired a generation of young Romanians. Even today, decades after the fact, the events on the Moldavian battlefields in 1917 and their attendant consequences remain an important influence on modern Romanian nationalism.[38]

15
Between War and Peace: September 1917–January 1918

The battles of Mărăşeşti and Oituz marked the end of offensive operations on the Romanian Front. A proposal of Seeckt and Archduke Josef for a new attempt to conquer Moldavia was rejected by Ludendorff and Arz. Their focus now was on France and Italy. An Entente request for a Russo-Romanian attack to aid the Italians in crisis at Caparetto received only perfunctory consideration from Shcherbachev and Prezan. Berthelot decisively rejected it: simply to hold the front would require "a miracle of equilibrium."[1] Consequently, both sides hunkered down for the winter. Russo-Romanian forces were realigned. Units of the Russian 4th Army standing between the two Romanian armies were withdrawn, giving the Romanians a continuous front of 120 kilometers running from the Uz valley in the north, south to Iveşti, then southeast to Suraia on the Siret. Ten Romanian infantry divisions and one cavalry division were in the line, with five infantry divisions and one cavalry division in reserve. Those that had suffered in the heavy combat of summer were being replenished and rebuilt under the supervision of the MMF. Flanking the Romanians to the north were the Russian 4th and 9th Armies, to the south the 6th Army. These armies, including the 8th Army in Bukovina, totaled 59 infantry and eight cavalry divisions. However, their units were undermanned and their discipline undermined by pacifism and revolutionary indiscipline. The Central Powers, for their part, continued transfers to other fronts. In addition to the Alpine Corps, the Württemberg Mountain Battalion, and the Austrian 13th ID announced earlier, six other major units departed in the period September–November 1917. Only one German and two Austro-Hungarian battle-weakened divisions were sent to replace them. Consequently, on paper, the Central Powers were heavily outnumbered, 2 to 1 in infantry divisions. Given the condition of the Russian divisions, which were incapable of offensive action and increasingly questionable for defense, a rough balance of forces existed on the Romanian Front.[2]

BEHIND THE FRONT: THE PROPAGANDA WAR

The cessation of combat enabled the Central Powers to target the Romanian army with the propaganda campaign that had proved so successful with the Russian Army. The Austro-Hungarian 1st Army set up four new propaganda centers at the front in addition to the 12 already in existence. One purpose of these centers and similar ones of the German 9th Army was to distribute printed material. Included were newspapers and periodicals from Bucharest, including *Gazetă Bucureştilor*, *Lumină*, and *Săptămână Ilustrată*. This literature was handed directly to Romanian soldiers where possible, thrown over the lines, or deposited at established locations in no-man's-land.[3] Manifestos to encourage desertion were also distributed. One signed "Romanian Patriots in the Occupied Territory" contained a special offer to soldiers native to Wallachia, who composed a majority in the Romanian army. Deserters, but not prisoners of war, could avoid imprisonment and return immediately to their home and employment. It closed with an emotional appeal: "Come home, your wives and children, your parents and your native land await you with opens arms." Photos of deserters who accepted the offer were then published in *Săptămână Ilustrată*.[4]

Austro-German intelligence reported that the number of desertions increased in September. The motives most frequently mentioned during interrogation were poor living conditions, mistreatment by officers, and war weariness. A number also referred to the offer of repatriation. Photos of returnees appearing in *Săptămână Ilustrată* "made a great impression," an Austrian evaluation concluded. "In my experience," another analyst related, "most deserters are coming from *ersatz* units."[5] Hard evidence on the actual number of deserters is fragmentary. Group Gerok, facing the Romanian 2nd Army, reported 111 desertions in the period 1–25 September. Mackensen's 9th Army, opposite the Romanian 1st Army, counted 84 desertions during the second week of September, 23 for 19–21 September, and 30 for 18–24 November. The evidence is insufficient to draw a firm conclusion, but if these figures are extrapolated and then compared with the number of troops involved, it would indicate the Romanian desertion rate in the autumn of 1917 was not high. Division-by-division reports by French liaison officers termed morale "good" to "excellent" and gave no indication that desertion was a serious problem.[6]

The failure to induce mass desertions from the Romanian army, according to enemy intelligence, was due to "severe countermeasures [that] make desertion very difficult, often impossible." Deserters reported that the men were closely watched by their officers; removing a gun belt raised suspicion. Reportedly men were offered money to snitch on the plans of their comrades. The Romanian command used positive as well as negative reinforcement. General Petala (I AC) ordered his officers to "speak with troops in the line daily," praising their achievements at Mărăşti, Mărăşeşti, and Oituz and promising that "in the course of the next year our suffering will end. . . . Romania will be integrated with territory from Austria-Hungary." Petala also included a stern warning: "Traitors must be judged and sentenced to death. . . . Loyal fighters on the other hand be they living or fallen on the field of battle . . . will be covered with glory. . . . Traitors, conversely will pile shame on their name, paying for their sin."[7]

Although it appears that relatively few Romanian soldiers deserted, many, including officers, fraternized. A second function of enemy propaganda centers was to send Romanian-speaking agents called "negotiators" across the line. They reported contact with virtually every Romanian division at the front. The IV AC (2nd Army) was characterized as "very accessible"; newspapers circulated "everywhere" and were "eagerly read." In the 12th ID, "soldiers received newspapers, schnapps and photographs . . . a Romanian officer bought a watch." In the same division, "a Romanian . . . came for a short conversation and gave me a friendly letter and post for relatives in the occupied area." Letter traffic soon began in both directions. On 19 September, according to an Austrian report, a lieutenant colonel of the 12th ID "listened intently to our negotiator and wrote down some things. . . . He intended to discuss them with the commanding officers of the 12th ID without the knowledge of the French officer attached to the division." At the departure of the negotiator, the guards of the Romanian outpost saluted, and their commander cried out in German, "Hoch

Deutschland." Five days later, a Romanian sergeant delivered a letter: "The higher command of the regiment and division did not want to negotiate and nothing more would be received." In some units, soldiers continued to accept propaganda: "The Romanian 6th, 7th, 8th infantry divisions pick up our newspapers in almost every location," an enemy report affirmed. Also during October and November, enemy negotiators reported that conversations were refused and propaganda patrols were fired at as they distributed literature. Near Magură Cașin, a Romanian officer threw over a message that said "further propaganda was useless." "The Romanians appear successful in countering propaganda . . . [by] seizing our news broadsheets," lamented one Austrian report.[8]

At the end of October, the Romanians began a propaganda campaign of their own, which is reflected in excerpts from Austrian intelligence reports. A soldier of the 12th ID "gave over Romanian counter propaganda in the course of a conversation." It called attention to the impending arrival of American troops in France, a German defeat at Riga, and the threat of starvation in the Central Powers. "Near Varnița, the Romanians posted a placard on which was written we could not win the war." Elsewhere another placard appeared with "exaggerated reports over the battle of Cambrai, the resurgence of the Italians, and the success of the English in Palestine." In mid-November, the Romanian 3rd ID "took down placards set up by us at night and put on them a new inscription: 'All lies. In Germany revolution.'" At the end of November, *Kriegswoche*, a four-page German-language weekly, began to appear along the Austro-German lines. It contained news from all the battlefields as well as information on the military and the political and economic problems of the Central Powers, including declining morale in the German army, peace protests in Berlin, and the decline in the value of the mark. It was soft propaganda whose reasoned arguments were designed to subtly undermine German and Austrian morale. Distribution continued until peace negotiations in March 1918, much to the displeasure of the Austrian-German commands.[9]

A unique Romanian propaganda initiative was an appeal to Transylvanian Romanians serving in the Habsburg army to desert and follow the example of the Transylvanian legion. Several battalions of the latter, recruited from the more than 100,000 Habsburg Romanians in Russian prison camps, had already arrived in Moldavia. In the autumn of 1917, Austrian intelligence discovered broadsheets at the front signed "Transylvanian and

Bucovinian Volunteers in the Romanian Army." It recounted the past sins of the Hungarians, calling for "death to the Germans and Hungarians. They are our enemies and tyrants." Because by design few Habsburg Romanians were posted against the Romanian army, readers were told, "Surrender to the Russians. . . . [They] will send you to Romania where you will fight under the Romanian king." The number who responded to this broadsheet is not known, but the appeal, in and of itself, raised concern in the Habsburg command.[10]

THE FOCŞANI ARMISTICE

Throughout the autumn of 1917, the state of the Romanian army gave Entente leaders cause for optimism. Its depleted divisions were being filled out and retrained. French officers continued to rate their morale high. Berthelot had no reservation about their capacity for combat. Enemy analysts agreed. Romanian soldiers were described as "under the control of their officers. . . . Hitherto, discipline has not suffered." The combat value of the Romanian army was being restored "through the authority of the officers, improved training and armaments, in addition to well functioning troop reserves."[11] In contrast, the Russian armies were rapidly falling into anarchy. Replacements arriving at the front, especially young officers, introduced more radical ideas. Bolshevik influence, pacifism, and disorderly conduct increased. Reports of General Shcherbachev and French and Romanian liaison officers, as well as enemy intelligence, agreed on the details: "a burning thirst for peace"; officers disobeyed and intimidated; reluctance to work on fortifications; resistance to entering the line; and increasing desertion from the front. The degree of indiscipline varied from unit to unit and army to army. The 9th Army in the north, where Ukrainian soldiers predominated, and the 4th Army, which had fought with success alongside the Romanian army, were considered the most reliable; the 6th Army, which manned the southern wing of the front, was the least reliable. The latter's IV Army Corps, responsible for defending the crucial Nămoloasa bridgehead, had become a leading center of Bolshevik influence. French officers addressing units of its 30th ID were met with shouts of "Russians make war for France" and "Peace and nothing more." Their reports described Russian officers as demoralized and humiliated. In the 117th Regiment, officers of one battalion

Russian soldiers in Romania, 1917. "Long Live the People, Land, Freedom, Peace." From Glenn E. Torrey, *Armata Revoluționară Rusă și România, 1917* (Bucharest: Editura Militară, 2005)

were arrested by their men and forced to march at command. Men of the 119th Regiment stormed their officers' mess, sacked the place, and forced its occupants to flee out a window. "Division 30 is not the only [Russian] division . . . in a state of anarchy," Colonel Antonescu commented. "The Russian 6th Army does not wish to fight and the troops of this army . . . would retreat at the first move of the enemy."[12]

Consequently, Romanian reserves were channeled into strategic areas behind the 6th Army. Neighboring Romanian commanders made contact with their Russian counterparts to work out a plan of operations in the event of an enemy attack. On 13 November, after one regiment of the 30th ID left the line and its replacement refused to man it, a Romanian regiment took its place. The next day plans were made to replace the entire division. Virtually the same problem arose with the 40th ID. The Romanian MCG believed it had enough reserves to replace part or all of the Russian 6th Army, but if the departure of Russian troops increased, the front could not be held. Contingency plans were made for a retreat all the way to the Prut if an enemy attack made this necessary. Still, Berthelot was hopeful that the Russian armies could hold up through the winter, possibly with the aid of new divisions being created from among Czech and Serb volunteer units in Russia. He met with the Czech leader Thomas Masaryk in Iaşi in late October to discuss the issue. After giving some encouragement, Masaryk decided military and provisioning conditions were too insecure to send Czech troops to the Romanian Front.[13]

The hope of Berthelot and the Romanians that the status quo at the front would hold through the winter of 1917–1918 was shattered by Lenin's seizure of power in Petrograd and his order on 21 November for the Russian armies to conclude an armistice. Shcherbachev, with the backing of the Entente ministers and the Romanians, rejected Lenin's order. He intended to continue the war under the quasi authority of the embryonic Ukrainian Republic. The majority of the soldiers, infected with the toxin of peace and encouraged by Bolshevik agitators, followed Lenin's instructions to arrange ad hoc local armistices. Shcherbachev, if he was to maintain any control at all, was forced on 4 December to ask Mackensen and Archduke Josef for a meeting at Focşani to discuss an armistice on the Romanian Front.[14] The Romanians now faced a painful dilemma. To fight on alone would lead to disaster either in a "triangle of death" in Moldavia or in a retreat into Bolshevik Russia. On the other hand, an armistice would lead, almost certainly, to a separate peace. The latter, French premier Georges Clemenceau had already warned, would jeopardize Romania's war aims as promised in the treaty of 1916. With the hope that their allies would grant approval after the fact, the Romanian cabinet authorized Prezan on 4 December to send delegates to Focşani. Orders went out that evening for units at the front to send parliamentarians to the enemy lines and arrange a cease-fire beginning at 8:00 A.M. on 5 December. To emphasize the strictly military nature of the negotiations and to avoid implicating the king, the supreme command of the army was transferred to Prezan. Averescu, prevented by pride from serving under his rival, asked to be relieved of command of the 2nd Army. Refused, he ended up accepting a "furlough," which served as a transition from his military to his political career.[15]

The Central Powers responded eagerly to the call for negotiations, which began on 7 December. The German delegation at Focşani was headed by General Curt von Morgen, commander of the I Reserve Corps. General Oskar Hranilovici, onetime Habsburg military attaché in Bucharest, led the

Austro-Hungarian delegation. Bulgarian and Turkish delegates were also present. For the Germans, their priority was to secure freedom to transfer troops to the west to participate in Ludendorff's spring offensive; for the hunger-conscious Austrians, it was the opening of the Danube for food imports from South Russia. The Russian delegation was led by the 9th Army commander, General Anatoli Kelchevskii, the Romanian by Vice-Chief of Staff Alexandru Lupescu. The Russo-Romanian delegations, which acted in unity, were adamant that they did not recognize Lenin's government and would not accept the unfavorable terms of the armistice the Central Powers were forcing on the Bolsheviks at Brest-Litovsk.[16] The most disputed issues at Focşani were three the Central Powers tried to carry over from the Russian negotiations: freedom to transfer troops to other fronts, freedom of shipping on the Danube and Black Sea, and freedom of movement in the neutral zone. On the first issue, Lupescu had orders to secure "at any price" a prohibition of transfers in order to protect Romania's allies. Deadlock on this issue led to suspension of negotiations for one day. Then on 9 December, a compromise was worked out. Only troops already under transit orders on 5 December could leave the front. Hranilovici reported to AOK that "it was the Romanians who opposed [our position] with such determination . . . that it had to be changed to our disfavor." In the end, the German OHL was able to turn this formula to its own advantage, alleging transfer orders had gone out for the entire Eastern Front before 5 December. The Romanian command accepted this interpretation, rationalizing that troops already under orders could be considered no longer existing at the front. Both sides proceeded to apply this "self-enforcing" clause liberally.[17]

On the issue of freedom of shipping on the Danube, the Romanians were willing to open the river to Galaţi, which they controlled, but not downstream or on the Black Sea coast. This meant that the main avenue for the Central Powers to access food supplies in the Ukraine would remain closed. Lacking an agreement at Focşani, the issue was referred to a special commission to meet later at Brăila. There a convention was signed that established a line of demarcation between opposing naval forces, but the Romanians refused to concede the desire of the Central Powers for free navigation.[18] The Central Powers considered freedom of movement in the neutral zone on the front "absolutely necessary." As Hranilovici explained to AOK, "It is necessary to promote energetically, with all means, propaganda among the Romanian troops." The Romanians opposed freedom of movement and es-

Kelşewsky   Hranilovici   Morgen   Lupescu   Hentsoh

Armistice negotiators at Focşani, 9 December 1917. From Constantin Kiriţescu, *Istoria războiului pentru întregirea României*, 2nd ed. (Bucharest: Editura Casei Şcoalelor, 1925)

sentially got their way. Articles 10 to 13 established a neutral zone into which entry was forbidden and the sale and consumption of alcohol banned. The Romanians made it clear they would oppose entry with force, but would arrest rather than shoot violators. The final draft of the armistice was signed on 9 December, with all the delegates posing shoulder to shoulder for a group photograph. Military comradeship and common concern about Bolshevism had created a degree of mutual empathy. Kelchevskii's chief of staff, "emotionally moved," gripped Morgen's hand at departure: "I wish, Your Excellency, that you do not experience in your country and in your army the same conditions that now exist with us."[19]

IMPACT OF THE ARMISTICE

The armistice exacerbated the yearning for peace on both sides of the front. Romanian parliamentarians reported its manifestations as they visited enemy positions: "A [German] colonel wept before me saying he had lost two sons in battle. . . . Another colonel complained about the heavy losses at Mărăşeşti." An Austrian lieutenant and his men on the front of the 1st Army voiced their hope of peace and a return home: "We love the young Kaiser Karl, but the wolf of Berlin, who perseveres in continuing the war, we would wring his neck." One Romanian delegate at Focşani reported being cheered by 150 German soldiers. One asked him to see that the armistice was of long duration; "otherwise we will go to the Western Front." Nevertheless, the parliamentarians reported that German discipline was strong and the men under control of their officers.[20]

The Romanian command was concerned about the impact of the armistice on its own soldiers as enemy propaganda teams continued to fraternize, deliver newspapers and packets of letters from the occupied zones, and "manifestos . . . inviting our troops to become traitors and our people to revolt."[21] To combat the growth of pacifism, officers were reminded of "the necessity of impeding, at any price, conversations or fraternization" at the front; newspapers "thrown over are to be burned." Counterpropaganda teams were to be formed in each unit. Gatherings of even small groups of soldiers were forbidden, "as are discussions about the situation we are in." Violators "will be immediately sent before a court-martial." Surveillance required "officer observers for every subsector and at night an officer listener with every company in the trenches." Positive initiatives included patriotic religious services and distribution of copies of the armistice, with officers explaining to their men that "an armistice is not the same as concluding peace, hostilities could resume at any time." Other talking points were exhortations to "patriotism and sacrifice," "keep the faith," and "final victory will ultimately be ours and that of our allies."[22] These efforts appear to have been successful, at least initially. "Due to the strict implementation of the Focşani armistice and the invariably strict discipline with the Romanian troops," an Austrian analyst complained on 29 December, "propaganda could make no progress." The Romanians even "take every opportunity to interrupt our traffic with the Russians." Desertions were reported to be down, but fraternization continued throughout the armistice. Brătianu's son, Gheorghe, describes in detail how he and an officer friend visited enemy lines near Cireşoaia late in December. They exchanged news, letters, cigarettes, and newspapers with an Austrian officer, a Transylvanian Romanian. As the armistice continued, the morale of the

Romanian troops was increasingly affected by the growing desire for peace. "Officers and men constantly express their desire for peace," enemy intelligence reported in January. "The mood of the officer corps is depressed and, although indeed thoroughly disciplined and possessing vital patriotic feeling, . . . view their war as lost because of the Russian breakup." Another analyst warned that the fighting ability of the Romanian army "has not suffered and must be reckoned with."[23]

In the Russian armies, however, the armistice served as a catalyst for an exuberant implementation of the revolutionary slogan, "Peace, Demobilization and Return to the Homeland." Anarchy ruled in many Russian units. Austrian parliamentarians visiting the 48th ID and XXIV AC headquarters on 5–6 December were greeted by "about 600–800 soldiers with music, lifted out of the automobile and taken on the shoulders of the soldiers to a hall where, in the presence of a great number of soldiers, the Revolutionary Military Committee of the 48th ID greeted us in a long, passionate speech as 'messengers of peace.'" The visitors learned that two days earlier, both unit commanders had been arrested and replaced by young revolutionary officers. A few days later, 4th Army commander General Ragoza was replaced in a similar coup. At Galaţi, the 6th Army Military Revolutionary Committee took control from their commander General Tsiurikov. The attempt to overturn General Kelchevskii at 9th Army headquarters failed when Ukrainian soldiers, strongly represented in his command, rallied to his support.[24]

The next target was Shcherbachev himself. On 15 December, Senen Roshal, appointed by Lenin as commissar of the Romanian Front, led a Bolshevik takeover of the Front Revolutionary Military Committee with the help of the Russian garrison at Socola, a suburb of Iaşi. When the revolutionaries conspired to arrest Shcherbachev and assume command of the Russian armies, the general demanded the Romanians take action. Berthelot proposed to go even farther, "to arrest all of the marximalists en masse." Brătianu was hesitant, fearing it would trigger a march of Russian troops on Iaşi and other cities and retaliation from Lenin, even war. After an all-night cabinet debate on 22 December, Prezan was authorized to use force against Bolshevik centers at Socola and elsewhere in Moldavia. A strike by Romanian troops, aided by a few Ukrainians, disarmed a force of 3,000 Russian soldiers at Socola "without the least shedding of blood." At other commands taken over by Bolsheviks, the usurpers, disorganized and poorly led, were also quickly suppressed. Ragoza, along with other Russian generals, was restored to his command.[25]

DEPARTURE OF THE RUSSIAN ARMY

Although a Bolshevik takeover of the higher Russian commands had been defeated, the fact remained that Russian divisions could not be counted on to defend the front. Soldiers left their positions in droves. Large gaps appeared in the line. In an example of what was to come, the Romanian 5th ID reported in mid-December that with its neighboring Russian division, only one soldier per kilometer remained in defensive positions. The majority were "wandering in the villages," posing a threat to internal security. "Isolated individuals and organized bands," read a circular order from MCG, "openly commit robberies, pillaging and even felonies, terrorizing the population with guns, grenades and all manner of violence." Anarchic Russian troops had now become a more immediate threat than the enemy. Consequently, Romanian leaders decided to allow them to leave, but only under strict guidelines to ensure an orderly evacuation: authorization of the Russian command, disarmament, and travel by train or by foot along established routes with adequate depots of supplies. "Otherwise they will turn to plundering to live. . . . No plundering will be tolerated and violators, however numerous, will be punished according to Romanian law," read Colonel Antonescu's directive. Romanian military units were assigned to control the evacuation.[26]

Many Russian units decided to submit to the guidelines, but some decided to defy them, moving eastward on their own and under arms. The situation was exacerbated when, on 2 January, Ensign Krylenko, Lenin's new chief at STAVKA, ordered Russian units to withdraw from the front, by force if necessary. MCG, fearful not only of systematic devastation in Moldavia but of disruption of depots and supply lines in Bessarabia, was determined to enforce its guidelines. All or part of seven Romanian divisions, either from reserves or withdrawn from the line, were positioned behind the front, eastward to the Prut. Some Russian units were turned back without major bloodshed. However, several large-scale pitched battles occurred. At Galaţi, the 9th ID and 10th ID of the IV Siberian Corps engaged the Romanian 4th

ID in two days of fighting on 20–21 January 1918. After experiencing some success and taking a number of Romanian prisoners, the Russians were thrown into disorder by a determined Romanian use of bayonets, artillery, and fire from Danube monitors. This convinced the 9th ID to submit to disarmament and seek refuge in German lines to the west on 22 January. Two days later, the 10th ID also agreed to disarm and was escorted across the Prut into Bessarabia.[27] A similar confrontation in northern Moldavia is summarized in an Austrian intelligence report of 2 February:

> the II [Russian] Army Corps in an attempt to march through to Bessarabia . . . was routed and, in the most part, disarmed. A portion, about 1000 men, went over to us. . . . Armed transit of XVIII and XL Army Corps has likewise failed. Battles near Sereth and Mihaileni with Romanians ended in disarming of troops. Only part of the 43rd Infantry Division has fought through to Russian territory. Approximately 800 men . . . as well as 50 trucks and 20 motorcycles . . . deserted to us. Greater part of both corps, thrown into disorder, may seek to reach the border unarmed. II, XVIII, and XL Army Corps can be considered dissolved. . . . The 9th Romanian Division takes over this sector. . . . VIII Army Corps, because of Romanian opposition to transit to Russia, has returned to its old position.[28]

Although one can hardly speak of organized demobilization as Shcherbachev and the Romanians originally intended, the Russian army, whether peacefully or violently, quickly evacuated Moldavia. Between 14 December and 17 January, the XXX Army Corps, for example, shrank from 24,000 to 2,000. From the beginning of November until the end of January, the overall Russian troop strength on the Romanian Front declined from over 1,200,000 to about 50,000. At the beginning of February, MCG reported that "the entire front, previously defended by [Russian] armies 8, 9, 4 and 6, is now with rare exceptions almost completely exposed. The Russian units are completely disorganized and with reduced effectives have retreated on their own initiative behind the front, where they continue demobilization."[29] After 1 January, Russian troops were no longer counted in the troop strength of the Romanian Front, and at the beginning of February, MCG proclaimed that the "Russian army no longer exists." During February and

March, large numbers of unattached Russian soldiers wandering about were rounded up, gathered in detachments, and transported into Russia. Soon, only commissions to liquidate depots of Russian supplies remained. However, there was still evidence of the once mighty Russian Army in Romania. As Colonel Antonescu put it, "Moldavia was full of abandoned horses, cannon, guns, and wagons."[30]

16
Bessarabia and the Peace of Buftea: January–March 1918

BESSARABIA

Lenin's decision for peace and the rapid decomposition of the Russian army left the Romanian army as the only disciplined Allied military force on the Eastern Front. Despite the Focşani armistice, Allied leaders, especially the French, still hoped to use it as a *môle de résistance*, a nucleus around which to build an anti-Bolshevik coalition to continue the war in South Russia. The Ukraine, the Don Cossacks, and various "volunteer" groups under former tsarist generals were considered as other prospects. Berthelot, who was selected to lead this endeavor, expressed to Clemenceau his skepticism but agreed to "attempt the impossible." Stability in Bessarabia was a sine qua non for this plan as well as for the survival of Romania itself. As the rear area of the front, it provided access to food, armament depots, and the outside world. Moreover, it was the designated place of refuge should a new offensive of the Central Powers necessitate the abandonment of Moldavia. The flight of Russian troops eastward, as Brătianu had anticipated, transferred the problem of revolutionary disorder from Moldavia to Bessarabia, which was ill-prepared to deal with it.[1]

THE MOLDAVIAN REPUBLIC

During 1917, Bessarabia had been undergoing a political and socioeco-
nomic revolution as it sought to implement its goals of the March revolution: provincial autonomy, democracy, and land reform. The political
process was dominated by intellectuals from the majority population, Romanian in ethnicity, language, and culture. Many Bessarabians had developed an independent Moldavian sense of identity and were skeptical of
restoring the province's historical connection with Romania. Minority
groups (Ukrainian, Russian, Gaugaz-Bulgarian, Greek, Jewish) were
strongly opposed to union. For peasants, the overriding concern was land
reform. During 1917, local peasant assemblies demanded the breakup of
the large latifundia and the distribution of land to the agricultural masses.
Many peasants had already stopped fulfilling obligations of rent and labor
to the landlord. Some had seized land and/or engaged in violence. Even
the lands of the monasteries and churches had not been exempt.[2]

In November 1917, Moldavian military officers and political leaders
took the initiative in creating an interim Bessarabian parliament called the
Sfatul Ţării (National Council). Seats were allotted on the basis of nationalities as well as special interest groups. Ethnic Moldavians formed a majority. The Sfatul Ţării met for the first time on 4 December in Chişinău and
on 15 December declared Bessarabia to be the Moldavian Autonomous Republic within a federated Russia. The most pressing of its many problems
was maintaining public order in the face of peasant unrest, minority discontent, and now the influence of unruly revolutionary Russian soldiers.
A recently formed Moldavian regiment proved unable to provide security.
It lacked discipline and leadership, eventually coming under Bolshevik influence.[3] With growing disorder putting its own existence in jeopardy, the
Sfatul Ţării turned to Allied representatives in Iaşi for assistance. Berthelot
promised money, armaments, and French instructors to create a Moldavian
army. This required time; the need was immediate. Widespread suspicion
of Romanian annexationist intentions made it impolitic for the Sfatul Ţării
to ask for the assistance of the Romanian army directly. Hence an initial request was made for Czech, Serb, or Transylvanian units from Kiev. The first
two were unavailable. Although a contingent of Transylvanians prepared
to travel to Chişinău, it was clear in Iaşi that this ad hoc force would be un-
equal to the task. After much hesitation, the Sfatul Ţării asked Shcherba-

chev, as front commander, to send "a division from among the troops he disposes." "It is up to us, you and me," Berthelot wrote Prezan on 5 January, "to bring General Shcherbachev to decide that this division be Romanian." Shcherbachev agreed and met with Berthelot and Prezan on 12 January to prepare the operation.[4]

The Romanian cabinet, however, hesitated before giving its approval, weighing the risks involved: further weakening of the Siret Front, tempting the Central Powers to attack, and inciting a declaration of war from Lenin. The cabinet preferred sending smaller, lower-profile detachments. But MCG, as Colonel Antonescu explained to the French mission, insisted on a major operation with an experienced division in order to preclude an embarrassment at the hands of the Bolsheviks. On 16 January, Brătianu and his cabinet approved the operation. Although the immediate Romanian motive was military necessity, the historic hope of uniting Bessarabia with the *Patria Mamă* was not absent. It had been reawakened by recent indications that a breakup of the Russian empire was at hand. At the same time, the Central Powers were encouraging the Romanians to lay hands on the province as a quid pro quo for giving up Dobrogea. Brătianu, looking far ahead, recognized the value of a military presence there as a bargaining chip in postwar peace negotiations or as compensation if Romania's war aims could not be achieved in Austria-Hungary. Then, "it could not be said that we had fought and suffered for nothing."[5]

While Romanian intervention was being organized, the situation in Chişinău reached a crisis. Bolshevik-inspired forces seized power on 18 January with the help of the Russian garrison. They disarmed a contingent of Transylvanian volunteers who finally arrived to aid the Sfatul Ţării. Two members of Shcherbachev's staff who accompanied them were brutally beaten to death. Some leaders of the Sfatul Ţării fled to Iaşi or went into hiding. "What should have been a police action," Berthelot commented, "now becomes a military operation which necessarily involves the shedding of blood."[6] On 21 January, MCG ordered the Romanian 11th ID to advance into Bessarabia. Its mission was "to assure the transport of supply trains on the Bender–Socola line" and "to assure order in Chişinău and Bender." In preparation for any eventuality, three additional divisions were positioned along the Prut, the 13th ID, the 2nd CD, and the 1st CD. All four divisions were soon organized as the VI Army Corps, commanded by General Ion Istrate. General Prezan issued a proclamation assuring Bessarabi-

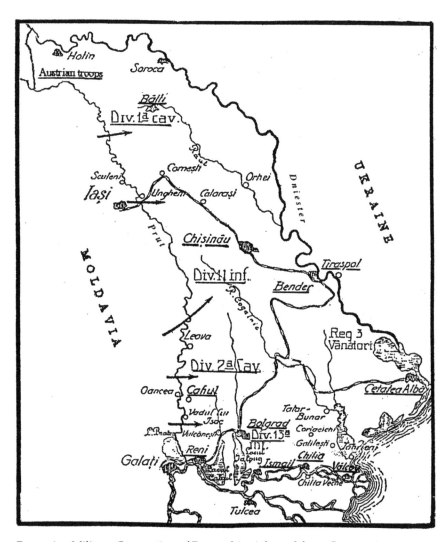

Romanian Military Occupation of Bessarabia. Adapted from Constantin
Kiriţescu, *Istoria războiului pentru întregirea româniei,* 2nd ed. (Bucharest: Editura
Casei Şcoalelor, 1925)

ans that Romanian intervention, undertaken at the request of General
Shcherbachev, was only to restore order and protect transport of supplies.
The Romanian army would be withdrawn when replaced by other forces;
it posed no threat to the Moldavian state. Prezan's pledge appeared in the
press and was disseminated by airplane. Berthelot and French minister
Saint-Aulaire gave similar public assurances.[7]

OCCUPYING BESSARABIA

On the night of 23 January, the 11th ID crossed the Prut. One brigade traveled by train directly to Chişinău, the other by foot, approaching the city from the southwest. Neither met significant resistance. The first contingent entered the city quietly on 26 January, accompanied by two leaders of the Sfatul Țării. Revolutionary forces fled east to Bender. The Bolshevik committee of Chişinău, from its refuge there, sent a radiogram to all Russian troops still on the Romanian Front calling on them for aid, urging them to "[take] the road to Bessarabia with their guns." On 27 January, the pompous commander of the 11th ID, General Ernest Broşteanu, arranged his triumphal entry into Chişinău, accompanied by a band and artillery salvoes. In an address to a special session of the Sfatul Țării, he promised not to interfere in its work in organizing the new republic but to defend the life and property of its citizens from anarchy.[8]

Lenin reacted angrily to the Romanian intervention in Bessarabia, breaking off diplomatic relations, confiscating the Romanian treasury held in Moscow, and imprisoning and then expelling the Romanian minister. In Odessa, the Rumcherod, a Bolshevik military–revolutionary committee influenced by Romanian socialist Christian Rakovskii, who had been co-opted into Soviet leadership, initiated a reign of terror against the large number of Romanian citizens who had taken up refuge there. Throughout February, the Romanian government, with the mediation of Entente representatives in Odessa, and especially Colonel Joe Boyle, a Canadian, negotiated with Rakovskii and the Rumcherod to rescue the hostages and avoid a military confrontation with the Bolsheviks. The latter appeared necessary because the Central Powers were now threatening to denounce the armistice.[9]

After securing Chişinău, Broşteanu sent detachments to surrounding cities, including Orhei, 45 kilometers to the north. A larger unit in battalion strength with artillery and cavalry advanced 60 kilometers southeast along the railroad to Bender. After receiving hostile fire from hills and villages en route, the detachment commander delayed his attack on the city pending the arrival of substantial reinforcements. On 2 February Bender was easily occupied, with the defenders retreating east across the Dniester to Tiraspol. Inexplicably, the Romanians failed to secure the bridge or disarm the local Russian–Ukrainian population. Consequently, their opponents counterattacked and retook the city, assisted by Russian soldiers, a Ukrainian unit, and 200 members of a Romanian revolutionary battalion recruited from among deserters and workers in Odessa. Embarrassed, MCG ordered the 1st CD to send aid to the 11th ID "as much and as soon as possible." On 7 February, a Romanian force of six battalions of infantry with artillery and a brigade of the 1st CD launched a new attack. By noon, the defenders and many of the local population again retreated over the Dniester to Tiraspol. This time the Romanians properly secured the city, including its medieval fortress. Three Romanian officers and 38 soldiers were killed in the battle of Bender. "A bloody reprisal followed against the bands of the city," according to the Romanian historian Kirițescu.[10]

While the 11th ID was pacifying Central Bessarabia, the three other divisions of the VI Corps had been given missions in other regions. On 24–25 January, two detachments of the 13th ID crossed the Prut. One followed the river south to the southern Bessarabian rail terminus of Reni. The other headed southeast to Bolgrad, the erstwhile headquarters of the Russian 6th Army. Both cities were easily occupied and order was restored. Army commanders characterized Romanian populations as "benevolent" but the majority Bulgarian residents of Bolgrad as "very upset because a Bulgarian republic had already been proclaimed." There "ten bandits" were reported executed.[11] From Reni and Bolgrad the 13th ID moved systematically down the Danube and then along the Black Sea coast. The populations of this region were primarily non-Romanian, and the major cities were under the control of "Soldiers, Workers and Peasants Soviets." They were supported by revolutionary elements of the Russian Danube flotilla and by deserters from the Romanian army and navy organized as Red Guards. Ismail, the first objective, was easily occupied on 3 February. Soviet sources reported that "14 sailors were executed." After leaving a security battalion at Ismail, detachments of the 13th ID continued on to Chilea. Here several ships had been taken over by Romanian deserters, and Russian revolutionaries had burned a great part of the city. With the assistance of marines from Romanian Danube monitors, Chilea was occupied on 8 February. Next was Vâlcov, which harbored the majority of the Russian Danube flotilla. This city was expected to offer strong resistance because a new contingent of Romanian Red Guards had been sent from Odessa. On 18 February, after several days of exchanging artillery and monitor fire, the defenders boarded the Russian ships and left. The last objective of the 13th ID was Cetatea

Alba (Akerman), located where the Dniester entered the Black Sea. During its 150-kilometer advance from the Romanian frontier, the division had been diminished by several security detachments left along the way. Consequently MCG ordered it be assisted by elements of the 11th ID and 2nd CD. After a march of 60 kilometers in four days, the Romanian forces entered the city without fighting on 8 March.[12]

Although the organized centers of resistance in southern Bessarabia had now been neutralized, opposition to the Romanian occupation continued in outlying areas. It was supported by peasant discontent and encouraged by the Rumcherod from Odessa. The 2nd CD was given the task of pacifying the countryside. Its first order of the day was to complete the mandate given when the Romanian army first crossed the Prut: "No armed Russian unit is to be left behind. . . . All fugitive Russian soldiers will be expedited . . . across the Dniester." Additionally, the 2nd CD was charged with disarming the civilian populations and, if hostile, "bringing them to obedience." In the absence of adequate local police and gendarmes, Romanian divisions had to assume administrative and security responsibilities.[13]

On 30 January, MCG ordered the 1st CD, commanded by General Mihai Schina, to occupy northern Bessarabia, concentrating its activity in the vicinity of Bălți. After a march of almost 200 kilometers, advance units reached this city on 3 February. Organized opposition to Romanian intervention had already appeared in this region among the predominantly Russian–Ukrainian population. On 22 January, the Bălți Soviet had denounced the Sfatul Țării. On 27 January, a regional peasant assembly did the same and protested to the Romanian government "against the flagrant intervention of a foreign country in our internal affairs." The assembly proposed sending agents to other regions to promote the organization of military units. "In the Bălți region," concluded a report of the Romanian security services, "among the peasants a spirit of revolt and agitation against the entrance of Romanian troops into Bessarabia dominates." Because of the mood in Bălți, Schina decided to await the arrival of all of his forces before attacking the city. On 5 February, the "Bolshevik" defenders, peasants, and Russian soldiers, led by a Moldavian officer, were easily overcome and disarmed. Schina thereupon sent detachments into the surrounding regions, disarming the civilian population, which was well endowed with weapons looted from depots or received from departing Russian soldiers.

At Ocniţa, the division reported, "Bolsheviks expelled after a short fight with many arrested. Fifteen were executed." On 8 March, Schina declared the entire area "cleansed of hostile elements." However, Romanian patrols continued to draw gunfire from a number of villages for weeks thereafter.[14]

The penetration of the Romanian army into northern Bessarabia reached as far as the line Ocniţa–Mogilev–Soroca. Farther north, Austrian forces from the command of General Hermann Kövess had already entered Bessarabia as the Russian forces evacuated. On 24 February, the Austrians pushed forward to the Nowosielica–Hotin line to counter the Romanian advance. Three days later, they reached their goal, the railroad transversing northern Bessarabia, which they intended to use to transport troops to occupy Odessa. On 2 March, a Romanian unit confronted an Austrian troop train. Its commander asked the Romanians to withdraw. A potentially serious incident was avoided when MCG decided not to withdraw, but also not to oppose by force the Austrian transit. Because negotiations between Romania and the Central Powers were already under way for concluding peace, a mutual desire to avert an armed conflict prevailed. With the exception of this northern region, which included the historic Romanian fortress city of Hotin, by the end of March, the Romanian army had completed the occupation of Bessarabia. The human cost had been relatively small: three officers and 122 men killed; 12 officers and 300 men wounded; 151 men missing.[15]

RULING BESSARABIA

Although occupying Bessarabia had been relatively easy, ruling it was not. In a memorandum of 15 February, Prezan stated, with a measure of insight, his view of the problems. First, the leaders of the Sfatul Ţării were "educated men of great enthusiasm but without . . . political experience." Second, the agrarian question would be a continuing problem because "most of the latifundia have been confiscated. . . . One could not restore former properties other than with great risk." The cultivation of the land should be undertaken "starting from the present *de facto* situation." Third, the present Moldavian army was a "latent volcano, they do nothing. . . . Being contaminated with revolutionary ideas . . . they are actually dangerous. . . . It would be good to renounce for a moment the formation of a special Moldavian Army." Finally, "Police and gendarmerie do not exist. . . . There is an imperative need to organize these two services." The conduct of the Romanian army in implementing this policy was controversial and was met with considerable suspicion and hostility from broad segments of the population. Moldavian nationalists and the minorities feared their embryonic democracy would be throttled. Peasants were apprehensive that agricultural reform would be reversed. These concerns were exacerbated by the initial behavior of some Romanian officers, especially General Broşteanu. In Chişinău, he ruled with an iron hand, ignoring the Sfatul Ţării for the most part. He instituted a severe regime of martial law, including use of the death penalty. When the president of the Sfatul Ţării informed him that execution had been forbidden in the Moldavian Republic, Broşteanu is alleged to have replied, "I am the judge and for all crimes serious punishment will be applied." Crimes liable for court-martial included "insults, oral or written, of Romanian officers and soldiers."[16]

Three days after the arrival of the Romanian army, Captain Sarret, the French consul in Chişinău, began sending Saint-Aulaire reports highly critical of Broşteanu. He accused him of supporting only the program of the Moldavian National Party "leading to the annexation of Bessarabia [by Romania]." He passed on a host of complaints of arbitrary arrests, brutality, and anti-Semitism. "One feels the troops of General Broşteanu treat Moldavia a little like a conquered country," Berthelot commented. Broşteanu's arbitrary behavior was most evident in his treatment of the Moldavian Peasant Party. At its congress in Chişinău on 30 January, Sarret reported, "a small Romanian detachment surrounded the hall, setting up machine guns in the surrounding streets. At 2:00 P.M., a Romanian major, accompanied by M. Erhan [a director of the Sfatul Ţării] entered the hall with armed soldiers and declared the session over." When questioned later, Broşteanu declared he did not consider his behavior a violation of the Romanian promise not to mix in the internal affairs of Bessarabia. He justified other repressive actions by insisting his purpose in coming was to "fight Bolshevism and no one could impede him in this battle." Berthelot felt it necessary to instruct General Charles Vouillemin, his chief of mission in Chişinău, to intervene more actively with Broşteanu "to protect Bessarabians against possible violence of the Romanians."[17]

While coercion quickly restored order in Chişinău and other cities, the Romanian army continued to encounter hostility and peasant unrest in the countryside. General Schina records that in the Balți region peasants "expressed hate toward us. They cried out that we had come to reinstate the large landowners in their rights and to subject the peasants to our [Romanian] agrarian system, conforming to which the peasant is obligated to work without pay for the boyars five days a week while he is permitted to work for himself only one day." Initially, in some regions at least, the army did intervene, as a Romanian official reported, "taking the part of the proprietor and obligating the peasant to restore everything." On 12 February, Colonel Anastasiu warned MCG from Chișinău that it was "absolutely necessary to stop the action of turning back the property of the great estates which the peasants received." General Lupescu immediately ordered that the army "no longer intervene in relations between proprietors and peasants other than to prevent new devastations and plundering." Another peasant complaint was the army's requisition of food at "miserable prices." "Romanian soldiers take forcibly from the peasants as much bread as they need" was a charge in the Bessarabian press. This issue was exacerbated by a poor harvest, looting by Russian soldiers, and the acute shortage of food in Moldavia, which forced the army in Bessarabia to "live off the land."[18]

UNION WITH ROMANIA

While pointing out that the action of the Romanian command in Bessarabia was often arbitrary, it is important to emphasize that the army entered a province already beset with anarchy and where the infrastructure of administration and justice had broken down. "Most villages and towns," Colonel Anastasiu wrote, "are still in the situation created by revolutionary militia . . . [which] is worse than the police and authorities that preceded. . . . Many gendarmerie personnel of the highest order are needed." He urged the High Command to set up a complete military system of administration and justice. Critics point out, however, that by dismissing Russian-appointed incumbents, the Romanians contributed to the problem of public order. In evaluating the Romanian presence, it is also important to keep in mind that it was welcomed by many, especially the unionists in the Moldavian National Party. Even those who suspected Romanian intentions were pragmatic enough to admit that the survival of their republic was dependent on the Romanian army. As a leader of the Sfatul Ţării acknowledged publicly, "In the districts where there are Romanian troops, quiet rules. . . . However in the districts where there are no troops . . . anarchy dominates."[19] Most of the great landowners were, of course, grateful. The Russian A. N. Krupsensky, who later bitterly criticized the Romanians, wrote to General Istrate on 14 April, "After a year of Bolshevik horror, . . . thanks to the Romanian Army order has been restored." Not a few state employees also welcomed Romanian rule. A railroad worker told a Romanian diplomat that he and his coworkers, weeks in arrears in wages, "want to ask the Romanian government that in case they have the intention to annex Bessarabia that they act and also incorporate the functionaries, paying them their salaries."[20]

By mid-March, Romania's decision to open peace negotiations, the entry of Austro-German troops into South Russia, and especially the territorial pretensions of Ukraine on Bessarabia, created a dangerous situation for the Moldavian Republic. Its only practical option was a more formal connection with Romania, the single protector it could count on. Therefore, pragmatism rather than popular enthusiasm motivated the Sfatul Ţării on 9 April to approve a conditional union. The divided vote on the Act of Union (86 for, 3 against, and 36 abstentions) indicated that, for many members, it was a necessary but not ideal solution. Internal discontent and hostility toward Romania persisted, encouraged by propaganda and agents originating from Bolshevik Russia, the Ukraine, and tsarist émigrés. The Romanian secret service was extended widely into Bessarabia during 1918, and the province continued to be ruled by a military governor under a state of siege.[21]

THE PEACE OF BUFTEA

The Austro-German commands had watched with keen interest the exodus of Russian troops from the front and the diversion of Romanian divisions to control them. These developments restored to them the option of using military action to force Romania to sign a peace treaty. Mackensen had hoped to accomplish this politically by using Germanophile politicians in Bucharest to overturn Brătianu and King Ferdinand with the acquiescence of the Romanian army. At Focşani, however, it had become clear that

Premier Alexandru Marghiloman (center) with Sfatul Țării at signing of the Act of Union of Bessarabia with Romania. From *Lui Alexandru Marghiloman. Omagiu* (Bucharest: Tiparul Cultura Națională, 1924)

the latter was committed to the king and prepared to resist. As Captain Horstmann, chief political officer at OKM, informed Berlin on 1 January, "All attempts to establish contacts with its [army] leaders to support a political coup have failed." But Mackensen was still reluctant to renew the fighting. He held the Romanian army in high regard. His own 9th Army had been weakened by transfers, including some of its best units and its heavy artillery. The Austro-Hungarian command was in the same position. Reports given at AOK in January stressed the value of the Romanian army and, in contrast, the weakness of Habsburg units. The latter's morale, training, and nourishment were low; insufficient horses remained to move the artillery.[22] However, by the end of January, with the complete disintegration of the Russian army, the equation had changed. The Romanian army alone could not possibly cover the front. Even if all of its 15 infantry divisions were available, an Austrian analysis concluded, each would be required to defend a segment of 22 kilometers, "a situation of no military value."[23] Furthermore, as we have seen, Lenin's January threats directed at Iași raised the possibility the Romanian army could face war on two fronts.

THE ULTIMATUM OF THE CENTRAL POWERS

Consequently, on 24 January Mackensen wired Ludendorff: "This may be the time to force Romania to peace." He proposed sending an "ultimatum demanding peace [negotiations] within 24 hours, otherwise the armistice will be denounced." Ludendorff found this "militarily correct" and telegraphed Arz: "OK Mackensen believes that with its present power it can carry out a successful operation on the lower Siret if, at the same time, the Army Group Kövess could push in the direction of Târgu Ocna-Onești with the strongest power possible." Arz bought into the idea and planning was initiated for a joint operation under the code name Halali. In addition to the attack of Mackensen's Army Group on the Siret and that of the Austro-Hungarian 1st Army over the Carpathian passes, the Austro-Hungarian 7th Army would invade northern Moldavia from Bukovina.[24] Mackensen anticipated sending an ultimatum at the end of January. However, General Max Hoffmann, leader of the peace negotiations with Bolshevik Russia at Brest-Litovsk, requested a direct threat be postponed until after the impending conclusion of a peace treaty with the Ukraine. Consequently, the radiogram Mackensen sent to Iași on 31 January contained only a summons to meet at Focșani on 4 February to discuss "Russo-Romanian troop changes which have rendered impossible the maintenance of the [Focșani] convention." When Ludendorff asked Mackensen's command what it would do if no Romanian negotiators showed up, General Hell replied, "Denounce the armistice immediately! What follows is conditional."[25]

To prepare the basic conditions of peace to be presented to Romania, German and Austrian Foreign Ministers Richard von Kühlmann and Count Ottokar Czernin met with Ludendorff in Berlin on 4 February and agreed on the following points:

Political—dismissal of the Brătianu government.
Territorial—cession of the entire Dobrogea to the Central Powers
    jointly, and frontier cessions to Austria-Hungary; in return, the Cen-

tral Powers would support Romania's territorial acquisitions in Bessarabia.

Military—demobilization of the Romanian army except for the divisions facing Russia; dismissal of Entente military missions.

Dynastic questions—to be considered an internal affair of the Romanian people.

Economic—imprecise demands but of far-reaching consequence.

Occupation—continuation indefinitely of the German administration in Wallachia.

To entice the Romanians to the table, the full extent of these demands were not to be revealed to them until after the negotiations began.[26]

Mackensen's radiogram was received in Iaşi like a long-expected announcement of doom. Berthelot, under orders from Paris to keep Romania in the war, tried to portray it as a bluff. But Romanian political and military leaders perceived it for what it was: the preliminary to the denunciation of the armistice. Brătianu, convinced for some time that peace was inevitable, had already contacted Entente ministers seeking tacit approval to enter into negotiations. Otherwise, he pleaded, Romania would be "condemned to suicide." A crown council, meeting on 2 February authorized a delegation headed by General Lupescu to go to Focşani to "determine the enemy's intentions." Anticipating the denunciation of the armistice, MCG prepared operational instructions, which were issued on 3 February. It estimated—quite accurately, as German sources prove—the strength of the German, Austro-Hungarian, and Bulgarian forces at 20½ divisions of infantry and 9½ divisions of cavalry, a total of 159,400 "bayonets." It also recognized that the fighting capacity of the Habsburg divisions was "very weak," their morale "low," and that some German divisions had been weakened since the armistice by transfers of isolated subunits, plus younger officers and men. On the other hand, the order continued, "The present front is much too extended for our total means . . . [and] cannot be maintained. . . . In case the enemy attacks with superior force, all terrain west of the Siret will be disputed step by step but only through rearguard fighting and maneuver. True resistance will be executed from positions . . . organized . . . between the Siret and Prut." Reminding his army of "our total isolation and reduced means," Prezan called for "spiritual perseverance, courage, and tenacity . . . to continue the battle, to avenge the past, and to assure the future."[27]

When the negotiations opened at Focşani on 4 February, General Hell insisted that the existing armistice was no longer viable as a result of the removal of Russian and Romanian troops from the front. The time had come for a "clarification of Romania's intentions from both the military and political point of view." General Lupescu responded that he was authorized to negotiate only on military matters but would ask for instructions. During the night, he spoke "long and often" via telex with Iaşi. His only guidance from Prezan was to prolong the negotiations. Consequently, all he could say in the session on 5 February was that he had received no instructions regarding the attitude of his government. However, in a personal conversation with General Hranilovici, the Austro-Hungarian delegate, Lupescu remarked that it was his feeling that a change of opinion in favor of peace was under way in Iaşi. Frustrated and impatient, Hell demanded that Lupescu return within four days accompanied by a political plenipotentiary. The Austro-German commands reaffirmed their determination to denounce the armistice and attack if Romania did not begin negotiations for peace immediately.[28]

AVERESCU AND THE CENTRAL POWERS

Brătianu was, in fact, already orchestrating a response to an anticipated ultimatum. Well aware he was persona non grata to the Central Powers, and unwilling to accept the odium of capitulation personally, he had been arranging for Averescu to succeed him as prime minister. The general's prestige and popularity in the army and the civilian population would be a stabilizing influence as the nation paid the painful price of peace. Averescu, politically ambitious, naively believed he could exploit a personal friendship with Mackensen that dated back to his years (1895–1897) as military attaché in Berlin. From the beginning of the war, Averescu had favored peace over a military *Götterdämmerung*. Since December, he had actively advocated peace negotiations. On 7 February, Brătianu invited the general to lunch and laid out in detail his guidelines for peacemaking: drawing out the negotiations as long as possible, then a settlement that preserved the

dynasty and territorial integrity, except for Dobrogea. The next day, Brătianu resigned, and the king asked Averescu to form a new government.
What the general did not know was that Brătianu and the circle around the
king viewed his government only as a transition to a future regime led by
Alexandru Marghiloman and other conservative politicians in Bucharest.[29]

The governmental change in Iaşi forced the Central Powers to extend
until 13 February their deadline for a Romanian plenipotentiary to arrive
in Focşani. The signing of the peace treaty with Ukraine on 9 February increased their hope for an agreement with Romania "on the diplomatic
route"; if not, then "a decision through the sword." Averescu immediately
dispatched three delegates to Bucharest to seek an additional 20-day pro-
longation of the armistice. One of them, his longtime *chef de cabinet*, Colonel
Ressel, requested a personal meeting between Averescu and Mackensen.
The field marshal readily agreed to meet the new premier on 18 February.
An extension of the armistice until 22 February was granted despite the reluctance of OHL and AOK. To the former, it meant a delay in troop transport; to the latter, it meant delay in grain imports from South Russia
recently made possible by the treaty with Ukraine. Austro-German negotiators were encouraged by Ressel's private assurance that Averescu intended to conclude peace, "repeating three times, he will."[30]

The field marshal received Averescu with great cordiality at his headquarters, located in Prince Ştirbey's palace at Buftea, just outside Bucharest.
Mackensen, who was vainly proud about his own physique, described
Averescu as "noticeably aged but in body and spirit, however, not senile."
The atmosphere was comradely as they exchanged memories of their contacts 20 years previously. The premier, Mackensen noted, "spoke again and
again" about his connections with Germany. In this conversation and one
that followed with Hell and Horstmann, Averescu was given only a general statement of the enemy's terms; he received the impression that there
was room for negotiation. However, on one issue Averescu himself was
adamant: a demand to cede all of Dobrogea would wreck the peace negotiations. The Germans received the impression that if only the region south
of the Cernavoda-Constanţa railroad were demanded, Averescu would accept all the other conditions. It was clear that Dobrogea was the Gordian
knot of the negotiations. While Germany, Austria-Hungary, and Turkey
were not averse to a compromise on this issue, the Bulgarians were. They
insisted with emotional fervor that all of Dobrogea was their rightful booty.

Averescu, now premier, arrives at Buftea to meet with Mackensen, 18 February 1918. From *The Times History of the War* (London: The Times, 1917–1919)

To deny it to them risked driving Bulgaria into the arms of the Entente. Berlin and Vienna were on the horns of a dilemma.[31]

Before returning to Iaşi, Averescu requested an opportunity to meet directly with Kühlmann and Czernin. Still involved in the Brest-Litovsk negotiations, they were not inclined initially to give their attention to Romania until finished with the Russians. Arz gave voice to his impatience, shared by Ludendorff, to determine Iaşi's intentions: "It is essential to clear up immediately the Romanian situation. . . . Whether it results in peace or renewal of war . . . makes no difference." Resolution of Romania's attitude was more important than "peace with Lenin and Trotsky." Persuaded, the two foreign ministers traveled together to Bucharest to meet with Averescu on 24–25 February. Briefed beforehand, Kühlmann was surprised to learn Mackensen and his staff valued the Romanian army "very highly." Hell warned that conquering Moldavia would be no *Spaziergang* but would involve "a difficult and costly operation." "This does not correspond to the view we came here with," Kühlmann wrote to the Reichschancellor in Berlin, "according to which the final defeat of Romania would be hardly more difficult and costly than the military promenade against the Bolsheviks." Privately, he questioned "if it was responsible . . . to sacrifice German blood in great quantities to force Romania to cede all of Dobrogea to Bulgaria."[32]

Nevertheless, Kühlmann allowed Czernin to dominate the meeting on 24 February with Averescu and to present the full demands of the Central Powers in "a manner which will leave no doubt that if they are refused we will attack." Averescu was shocked upon hearing their conditions, some of which had been omitted or at least minimized in his earlier interview with Mackensen. "Very upset," Averescu hardened his own attitude, declaring the cession of Dobrogea "especially impossible." The meeting was unproductive and lasted only two hours. The general left for Iaşi that night. Colonel Ressel explained privately to Hranilovici that the premier would be immediately overthrown in Iaşi if he agreed to the cession of all of Dobrogea. But, he added, "one could, in the end, . . . live with" the cession of southern Dobrogea up to the Cernavoda–Constanţa railway. The cession of the railway, the port of Constanţa, and Northern Dobrogea would be completely unacceptable. "As far as he [Ressel] could see," Hranilovici reported, "the war would be continued."[33]

As their meeting ended, Czernin had asked Averescu to arrange for him a personal interview with King Ferdinand. This meeting took place on 27 February near Mărăşeşti on the royal train. In a 45-minute conversation "under four eyes," Czernin "did not spare him anything," demanding acceptance of all conditions within 48 hours. Otherwise the resumption of the fighting would "mean the end of Romania and the dynasty." Ferdinand, intimidated and crying at times, said he would allow negotiations on the basis of Old Dobrogea, but the entire province could not be ceded. He could not find a cabinet to accept it. At this point, Czernin suggested Marghiloman. In conclusion, he reiterated his 48-hour deadline. The king promised a reply by the afternoon of 1 March.[34] After Czernin's visit, with war increasingly possible, Averescu signed off on an agreement with the Rumcherod designed to release Romanian hostages in Odessa and reduce the threat of hostilities with Bolshevik Russia. This so-called Rakovskii accord also provided for the retreat of the Romanian army into Russia if necessary.[35]

On 28 February Ludendorff ordered Mackensen to implement operation Halali. OKM was given permission to utilize the five German divisions under order to entrain for the west; the attack could begin in four to seven days. Arz ordered Kövess to begin his operations 72 hours after Czernin's ultimatum expired. However, Austro-Hungarian participation was thrown into question by Kaiser Karl, who objected to resuming the war over Dobrogea simply to "satisfy Bulgaria's unrestrained desire for conquest." Czernin tried to overcome his monarch's resistance, but Karl came back with a direct command. Only if the Romanians refused a settlement guaranteeing them northern Dobrogea would he allow the participation of Austro-Hungarian forces.[36] Alarmed, Mackensen warned that without Austrian cooperation, a successful outcome could not be counted on; the offensive would, in a short time, come to a standstill. The result "would appear as a victory of the Romanians." OHL agreed that without Austrian support the operation would be hopeless. Kühlmann added in a letter to the Reichschancellor that inability to enforce an ultimatum would put the Central Powers in a "laughable and dangerous position." To break Karl's resistance, Kaiser Wilhelm wired an appeal to his colleague to join him in "immediate and decisive action" if Romania rejected Czernin's ultimatum. Karl finally agreed to commit Habsburg troops, but only after Czernin promised that if Romania continued its refusal, Conservative leader Alexandru Marghiloman be sent to Iaşi with a compromise offer in which Romania could keep Northern Dobrogea. "This would place us in a difficult position vis-a-vis the Bulgarians," Czernin admitted, "but we will use it as a last resort."[37]

ROMANIA SUBMITS

Meanwhile, in Iaşi, turmoil reigned as Romanian leaders wrestled with a response to Czernin's ultimatum. Averescu tried to stall for time, first by asking for direct contact between Ferdinand and Karl. Czernin demanded prior acceptance of all conditions. Next, Averescu sent a list of his delegates for the peace negotiations, including several out-of-country diplomats, which would necessitate a delay. Again Czernin's answer was negative. But when informed a Romanian crown council was scheduled to meet in Iaşi, he did extend the deadline until noon on 4 March. Orders had already gone out for Halali, with hostilities to begin at noon the next day if the Romanian answer was unsatisfactory.[38] On 2 March, the first of three crown councils was convened by King Ferdinand. An atmosphere of tragedy pervaded the meeting. The monarch was so emotional he could hardly speak. His presentation ended in tears. The majority agreed that peace was inevitable, but no one wanted to accept responsibility for a peace settlement so damaging to the nation. Brătianu suggested that Averescu negotiate with "hand on sword." The premier pleaded that he lacked a sufficient political base and urged Brătianu to undertake the negotiations. The latter refused and suggested calling Marghiloman. No decision was reached. Immediately after the crown council, a telegram arrived denouncing the armistice.[39]

Meanwhile, the Romanian MCG had been preparing for the resumption of fighting. On 2 March, army commands were warned to let the enemy initiate any hostile action. The next day, new operational instructions for responding to an enemy attack were issued. The analogous order issued a month earlier had provided for a retreat into the area between the Siret and Prut. Now, with Bessarabia secure, MCG envisioned withdrawing the Romanian army farther east. It would concentrate between the Prut and the Dniester, south of a line running approximately Soroca–Bălți–Rădăuți. The retreat would commence as soon as the enemy began hostilities. Withdrawal of artillery was already under way. Supplies and equipment that could not be withdrawn were to be destroyed. In Antonescu's eloquent words, Prezan challenged his army: Romania was in an isolated military situation "without precedent in history," but "we must fight to save the honor, integrity and independence of the country." With Austro-German forces already in the Ukraine, the military situation of Romania was clearly hopeless. If the enemy attacked, Berthelot wired Paris, "The Romanian Army will make them pay dearly but their success is not in doubt. It will be only a matter of weeks."[40]

The denunciation of the armistice added to the panic in Iași as the government tried to come up with a response without making an abject capitulation to the enemy demands. After a conversation with the king following the crown council, Averescu wired Kühlmann and Czernin, arguing that his naming of a Romanian negotiating team "implicitly" implied an acceptance of their demands as "a basis" for negotiations to follow "in a spirit of conciliation and reciprocal concessions." The answer from Bucharest, which arrived during a second, again inconclusive, crown council, welcomed Averescu's response. It also insisted that before the armistice could be extended, a Romanian plenipotentiary must sign by noon on 5

March an acceptance of all demands of the Central Powers. Now added to the fundamental territorial and economic demands were three new military conditions: immediate demobilization of at least eight divisions; assistance in the transit of Austro-German troops to Odessa; and the immediate departure of the Allied military missions.[41] Averescu, especially upset over the demobilization demand, resigned, but the king refused to accept it. After a third crown council on the morning of 4 March, and another unsuccessful attempt to resign, Averescu telegraphed to Kühlmann and Czernin an acceptance of their conditions. It promised that Justice Minister Constantin Argetoianu, with full plenipotentiary powers, would arrive in Bucharest the next day to sign the desired document. Orders to Austro-German forces to implement Halali were suspended.[42]

Argetoianu, accompanied by a few economic and legal advisors, left Iaşi hurriedly on the night of 4 March. He lunched with General Morgen as he changed trains in Focşani. At the station, onlookers shouted, "Hurrah, Peace, Peace." Arriving at the Buftea station at 7:00 P.M. on 5 March, he discovered the Central Powers intended to make a spectacle of the signing ceremony. Conducted immediately to the Ştirbey palace, he was met on the steps by Mackensen, Hell, and Hranilovici. In the Great Hall, he found 120 enemy representatives already in place. "Without discussion worthy of the name," Argetoianu stepped to the table and signed the document, followed by Kühlmann, Czernin, and then the Bulgarian and Turkish representatives. As decided in Iaşi, all conditions were accepted without objection. The only exception was the new demand that Romanian troops evacuate all Austro-Hungarian territory immediately. Argetoianu signed this point ad referendum.[43] The Preliminary Peace of Buftea, as the document signed on 5 March came to be known, can be summarized in the following points.

1. Romania cedes Dobrogea to the Danube to the Central Powers.
2. The Central Powers will be "concerned" to maintain for Romania a trade route to the Black Sea via Constanţa.
3. Romania "concedes in principle" the boundary rectifications demanded by Austria-Hungary.
4. Romania "concedes in principle" measures in the economic realm "corresponding to the circumstances."
5. Romania will immediately demobilize at least eight divisions. When peace is reestablished between Russia and Romania, the

remainder of the Romanian army will be demobilized insofar as is not necessary for security on the Russian–Romanian frontier.

6. Romanian troops are obligated to evacuate the districts of Austria-Hungary they occupy.

7. The Romanian government commits itself to support the transport of troops of the Central Powers through Moldavia and Bessarabia to Odessa.

8. The Romanian government commits itself to dismiss Entente military officers serving in Romania.[44]

The next day, Argetoianu met with Kühlmann and Czernin to agree on a working plan for negotiating the details of the open-ended clauses, which were nothing less than a blank check. Four mixed commissions (political, military, legal, and economic) were proposed with the first plenary session to begin at the Cotroceni palace in Bucharest on 8 March. "We hope to finish things quickly," Czernin wrote to Vienna. His optimism ignored the complexity and controversy inherent in such issues as Bulgarian claims to Dobrogea, frontier rectifications, financial reparations to be paid by Romania, a trade agreement to exploit Romania's resources, especially oil, remodeling of the Danube commission to the favor of the Central Powers, and Jewish emancipation. Negotiations on the details of these issues would require almost two months as the Romanians fought to limit the exorbitant demands of their enemies and as serious differences arose among the Central Powers as they vied to profit at Romania's expense.[45]

17
Peace, Demobilization, Reentry: March–November 1918

While details of Romania's other concessions were being negotiated, the implementation of the military provisions of the Treaty of Buftea, which is the main concern of this study, began immediately. On 6 March, Averescu instructed MCG to evacuate Romanian troops from the Austro-Hungarian territory that they had occupied during the fighting or later as Russian troops left. Those in Bukovina began to depart the next day; others in Transylvania were gone by 12 March. Equally rapid was the departure of the French military mission and other Allied military personnel. Berthelot had begun preparations soon after Averescu's assumption of power told him that peace was inevitable. During the critical crown councils of 2–4 March, he was prepared to send his officers back to their Romanian units if resistance was decided on. He rejected Mackensen's offer of transit through Austria-Hungary, with a four-week quarantine in Wallachia, as demeaning. Instead he chose a long trek by train through the chaos of Bolshevik Russia. The departure of more than a thousand officers and men who had stood alongside their Romanian comrades in the heat of war was preceded by two days of emotional leave-taking. "The last word has not been spoken," Berthelot promised Romanian leaders. "France will never recognize this odious peace." The king and queen joined thousands at the station for a tearful farewell on 9 March. Impetuous Queen Marie, we are told, "threw herself sobbing on Berthelot's chest." The last of five trains departed Iași and headed for Odessa just after midnight amid heartfelt cries of "au revoir."[1]

The day before Berthelot's party departed, German troops in more than 100 trucks set out from Galați to cross Bessarabia, also en route to Odessa. Their mission was to establish a presence in this Black Sea port, the key to accessing the resources of the Ukraine, before the arrival of the Austrian column advancing down the Dniester from Bukovina. Fulfilling the obligation assumed at Buftea, Romanian officers helped organize the expedition and supplied it from Romanian army depots en route. The German column had no intention of intercepting the MMF, but King Ferdinand, upset by rumors to the contrary, ordered Averescu to warn Mackensen that its safe conduct was "a point of honor." Interfering with it would "endanger" the peace negotiations. In addition, MCG ordered Romanian army units in Bessarabia to impede the German advance, if necessary. This, in turn, called forth a threat from Mackensen to advance by force. The issue disappeared as the last train, with Berthelot on board, remained five hours ahead of the Germans on the route to Odessa. Romanian cooperation with the transit and supply of Austro-German units in the Ukraine continued throughout March and beyond.[2] Their presence proved to be in Romania's interest, helping to control anti-Romanian forces on the Dniester and to suppress the Bolshevik disorder in Odessa.

The immediate demobilization of a significant proportion of the Romanian army was Mackensen's prerequisite for the release of additional German divisions for the western offensive scheduled to open on 19 March. Also, as Ludendorff pointed out, once demobilization began, the Romanians would have less leverage in resisting far-reaching German economic and financial demands. On the other hand, Ludendorff did not desire the total demobilization of the Romanian army immediately. Its presence, especially in Bessarabia, was a useful counterweight to the Bolsheviks, covering the back of German and Austrian forces in the Ukraine.[3] Consequently, in discussions of the Mixed Military Commission at Focșani on 8 March, General Emile Hell, Mackensen's chief of staff, asked that only five of the 15 Romanian infantry divisions be demobilized initially. Fifty thousand men from these divisions must pass into Wallachia. Reserve officers could accompany them, but active officers were required to remain in Moldavia. Of the other divisions, the two infantry divisions (plus the two cavalry divisions) in Bessarabia could remain fully mobilized. After

King Ferdinand and Queen Marie review troops as demobilization begins, March 1918. Arhivele Istorice Naţionale Centrale

the signing of the final peace treaty, eight more infantry divisions must be demobilized. As proof of Romania's intentions, Hell asked that the first contingent of demobilized soldiers cross the demarcation line within five days. Allowed to select the divisions to be demobilized initially, MCG issued an order on 12 March designating divisions 11 to 15, which were composed primarily of men native to Wallachia. Two contingents of the 14th ID, numbering some 3,500 men each, crossed the front during the third week of March. Thousands more would follow.[4]

As demobilized troops departed Moldavia for their homes in the occupied area, they were cautioned to "avoid manifestations and conflict that might offend Germany and Austria-Hungary. The terms of Romania's future might depend on this." They traveled by train and by foot. The latter were greeted in villages along the way by women who waited "hour by hour," hoping to catch sight of husbands and sons. Those who traveled by train, though unannounced, were greeted by thousands at Bucharest's Gara de Nord with flowers and shouts of "hurrah" and "long live Romania." The occupation authorities reacted with a decree forbidding such "manifestations and ovations." Nonetheless, the returnees continued to receive a hero's welcome. However, homecoming was not a pleasant experience for all. Some found themselves unemployed, others their houses requisitioned for enemy use. One young lieutenant, upon arriving at his home, was shocked to find German soldiers tending his two young children. His wife was away on a trip with their superior, a German officer, who had been quartered with his family.[5] Occupation authorities quickly concluded that demobilized soldiers were stimulating Romanian national pride and a spirit of resistance. "Returning soldiers enthusiastically tell of their victory over the Germans at Mărăşeşti," an Austrian official at Brăila reported on 30 March. The Austrian consul at Craiova noted a rise in patriotism and attributed it to the return of village schoolteachers. "Because of agitation by returning demobilized Romanians," the AOK liaison in Bucharest reported on 17 April, "the peasants in the occupied zones are hesitating to give corn and grain stocks so that continuing exports and present quantities are threatened. OK [Oberkommando] Mackensen asks for help and troops from Austria."[6] As the number of returnees increased to more than 200,000 during the spring and summer, so did Austro-German concern.

THE MARGHILOMAN GOVERNMENT

Just as demobilization got under way, Averescu resigned and was replaced by Alexandru Marghiloman, the leader of the Conservative Party who had remained behind in Bucharest in December 1916. Averescu had come under criticism, much of it unjust, on a variety of issues: the MMF evacuation crisis; the accord he had signed with the Bolsheviks over Bessarabia; and, above all, for allegedly being too compliant in accepting the terms offered at Buftea. Brătianu, who was "still the spiritual rector of Romania," arranged for Marghiloman to come to Iaşi for an interview with the king on 11 March. On the same day, the sovereign made it clear to Averescu that the time had come for him to go. The general submitted his resignation but then made a bizarre attempt to keep his position by soliciting Mackensen's support. The field marshal refused to go this far, but he did send a telegram to Ferdinand suggesting Averescu be retained as head of the army. This advice was ignored, of course. On 18 March, Marghiloman, who had the en-

Alexandru Marghiloman,
premier March–November
1918. From *Lui Alexandru
Marghiloman. Omagiu*
(Bucharest: Tiparul Cultura
Naţională, 1924)

dorsement of the Central Powers, was asked to form a new government.
The hope in Iaşi was that he might be able to lessen the severity of the peace
terms.[7]

Upon Marghiloman's return to Bucharest on 21 March, the Central Powers insisted he sign a second preliminary agreement specifying the frontier
rectifications and economic concessions left undefined in the Treaty of
Buftea. Under the rubric of "a defensible frontier," AOK presented a map
claiming not only the Carpathian passes but beyond, encompassing valuable timberlands, the key Danube port of Turnu-Severin, and Târgu Ocna
with nearby oil fields. "Under no circumstances," Marghiloman maintained, could he accept these extreme demands, which even OHL characterized as "colossal." Obstinate resistance by Romanian military negotiators was aided by the determination of both Ludendorff and Kaiser Karl
that the peace negotiations not be prolonged over this issue. Ultimately,
these demands were reduced by almost 75 percent, much to the displeasure of AOK and the Hungarians. Nevertheless, more than 5,000 square kilometers and 20,000 inhabitants were included. Reaching agreement on the

economic concessions was more complex, necessitating seven subcom-
missions working simultaneously. Ludendorff demanded that the details
on fundamental issues be committed to paper and initialed preliminary
to the departure of German divisions to the Western Front. Lacking an
agreement by 28 March, military measures against Romania would be prepared. On 25 March, Marghiloman was told that if he did not initial an
agreement that very night, the armistice would be denounced. At 4:00 A.M.
on the 26th, after hours of frenzied negotiation, the premier, surrounded
by a battery of military and diplomatic officials of Germany, Austria-
Hungary, Bulgaria, and Turkey, signed the desired document. "I was alone
and they were many," he wrote in his journal.[8] The Germans, now convinced that "by statement and by action the Romanian government has
given up any idea of further fighting," began troop transport with the 76th
ID on 27 March. It was followed at about ten-day intervals by the 109th ID,
the 216th ID, and the 115th ID. These divisions and others from Russia were
not available during the early weeks of Ludendorff's offensive. This has
led to speculation that the delay in concluding peace with Romania and
Russia may have contributed to its failure.[9]

Marghiloman, who commuted back and forth between Iași and Bucharest,
had a difficult task governing the still bifurcated nation. In Wallachia,
Mackensen's military administration remained in firm control, although
most Romanian ministries, including the War Ministry, established adjunct
departments in Bucharest. In fact, foreign minister Constantin Arion spent
most of his time there. But Marghiloman's authority was tightly circum-
scribed. If it could be said that in Wallachia he hardly ruled, in Moldavia,
the premier found it hard to rule. Viewed by many with suspicion and by
some as a traitor, Marghiloman encountered resistance to his authority, especially within the army. During the war, MCG under Prezan and Antonescu had become almost autonomous of the civilian government. To
gain control over the military, the new premier chose as minister of war the
retired general Constantin Hârjeu, another Conservative who had remained in Bucharest. Prezan was uncooperative, particularly in implementing demobilization and bypassing Hârjeu in nominating new generals. The king was complicit in the insubordination at MCG. For over a
month, he refused Marghiloman's request that Prezan be replaced by General Christescu. Finally, on 18 April, after the premier threatened to resign,
the monarch gave in. Prezan retired to his estate near Vaslui, and An-

tonescu was assigned to command a regiment remote from Iaşi. The army command was completely reorganized. MCG was eliminated, and its functions reverted to five army corps reporting directly to the General Staff (MSM). Three senior generals, Văitoianu, Coandă, and Grigorescu, were given the honorific title of inspector general.[10] Active-duty officers were divided over supporting Marghiloman and his policy of accommodation with the Central Powers. Some resigned in protest; a few emigrated to France. Officers, in the majority, were and remained Francophile. There were few true Germanophiles. Those like Christescu, who implemented Marghiloman's policy of accommodation, were motivated primarily by patriotism and pragmatism rather than a commitment to Germany. Even Francophiles like Grigorescu found it convenient to be pragmatic. Initially, the "hero of Mărăşeşti" had loudly advocated continuing the war à outrance. In June, he publicly toasted Marghiloman and proclaimed the peace settlement the "best possible" under the circumstances.[11]

At the same time as he was struggling to gain control of the army, Marghiloman and his negotiators were battling the Central Powers over the final details of the complex economic, financial, and legal clauses of a final peace treaty. The Romanians fought hard but had only limited success in whittling down their enemy's rapacious demands. The Treaty of Bucharest, signed on 7 May, confirmed and specified concessions agreed to earlier: the cession of Dobrogea to a condominium of the Central Powers; the cession of Carpathian passes to Austria-Hungary; the right to exploit some of Romania's most valuable natural resources, especially oil; unfavorable trade and financial arrangements; and partial emancipation to the nation's Jewish population. The military clauses, which are our concern here, were essentially unchanged from what had already been agreed on in March.[12]

DEMOBILIZATION UNDER THE TREATY OF BUCHAREST

With the signature of the treaty, the Romanians were obligated to begin demobilizing the remainder of their army, except for the divisions in Bessarabia. Mackensen sent Colonel Brandenstein, one of his staff officers, to Iaşi with a sizable staff to scrutinize the process. The Austrian High Command planned to send their own representative also, but German opposition delayed his arrival until October. At the War Ministry, Brandenstein reported,

Hârjeu received him "very cordially" and said he "looked forward to going hand in hand with Germany to the salvation of Romania." Christescu likewise pledged "very heartily" to cooperate completely: "All orders issued by him are at my disposal." Brandenstein thought it significant that each man received him alone, without witnesses. Colonel Carol Ressel, Averescu's *chef de cabinet* and an ethnic German who was assigned as Brandenstein's liaison with MSM, was less ingratiating. He termed the peace treaty "very hard" and expressed hope that "the last word for Romania was not yet spoken." "The idea that with the general peace conference more favorable conditions . . . for Romania would be achieved, one hears spoken repeatedly here," Brandenstein commented in his report.[13]

On 14 May, MSM issued an order for the demobilization of the eight infantry divisions in Moldavia. Complementary instructions for the marine and aviation services soon followed. Termination of the demobilization process was scheduled for 14 June. This target date proved to be unrealistic. Processing and transport of divisions 11 to 15 were still uncompleted. The addition of the thousands more exacerbated these problems. "Demobilization transport has virtually ceased," Austrian intelligence reported in June. In an attempt to bring demobilization into alignment with transportation, MSM extended the completion date to 14 July. In reporting this delay to Mackensen, Brandenstein urged forbearance: "The Romanian General Staff and War Ministry find themselves in a difficult position which threatens to grow if demobilization is not extended. . . . As far as I can see, it does not lie in the German interest to increase the demobilization difficulties." Although de jure demobilization was declared terminated on 14 July, de facto demobilization continued, by default or design, throughout the summer, and in fact was never fully completed.[14]

A lack of planning and preparation exacerbated the difficulties inherent in demobilizing an army of more than 300,000 men and officers. The result was chaos, suffering, and discontent. Except for one month's pay, demobilized soldiers received no assistance. Those returning to their homes in Wallachia were largely on their own in arranging transportation. On his trip to Iaşi in mid-May, Brandenstein noted how appalling the situation was: "At all stations numerous demobilized [soldiers] drifted around appearing to wait for a travel opportunity. . . . Chaos ruled. . . . Among the demobilized, one sees many invalids for whom their homeland apparently is little or not at all concerned." The lot of the demobilized who remained in

Moldavia differed little. In Iaşi, Brandenstein also observed many who "lolled about, not working and soon their maintenance and wages were used up." Upon asking Colonel Ressel what these men would do, he was told, matter-of-factly, "they will steal." Some may have joined with deserters in bands, which, according to Austrian intelligence, "rove about Moldavia. Through the stealing of food they have become a veritable plague on the population."[15]

For soldiers eager to return to their homes and families, denial or delay of demobilization often triggered discontent and sometimes disobedience. A number of diverse protests can be cited. The most unusual was the petition the 75th Territorial Battalion in Bârlad sent to Brandenstein requesting German help in getting home, "since our military authorities will not demobilize us." On 13 July, some men of the 1st Heavy Artillery Regiment, the commander reported, "did not want to follow the battery to a new cantonment, coming as a group . . . requesting demobilization. Although I spoke with them showing the reasons for the delay . . . it was impossible to convince them and in a group they departed for Mărăşeşti. Having a restricted force, I was not able to take any immediate measures against them."[16] Both Romanian security police and Austro-German intelligence reported similar protests in units stationed in Bessarabia. The latter records: "Younger soldiers in regiments stationed in Bessarabia refuse orders and demand immediate demobilization." Demobilization was not the only cause of declining morale in the Romanian army. "As the consequence of poor nourishment and strenuous work," Austrian intelligence reported in August, "hitherto more than 400 men of the 33rd Infantry Regiment have deserted." Lack of concern, inefficiency, and corruption by officials and officers played their role, but the underlying reason for poor nourishment was the near-famine conditions in Moldavia, under which the civilian population suffered as well.[17]

Demobilization was traumatic for officers as well. Treaty limitations meant that most reserve and some active officers lost their positions. Limited numbers took service in the *grăniceri* and gendarmerie, which were being expanded. A few found positions in the civilian bureaucracy. A handful stood for election to parliament. Many struggled to provide for their material needs. One group of reserve officers petitioned Marghiloman for help—recall to duty or a job in the bureaucracy, but "until this is possible," relief in the form of stipends, access to military mess, and money or food for their families. In its selection of active duty officers for retention, the War Ministry gave preference to experience which tilted the balance toward the higher ranks. "Today majors are platoon leaders," a deputy complained in parliament. Depression and discontent grew among the highest ranks, crowded with colonels. "The War Ministry," Brandenstein observed, "is figuratively stormed daily by dissatisfied higher officers who through their complaints and requests create an uproar." Yearly promotions, announced on 30 May, advanced 17 colonels to general and 54 generals and colonels to command positions. A deputy asked in Parliament "why the reduced army now had 135 generals when in peacetime there had been only 35? . . . Generals are now office clerks in the [War] Ministry." Hârjeu replied that to avoid "rebellion" and social unrest, such as had occurred in France after the defeat of 1870, he endorsed the "principle of accommodation" until the opening of corresponding positions matched the need.[18]

At the end of summer, 1918, despite the impact of demobilization, the Romanian army still numbered over 100,000 men, including support and service units. Despite this, it was incapable of serious combat. The 9th ID, 10th ID, and the two cavalry divisions in Bessarabia were, in theory, fully mobilized. However, their units were dispersed, diverted into agricultural work, guarding supply depots, and maintaining public order in the face of serious nationalist, peasant, and Bolshevik opposition. Divisions 1 to 8 were being reduced to peacetime strength. Some counted fewer than 400 men per regiment. Training was "almost nonexistent." Elimination of command and staff infrastructure dictated by the Treaty of Bucharest had weakened cohesion and control within the army. Internal communication between the high command and field units had been paralyzed when, to satisfy the Germans, the civilian Post Telegraph and Telephone took over the military communications system. Its equipment and technical personnel were subsequently sent to Bucharest. Rapid communication for the army was reduced to four stations of carrier pigeons. Horses were seriously deficient. Rail transportation was crippled for lack of fuel.[19] Reports reaching Paris confirmed the weakness of the Romanian army. Colonel Rosetti, who emigrated to France at the end of June, told the French High Command that the Romanian army, for the moment, "is reduced to complete impotence." The dispatches of French military attaché Colonel Pierre Lafont were equally negative: morale was low; "the final victory of the Entente is seen as the last chance for the salvation of the country. Everyone has their eyes on the Western Front." In mind were German attacks during May and June, which had opened a salient 60 kilometers deep in French lines, captured Soissons, and reached the Marne river 50 kilometers from Paris. After a pause, Ludendorff resumed the attack on 15 July, crossing the Marne and imperiling the position of the French 5th and 6th Armies. Military and civilian morale in Romania reached its nadir.[20]

THE TIDE OF WAR TURNS

The Second Battle of the Marne proved to be Ludendorff's last offensive. On 20 July, word reached Iași that the Germans had been stopped and forced to retreat back across the river, surrendering 17,000 prisoners and 360 cannon. "The recent French offensive has stirred the Romanian people," OKM reported to Berlin on 8 August. There was other good news for the Romanians. Thousands of American troops were now arriving daily in France. On the Italian Front, the Austrians admitted failure of their Piave offensive. Concurrently, Czech and Yugoslav groups made declarations of national self-determination. All of these developments resonated in Romania. "In all of Moldavia," an Austrian intelligence report read, "there are rumors about civil war in Austria-Hungary," that the "long awaited breakup of the Austro-Hungarian Monarchy begins."[21] Despite censorship of the press, confirmation came as details were disseminated by Allied diplomatic missions and widely spread in broadsheets and by word of mouth. German intelligence was especially upset by the role of demobilized officers who, it alleged, were "spending time in coffee houses creating anti-German feeling."[22]

In Wallachia, news from abroad spread rapidly also. Excerpts from German police reports describe the response. "Street life in Bucharest gives a mirror of the deteriorating frame of mind: lively, open discussion of war maps, lack of respect from hitherto polite Romanian [street] cleaning crews"; "when German and Austrian officers appear on the streets in uniform, insults are called out, especially frequently the word *Boche*." Demobilized soldiers were again singled out as the provocateurs of resistance. A strike of 350 workers at a facility in Turnu-Severin was "traced back to the instigation of Romanian soldiers from Moldavia." Rumors circulated that reserve officers recruited into the gendarmerie were planning to arm demobilized soldiers and lead an uprising in connection with an attack by the Romanian army across the Siret. There is no evidence of such a plan at that time, although later it was suggested as an adjunct to Romanian re-mobilization. Strangely, Marghiloman failed to draw the appropriate con-clusion from the events on the battlefield even though he was well in-formed, as his journal reveals. He clung to his conviction that Romania's future lay in a close relationship with Germany and Austria-Hungary. For that reason, he continued to advocate the ratification of the Treaty of Bucharest by the king in a form that included many of its demands on Ro-mania. But Ferdinand, gaining new hope from events on the Western Front, resisted German pressure to give his assent, without which the treaty would have no legal validity under Romanian law.[23]

With growing evidence of Romanian resistance, and especially the con-tinued refusal of Ferdinand to ratify the Treaty of Bucharest, the anger and frustration of the Central Powers mounted. From Berlin came talk of a "thorough housecleaning" in Iaşi, including replacement of the dynasty, under threat of military action. However, Mackensen's command was not eager for a confrontation. Captain Horstmann warned Berlin that "the Ro-manians could put up 350,000 men, among them 175,000 ready for com-bat." Against them could be sent "only four German divisions of the oc-cupation army which are not strong and are comprised for the most part from men not capable of combat. . . . Even if one adds the two Austrian oc-cupation divisions, the total power for a serious confrontation would be extremely weak." Horstmann's exaggerated estimates of the capability of the Romanian army were echoed in an analysis prepared at OHL. Never-theless, Ludendorff met with Arz at German headquarters in Spa on 14 Au-gust to plan a military operation under the code name Fangstoss. By the beginning of September agreement was reached on the following details: Austro-German forces of Ober-Ost (High Command East) would attack Moldavia on the upper Dniester and through Bukovina; Austro-Hungarian troops from the Ukraine would invade Bessarabia over the lower Dniester at Tiraspol; and Mackensen's forces would advance over the Siret. Defen-sive forces in Transylvania would also be increased. An ultimatum was pre-pared, and on 13 September OHL ordered Mackensen to prepare to march.[24] Three days later, however, Arz informed Ludendorff that as a re-sult of Austro-Hungarian peace initiatives, Kaiser Karl had forbidden the participation of Habsburg forces. Even unilateral German action would be "undesirable." Ludendorff canceled Fangstoss but expressed his displeasure by warning Arz that all future "complications" with Romania must be borne by Austria-Hungary alone. German troops were being diverted elsewhere, and there would be no German help provided, as in 1916.[25]

On 15 September, General Louis Franchet d'Esperey launched the long-awaited offensive of the Allied army of the east from Salonika. Two French divisions and a single Serbian one attacked on the front of the German 11th Army, now composed largely of Bulgarian forces. Within two days, all three Bulgarian defensive lines had been penetrated. The Bulgarian army retreated, sometimes in full panic, over the next week. On 28 September, its High Command asked for an armistice. This was signed at Franchet d'Esperey's headquarters in Salonika the next day. Its terms granted Allied troops free passage through Bulgarian territory. During October, British and French troops advanced northward, slowed only by their own logistics and by inadequate roads and rail lines. The Romanian Front would soon be reestablished on the Danube.[26]

News of the Bulgarian collapse spread quickly throughout Romania. In Bucharest, initial reports were received with skepticism as "too good to be true." However, confirmation came from indiscretions of German occupation personnel and foreign sources. In Iaşi, again detailed information was supplied by the Allied diplomatic missions. The Serbian minister briefed Marghiloman personally. On 27 September, Horstmann acknowledged the Bulgarian defeat, asking Marghiloman to delay publication in the press. "This confirms that the front is completely broken," the premier concluded. The next day, as Christescu handed Marghiloman a copy of MSM's weekly political–military report prepared for King Ferdinand, he added, "The game is up for the Germans." Nevertheless, the premier still could not envision the decisive defeat of Germany or the dissolution of Austria-Hungary. For Brătianu, the circle around the king, and higher military leaders, it was time to position Romania to benefit from their enemies' misfortunes. Ferdinand ordered Marghiloman to make no commitments on ratification. Brătianu made it clear to the Entente ministers that he maintained fidelity to their cause. Christescu and MSM became more proactive in preparing for remobilization and possible entry into the war.[27]

General Constantin
Christescu, chief of the
General Staff, March–
November 1918. Muzeul
Militar Naţional

REMOBILIZING THE ROMANIAN ARMY

The first steps to rebuilding the Romanian army had been taken in July at the time of the Second Battle of the Marne. Marghiloman gave neither support nor blessing at first. War minister Hârjeu, ailing and lethargic, provided no leadership. The initiative came from Christescu and his staff. Their planning was secretive, *en bureaux*, and orders were verbal. The lack of a paper trail has made it difficult to discover and document what was done in this initial stage. But it appears that about all that was accomplished was to slow the demobilization process and ensure that the best men and officers were retained. At the beginning of September, according to Romanian estimates, 160,000 to 170,000 men and officers were still under arms—40,000 to 50,000 more than allowed by the treaty. A German analysis put the figures at about 120,000 and 33,000, respectively. The Romanians were even more successful in retaining arms and ammunition, in violation of the Treaty of Bucharest. It was not until 28 August that agreement was signed with the Central Powers that established a procedure for their surrender. It permitted the Romanian command to inventory their own holdings and select those weapons to be given up. The Romanians cleverly exploited this self-policing system. First, they kept two sets of books, which concealed what they actually possessed. Second, in fulfilling the quota to be surrendered, they selected a preponderance of weapons that were obsolete or lacking in ammunition. This chicanery allowed the Romanians to retain about 60 percent of their existing armaments, and the best at that. The Romanian army was able to reenter the war in November with sufficient basic weapons for all its divisions and munitions for 15 to 20 days of combat for the nine divisions they eventually mobilized.[28]

The next stage in the resurrection of the Romanian army came late in September with the collapse of the Bulgarian Front. Christescu ordered the operations and administrative sections of MSM to develop a detailed plan of mobilization "as rapidly as possible" but "with the greatest discretion so that the German command not discover anything about the preparation of such a work." Their proposals, which formed the basis of the plan eventually implemented, distinguished two groups in the process of mobilization. Group One, which could be assembled quickly, was comprised of divisions with a majority of reservists at hand in Moldavia. It included also the divisions in Bessarabia. Group Two was composed of divisions belonging to Army Corps II and III, most of whose personnel had passed into Wallachia. They were to be assembled in skeleton form in Moldavia, their ranks filled out as additional men and officers were able to return. The need for officers in both groups was particularly great.[29]

During September and early October, German intelligence received many reports that indicated measures preliminary to mobilization: active-duty officers denied furloughs; military doctors recalled from the occupied areas; increasing numbers of officers appearing at the War Ministry office in Bucharest requesting permission to travel to Moldavia. Brandenstein forwarded a report that men in Moldavia had been ordered to register in order to prepare military registration lists. Other reports indicated that Romania was looking forward to cooperating with Entente forces now entering Bulgaria. "The Intelligence Service of the Romanian General Staff has recently developed a very active service in the occupied area," read a report of Mackensen's political police early in October, with "special interest in Danube crossings and the status of Austro-German troops in Wallachia."

On 9 October, Christescu ordered all detached military personnel to return to their units by 14 October. After the Bulgarian armistice, calls arose within the Romanian army to mobilize and reclaim Dobrogea. "The troops of the V Army Corps are indeed eager to fight and desire to take revenge on the Bulgarian population of Dobrogea," a "reliable source in the Romanian Army" was quoted in German intelligence. Marghiloman even proposed to Horstmann the occupation of the province by a Romanian or a joint Romanian–German contingent. The Germans were agreeable to the former, provided Romania only mobilized "the least number of troops necessary."[30]

The German willingness to return Dobrogea highlights their concern that Romania would reenter the war and threaten Mackensen's rear as he faced Entente forces on the Danube. "For me," the Field Marshal had journaled on 4 October, "the chief question now is 'What will Romania do?'" He continued his train of thought in a telegram to OHL: "If she [Romania] once again joins the Entente . . . then the Balkans and perhaps the entire war are lost for us. . . . Nothing must be undone to win Romania for us." One option, he wrote, was the revival of Fangstoss. "But my power is not sufficient," he added. Ludendorff, with monumental crises on other fronts, was powerless also. He told Mackensen to concentrate on defending the Danube line against Entente forces as long as possible. Without Romanian oil, the war could not be continued in the west. Mackensen's second suggestion to OHL was, "If we offer Romania all of Dobrogea plus the [old] frontier with Austria-Hungary, she may join us." In extended discussions with Marghiloman, Horstmann made it clear that Romania in return must ratify a modified treaty, promise neutrality and friendship toward the Central Powers, and "expressly renounce Transylvania, asking, perhaps in case of need, local autonomy for it."[31] On 13 October, the premier recommended to the king that he accept these proposals, arguing that "the economic future of Romania dictates friendship toward the Central Powers." He insisted that the Entente was "not disposed to dismember Austria-Hungary," pointing to President Wilson's speech in January, which spoke only of autonomy for the peoples of the Dual Monarchy. "Romania cannot receive Transylvania. If this province is to obtain autonomy, there must be good relations between Romania and Hungary." Ferdinand rejected Marghiloman's argument, which ignored the direction the war was taking and which was soon invalidated by Wilson's 19 October statement endorsing national self-determination for the peoples of Austria-Hungary. The king and those around him were now eagerly awaiting the arrival of Allied armies on the Danube and, with their support, the liberation of their homeland. The fulfillment of the promises for which they had entered the war appeared possible.[32]

ROMANIA REJOINS THE ENTENTE

With the collapse of Bulgaria, Romania reappeared in the strategic plans of the Allies. On 30 September, the day after the Bulgarian armistice, Clemenceau abruptly recalled Berthelot from his command of the 5th Army on the Western Front. He was ordered to Salonika to lead a new "Army of the Danube" in occupying Bulgaria and rousing Romania to action. The Romanian army was counted on to play a central role in subduing Mackensen's forces, occupying Transylvania, and cooperating with Allied contingents intervening in South Russia against the Bolsheviks. Berthelot arrived in Salonika on 13 October. In conjunction with Franchet d'Esperey, he drafted a letter for Saint-Aulaire, which was delivered in Iaşi on 22 October, via a French airplane, by Victor Antonescu, the former Romanian ambassador in Paris. The letter revealed Berthelot's plan to cross the Danube with his army "about the middle of November." "It is indispensable for Romania to take up arms," it warned, "in order to prove its unshakeable fidelity to the Entente, to liberate its territory, and to win once again the rights to the realization of its national claims." Berthelot also requested detailed information about the Romanian forces that could be expected to intervene, as well as details about enemy forces. Saint-Aulaire commissioned Colonel Lafont to answer the military questions while he and Antonescu discussed the political implications of mobilization and reentry with Brătianu who, as it happened, lived next door. Lafont described Romanian civilian and military morale as high, but the army as "completely disorganized." Nevertheless, Lafont believed that six divisions could be "ready to march" in about eight days, two and perhaps four more in 20 days, and two others in 30 days or six weeks. Events would prove that Lafont's estimates were wildly optimistic.[33]

Meanwhile on 22 October, Saint-Aulaire, Antonescu, and Brătianu had continued their discussion on the issues raised by Berthelot's letter "until

late in the night, examining all hypotheses." The next day Prezan was recalled from his estate near Vasliu to join the deliberations. He "raised objections from the military point of view" to immediate mobilization. Other
army commanders in Iași were also consulted. They agreed that mobilization would be difficult. Averescu, however, advised the king to change the
government and mobilize immediately, "so that the general peace will find
us with guns in hand and, if possible, feet in the territory we claim." The
king then requested that Colonel Antonescu be ordered to return to Iași,
ostensibly to assist him "in a study related to the past campaign." Marghiloman, Hârjeu, and Christescu reluctantly granted his request, but the latter warned of a repetition of 1916, "when the General Staff was left out and
everything was arranged behind the scenes." "A mobilization today would
be suicide," Christescu added. "The Germans would crush us in three
weeks."[34]

Under Prezan's signature, Antonescu prepared for Ferdinand a 15-page
memorandum entitled "General Assessment on the Possibilities and Op-
portunities of our Entry into Action against the Central Powers." Its contents presented a "distressing" picture of the Romanian army that, in part,
was a criticism of Christescu's stewardship. The men who had distinguished themselves at Mărășești "are today naked, barefooted, hungry and
demoralized." Units "are completely lacking in cadres, above all those of
officers." The memorandum envisioned that only eight divisions could be
mobilized initially, giving the enemy a "vast superiority" when counting
all the Austro-German divisions surrounding Moldavia. But "this figure
must not frighten us because not all are immediately dangerous." Most of
those to the east were too far away, and the majority of those in Wallachia
"must face Entente forces advancing from the south toward the Danube."
The memo was realistic in playing down the enemy threat. According to
German assessments, Mackensen's occupation divisions were without
heavy artillery and composed largely of men over 35 years of age. Undermanned Austro-Hungarian divisions were in a "state of decomposition";
mutinies had already occurred in Wallachia and east of the Dniester. The
"decisive factor" for Romanian mobilization, the Prezan memorandum
continued, must be the Allied army advancing from Salonika, "especially
if it has the power and intention to force the Danube." It must provide the
Romanian army with "an indispensable base of operations." "No move

must be undertaken if it is not certain that during the time of our mobilization, 10–15 days, Allied troops assure us this base." Their role was not
only to provide support for Romanian military operations, but eventually
to provision troops, horses, and the civilian population. The Prezan memo
also went into detail on the technical details of mobilization. Of prime interest for the king and Brătianu was its conclusion as to when the Romanian army could make "the supreme move." "Soon yes, but immediately
no." It would require 15 days of advance preparation and then 15 days to
mobilize under the protection of Allied forces on the Danube.[35]

As the Romanian leaders debated what to do, the war entered its final
days. The German army was beaten back on the Western Front, Ludendorff
was dismissed, the German navy mutinied, revolution and nationalist revolt broke out in Austria-Hungary, and the Italian Front collapsed, forcing the Austrian High Command to sign the Armistice of Villa Giusti at
Padua (4 November). The latter required German troops to evacuate Italy,
the Balkans, and Austria-Hungary within 15 days or be interned. On 5 November, foreign minister Arion telegraphed from Bucharest that German
troops were preparing to leave and that anarchy might follow. "It is necessary we have gendarmes immediately at hand and, within a short time,
Romanian troops." On the same day, Marghiloman solicited and received
Ferdinand's approval to send troops of the 8th ID into Bukovina, as requested by the Romanian National Council in Cernăuţi.[36] Also on 5 November, Christescu delivered to the five army corps commanders "Secret
Instructions Concerning the Mobilization of the Army." On 6 November,
the king replaced Marghiloman with General Coandă, a proxy for Brătianu.
A decision on mobilization and entering the war became imperative when,
on 7 November, the German government decided to open armistice negotiations on the Western Front. The next day Brătianu summoned Saint-
Aulaire, Colonel Lafont, Coandă, Prezan, and Colonel Antonescu to his
house. The discussion was "lively and spirited." The French insisted on immediate action. Prezan maintained that it was impossible to gather even
the necessary provisions for the army in fewer than 25 days. Brătianu, as
was his custom, temporized, weighing the consequences. A military operation would strengthen Romania's position at the peace conference. On the
other hand, premature and ineffective action could be perilous, allowing
the enemy to carry out destruction in the occupied territory. In the end, it

was decided to send a general to Bucharest to investigate the situation there and to confuse the Germans about Romania's intentions. In addition, steps preliminary to mobilization already begun by Christescu would be extended.[37]

Meanwhile, Franchet d'Esperey and Berthelot, having heard little from Iaşi since Lafont's report, were becoming impatient with Romanian timidity. Berthelot had reached Sofia on 6 November with the intention of attacking over the Danube two weeks later. However, Franchet d'Esperey, under orders from Paris to intercept Mackensen's army before it could escape, decided to force the Romanians' hand. He ordered French forces to begin crossing the river on the night of 8–9 November. Berthelot had already prepared an emotional call to arms to be dropped by French aircraft: "The hour of vengeance or rather the hour of justice has struck. . . . Peasants take up your pitchforks and scythes and rise up against the invader. . . . Rise up Romanian brothers and fall on the enemy." Berthelot also sent a message to Iaşi on 8 November announcing the crossing and containing this blunt advice: "I earnestly request that the Romanian Army be mobilized immediately. Any later will be too late." This radiogram ended Romanian temporizing. On 9 November, Ferdinand authorized general mobilization. An ultimatum was sent to Mackensen with the impossible demand that his forces evacuate Romanian territory within 24 hours or disarm. The next day the Romanian government declared war on Germany, less than 24 hours before the armistice in the west went into effect at 11:00 A.M. on 11 November.[38]

Meanwhile, the crossing of the Danube, so important as a symbol, proved to be a minor military operation. Only six battalions of Berthelot's Army of the Danube had reached the river before the armistice. The plan to cross on the night of 8–9 November miscarried because Bulgarian boatmen refused to cooperate. It was not until daybreak on the 10th that a French detachment established at Giurgiu became the first Allied presence on Romanian soil. The rearguard of German forces, already in retreat, offered little resistance: scattered rifle fire, a few salvoes of artillery, and an attack by a German aircraft. In order to impede the French advance, Mackensen, as he had already warned Iaşi, had several bridges over the Argeş river destroyed. When official news of the armistice in the West arrived on 12 November, both sides suspended military operations.[39] Although officially hostilities with the Central Powers had ended, the Romanian army continued its remobilization for the tasks ahead: first, ensuring the retreat of Mackensen's Army and reestablishing Romanian sovereignty in Wallachia and other occupied areas; second, the occupation of Transylvania and the adjacent regions promised in the treaty of 1916. The story of the First World War on the Romanian Front would be incomplete without a brief consideration of these issues.

Epilogue

THE RETREAT OF MACKENSEN'S ARMY

The Armistice of Villa Giusti obligated German troops to evacuate by 19 November. Already on 26 October, General Wilhelm Groener, who had succeeded Ludendorff at OHL, ordered Mackensen to make preparations to retreat through Hungary to German territory. Because revolutionary disturbances had already disrupted his projected lines of communication, OHL authorized Mackensen to occupy railroads in Transylvania as well as its key transport and supply centers of Braşov and Sibiu. Horstmann assured the Romanians that this was a temporary military measure, not a support of continued Hungarian control. The German foreign office, anticipating the breakup of the Dual Monarchy and anxious to establish good relations with postwar Romania, repeated to Mackensen that the retreat must be carried out "in good will," making it clear that "Germany does not stand in the way of Romania's national aspirations." In order to avoid possible conflict with Romanian troops that might advance into Transylvania, Mackensen proposed to General Mircescu, the Romanian liaison at OKM, a line of separation along the Predeal–Cluj railroad. Mircescu arranged for Marghiloman to travel to Focşani on 6 November to meet with Colonel Maximilian Schwarzkoppen, Mackensen's chief of staff, to discuss the arrangements for a peaceful and orderly evacuation. But the premier was dismissed before he could depart for the meeting. With the advent of the new government, the Romanian declaration of war, and especially the involvement of the French, this cooperative spirit was replaced by an adversarial one.[1]

For this reason, the evacuation of the German army was more difficult than either the Romanian or the German government had originally envisioned. Controversies quickly developed over two issues: responsibility for the disorder in Wallachia that accompanied Mackensen's retreat, and the timetable for the evacuation. Berthelot, designated by the Allied Powers to enforce the armistice in Romania, instructed Romanian prefects to report all enemy violations of its terms. He soon had a long list. On 18 November, he sent a radiogram to Mackensen charging retreating German troops with "wanton destruction" of bridges, railroad stations, and food deposits, as well as forced requisitions and violence against Romanian gendarmes and civilians. He threatened to hold Mackensen personally responsible. The field marshal denied the charges in a feisty reply.[2] However, his journal and other German sources acknowledge a weakening of discipline; some soldiers, demoralized by defeat and desperate to get home, had taken personal property by force, including food, horses, carts, and vehicles. But it is also true, as Mackensen pointed out in his reply, Romanians also bore responsibility for the disorder that accompanied the evacuation. Understandably, after two years of harsh occupation, some citizens, particularly in Bucharest, vented their anger by harassing German military and civilian personnel and by destroying or stealing their property. As Romanian sources testify, mobs of looters plundered not only German but Romanian depots, shops, businesses, and factories in an orgy that lasted several days. When German troops intervened to maintain order, in some cases shots were fired. At the Obor food depot, reportedly six died when German soldiers fired on looters. In Bucharest, a total of 21 casualties are alleged to have occurred.[3]

A second controversy developed over the failure of Mackensen's forces to complete their evacuation by 19 November, as required by the Armistice of Villa Giusti. The evacuation began in earnest on 7 November. Mackensen and his staff left Bucharest on the night of 11 November, and the last German units departed the capital hurriedly the next day. However, railroad capacity was insufficient for 160,000 soldiers, economic–administrative personnel, civilian workers, and dependents. Travel by road in winter was extremely difficult. Consequently, when the deadline of 19 November passed, thousands of Germans were still on Romanian soil. Berthelot forwarded to Paris erroneous reports that German troops were being installed for the winter in the Prahova valley in order to retain control of Romanian oil. He then sent an ultimatum to Mackensen inflicting a fine of 500,000,000 marks plus 50,000,000 for each additional day the evacuation was prolonged beyond the deadline. Mackensen, on instructions from his government, took the position that the more flexible evacuation injunction contained in the 11 November Western Armistice, "to return immediately to the frontiers of Germany," took precedence over Villa Giusti, to which Germany had not been a party. Allied supreme commander Ferdinand Foch, eager to humiliate his enemies, insisted on applying the latter.[4]

To resolve these issues and others relating to the evacuation, Berthelot sent a Romanian–French delegation headed by General Mircescu to Sinaia on 24 November to meet with Mackensen's representatives. The latter conceded on a number of issues, admitting that "destruction" and "abusive requisitions" may have been committed by men and officers "confused" and "disoriented" by Romania's unexpected declaration of war. They expressed Mackensen's "profound sorrow" and "regrets" and gave his assurance that "the most rigorous measures would be ordered once again to avoid a reoccurrence." In his report of the meeting, French major Mablais expressed some understanding of the enemy dilemma: "The Germans retreat in good enough order and they seem to respect property and inhabitants. . . . Still it is evident that discipline sinks in the German Army, the officers are no longer much respected." On the evacuation timetable, the Germans called a new deadline from Berthelot to complete their departure in five days a "technical impossibility." When asked to estimate the termination of evacuation, they replied not before 5 December for Romania, and not before 25 December for Transylvania. Overall, the meeting was productive, and with an agreement to meet again later, a compromise appeared possible. However, as the delegates were departing, a French officer arrived from Bucharest with a peremptory order from Foch that Mackensen's forces must be immediately disarmed and interned. General Kosch, the ranking German delegate, stormed out of the room in anger. However, at a second negotiating session at Râmnicu-Vâlcea on 1–2 December, a sensible and pragmatic attitude prevailed. Mackensen, under orders from Berlin, agreed to the demand for disarmament and internment in an "honorable manner." Because virtually all German forces had by now crossed into Transylvania, the Romanian–French delegation declared their "disinterestedness" in the issue, which henceforth would be the responsibility of the Hungarian government.[5]

During simultaneous negotiations in Budapest, Mackensen had come to believe the Hungarians would demand only a symbolic disarmament and internment involving a minimal delay in reaching Germany. Unofficial statements of the Hungarian War Ministry and a comment by the French representative at the armistice commission on the Western Front encouraged Mackensen to continue his race toward home. During the first two weeks of December, a large portion of the German forces was able to cross Transylvania into Hungary proper. But then, Hungarian premier Count Mihály Károlyi gave in to French pressure and agreed to enforce immediate disarmament and internment. Mackensen protested and attempted to prolong negotiations until more of his troops reached Austria. The absence of credible Hungarian military power and the cooperation of lower officials allowed the retreat to continue. On 16 December, as the field marshal and his staff were passing through Budapest, his train was blocked and he was summoned to a meeting with Károlyi. When they met, the premier immediately demanded that Mackensen allow himself to be interned and order his troops to disarm. Otherwise all German troop trains would be blocked. Mackensen reluctantly agreed to this demand because it would allow the retreat of his troops to continue. On 1 January 1919, the last train bearing German troops reached friendly Austria.[6]

Meanwhile, the field marshal and his personal staff began their internment at a private villa outside Budapest under Hungarian custody. He believed his confinement would be short. However, on 31 December a detachment of French cavalry surrounded the villa. Four days later, Mackensen was given the choice of moving, willingly or under force, to a new, unnamed place of internment under French custody. Because there was really no alternative, he submitted. As justification for their action, the French suggested that he was intending to escape on the last German train. He was not physically mistreated, yet Mackensen felt betrayed and humiliated. Even his horse was taken from him. The field marshal, with his personal staff, was moved several more times, with Salonika his eventual destination. Here he was held not only until Germany had ratified the Paris Peace Treaty, but until many of the Allied Powers had done so as well. It was not until 1 December 1919 that he was able to return to his homeland.[7]

While the evacuation of Mackensen's forces from Wallachia unfolded,

King Ferdinand and his government remained in Iaşi. Almost three weeks elapsed after the armistice before they returned to Bucharest and reasserted their authority over the occupied area. They were delayed by the political and military disorganization then existing in Moldavia, which had been exacerbated by the change in government and the unexpectedly sudden ending of the war. As already mentioned, serious difficulties were encountered in remobilizing the army. The process was impeded by bad weather, the wretched conditions of the railroads, a shortage of matériel, and the lack of precise knowledge of where demobilized soldiers were located. Because so many men and officers had passed into Wallachia, only four infantry divisions (approximately 10,000 men each), plus two smaller divisions of light infantry could be mobilized initially. These were in addition to the four divisions in Bessarabia and the one in Bukovina, all of which were in weakened condition themselves.[8]

In the interim before his return, the king empowered Berthelot to administer and keep order in Wallachia in his name. He also asked the general to delay his own appearance in the capital until they could enter together triumphantly. Consequently, Berthelot established a temporary headquarters in Giurgiu on 16 November, from which he exercised authority with Ferdinand's mandate. As the days passed without an indication of when the Romanians would return, Berthelot grew increasingly impatient. "Here, eight days since I requested them to come," he complained to his nephew Georges on 24 November. "They are still in course of discussing, I know not what, protocol. Yesterday I sent two of my officers to Iaşi to take them by the collar and bring them, cost what it may." In response, General Prezan and Colonel Antonescu arrived in Giurgiu on 26 November. Agreement was reached on a course of action regarding Bukovina, Dobrogea, Transylvania, and the reoccupation of Wallachia, as well as the return of the king, which was set for 1 December. Berthelot also requested that 16 Romanian infantry battalions be put at his disposal immediately for collaboration with the Allied intervention in South Russia, which Berthelot was directing. On 28 November, Berthelot and his staff relocated to the capital, "ostensibly incognito."[9]

On the morning of 1 December, the king and his party detrained at the suburban Bucharest station of Mogoşoaia. Berthelot joined them there and at Ferdinand's wish took his place on the monarch's right, with Queen Marie on the left, for their entry into the capital on horseback. They were

Victory parade in Bucharest, 1 December 1918. From left: Berthelot, Ferdinand, Marie, Prince Nicolae. Arhivele Istorice Naționale Centrale

followed by symbolic units of Romanian, French, and English troops with French Nieuports performing aerobatics overhead. The huge crowds that thronged the streets were in utter delirium, shouting and crying, waving flags, placards, and handkerchiefs. Flowers covered the Calea Victoriei. "The town had absolutely gone mad," Marie wrote in her journal. As the day's ceremonies continued, Romanian leaders were jubilant. On the second anniversary of their flight from Bucharest in defeat and despair, they were returning in triumph, confident, as Queen Marie expressed it, of "having accomplished the dream of the Ages, Romania's Golden Dream. We had come back as King and Queen of all the Romanians."[10] That evening Ferdinand hosted a victory banquet at Cotroceni palace in the same room where the humiliating Treaty of Bucharest had been signed eight months before. The monarch, once viewed as dull and weak-willed by some, was now looked on with respect and held in high esteem. He had demonstrated unexpected strength in supporting Brătianu's decision to intervene and then in persevering in this course through the dark days of the war. In so doing, Ferdinand secured for himself a place of honor among the founders of modern Romania.

OCCUPYING THE PROMISED LAND

On the same day that Bucharest celebrated the return of the king, a Romanian national assembly meeting in Alba Iulia proclaimed the union of Transylvania with Romania. Proclaiming the union was one thing; realizing it was another. Hungarians were not reconciled to the partition of the historic lands of the Holy Crown of St. Stephen, but their focus initially was on their internal political and social revolution. Under the pressure of a liberal–democratic reform movement, Kaiser Karl had appointed its leader, Count Milhály Károlyi, to head a new government on 31 October 1918. In addition to proclaiming the independence of Hungary from the Dual Monarchy (16 November), the Károlyi government initiated democratic reforms. Included were generous concessions to the minorities designed to persuade them to stay. It was too little, too late. Like the Romanians, the Serbs, Slovaks, Croats, and other minorities had already opted to secede. Károlyi and his supporters then placed their hope for limiting the extent of their losses in the deliberations of the Paris Peace Conference, which would convene in mid-January 1919. Meanwhile, opposition to Károlyi appeared on the right and the left. Political conservatives viewed his political program as too radical. Some officers of the military were beginning to form secret organizations to oppose him as well as to defend the integrity of the fatherland. On the extreme left, the embryonic Communist Party was growing by feeding off economic and social distress as well as the general disappointment of the population over the cost the nation was paying for having been involved in a war many of them had not wanted.[11]

These political tensions were felt in Transylvania as well, where advocates of various social and political agendas agitated the population. Strikes occurred among miners, railroad personnel, and postal workers. In addition, there were ethnic tensions as Romanian, Saxon, Szekler, Ukrainian, Hungarian, and other national groups asserted their claims, sometimes provocatively. Several formations of armed "guards" were organized to protect their interests. The province was in ferment, public order was disrupted, and acts of intimidation and violence were reported. The Romanian National Council announced on 7 November that it was taking over administration of more than 20 Hungarian counties, and on 10 November, its Conciliul Dirigent (Directing Council) called for the quick intervention of the Romanian troops. The Allied Powers had long intended to use the Ro-

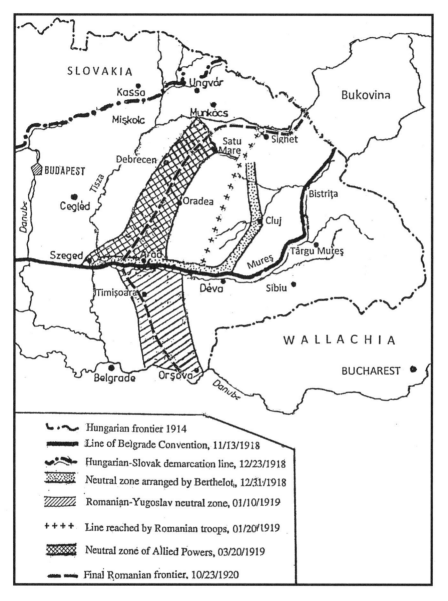

Demarcation Lines in Transylvania, 1918–1919. Adapted from Mária Ormos,
From Padua to the Trianon (Boulder, Colo.: East European Monographs, 1990)

manian army to disarm enemy troops and assist in the occupation of Hungary, a task for which their own forces were not sufficient. At the same time, however, they were reluctant to allow the Romanians to occupy all of the territory promised in the treaty of 1916, which they considered excessive. Furthermore, they held that this agreement itself had been abrogated by Romania's separate peace. They intended to satisfy Romanian claims—partially, at least—but reserved a decision for the Paris Peace Conference. The Romanians, on their part, felt it imperative to hasten their occupation of the province, not only to protect their co-nationals but to lay physical claim on their desiderata.[12]

The advance of the Romanian army into Transylvania proceeded gradually, in several successive stages, beginning in the latter part of November. Divisions already mobilized were committed to Bessarabia and Bukovina to maintain order and guard against nationalist and Bolshevik threats from the Ukraine. Remobilization of additional divisions, as has been pointed out, was slow. Consequently, only relatively small avant guard forces crossed the frontier by the end of November. Deployment was also hindered by winter weather, with Romanian troops reaching only the Mureş river by the middle of December. The river marked the demarcation line established by the Belgrade Convention, which General Franchet d'Esperey had negotiated with the Hungarian government on 13 November. This line, intended to prevent conflict between Romanian and Hungarian forces, allotted only about one-half of Transylvania to Romanian occupation.[13] The Romanians refused to recognize the terms of the Belgrade Convention because they had not been a party to its conclusion and because Franchet d'Esperey at the time had been unaware of the Entente's prior commitments to Romania in the treaty of 1916. Consequently, with the encouragement of Berthelot and others in the French military, the Romanians continued their advance in December beyond the Mureş river. Citing "alarming" reports about the situation in Cluj and elsewhere in Transylvania, the Romanian High Command ordered the Command of Troops in Transylvania (CTT) on 17 December to advance to the line Cluj–Turda–Aiud–Alba Iulia. The Allied Powers acquiesced in this and later advances with corresponding changes in the demarcation line because they had insufficient troops to supervise the region and because the Romanians presented them with a fait accompli. Also, the Allied Powers, above all the French, were anxious for the Romanian government to follow through on its earlier commitment to provide 15 battalions for their intervention against the Bolsheviks in South Russia. Brătianu had warned them directly on 23 December that failure to fulfill the promises of 1916 "will make it impossible for Romania to furnish its cooperation in the Allied action in South Russia." By the end of January, Romanian forces had reached the Apuseni Mountains. At this point, the occupation of the province of Transylvania, strictly speaking, was completed, but beyond lay regions heavily populated by Romanians. The Romanian army paused throughout February and March as the Romanian delegation at the Paris Peace Conference, headed by Brătianu, presented their case for fulfillment of the treaty of 1916. The premier, obstreperous and inflexible as usual, had a stormy relationship with the representatives of the Great Powers.[14]

Meanwhile, Károlyi continued to trust that the Allied Powers in Paris would accept his argument that the new Hungary should not be penalized too harshly for the sins of the old. However, after considerable testimony and debate in Paris during February, the Council of Four (representatives of France, Great Britain, Italy, and the United States) decided to establish a neutral zone whose western limit was not far from the line promised to Romania in the treaty of 1916. On 20 March, the council directed the Hungarian government to withdraw its forces a few kilometers behind this zone, which included most of the Hungarian provinces of Crişana, and Maramureş. Although this decision was not a delineation of a final frontier, the Hungarians saw the handwriting on the wall and were devastated. Károlyi resigned in protest, and a revolutionary socialist/communist regime headed by Béla Kun took power and proceeded to establish a Soviet republic.[15]

Kun, a native of Cluj and a former sergeant in the Habsburg army, had become a Bolshevik while a prisoner of war in Russia. His activity in recruiting other soldiers and his ability as a communist agitator and publicist in the Russian Revolution gained him some attention. When he returned home, his reputation as an associate of Lenin led to his being acknowledged as the leader of the Hungarian Communist Party. The details of his political agenda are not our primary interest here, but rather his role in the conflict with Romania. As a son of Transylvania, he undoubtedly had a personal interest in opposing the expected advance of the Romanian army into the neutral zone. This aspect of his agenda resonated with Hungarians, even those who did not agree with his internal political revolution. Included among the latter were remnants of the former Habsburg army. Some were already being consolidated and were reportedly ready to fight to prevent the radical dismemberment of the lands of historic Hungary. In addition to promoting the creation of a Hungarian Red Army, Kun's regime recruited contingents of revolutionary Red Guards. However, some of the consequences of Kun's dictatorship of the proletariat were to cause discontent among veteran soldiers: the abolition of military ranks and decorations, the loosening of discipline, the appearance of Red Guard formations and political commissars among them, as well as the political sermons delivered by agitators from local directories. What the soldiers wanted were uniforms, guns, and ammunition to meet the incursions of Romanians from the east and the Czechs from the north.[16]

Romanian political and military authorities were thoroughly alarmed, not only by the appearance of a Bolshevik regime in Hungary and its preparations to resist the Romanian advance, but also by Kun's boast that Bolshevik forces in the Ukraine were prepared to march against Romania and link up with Hungary. The conviction in Bucharest was unanimous that it was imperative to advance into the neutral zone. The appearance of Kun's regime also created sympathy among Allied leaders for Romanian action. General Franchet d'Esperey, who had long been obsessed with leading a march up the Danube, met with Berthelot and Romanian leaders in Bucharest on 6 April. There it was decided "to settle the Hungarian question immediately." The advance was encouraged indirectly by the acquiescence of the French General Staff, even though approval of the Council of Four in Paris was lacking. On 10 April, the Romanian command prepared operational orders for the occupation of the neutral zone and brought newly activated divisions to war footing. As early as February, the Romanian army had been supplementing its ranks by co-opting men and officers of Romanian and German descent from veterans of the Imperial Army. Of necessity, many were clothed in their old Austro-Hungarian uniforms, and some regiments even retained German as the language of command. Two divisions had former Habsburg officers as commanders and chiefs of staff. One, the 18th ID, was led by General Dănilă Papp, who had served as a member of the Austrian General Staff, a professor at the Austrian military academy, and more recently a prominent field commander on the Russian Front.[17]

The Romanian advance into the neutral zone, which began early on 16

April, met only temporary resistance from Hungarian forces, many of whom fled or retreated, some as much as 50 kilometers a day. Political commissars and officers who attempted to stop them were threatened with death. A few formations of Red Guards mutinied and fought with other revolutionary units. In some areas, armed citizens of Romanian descent or counterrevolutionary Hungarians aided the Romanian forces. By April 23, the Romanians had reached a line near the western edge of the neutral zone, which encompassed the important Hungarian center of Debrecen. After the revolutionary directory controlling the city fled, former city officials cooperated with the Romanian commander. Hungarian police officers remained at their posts, and Hungarian officers and noncommissioned officers from the local garrison were permitted freedom of movement in the city, in uniform but without arms.[18]

The Romanian government and military paused for a few days again as they pondered the continuation of their advance beyond the neutral zone to the Tisza, a natural line of defense. When asked his opinion, Franchet d'Esperey again urged that they continue. This was also the view of Foch and other Allied leaders in Paris, although the Council of Four continued to withhold approval. On 25 April, the Romanians resumed their march. Hungarian resistance again melted away almost immediately. Regular army troops wanted to go home. Whole divisions surrendered. Revolutionary units from Budapest fled the front and engaged in pillaging. But near Solnok, the Romanians did encounter resistance from a large group of Red Guards as well as increased hostility from the Hungarian population. By 30 April, the Romanian army had reached the Tisza river, far beyond the line envisioned in the treaty of 1916.[19]

Firmly established along the east bank of the Tisza, the Romanians then faced another decision. Some Allied leaders, particularly the French military, favored a continued Romanian advance to Budapest in order to disarm Kun's increasingly troublesome regime. The Romanians hesitated. They did not want to act alone and open themselves to charges of imperialism. Also, they were facing trouble on their eastern ramparts, where renegade Romanian socialist Christian Rakovskii, now the Soviet commissar for the Ukraine, was threatening to invade Bessarabia. When his forces succeeded in driving Allied interventionist forces out of Odessa early in April, this threat appeared credible. After transferring troops to the east, the Romanians stood on the Tisza during May, June, and most of July while Al-

General Prezan (center, with Antonescu close behind) with Command of Troops in Transylvania, 1919. Muzeul Militar Naţional

lied leaders in Paris attempted to come to an agreement on how to deal with the Hungarian situation. The Romanian army relaxed during this period as Kun and his military leadership turned their attention from their eastern campaign on the Tisza to the northern campaign against Czech forces in Slovakia. On 29 May, fighting broke out on the latter front.[20]

During the first days of June, the Hungarian Red Army enjoyed some success against the Czechs, but in response to an order from the Council of Four in Paris, Kun ordered his army to evacuate their gains. The initial success in the northern campaign encouraged Kun and his military advisors to believe that by shifting forces, an offensive across the Tisza against the Romanians could also be successful. They persisted in the false hope that an offensive of Bolshevik forces from the Ukraine would threaten Romania and even establish a direct link with Hungary. Consequently, on 20 July, after shifting forces to the Romanian Front, the Hungarian Red Army attacked across the Tisza. The Romanian command had blown up bridges over the Tisza but grouped the majority of its 90,000 troops some distance behind the front. Consequently, with the aid of surprise, the Hungarians were able to cross the river at several points and push back the lightly held Romanian Front by up to 50 kilometers. However, Kun's decision to evacuate the hard-won gains they had made in Slovakia had broken the spirit of resistance that still existed in the Red Army. Experienced, capable commanders and officers resigned, soldiers quit, and discipline declined even more. When orders were given for the new offensive, about the only soldiers who fought with fervor were those whose homes were in the territory occupied by the Romanians. The Romanians responded quickly with their reserves, and in four days, they had completely routed the Hungarians. On 1 August, the Romanians crossed the Tisza with much pomp and ceremony. King Ferdinand and Queen Marie came from Bucharest to observe it. The road to Budapest was open. Kun's attack had ended the indecision in Paris. With widespread Allied approval, the Romanian army marched virtually uncontested into Budapest on 3 August 1919.[21]

After a controversial occupation that lasted until November, the Romanians withdrew gradually to the line promised in the treaty of 1916. A frontier about 50 kilometers to the east of this line was incorporated into the final peace settlement, the Treaty of Trianon (March 1920). In other decisions of the council, Romania received Bukovina and half of the Banat, which was divided with Yugoslavia. Even with the reductions, Romania received the greatest part of what it had been promised in 1916. In addition, the Allied Powers formally recognized its annexation of Bessarabia.[22] These gains radically transformed prewar Romania. Its territory increased from about 150,000 square kilometers to almost 300,000 square kilometers. Romania was then the largest country in Southeastern Europe. Her population grew from about 8 million to over 15 million. The nearly 3 million ethnic Romanians living in prewar Hungary had been reduced to 254,000 (including those now in Yugoslavia). Only 24,000 remained in postwar Hungary. At the same time, over 1,500,000 Hungarians had been incorporated into Greater Romania, where they formed almost 10 percent of its population. Taken together with other minorities, the non-Romanian population amounted to 30 percent of the total, compared with 8 percent before the war. With these additions came corresponding increases in economic resources and potential.[23] However, serious problems accompanied these gains, including alienated minorities and angered neighbors, which affected Romanian internal and foreign policy in the interwar era and beyond.

In Conclusion

Romania's intervention in the First World War was not primarily a reaction to the military situation in the summer of 1916, even the Brusilov Offensive. It was the consequence of a calculated political decision to take a critical step forward in the nation's quest for national unification. After two years of hard-nosed negotiating, Premier Ion Brătianu had succeeded in committing the Entente powers to diplomatic and military support for his nation's annexation of the Romanian-inhabited provinces of Austria-Hungary. Certainly, the success of the Brusilov Offensive was one factor that determined the timing of Brătianu's decision to act. He did not expect or require that the advance of Brusilov continue, only that Russian forces maintain their positions, especially in Bukovina. Equally important along with the military situation was his conclusion that it was "now or never" diplomatically. First, he realized that the patience of the Entente leaders had been exhausted by his vacillation and by his haggling over the terms of the alliance. He took seriously a warning that they might end the negotiations. Second, he feared Romania's opportunity would also be lost if a general or separate peace occurred. "The moment before us is decisive," he remarked to his son, "if peace is concluded without us, we would be squashed between a great Hungary and a great Bulgaria."[1] These political considerations also explain Brătianu's resolve to intervene even when changes in the military situation during August increased the possibility that Romania would experience defeat. His study of Italian and German unification had suggested to him that a defeat could be a step toward victory.

328

Romania's defeat was predictable to those who understood the nation's strategically vulnerable geographical position, its poorly trained and inadequately equipped army, the incompetence of its high command, and the questionable promises of support from its allies. No doubt these factors were on the mind of the British military attaché when, with a guilty conscience, he remarked to his French colleague shortly after they had signed the military convention, "I feel like a hired assassin."[2] Romania's planning for war, based on premises of a political nature, added to the above problems by giving little consideration to the strategic options of a defensive stance along the Carpathian frontier and/or a retreat in Dobrogea. Under any option, Romanian success would have required the cooperation of powerful Russian forces and an Entente offensive from Salonika able to seriously threaten Bulgaria. Neither of these occurred. STAVKA declined to revive the Brusilov Offensive in Bukovina to complement the advance of the Romanian army across the Carpathians. British–French conflict over the role of the Allied Army of the East, Brătianu's delay in signing the military convention, and Mackensen's preventive strike made it impossible for General Sarrail to provide substantial support for Romania until it was too late.

Romania's intention to intervene was no secret to the Central Powers. Only its exact timing was uncertain, most crucially in the mind of Falkenhayn. His miscalculation had only a minimal impact on the military response of the Central Powers. They had already taken most of the precautionary measures possible, short of provocative actions toward Romania or prematurely weakening operations on other fronts. However, Falkenhayn's misjudgment had serious consequences in the political realm. It precipitated his replacement at OHL with the silent dictatorship of Hindenburg/Ludendorff, which decisively altered the relationship between the political and military authorities in imperial Germany. It initiated, as Gerhard Ritter has argued, the triumph of the sword over the scepter.[3] Ludendorff's policy of total war eventually exhausted Germany and led to its total defeat. The Romanian crisis also accelerated the centralization of military leadership within the Central Powers. Cooperation of their four military chiefs in July and August over the Romanian threat was formalized on 6 September with the establishment of four-power supreme war leadership, behind which stood the OHL. Mackensen had already taken command of German–Bulgarian–Austrian–Turkish forces on the Dobrogean

Front, a unique example of their joint operations during the war. The creation of the new German 9th Army, which took control of operations on Austria-Hungary's own frontier, was another step in the latter's growing dependency on its ally. Centralization of command under the German aegis increased intra-alliance tensions, but it was also one of the keys to the initial defeats inflicted on the Romanians. The Central Powers were able to respond immediately with an attack on Dobrogea and, thanks to Hungarian railroads, assemble quickly in Transylvania a force sufficient to expel the Romanians.

The decisive and coordinated response of the Central Powers stands in contrast to the vacillating and uncoordinated prosecution of the war by Romania and its allies. In addition to failing to cooperate by attacking alongside the Romanian North Army, the Russians did not take seriously their obligation to provide effective support for the Romanian forces in Dobrogea. The XLVII Corps of General Zaionchkovskii was much weaker than promised, and its commander was reluctant to fight for the Romanians, for whom he had contempt. However, it was the Romanian command that mismanaged most grievously the opening campaigns. Among its many errors was the failure to evacuate the vulnerable bridgeheads of Turtucaia and Silistria, slowing and then aborting the advance in Transylvania, and then undertaking the ill-advised Flămânda Maneuver.

The last two decisions gave the German 9th Army time to organize unmolested in Transylvania and then launch a successful counteroffensive. Falkenhayn's attempt to follow this up immediately with the invasion of Wallachia was stymied throughout October and November by the rugged terrain of the Carpathians and the sacrificial resistance of Romanian soldiers in its passes. This gives some support to speculation that, from a military point of view, a Romanian war plan based on defense in the north might have been a better option than Hypothesis Z, at least in gaining additional time for the development of support from military operations of Romania's allies. Once the Carpathians were penetrated and enemy forces were free to conduct a war of movement, the defense of Wallachia became impossible, especially because Mackensen was poised to cross the Danube. At that point in the war, it would have been strategically advisable for the Romanians to follow Russian advice and carry out a controlled withdrawal east to Moldavia. Political and emotional factors dictated a counteroffensive with the Prezan/Antonescu "mass of maneuver." Compromise of its

secrecy and delays in its execution sealed the fate of this unrealistic operation. Under the impact of the combined attack of Falkenhayn and Mackensen, it ended in a disorderly and costly flight to the east.

By their victory over Romania, the Central Powers gained access to food
for their hungry populations and oil to fuel the German army and navy. It
is Norman Stone's conclusion that these imports from Romania enabled
the Central Powers to continue the war into 1918.[4] The defeat of Romania
reduced the possibility of a negotiated peace. The Allies were not anxious
to negotiate from a position of weakness, and it was a catalyst for the timing of Ludendorff's decision to resume unrestricted submarine warfare.
The consequences of his decision need no elaboration.

In contrast to the optimism created among the Central Powers, the defeat of Romania triggered "buyer's remorse" among the political and military leaders of the Entente powers, who had hoped Romania's intervention would tilt the war in their favor. The direct burden of rescuing
Romania fell on the Russians, who eventually sent more than 1,000,000
troops to cover an extension of their frontier, which had heretofore been
shielded by a neutral Romania. Anger directed toward the tsar and his government over the Romanian fiasco must be considered one of the catalysts
of the March Revolution. Other Entente leaders also paid a political price
over the Romanian tragedy. Nevertheless, the Western Powers did reap
benefits from Romania's intervention. The diversion of more than 40
Austro-German divisions to the Romanian Front certainly was of benefit
to Allied armies on other battlefields. The impact of these transfers is impossible to quantify precisely. For example, on 2 September 1916 Ludendorff ordered that all offensive operations cease at Verdun in order to release additional men and supplies for the Somme and Romania. However,
fighting at Verdun had already passed its critical stage, and it cannot be
said that Romania's entry "saved" Verdun. On the other hand, it is obvious that the opening of a new theater of operations further splintered the
dwindling military strength of the Central Powers.[5]

As for the Romanians, the campaign of 1916 cost them 250,000 casualties, placed two-thirds of their country under a harsh occupation regime,
and depressed the morale of soldiers and civilians to the point that some
doubted that the war should be continued. Fortunately, the shield provided
by the Russian army and the strategic priorities of the Central Powers elsewhere provided the Romanians with a reprieve of six months in which to

regroup and rebuild their shattered army. At the base of the resurrection of this army—certainly the most remarkable of the entire war—was, of course, Romanian self-effort. Also essential were the supply of abundant military equipment by the Entente and the mentoring of General Berthelot's mission. Not all of its faults had been corrected, but in contrast to the mismatch of 1916, the Romanian army of 1917 was able to stand on virtually equal ground with its opponents in most military categories. The acquisition of new weapons and new skills elevated morale, as did the confidence imparted by Berthelot and his men. Their presence among the Romanians, fighting for them and in some cases dying with them on the field of battle, was a vivid demonstration that Romania was supported by powerful allies in the west.

The Austro-German command approached the campaign of 1917 under their impression of the Romanian army of 1916. They had doubts about its transformation and ability to withstand a major attack. They also underestimated the number of Russian soldiers who, despite the impact of revolutionary pacifism and disorder in their ranks after the March Revolution, would support their Romanian allies, in defense if not in attack. These misconceptions underlay the plans of the Central Powers for their operations in 1917. Transfers to other fronts had weakened their own forces, and adequate replacements had not arrived. After the fighting began, Austro-German commanders and their men at the front were surprised at the willingness of Romanian soldiers, and some Russians, to resist and counterattack, even in the face of heavy losses. The former, defending the last slice of their homeland, fought with a courage born of desperation. They were aided by a terrain that was unsuited for the war of maneuver, which had favored the Central Powers in 1916. Although the Romanian success in the summer of 1917 was a defensive victory, it frustrated the plans of the Central Powers to force Romania out of the war and release troops for other fronts. As virtually the only significant military success of the Allies in 1917, the battles of Mărăşti, Mărăşeşti, and Oituz won their admiration and reestablished Romania's credibility in their eyes. To have defeated enemies traditionally held in fear and awe increased Romanian self-confidence and has remained a major focus of national pride ever since.

What the armies of the Central Powers could not do on the battlefield was accomplished by Lenin's order to Russian armies in November 1917:

to conclude an armistice. The Romanians had no choice but to do likewise. The consequent withdrawal of Russian troops and the diversion of Romanian troops to control them in Moldavia and Bessarabia precipitated the demand of the Central Powers for a permanent settlement of the war. This confronted the Romanians with a cruel dilemma: conclude a separate peace that would release the Allies from their promises of 1916, or face a bloody and ultimately hopeless resumption of hostilities. With Brătianu still manipulating events in Iaşi, the Romanians drew out the negotiations as long as possible before concluding a preliminary peace (5 March) and a final treaty (7 May). This delay forced the Central Powers to postpone an additional transfer of troops they needed on other fronts. During the peace negotiations, serious tension and conflict arose among the Central Powers: between Bulgaria and its allies over the disposition of Dobrogea and between Austria-Hungary and Germany over their own territorial and economic compensation. The territorial losses they forced on Romania were severe, but those of an economic nature were even more significant as they submitted the nation's resources to long-term German exploitation. Austro-German support for the annexation of Bessarabia was scant compensation for all these losses. Furthermore, Romanian rule in this province proved to be controversial and involved ongoing conflict with Soviet Russia.

Peace and demobilization required by the treaties of Buftea and Bucharest temporarily emasculated the Romanian army and crippled its immediate ability for combat. Still, when remobilization became possible in November 1918, a remnant of over 100,000 soldiers remained under arms, and with the help of some clever bookkeeping, the Romanian army had retained sufficient armaments to equip them. Isolated between Austro-German forces in the Ukraine and Mackensen's divisions on the Siret, it is understandable why the Romanians hesitated to take overt steps toward reentering the war, even after it became clear in the autumn of 1918 that the Central Powers would be defeated. It took a stern warning from Berthelot to move them to remobilize and declare war on Germany, only hours before the armistice in the west. These last-minute actions gave the Romanians a plausible argument that their treaty of 1916, and therefore its promises, remained valid.

This issue was hotly debated at the Paris Peace Conference as Brătianu argued for the complete fulfillment of the treaty in his customary inflexible and confrontational manner. His behavior alienated Allied leaders and destroyed some of their sympathy for Romania's cause generated by its suffering in 1916 and courageous stand in 1917. On the other hand, Romania's position was strengthened by the desire of the Allies, especially the French, to use the Romanian army to stabilize the postwar situation in Southeastern Europe and participate in a cordon sanitaire against Bolshevism. The rise to power of Béla Kun in Hungary appeared to make the Romanian army indispensable and solidified support for Romania's claims. In the end, the Paris Peace Conference approved territorial gains for Romania that, with the exception of the division of Banat with Yugoslavia, included by and large what had been promised in 1916. In addition, the annexation of Bessarabia was recognized.

The Greater Romania that emerged from the First World War was almost exactly twice the size of the prewar Old Kingdom, both in territory and in population. But this growth left the nation with dissatisfied minorities and hostile, irredentist neighbors. The Soviet Union, Bulgaria, and Hungary would take their revenge during the summer of 1940. Under successive threats from these nations, who had the approbation or acquiescence of Nazi Germany, Romania surrendered Bessarabia, Northern Bukovina, Southern Dobrogea, and a large wedge of Transylvania. These losses totaled one-third of its interwar territory and population.[6] Only Transylvania was restored after World War II. Nevertheless, contemporary Romania remains a reasonable fulfillment of the vision of a Greater Romania for which the nation went to war in 1916.

Notes

PREFACE

1. Glenn E. Torrey, "The Romanian Campaign of 1916: Its Impact on the Belligerents," *Slavic Review* 39, no. 1 (March 1980): 27–44.

1. THE ROAD TO WAR: 1914–1916

1. For an authoritative survey of Romanian history of this period, see Keith Hitchins, *Rumania, 1866–1947* (Oxford, U.K.: Clarendon Press, 1994), chap. 1. Romanian attitudes toward Dobrogea changed as immigration and economic development, including the building of a major seaport at Constanța and a railroad bridge over the Danube river to connect it with the interior, turned this frontier region into a Romanian California. Constantin Iordaci, "'Rumyskata Kaliforniia': Integriraneto na Ceverna Dobrudzha v. Rumyniia, 1878–1913 g." *Istoricheski Pregled* 46, no. 3/4 (2001): 50–78.

2. Hitchins, *Rumania*, 1–10, 40–54, 137–153, 203–230. For a brief survey of this period, see Jean-Noel Grandhomme, *La roumanie de la Triplice à l'Entente, 1914–1919* (Paris: Soteca, 2009), 25–38.

3. Şerban Rădulescu-Zoner, *România şi tripla alianţă la începutul secolului al XX-lea 1900–1914* (Bucharest: Editura Literă, 1977), chap. 2; Grandhomme, *Triplice*, 40–42.

4. Katrin Boeckh, *Von der Balkankriegen zum Ersten Weltkrieg. Kleinstaaten Politik und ethnische Selbstbestimmungen auf dem Balkan* (Munich: Oldenbourg, 1996), 60. Francois Bocholier, "La Dobroudja entre Bulgarie et Roumanie (1913–1919). Regards française," *Études balkaniques* 37, no. 1–2 (2001): 65–69, reflects Bulgarian concerns. Lascu Stoica, "Din istoria Dobrogea de sud în cadrul României întregite 1913–1940," *Revista istorică* 6, no. 11–12 (1995): 957–975, summarizes the Romanian point of view.

5. Hitchins, *Rumania*, 153–154; Ottokar Czernin, *Im Weltkrieg* (Berlin: Ullstein, 1919), 106–107.

6. Vasile Vesa, *România și Franța la începutul secolului a XX-lea 1900–1916* (Cluj: Editura Dacia, 1975), 48–49, 58; Anastasiu Iordache, *Ion I. C. Brătianu* (Bucharest: Editura Albatros, 1994), 157, 202; Zoltan Szaz, "The Transylvanian Question and the Belligerents, July–October 1914," *Journal of Central European Affairs* 13, no. 4 (October 1953): 339; Ester Uribes, "La rencontre de Constantza du 14 juin 1914," *Revue roumain d'histoire* 7, no. 2 (1968): 233–246. The visit was initiated by the Romanians. Ion Oprea, *România și imperiul rus, 1900–1924*, vol. 1 (Bucharest: Editura Albatros, 1998), 60–64.

7. Czernin to Vienna, 1 August, Österreichisches Staatsarchiv, Haus-, Hof-, und Staatsarchiv [HHStA], Politisches Archiv [PA] XVIII, Gesandtschaftsarchiv Bukarest/1914; Anastasie Iordache, "La declaration de neutralité la première guerre mondale," *Revue roumain d'histoire* 13, no. 1 (1994): 131–151; Glenn E. Torrey, *Romania and World War I: A Collection of Studies* (Iași: Center for Romanian Studies, 1998), 56–57, 65.

8. Ion Gheorghe Duca, *Amintiri politice*, 3 vols. (Munich: Jon Dumitru Verlag, 1981), 1:117, 121; Dumitru Suciu, *Monarhia și faurirea România Mare* (Bucharest: Editura Albatros, 1977), 165; Hannah Pakula, *The Last Romantic: A Biography of Queen Marie of Romania* (New York: Simon and Schuster, 1984), 134; Eugen Wolbe, *Ferdinand I. Der Begründer Grossrumäniens* (Leipzig: Verbano, 1938), 17.

9. There are many examples in Marie's unpublished "Memorii," Arhivele Naționale Istorice Centrale [AN (Bucharest)], Fond Regina Maria, i.e., 12/25 November 1916; Alexandru Sturdza, "Jurnal," 19/2 December 1916, AN (Bucharest), Fond Sturdza; Pakula, *Last Romantic*, 134, 191.

10. Wolbe, *Ferdinand*, 109; Czernin to Vienna, 7, 30 September 1914, HHStA, PA I, Karton 517. "I had to be something of a 'soul doctor' to prepare him little by little, to strengthen his will, to uphold his spirit, to smooth the way," Marie, Queen of Romania, *Ordeal: The Story of My Life* (New York: Charles Scribner's Sons, 1935), 7.

11. Wolbe, *Ferdinand*, 114; Suciu, *Monarhia*, 166–167; Marie, "Memorii," 13 October; Ioan Lupaș, *Zur Geschichte der Rumänien* (Sibiu: Krafft und Drotleff, 1943), 566.

12. Constantin Argetoianu, *Pentru cei de mîine. Amintiri din vremea pentru celor de ieri*, 10 vols. (Bucharest: Humanitas-Machiavelli, 1991–1997), 2:138; Ion Gheorghe Duca, *Portrete și amintiri*, 2nd ed. (Bucharest: Cartea Românească, n.d.), 39–40.

13. Ioan Scurtu, *Ion I. C. Brătianu* (Bucharest: Editura Museion, 1992), 3, 101; Iordache, *Brătianu*, 213; Radu R. Rosetti, *Mărturisiri, 1914–1918* (Bucharest: Editura Modelism, 1997), 80, 99; Terrence Elsberry, *Marie of Romania* (New York: St. Martin's Press, 1972), 217.

14. Frank Rattigan (Bucharest) to Foreign Office [FO], 22 February 1917, Public Record Office (London) [PRO], FO, class 371, file 2883 [371/2883]; Torrey, *Romania and World War I*, 107; Scurtu, *Brătianu*, 99; Vesa, *România*, 37; Duca, *Portrete*, 45.

15. Demetre Ghika, "Souvenirs de carrière, 1890–1940," 614 (manuscript copy in Hoover Institution Archives, Stanford, Calif.); Saint-Aulaire to Paris, 21 August

1916, Archives Diplomatiques, Ministère des Affaires Étrangères (Paris) [AD], Guerre 1914–1918, Balkans, Roumanie, vol. 112, 2; Bussche (Bucharest) to Auswärtiges Amt [AA], 26 November, Archiv des Auswärtigen Amts (Berlin) [AA], PA, file Deutschland 128, no. 2; Iordache, *Brătianu*, 236.

16. Pakula, *Last Romantic*, 147–149, 157–158, 203, 206, 208; Argetoianu, *Pentru cei de mîine*, 3:174–176; Alexandru Marghiloman, *Note politice, 1897–1924*, 5 vols. (Bucharest: "Eminescu," 1927), 1:240. Ioan Scurtu, "Eminențe cenușii: Barbu Ştirbey," *Magazin istoric* 33, no. 6 (1999): 54.

17. Duca, *Amintiri*, 1:125, 264; Scurtu, "Barbu Ştirbey," 54, 58; Rattigan to Curzon (London), 21 May, 1 July 1919, PRO/FO 608/49; Jean Naum Manuscript, Biblioteca Academiei [BA (Bucharest)], Fond Palatului.

18. Constantin Nuţu, *România în anii neutralităţii, 1914–1916* (Bucharest: Editura Ştiinţifică, 1972), 172–176, 195–204, 210–212. See Torrey, *Romania and World War I*, 11–13, 20, and Grandhomme, *Triplice*, chap. 2; Blondel to Paris, 4 May 1915, AD, Guerre, Roumanie, vol. 111.

19. V. N. Vinogradov, *Rumyniia v gody pervoi mirovoi voiny* (Moscow: Nauka, 1969), 165. See also Ema Nastovici, *România şi puterile centrale în anii 1914–1916* (Bucharest: Editura Politică, 1979), chaps. 2, 4; Iordache, *Brătianu*, 213–215.

20. Oprea, *România şi imperiul rus*, 1:68–74, 87–89; Vesa, *România*, 112, 117.

21. "Proiect de convenţiune militară între Regatul Român şi Imperiul Rus," 18 July 1915, Biblioteca Centrală de Stat (Bucharest) [BCS], Fond St. Georges, Arhiva Coandă; Vinogradov, *Rumyniia*, 139–141; Vesa, *România*, 121–122.

22. Torrey, *Romania and World War I*, 22, 25; Nuţu, *România*, 264, 277–280; Nastovici, *România şi puterile centrale*, 207–208; Carl Mühlmann, *Oberste Heeresleitung und Balkan im Weltkrieg, 1914–1918* (Berlin: Limpert, 1942), 159–161.

23. Blondel to Paris, 29 June, AD, Guerre, Roumanie, vol. 98; Barclay to FO, 29 June, PRO/FO 371/2606; Blondel to Paris, 4 July, AD, Guerre, Roumanie, vol. 111; Torrey, *Romania and World War I*, 108. For a detailed survey of these negotiations, see Dumitru Preda, *România şi Antanta. Avatarurile unei mici puteri într-un război de coaliţie, 1916–1917* (Bucharest: Institutul European, 1998), chap. 1, "Preliminării." On the Brusilov offensive, see Timothy Dowling, *The Brusilov Offensive* (Bloomington: Indiana University Press, 2008), 150–159, and Norman Stone, *The Eastern Front, 1914–1917* (New York: Charles Scribner's Sons, 1975), chaps. 11 and 12.

24. Brătianu to Lahovari (Paris), 3 July, BCS, Fond St. Georges; Vinogradov, *Rumyniia*, 157; Briand to Blondel, 7 July, AD, Guerre, Roumanie, vol. 111; France, Ministère de la Guerre, *Les armées françaises dans la grande guerre*, vol. 8(1) (Paris: Imprimerie Nationale, 1934), annex 3, no. 1352, 26 June; Major Jules Pichon (Bucharest), "Historique des négociations poursuivies avec le gouvernement roumain en juin 1916," Service historique de l'armée de terre, Vincennes [SHAT], Serie 7N, Carton 1455 [7N1455]; Torrey, *Romania and World War I*, 109.

25. Resumé, Blondel-Brătianu, 29 June, AN (Bucharest), Fond Casa Regală, dosar 38/1916; Briand to Blondel, 7 July, AD, Guerre, Roumanie, vol. 111.

26. Duca, *Amintiri*, 1:251; Alexandru Oşca, Dumitru Preda, and Eftimie Arde

leanu, eds., *Proiecte şi planuri de operaţii ale marelui stat major român pînă în anul 1916* (Bucharest: Arhivele Militare Române, 1992), 90–91, 122–123, 172–173; Torrey, *Romania and World War I,* 144–151; Preda, *România şi Antanta,* 42–58. The Allied leaders concluded, correctly as it turned out, that a Romanian declaration of war on Austria-Hungary would be answered by a Bulgarian declaration of war or, failing that, that the Russian expeditionary force in Dobrogea could provoke a conflict. Briand to Paleologue (Petrograd), 31 July, AD, Guerre, Roumanie, vol. 112.

27. Joffre to Desprès, 8 August, AD, Guerre, Roumanie, vol. 99; France, Ministère de la Guerre, *Armées,* vol. 7(1): 524; William Robertson, *Soldiers and Statesmen, 1914–1918* (London: Cassell, 1926), 130, 141; Maurice Sarrail, *Mon commandement en Orient, 1916–1918* (Paris: Flammarion, 1920), 149; Ţenescu to Marele Stat Major (MSM), 11 August, BCS, Fond St. Georges, Arhiva Filodor; Barclay to FO, 30 July, PRO/FO 371/2607; Fasciotti to Rome, 1 August, Archivio Storico Diplomatico del Ministero degli Affari Esteri [AS (Rome)], 1914–1918, Telegrammi di Gabinetto in Arrivo, Anno 1916, vol. 441. The Romanians tended to discredit the reports of their military attaché in Athens, Lt. Colonel Constantin Crăiniceanu, because he was alleged to be a "fanatical Germanophile." Duca, *Amintiri,* 1:251.

28. Saint-Aulaire (Bucharest) to Paris, 4 August, AD, Guerre, Roumanie, vol. 99; Saint-Aulaire to Paris, 5, 21 August; "Protocole du 11 août 1916," AD, Guerre, Roumanie, vol. 112, 2.

29. Paleologue to Paris, 5 August, AD, Guerre, Roumanie, vol. 112, 2; Saint-Aulaire to Paris, 4 September, AD, Guerre, Roumanie, vol. 99, 2; Milne to Robertson, 14 August, Robertson to Hardinge (FO), 15 August, PRO/FO 371/2607; Torrey, *Romania and World War I,* 132–134.

30. Vinogradov, *Rumyniia,* 157; Fasciotti to Rome, 5, 10 August, AS (Rome), Telegrammi . . . Arrivo, vol. 441; Brătianu to Mişu (London), 11 August, Barclay to Grey, 11 August, GRC [Clerk] to Hardinge, 14 August, PRO/FO 371/2607; Blondel to Paris, 26 July, Pelle to Briand, 7 August, AD, Guerre, Roumanie, vol. 112, 2; Grande quartier général to Théâtre d'opérations extérieurs, "Note sur le concours roumain," SHAT, 16N3167.

31. Albert Pinguad, *L'histoire diplomatique de la France pendant la Grande Guerre,* vol. 2 (Paris: Éditions "Alsatia," 1938), 182, 194–195; Grey to Greene (Tokyo), 11 August, PRO/FO 371/2607; Briand to Isvolsky, 11 August, Fleurieu (London) to Paris, 12, 15 August, AD, Guerre, Roumanie, vol. 112, 2; Pichon to Joffre, 12 July, SHAT, 7N1455; Vesa, *România,* 195; V. N. Vinogradov, "Romania in the Years of the First World War," *International History Review* 14, no. 1 (August 1992): 461. Penelope, in Homer's *Iliad* and *Odyssey,* stalled her suitors for 20 years.

32. Fasciotti to Rome, 15 August, AS (Rome), Telegrammi . . . Arrivo, vol. 441; Duca, *Amintiri,* 1:257–259, 261; Constantin Giurescu, "România şi primul război mondial," in *Unitate şi continuitate în istoria poporului român,* ed. D. Berciu (Bucharest: Editura Academiei, 1968), 351. There is a photocopy of one of the hand drafts in Victor Atanasiu et al., *România în anii primul război mondial* [*RAPRM*], 2 vols. (Bucharest: Editura Militară, 1987), 1:151.

33. Duca, *Amintiri*, 1:263; Mavrocordat (Vienna) to Burian, 27 August, HHStA, PA I, Karton 882; *Universul* (Bucharest), 13/26 August.

2. THE ROMANIAN ARMY AND WAR PLAN

1. Costica Prodan and Dumitru Preda, *The Romanian Army during the First World War* (Bucharest: Univers Enciclopedic, 1998), 32. Statistics for the Romanian army during the war, like those for other belligerents, are to a degree estimates. Among the 400,000 subject to call were 150,000 men of the 1917, 1918, and 1919 classes; they were called later in the war.

2. Alexandru Ioanițiu, *Războiul româniei, 1916–1918* (Bucharest: Tipografia Geniu-lui, n.d.), 19–22; Ministerul de Război, MSM, Serviciul Istoric, *România în războiul mondial, 1916–1919* [RRM], 4 vols. + 4 vols., Documente-anexe [(D)] (Bucharest: Im-primeria Națională, 1934–1946), 1:58–59, 61, 64–65; Constantin Kirițescu, *Istoria războiului pentru întregirea româniei, 1916–1919*, 2nd ed., 3 vols. (Bucharest: Casei Scoalelor, 1925), 1:193; Gheorghe Dabija, *Armata română în războiul mondial, 1916–1918*, 4 vols. (Bucharest: Hertz, 1936), 1:337. Combatants composed only about two-thirds of the listed roster strength.

3. Reichsarchiv, *Der Weltkrieg, 1914 bis 1918*, 14 vols. (Berlin: Mittler, 1938–1954), 11:190; Hitchins, *Rumania*, 171; Duc de Luynes (Bucharest) to Philippe Berthelot (Paris), 6 September 1916, AD, Guerre, Roumanie, carton 14/I/23; Österreichisches Staatsarchiv, Kriegsarchiv [KA (Vienna)] Manuskripte Weltkrieg, Rudolf Kiszling, "Feldzug in Siebenbürgen und Rumänien in 1916," 1–2.

4. Dabija, *Armata română*, 2:336.

5. Alexandru Socec, *Zile de restriste din anii 1916–1918 și episodul din bătălia de pe Argeș*, 2nd ed. (Bucharest: Tiparnița de Arte Grafice, 1928), 8; Glenn Torrey, *When Treason Was a Crime: The Case of Colonel Alexandru Sturdza of Romania* (Emporia, Kans.: Emporia State University, 1992), 11; Arhivele Militare Române (Bucharest) [AMR], Fond Marele Cartier General [MCG], 1st Army, Dragalina (Division 1) to 1st Army, 10 October 1916; *RRM*, 1:79–80.

6. Alexandru Oșca, "Pregatirea armatei române pentru împlinirea idealului național," in V. F. Dobrinescu and Horia Dumitrescu, *1917 pe frontul de est* (Focșani: Editura Vantrop, 1997), 13; Dabija, *Armata română*, 2:339; *RRM*, 1:75, annex 4; Sterea Costescu, *Din carnetul unei capitan. Însemnări și amintiri din războiul pentru întregirea neamului 1 August 1916–1 April 1917* (Focșani: Tip. Învățătorul Român: 1927), 133.

7. Constantin Oprița et al., *Învățămîntul militar românesc: Tradiții și actualitate* (Bucharest: Editura Militară, 1986), 96–98; Duca, *Amintiri*, 2:15; Constantin Teodo-rescu, "Memoriu asupra caderei capului de pod Turtucaia," AN (Bucharest), Fond Casa Regală, 53/1916; AMR, Fond MCG, 1st Army, Dragalina to 1st Army, 10 Oc-tober 1916; Reichsarchiv, *Der Weltkrieg*, 11:190; *RRM*, 1:75.

8. Jean Nouzille, "La formation des officiers roumains en France entre 1870–1914," *Revue roumain d'études internationales* 27, no. 5 (1988): 403–409. France

was the preference of most young Romanian officers, but King Carol restricted their choice in favor of Germany.

9. See C. Soare, ed., *Istoria gîndirii militare româneşti* (Bucharest: Editura Militară, 1974), and C. Soare, ed., *Pagini din gîndirea militară românească* (Bucharest: Editura Militară, 1969). Intellectuals do not always make good leaders. When the war got under way, a number of commanders had to be replaced with officers who had fewer academic credentials. Ioan Anastasiu, *Răsboiul pentru întregirea neamului. Studiu critic* (Bucharest: "Bucovina," 1937), 48.

10. Foreign observers, especially the French, were highly critical. Glenn E. Torrey, ed., *General Henri Berthelot and Romania, 1916–1919: Mémoires et Correspondance* [hereafter cited as Berthelot, *Mémoires*] (Boulder, Colo.: East European Monographs, 1987), 33.

11. Dabija, *Armata română*, 1:16–18; George Protopopescu, *Arta militară românească în primul război mondial, 1916–1917* (Cluj: Muzeul de Istorie de Transilvaniei, 1973), 15–17; Vasile Alexandrescu et al., *Istoria militară a poporului român* [*IMPR*], vol. 5 (Bucharest: Editura Militară, 1988), 289–292; *RRM*, 1:30–33; Dumitru Iliescu, *Războiul pentru întregirea României. Pregatirea militară* (Bucharest: Imprimeriile "Independenţă," 1920), 5–6.

12. Soare, *Istoria gîndirii*, 192–193, 196–200, 202, 214; Soare, *Pagini din gîndirea*, xxxii, xliii; Marin Dragu and Mircea Dumitriu, eds., *Istoria infanteriei române* (Bucharest: Editura Ştiinţifică şi Enciclopedică, 1985), 2:76; *IMPR*, 5:354–355.

13. Rosetti, *Mărturisiri*, 70, 84n30. On the other hand, the military attaché in Berlin, Colonel Ludovic Mircescu, "frightened" by his personal observation of the destruction of Serbia, "continually pleaded" that a war not be undertaken against Germany.

14. Soare, *Istoria gîndirii*, 196, 200–202, 214; Dragu and Dumitriu, *Istoria infanteriei române*, 2:75; Dabija, *Armata română*, 2:335–340; Bayerisches Hauptstaatsarchiv, Kriegsarchiv [KA (Munich)], Alpenkorps, Abteilung 1a, Bund 35, Kriegstagebuch, 13, 19 September 1916.

15. *IMPR*, 5:202–203. Even munitions already purchased and some of them in the process of shipment were embargoed. Vasile Rudeanu, *Memorii din timp de pace şi război* (Bucharest: Editura Militară, 1989), 111–116, 129–142; Ioaniţiu, *Războiul româniei*, 20.

16. *RRM*, 1:65, 78; Romulus Scărişoreanu, *Fragmente din războiul, 1916–1918* (Bucharest: Tiparul Cavalerie, 1934), 77; report of Major Sancery, 1 November 1916, AMR, Fond MCG; Dragu and Dumitriu, *Istoria infanteriei române*, 2:73.

17. Ion Cupşa, *Armata română în campaniile din 1916–1917* (Bucharest: Editura Militară, 1967), 31; *RRM*, 1:66–67.

18. Oşca, "Pregatirea armatei," 32; Ioaniţiu, *Războiul româniei*, 27; *RRM*, 1:67–69; KA (Vienna), Neue Feldakten [NFA], 1st Armeekommando [1st Armeekmdo], Nachrichten Abteilung [NA], Faszikel [Fasz.] 33, Kriegsberichte, 2 November 1916; Protopopescu, *Arta militară*, 14.

19. Alexandru Lupaşcu-Stejar, *Din războiul româniei în lumea adevărului* (Bucharest:

Tipografia Serviciul Geografic, 1921), 11–12; *RRM*, 1:73; Costescu, *Carnetul*, 83. The memoirs of Erwin Rommel, *Attacks* (Vienna, Va.: Athena, 1979), reveal the effective use to which the Germans put field telephones in the Romanian campaign. See 103, 108, 139, 146, 159, 163.

20. AMR, Fond MCG, 1st Army, Dare de seamă, 28 August 1916, Raport, 9 September 1916; *RRM*, 1:72; Emilian Ionescu, *Pe Neajlov, într-o toamnă rece* (Bucharest: Editura Militară, 1976), 48–49; Iliescu, *Războiul*, 5; Kirițescu, *Istoria războiului*, 1:188.

21. Iliescu, *Războiul*, 5; Scărișoreanu, *Fragmente*, 32, 49; Bundesarchiv/Militärarchiv [BA/MA] (Freiburg), PH I/415, 89th Infantry Division, I. no. 8943, 18 September 1916; KA (Munich), Alpenkorps, 1a, Bund 34, "Einsatz in Rumänien und Siebenbürgen," 13 September 1916.

22. Captain E. H. Yates (Bucharest) to War Department, 1 September 1916, National Archives and Records Administration [NARA] (Washington, D.C.), War Department, Reports of the Military Attaché in Romania; *RRM*, 1:72–79; Șerban Rădulescu-Zoner and Beatrice Marinescu, *Bucureștii în timpul primul război mondial* (Bucharest: Albatros, 1993), 91.

23. Nicolae Bălotescu et al., *Istoria aviației române* (Bucharest: Editura Științifică și Enciclopedică, 1984), 89, 92; *RRM*, 1:70; Valeriu Avram, "Acțiunile aeronautici române în campania din 1916," in *ACTA III al III-lea colocviu internațional de istorie militară*, ed. Costica Prodan and Dumitru Preda [*ACTA*] (Bucharest: Comisia Română de Istorie Militară, 1997), 118; AMR, Fond MCG, 1st Army, 1st Division, Raport, 9 September 1916.

24. Nicolae Bîrdeanu and Dan Nicolaescu, *Contribuții la istoria marinei române* (Bucharest: Editura Științifică și Enciclopedică, 1979), 2:262, 266, 274; Olaf Richard Wulff, *Die österreichisch-ungarische Donauflottille im Weltkrieg* (Vienna: Braumüller, 1934), 82–83; N. Negrescu, *Rolul marinei în războiul pentru întregirea neamului și recompensa finală* (Bucharest: Gutemberg, 1920), 5–8.

25. Constantin Niculescu-Rizea, "Memoriu asupra activității mele în gradul de comodor cu privire la referatul domnului Amiral Bălescu," April 1918, BCS, Fond St. Georges; Negrescu, *Rolul*, 8, 7, 93; Berthelot to Ferdinand, 10 December, "Rapport du Colonel de Breda," BCS, Fond St. Georges; Vasile Scodrea, "Memoriu: situația flotei la 11 Januarie 1917," BA (Bucharest), Fond Palatului; N. Negrescu, *Comment on fit la guerre sur le Danube 1916–1918* (Bucharest: Imprimeriile Naționale, 1938), 32.

26. Oșca et al., *Proiecte și planuri*, 22, 25; Victor Atanasiu, "Atitudinea și rolul militar al româniei în perioada neutralității și în campania din anul 1916" (doctoral thesis, Academia Militară, Bucharest, 1975), 74–77. There were also plans for war with Bulgaria and even some preliminary consideration given to using an Austro-Russian war to occupy Transylvania.

27. Alexandru Oșca, Dumitru Preda, and Eftimie Ardeleanu, eds., *Istoria Statului Major General Român. Documente 1859–1947* (Bucharest: Editura Militară, 1994), 137; Atanasiu, "Atitudinea," 77; Rosetti, *Mărturisiri*, 49–50; Dumitru Iliescu, *Documente privitoare războiul pentru întregirea României* (Bucharest: Imprimirea Statului, 1924), 32–33.

28. Oşca et al., *Proiecte şi planuri*, 122ff; *RRM*, 1:84–95. "Romanian troops will not be able to undertake offensive operations or even defensive operations on a large scale in Dobrogea" (from a memorandum of the Operations Bureau, May 1916, quoted in Atanasiu, "Atitudinea," 103).

29. *RRM*, 1:95; Oşca et al., *Proiecte şi planuri*, 178; Rosetti, *Mărturisiri*, 79; *RRM*, 1 (D), no. 43; Prodan and Preda, *Romanian Army*, 27–28.

30. Hypothesis Z is analyzed in detail by Protopopescu, *Arta militară*, 19–27, and Dabija, *Armata română*, 1:67–100.

31. Oşca et al., *Proiecte şi planuri*, 172; Ţenescu (Sofia) to MSM, 28 July 1916, BCS, Fond St. Georges; Saint-Aulaire to Paris, 8 August, AD, Guerre, Roumanie, vol. 99; Barclay (Bucharest) to FO, 30 July, PRO/FO 371/2607; George Protopopescu, "Planul de campanie al MCG român pentru primul război mondial," *Acta musei napocensis* 9 (1972): 308–310; Dabija, *Armata română*, 1:166, 178.

32. In 1924, a "Commission to Establish the Truth in the Preparation of the Army 1914–1916" listed the statistical information about increases in numbers of men, officers, equipment, and supplies. It made no value judgments and confined itself to praising what had been achieved and reciting the obvious impediments to further accomplishment, such as lack of domestic production facilities and inability to purchase armaments. It is summarized in Oşca, "Pregatirea armatei," 12–34.

33. Oşca et al., *Istoria Statului*, 16–20; *IMPR*, 5:53–56; Anastasiu, *Răsboiul*, 26–29; Duca, *Amintiri*, 2:17; Rosetti, *Mărturisiri*, 83, 102; KA (Vienna), NFA, 1st Armeekmdo, NA, Fasz. 33, "Verzeichnis höherer rumänischen Offiziere," 24 October 1916.

34. Duca, *Amintiri*, 2:38–39; Rosetti, *Mărturisiri*, 83–84, 90; Iliescu, *Documente*, 39; E. Ardeleanu, ed., *Marele Cartier General al armatei române. Documente, 1916–1920* [hereafter cited as *MCG . . . Documente*] (Bucharest: Editura Militară, 1996), 8–9; Argetoianu, *Pentru cei de mîine*, 3:31.

35. Christescu was a graduate of L'école de guerre in Paris but was considered to be a Germanophile. KA (Vienna), NFA, 1st Armeekmdo, NA, Fasz. 33, "Verzeichnis. . . . Offiziere"; Bronsart (Bucharest) to AA, 29 March 1914, Bussche (Bucharest) to AA, 25 May 1916, AA, PA, file Rumänien 11; Czernin to Vienna, 15 August 1916, HHStA, PA I, Karton 520; Rosetti, *Mărturisiri*, 88, 101–102, 231, 237.

36. Iliescu, *Documente*, 37; Oşca et al., *Proiecte şi planuri*, passim; NFA, 1st Armeekmdo, NA, Fasz. 33, "Verzeichnis. . . . Offiziere"; Rosetti, *Mărturisiri*, 51–52, 82–83; Răşcanu had served as Romanian military attaché in Berlin during 1907–1911.

37. Duca, *Amintiri*, 1:262; Maria Georgescu, "Studiu introductiv," in Rosetti, *Mărturisiri*, 13, 15–16.

38. See "Studiu introductiv," in Alexandru Averescu, *Notiţe zilnice din război* [*NZ*], vol. 1, ed. Eftimie Ardeleanu and Adrian Pandea (Bucharest: Editura Militară, 1992); KA (Vienna), NFA, 1st Armeekmdo, NA, Fasz. 33, "Verzeichnis. . . . Offiziere."

39. Petre Otu, *Mareşalul Alexandru Averescu: militarul, omul politic, legenda* (Bucharest: Editura Militară, 2005), 77, 80, 88, 90, 102, 108, 112.

40. Averescu, *NZ*, 1:53, 71–73, 153–156. There are hints but no hard evidence that

Averescu proposed, before the war, that the principal action be in the south against Bulgaria.

41. Quoted in Rosetti, *Mărturisiri*, 59.

3. ON THE EVE OF WAR

1. Mühlmann, *Oberste Heeresleitung*, 169–170; Luckenwald (OHL) to AA, 1 August, AA, PA, Deutschland 128 no. 2. (For the contents of these intercepts, see dispatches of Luckenwald, Grünau [OHL], to AA, 15, 20, 24, 25, 26, 29, 31 July, 1, 4, 7, 8, 9, 10, 13, 18, 19, 27 August.) von Hötzendorf to Burian, 12 August, HHStA, PA I, Karton 520.

2. Hammerstein to Falkenhayn, 9, 10 August, AA, PA, Deutschland 128 no. 2; Karl-Heinz Janssen, *Der Kanzler und der General* (Göttingen: Musterschmidt Verlag, 1967), 241.

3. Admiralty Staff to AA, 26 July, Hammerstein to Falkenhayn, 3, 5, 11, 16 August, AA, PA, Deutschland 128 no. 2; BA/MA (Freiburg), RM 40, Marine Attaché (Constantinople) to Admiralty Staff, 9 August; Reichsarchiv, *Der Weltkrieg,* 10:601.

4. Luckenwald to AA, 5 August, Hammerstein to Falkenhayn, 11 August, AA, PA, Deutschland 128 no. 2; Evidenz Büro Armee Oberkommando [AOK], "Rumänien," 8 August, HHStA (Vienna), PA I, Karton 520.

5. Czernin to Vienna, 9 August, HHStA, PA I, Karton 520; Bussche to AA, 23 August, AA, PA, Deutschland 128 no. 2.

6. Hammerstein to Falkenhayn, 21 August, Bussche to AA, 25 July, 22, 24 August, AA, PA, Deutschland 128 no. 2; Titu Maiorescu, "Politica de neutralitate în conflictul european din 1914–1917," BA (Bucharest), Fond Maiorescu; Nuțu, *România,* 309–311; "Papers of General Hans von Seeckt," NARA, M-132/27, 4 September. Seeckt was the chief of staff of the Austrian Army Group Archduke Karl, which faced Romania.

7. Obrendorff (Sofia) to AA, 13 August, Bethmann Hollweg to AA, 21 August, AA, PA, Deutschland 128 no. 2; Reichsarchiv, *Der Weltkrieg,* 10:602; Erich von Falkenhayn, *Campania Armatei 9-a împotriva Românilor și Rușilor, 1916–1917,* translated by Al. Budiș and C. Franc (Bucharest: Socec, 1937), 15.

8. Thurn (AOK) to Vienna, 31 August, HHStA, PA I, Karton 520; Gerhard Ritter, *Staatskunst und Kriegshandwerk,* vol. 3 (Munich: Oldenbourg, 1964), 246–249; Janssen, *Kanzler,* 249–251. Seeckt commented sarcastically to his wife: "Was this the birthday of the Kaiser? If so, the Romanian declaration of war was a birthday present." Seeckt Papers, NARA, M-132/27, 27 August.

9. Mühlmann, *Oberste Heeresleitung,* 166.

10. Wulff, *Donauflottille,* 80; KA (Vienna), *Österreich-Ungarns Letzter Krieg, 1914–1918,* 7 vols. + 7 vols. Beilagen (Vienna: Verlag der Militärwissenschaftlichen Mitteilungen, 1930–1938), vol. 5, *Das Kriegsjahr, 1916,* 238, 244; Oskar Regele, *Kampf um die Donau* (Potsdam: Voggenreiter, 1940), 49–50; KA (Vienna), AOK, Bevollmächtigte Verbindungsoffiziere [VO], Fasz. 6270, VO/Oberkommando Mackensen [OKM], 27 July.

11. Thurn (AOK) to Vienna, 20 July, HHStA, PA I Karton 520; AMR, Fond Comandamentul Trupelor din Transilvania, Goldbach, "Grenzeverteidigung durch die Gendarmerie," 14 June 1915.

12. *Letzter Krieg*, 5:240–242; Reichsarchiv, *Der Weltkrieg*, 11:197; Rudolf Kiszling, "Feldzug," 3–4; Arthur Arz von Straussenburg, *Zur Geschichte des Grossen Kriegs, 1914–1918* (Vienna: Rikola Verlag, 1924), 104.

13. KA (Vienna), AOK, VO, Fasz. 6277, VO/OKM, 26, 31 July; Falkenhayn to Jagow (AA), 31 July, Bussche to AA, 17 August, AA, PA, Deutschland 128 no. 2; BA/MA (Freiburg), N 440/III, Ulrich von Henning, "Kriegs Erinnerungen," 61. Henning was the German liaison officer attached to the Bulgarian 3rd Army in Dobrogea.

14. Regele, *Kampf*, 51; Wolfgang Foerster, ed., *Mackensen. Briefe und Aufzeichnungen* (Leipzig: Bibliographisches Institut, 1938), 280–282.

15. KA (Vienna), AOK, VO, Fasz. 6270, VO/OKM, 25 July, 8, 17 August; Reichsarchiv, *Der Weltkrieg*, 10:598, 11:195; *Letzter Krieg*, 5:271; Foerster, *Mackensen*, 277.

16. KA (Vienna), AOK, VO, Fasz. 6277, VO/OKM, 13, 14 August, VO Fasz. 6408, VO/Bulgarian High Command [BGK], 16 August; Foerster, *Mackensen*, 278; Obrendorff to AA, 11 August, Bussche to AA, 13 August, AA, PA, Deutschland 128 no. 2; Nastovici, *România și puterile centrale*, 221.

17. Cyril Falls, *Military Operations: Macedonia*, 2 vols. (London: H.M. Stationery Office, 1933–1935), 1:140–144, 153–158; KA (Vienna) AOK, VO Fasz. 6270, VO/OKM, 17, 18, 21, 22 August, VO Fasz. 6408, VO/BGK, 17, 18, 24 August.

18. KA (Vienna), AOK, VO, Fasz. 6277, VO/OKM, 17, 20 August.

19. Wilhelm Groener, "Memoirs," NARA, M-137/2, 427, 29–30 August.

20. Duca, *Portrete*, 40; Gheorghe I. Brătianu, *File rupte din cartea războiului* (Bucharest: Editura "Cultura Națională," n.d.), 20–22; Langu to Rășcanu (MSM), 11, 21, 25 August, Arhiva Ministerului Afacerilor Externe Române (Bucharest) [AMAER], Fond 71/1914/E2, vol. 35.

21. Langu to Rășcanu, 23 August, Derussi (Sofia) to Bucharest, 6, 14 August, AMAER, Fond 71/1914/E2, vol. 35; Barclay to London, 16 August, PRO/FO 371/2623; Bertie Papers, PRO/FO/16/40, 17 August, PRO/FO 800/176; Fasciotti to Rome, 26 August, AS (Rome), Telegrammi . . . Arrivo, vol. 441.

22. Fasciotti to Rome, 20, 22, 24 August, AS (Rome), Telegrammi . . . Arrivo, vol. 441; Barclay to London, 22, 26 August, Buchanan (Petrograd) to London, 18 August, Grey to Buchanan, 18 August, PRO/FO 371/2623; Saint-Aulaire to Paris, 23, 24 August, AD, Guerre, Roumanie, vol. 99, vol. 112, 2.

23. Duca, *Amintiri*, 1:271–272; Victor Antonescu, "Memoriu," 27 August, BCS, Fond St. Georges, Arhiva Antonescu; Marghiloman, *Note politice*, 2:149–153; Iordache, *Brătianu*, 301.

24. Argetoianu, *Pentru cei de mîine*, 3:15; Constantin Kirițescu, *O viață, o lume, o epocă: memorii* (Bucharest: Sport-Turism, 1979), 211; Arhibald [pseud. (R. Rădulescu?)], *Porcii: impresii din timpul ocupației*, vol. 1 (Bucharest: "Poporul," 1921), 8; Christian Racovskii, "Arest și liberare," BA (Bucharest), Fond I. I. C. Brătianu. Gen-

eral Averescu, on the other hand, noticed "little enthusiasm" in the evening; the capital had a "lugubrious appearance." Averescu, *NZ*, 1:119.

25. Nicolae Iorga, *O viață de om*, vol. 2 (Bucharest: Stroila, 1934), 227; Duca, *Amintiri*, 2:24; Vasile T. Cancicov, *Impresiuni și păreri personale din timpul războiului României*, 2 vols. (Bucharest: Universul, 1921), 1:14–15; Arhibald, *Porcii*, 1:7.

26. Constantin Căzănișteanu and Dorina Rusu, eds., *Pe aci nu se trece!* (Bucharest: Editura Albatros, 1982), 55–57; "Pașiunea lui Ion Bulăcu: un țăran ca toți țăranii (1)," *Magazin istoric* 12, no. 9 (1978): 15; Traian Moșoiu, *Memorial de război (august–octombrie 1916)* (Cluj: Editura Dacia, 1987), 67.

27. Costescu, *Carnetul*, 10, 14; Sturdza, "Jurnal," 18/31 August; Averescu, *NZ*, 1:118; Duca, *Amintiri*, 2:9.

28. Cancicov, *Impresiuni*, 1:15; Vasile Bianu, *Însemnări din răsboiul româniei mari*, vol. 1 (Cluj: "Ardealul," 1926), 11; Ion Bulei, *1916: Zile de vara* (Bucharest: Eminescu, 1978), 230; Sturdza, "Jurnal," 18/31 August.

29. G. Brătianu, *File rupte*, 19–21; Marghiloman, *Note politice*, 2:159; Rădulescu-Zoner and Marinescu, *Bucureștii*, 54–57, 68–69. Much of this detail is recorded by the American military attaché. Captain E. H. Yates to War Department, 1 September, NARA, War Department, Reports of the Military Attaché in Romania.

30. *RRM*, 1:153–154, 160, 164, 166; Prodan and Preda, *Romanian Army*, 28–32; Dabija, *Armata română*, 1:105–106. Nevertheless, many delays did occur. The 1st Army command staff, for example, waited 12 hours on the platform for its train to Craiova. Many officers had trouble reaching their units. AMR, Fond MCG, 1st Army, "Raport rezumativ 29 August–12 September."

31. Mihail Aslan, *Memoriu asupra căderei capului de pod Turtucaia* (Iași: Ecoul, 1918), 5–6; Averescu, *NZ*, 1:116; Dabija, *Armata română*, 1:92–93, 163.

32. Ardeleanu, *MCG . . . Documente*, 76–78; Oșca et al., *Istoria Statului*, 23; Toma Dumitrescu, *Jurnal: războiul național (1916)*, ed. Petre Otu and Maria Georgescu (Bucharest: Editura Academiei de Inalt Studii Militare, 1999), 30; Rosetti, *Mărturisiri*, 94; Yates to War Department, 1 September, NARA, War Department, Reports of the Military Attaché in Romania.

33. Rosetti, *Mărturisiri*, 79, 96–99, 101–102; Duca, *Amintiri*, 2:17; Otu, *Averescu*, 131–132.

34. Marghiloman, *Note politice*, 2:176; Rosetti, *Mărturisiri*, 95–97, 104; Averescu, *NZ*, 2:66; Duca, *Amintiri*, 2:33.

4. THE INVASION OF TRANSYLVANIA

1. Rosetti, *Mărturisiri*, 79; *RRM*, 1 (D), no. 141; Argetoianu, *Pentru cei de mîine*, 3:18.

2. KA (Vienna), NFA, 1st Armeekmdo, NA, Fasz. 33, "Verzeichnis . . . Offiziere"; C. Căzănișteanu et al., *Comandanți militari. Dicționar* (Bucharest: Editura Științifică și Enciclopedică, 1983), 259–260. This stigma was reinforced by the perception that Prezan's advancement in the army was also due to his young wife, Olga, who was

one of Ferdinand's lovers. Prezan's biographer affirms that these relationships aided his rise in the hierarchy of the army but points out that Prezan's military record was comparable to that of many of his colleagues. Petre Otu, *Mareşalul Constantin Prezan. Vocaţia datoriei* (Bucharest: Editura Militară, 2009), 44–48.

3. Larry L. Watts, "Ion Antonescu and the Great War," in *Romania in the World War I Era*, ed. Kurt Treptow (Iaşi: Center for Romanian Studies, 1999), 77–98. Argetoianu (*Pentru cei de mîine*, 3:121) alleges, in jest, that Antonescu "led him [Prezan] by the nose." After the war, Antonescu tended to emphasize his own role almost to the point of portraying the general as a figurehead (Otu, *Prezan*, 161). Certainly Antonescu was the exclusive collaborator, if not the source, in all of Prezan's military planning. V. F. Dobrinescu and Gh. Niculescu, *Plata şi Răsplata Istoriei: Ion Antonescu: militar şi diplomat, 1914–1940* (Iaşi: Institutul European, 1994), 12–22.

4. BA/MA (Freiburg), RM 40, Kaiserliche Nachrichtendienst Bukarest, Berichte, 11 September; *Letzter Krieg*, 5:247; *RRM*, 1 (D), no. 146; *RAPRM*, 1:277.

5. *RRM*, 1:207–209, 315, 653, 834–836; *RRM*, 1 (D), nos. 107–108, 313–316; Rosetti, *Mărturisiri*, 120; Torrey, *Romania and World War I*, 241–242; *RAPRM*, 1:281; Stone, *Eastern Front*, 270.

6. *RRM*, 1 (D), nos. 146, 156; Dabija, *Armata română*, 2:266–267.

7. *Letzter Krieg*, 5:280–281; *RRM*, 1 (D), nos. 147, 149, 220, 221.

8. *Letzter Krieg*, 5:258, 260, 282–286; Curt von Morgen, *Meiner Truppen Heldenkämpfe* (Berlin: Mittler, 1920), 103; *RRM*, 1 (D), nos. 159, 222, 223.

9. Prodan and Preda, *Romanian Army*, 42; *RRM*, 1 (D), nos. 158–160; *RAPRM*, 1:284.

10. Dabija, *Armata română*, 2:284–285; *RAPRM*, 1:284, 294, 296.

11. Otu, *Averescu*, 131–132.

12. BA/MA (Freiburg), RM 40, Nachrichtendienst Bukarest, Berichte, 11 September; E. Ionescu, *Pe Neajlov*, 23; Kiszling, "Feldzug," 3.

13. *Letzter Krieg*, 5:249–251. The Szeklers were descendants of non-Hungarian-speaking peoples who had long since become completely Magyarized (integrated into Hungarian culture).

14. *RRM*, 1:289–295, 299, 379–380.

15. *RRM*, 1 (D) no. 139; *Letzter Krieg*, 5:288–289; *RRM*, 1:289–290, 379–380, 384–395, 400–401; Dabija, *Armata română*, 2:169.

16. *Letzter Krieg*, 5:280; *RRM*, 1:289–308, 389–405; *RAPRM*, 1:295; Prodan and Preda, *Romanian Army*, 44.

17. Duca, *Amintiri*, 2:35–36; Rosetti, *Mărturisiri*, 201; Ioan D. Culcer, *Note şi cugetări asupra campaniei din 1916* (Iaşi: Tribuna, 1919), 84.

18. Dragalina resigned his Habsburg commission in 1887 to enter the Romanian army, an action not uncommon during the early years of Romania's membership in the Triple Alliance. Nicolae Popescu, *Generalul Ion Dragalina* (Bucharest: Editura Militară, 1967), 11–13; Virgil A. Dragalina, *Viaţa tatălui meu, Generalul Ioan Dragalina* (Bucharest: Editura Militară, 2009), 70.

19. AMR, Fond MCG, 1st Army, Biroul de operaţii, Instrucţiuni Secret no. 1, 2

September, 1st ID, Dragalina, Raport, 25 August, 5, 7 September; *RRM*, 1:105, 232–233, 236–239; *Letzter Krieg*, 5:255–256; Popescu, *Dragalina*, 49, 54, 55.

20. Alexandru Sturdza to Zoe Sturdza, 1 September, BA (Bucharest), Fond Sturdza; Nicolae Defleury, *Divizia de la Cerna. De pe front și în captivitatea, 1916–1918* (Craiova: Editura Ramur, 1940), 47–48; Moșoiu, *Memorial*, 71–72.

21. Alexandru Niculescu, *Luptele de la Jiu* (Bucharest: Editura Militară, 1976), 12; *RRM*, 1:232–236, 321; *Letzter Krieg*, 5:254; Dabija, *Armata română*, 2:26.

22. *Letzter Krieg*, 5:278–279; AMR, Fond MCG, 1st Army, Biroul de operații, Instrucționii secret, 11 September; *RRM*, 1:305–306; Culcer, *Note*, 90–93; Niculescu, *Jiu*, 24–27; [KA (Munich)], Alpencorps, Abteilung la, Bund 4, Kriegstagebuch Siebenbürgen Rumänien, 8 September.

23. Kirițescu, *Istoria războiului*, 1:237; Adolf Reiner, "Erinnerungen aus dem Weltkrieg"; *Die Neue Zeitung* (Sibiu), 30 August, 6, 13 September, 4, 11 October 1936; *Letzter Krieg*, 5:253.

24. AMR, Fond MCG, 1st Army, Instrucțiuni Secret no. 1, 2 September; *RRM*, 1:100, 223; KA (Vienna), Manuskripte Weltkrieg, Rumänien, "Bruchstücke von Gefechtsberichte über den Feldzug 1916 in Siebenbürgen"; Reiner, "Erinnerungen," *Neue Zeitung*, 20, 27 September 1936; Dabija, *Armata română*, 2:39; *Letzter Krieg*, 5:253; Victor Atanasiu, *Bătălia din zona Sibiu-Cîneni* (Bucharest: Editura Militară, 1982), 39.

25. Arz von Straussenburg, *Geschichte*, 111; Reiner, "Erinnerungen," *Neue Zeitung*, 18 October 1936; *RRM*, 1 (D), no. 120; Atanasiu, *Bătălia*, 37–39; Moșoiu, *Memorial*, 29, 77–79; *RRM*, 1:230; *Letzter Krieg*, 5:254.

26. Reiner, "Erinnerungen," *Neue Zeitung*, 25 October 1936; Atanasiu, *Bătălia*, 43–44; Moșoiu, *Memorial*, 79; *RRM*, 1:231, 309–310; *RRM*, 1 (D), no. 124; Dabija, *Armata română*, 2:44–47; Goldbach, "Grenzeverteidigung," 15 June 1915.

27. "The remembrance of the terrible outrages committed by the Wallacheans [Romanians] in 1848–1849 enflamed their soul." Arz von Straussenburg, *Geschichte*, 109. For a balanced discussion of Transylvanian Romanians under Habsburg rule, see Keith Hitchins, *The Romanians, 1774–1866* (Oxford, U.K.: Clarenden Press, 1996), 198–230, 249–272; Hitchins, *Rumania*, 202–230.

28. AMR, Fond MCG, Raport rezumativ, 16–31/29 August–13 September; Moșoiu, *Memorial*, 75; Litz Korodi to Alfred Zimmerman (AA), 31 January 1917, in Ion Ardeleanu et al., *1918 la români. Desăvîrșire unității național statale a poporului român. Documente externe, 1916–1918*, vol. 2 (Bucharest: Editura Științifică și Enciclopedică, 1983), 882–885.

29. BA/MA (Freiburg), RM 40, Nachrichtendienst Bukarest, Berichte, 11 September; Reiner, "Erinnerungen," *Neue Zeitung*, 22 November; M. Rill and C. Göllner, "Die Erste Weltkrieg, 1914–1918," in *Die Siebenbürger Sachsen in den Jahren, 1848–1918*, ed. Carl Göllner (Vienna: Bohlau, 1988), 248–249.

30. AMR, Fond Comandamentul Trupelor din Transilvania, Goldbach to Siebenbürgische Gendarme Truppen, 10 August; Kiszling, "Feldzug," 8–9; Arz von Straussenburg, *Geschichte*, 108; *Letzter Krieg*, 5:256; KA (Munich), Alpenkorps, 1a, Bund 34, "Besondere Anordnungen für Truppen," 13 September.

31. BA/MA (Freiburg), RM 40, Nachrichtendienst Bukarest, Berichte, 11 September; Arz von Straussenburg, *Geschichte*, 109, 118; Kiszling, "Feldzug," 8–9; Rill and Göllner, "Erste Weltkrieg," 247; Reiner, "Erinnerungen," *Neue Zeitung*, 10 January 1937; Falkenhayn, *Campania*, 20.

32. Bianu, *Însemnări*, 1:27; Ioan Vlad, "The Welcoming of the Romanian Troops in Braşov on August 29, 1916," *Romanian Review* 30, no. 5–6 (1996), 76–77; KA (Vienna), AOK, VO, Fasz. 6281, VO/OKM, no. 25088/9, reproducing a captured Romanian decree of 15 September.

33. Bianu, *Însemnări*, 1:25; Vlad, "Welcoming," 78–79, 83–84, 87; Dumitru Preda and Costica Popa, "Romanian Battalions Cross the Carpathians," *Pages of History* 12, no. 4 (1987): 148–150; *Universul*, 30, 31 August; Cancicov, *Impresiuni*, 1:25, 31; Neli Cornea, *Însemnări din vremea războiului. Jurnal* (Bucharest: Steinberg, n.d.), 5; "Pasiunea lui Ion Bulăcu, 29 August–1 September," *Magazin istoric* 12, no. 9 (1978): 15–16; KA (Munich), Alpenkorps, Abteilung 1b, Bund 67, AOK Nachrichten, 1 November; Moşoiu, *Memorial*, 84; Căzănişteanu and Rusu, *Pe aci nu se trece!*, 62.

34. Liviu Maior, "Soldaţi români în armata Austro-Ungară, 1914–1918," in *Civilizaţia medievală şi modernă românească*, ed. Nicolae Edroiu, Aurdel Raduţiu, and Pompiliu Teodor (Cluj: Editura Dacia, 1985), 357–360; Liviu Maior, *Habsburgi şi români. De la loialitatea dinastică la identitate naţională* (Bucharest: Editura Enciclopedică, 2006), 127, 131–134; Günther Klein, "Die rumänische Offiziere in der k u k Armee. Sozial Aufsteig ohne Verlust de nationalen Identität?," *Revista istorică* 8, no. 3–4 (1997): 475–489; von Hötzendorf to Kriegsministerium, 18 November, KA (Vienna), AOK, Militär Kanzlei Seiner Majestät, Ops. no. 34/242; Morgen, *Meiner Truppen*, 103. Rodica Baluţiu, "Atitudinea soldaţi român faţă de primul război mondial," *Studii Universitatis Babes-Bolyai. Historia* 46, no. 1–2 (2000): 107–115; Gheorghe Bichicean, "Carnetul cu însemnări din primul război mondial ale învăţătorului Nicolae Curan," in Prodan and Preda, *ACTA*, 3:150–151; Dumitru Ciumbrudean, *Jurnal de front* (Bucharest: Editura Politică, 1976), 221–223.

5.THE WAR OPENS ON THE DOBROGEAN FRONT

1. KA (Vienna), AOK, VO, Fasz. 6270, VO/OKM, 30 August, 2 September; Foerster, *Mackensen*, 285; *Letzter Krieg*, 5:240. Berlin was concerned about reports that the Entente had approached Bulgaria with an offer of a separate peace. Jagow to Michahelles, 3 September, AA, PA, Deutschland 128 no. 2.

2. Henning, "Erinnerungen," 14, 16, 19, 30–31. Boris (1894–1943) reigned as king of Bulgaria during 1918–1943.

3. Stefan Popov, "Deistviiata na treta otdelna armiia v Dobrudzha prez 1916 godina," *Voennoistoricheski Sbornik* 65, no. 3 (1996): 152–153; Reichsarchiv, *Der Weltkrieg*, 10:202; KA (Vienna), AOK, VO, Fasz. 6270, VO/OKM, 2, 3 September; Boris Cholpanov, "Atakata ovladiavaneto na Tutrakanskatat krepost prez purvata svetovna voina," *Voennoistoricheski Sbornik* 59, no. 3 (1990): 128, 130; Henning, "Erinnerungen," 21, 24, 29.

4. Cholpanov, "Atakata," 106–112; S. Popov, "Deistviiata," 151; Petur Boichev, "Purvata svetovna voina 1915–1918 g. Bitaka za Tutrakan," in *Uchastieto na tutrakantsi vuv voinite: sbornik s izsledvaniia* [The Participation of Tutrakan in the War: Collection of Studies] (Tutrakan: Istoricheski Muzei, 1995), 134–135.

5. Averescu to Ferdinand, 9 September, AN (Bucharest), Fond Casa Regală, 1/1916; Ioanițiu, *Războiul româniei*, 44–45; Lupașcu-Stejar, *Din războiul*, 53; Costescu, *Carnetul*, 40–43, 47; Scărișoreanu, *Fragmente*, 32–49; Henning, "Erinnerungen," 40.

6. In a conscious act of deception, the Russians had worded their obligation as "two divisions of infantry and one division of cavalry" lest the weak strength of the Russian units force them to send more to total 50,000. Janin to Joffre, 28 July, AD, Guerre, Roumanie, vol. 112; Hanbury-Williams to Robertson, 28 July, PRO/FO 371/2607.

7. Although designated the "1 Serb Division of Volunteers in Russia," it probably encompassed additional Habsburg Slavic minorities. For a short history of this unit, see Miodrag Milin, "Operațiile diviziei 1 sârbe de voluntari în Dobrogea (august–octombrie 1916), după informații de arhivă iugoslave," in Prodan and Preda, *ACTA*, 3:105–110.

8. Andrei Zaionchkovskii, "Dobrudzha avgusta-oktiabr' 1916 goda," Tsentral'nyi Gosudarstvennyi Voenno-Istoricheskii Arkhiv (Moscow), Fond 69; "Russian Military Operations on the Romanian Front, October–December 1916" (report of Major Thornhill), PRO/FO 371/2883; Costescu, *Carnetul*, 122. Brătianu complained officially about "the deplorable effect produced by the Russian army in Dobrogea." Brătianu to Diamandy, 31 October, AN (Bucharest), Fond Casa Regală, 29/1916.

9. Zaionchkovskii to Alekseev, 23 August, Zaionchkovskii, "Dobrudzha," Tsentral'nyi Gosudarstvennyi Voenno-Istoricheskii Arkhiv (Moscow), Fond 69; Torrey, *Romania and World War I*, 235.

10. Argetoianu, *Pentru cei de mîine*, 3:33; Duca, *Amintiri*, 2:115. Aslan's chief of staff, General Gheorghe Mărdărescu, and his operations officer, Lt. Colonel Gheorghe Dabija, were both highly regarded.

11. Boichev, "Purvata svetovna," 103; Negrescu, *Comment*, 104–105; Dabija, *Armata română*, 1:179–185; Pamfil Șeicaru, *La Roumanie dans la grande guerre* (Paris: Minard, 1968), 304.

12. A French military attaché, visiting Turtucaia in June 1916, recognized the obsolescence of the fortifications, but out of concern for Romanian amour propre, he refrained from pointing this out to Colonel Rășcanu, who accompanied him. Pichon, "Historique de négotiations poursuivres."

13. KA (Vienna), AOK, VO, Fasz. 6270, VO/OKM, 7 September; Teodorescu, "Memoriu"; Kirițescu, *Istoria războiului*, 1:367; Negrescu, *Comment*, 113; *RRM*, 1 (D), nos. 270, 271; Dabija, *Armata română*, 1:252–253.

14. Duca, *Amintiri*, 2:15; Lupașcu-Stejar, *Din războiul*, 32.

15. Cholpanov, "Atakata," 112; Henning, "Erinnerungen," 16. His chief of staff was Colonel Stefan Noykov, who later served as chief of operations for the Bul-

garian High Command and after the war as chief of staff of the Bulgarian army. Ivan Stoichev, *Stroiteli i boini vozhdove na bulgarska voiska, 1879–1941* (Sofia: Todorov, 1941), 37, 41.

16. Ioanițiu, *Războiul româniei*, 48; Dabija, *Armata română*, 1:186; Ivan Popov, *Die Einnahme der Brückenkopffestung Tutrakan in Jahr 1916 und die Bulgarische Wehrmacht von heute* (Berlin: Heymann, 1940), 35; Cholpanov, "Atakata," 106, 112, 113; Boichev, "Purvata svetovna," 134–135, 142, 153.

17. Dabija, *Armata română*, 1:280–281; Costescu, *Carnetul*, 43.

18. KA (Vienna), AOK, VO, Fasz. 6270, VO/OKM, 4 September; S. Popov, "Deistviiata," 156–164; *RRM*, 1:488, 500, 530–534; Ioanițiu, *Războiul româniei*, 55–58; Dabija, *Armata română*, 1:283, 297–298.

19. Scărişoreanu, *Fragmente*, 38–40; Costescu, *Carnetul*, 44–47, 51. Arghirescu blames the inexperience of his men and the failure of his officers to carry out his orders. "Operațiile şi istoricul regimentului 9 vânători in războiul pentru întregirea neamul românesc 1916–1919," 51–55, BA (Bucharest), Manuscrise, A2085.

20. Dimitr Azmanov, "General Ivan Kolev," *Voennoistoricheski Sbornik* 65, no. 3 (1996): 78–97; Henning, "Erinnerungen," 16, 31–32; KA (Vienna), AOK, VO. Fasz. 6270, VO/OKM, 2 September; S. Popov, "Deistviiata," 152–153; Dabija, *Armata română*, 1:285. Scărişoreanu, *Fragmente*, 35–36.

21. Tarnowski to Vienna, 4 September, HHStA, PA I, Karton 995.

22. KA (Vienna), AOK, VO, Fasz. 6270, VO/OKM, 4 September; Negrescu, *Comment*, 141–142; Dabija, *Armata română*, 1:196–197; Popov, *Tutrakan*, 16; *RRM*, 1 (D), nos. 305, 306.

23. Iorga, *O viață de om*, 2:227; *RRM*, 1:474; Dumitrescu, *Jurnal*, 31; Aslan, *Memoriu*, 11; Kirițescu, *Istoria războiului*, 1:376.

24. *RRM*, 1:486; Henning, "Erinnerungen," 36; *RRM*, 1 (D), no. 332; Dabija, *Armata română*, 1:209; Aslan, *Memoriu*, 13; Rosetti, *Mărturisiri*, 110.

25. Cholpanov, "Atakata," 103; I. Popov, *Tutrakan*, 17–19; *RRM*, 1:553; *RRM*, 1 (D), nos. 325, 327, 328, 343; Dabija, *Armata română*, 1:211–212, 291; Zaionchkovskii, "Dobrudzha," 12; Cupşa, *Armata*, 69.

26. *RRM*, 1 (D), nos. 334, 342, 346, 348, 554; Lupaşcu-Stejar, *Din războiul*, 24, 46–62; *RRM*, 1:525–529, 558–561; Dabija, *Armata română*, 1:274–277. Cholpanov ("Atakata," 122) summarizes the battle from the Bulgarian perspective.

27. *RRM*, 1:509–511; Negrescu, *Rolul*, 25; Cholpanov, "Atakata," 119; Negrescu, *Comment*, 153–154; Dabija, *Armata română*, 1:216, 222; Henning, "Erinnerungen," 41.

28. Cholpanov, "Atakata," 117–118, 126; Lupaşcu-Stejar, *Din războiul*, 14; Kirițescu, *Istoria războiului*, 1:389; *RRM*, 1:516ff; Dabija, *Armata română*, 1:222–225; Henning, "Erinnerungen," 38–39.

29. *RRM*, 1:520–525; Dabija, *Armata română*, 1:232–233; Teodorescu, "Memoriu"; Negrescu, *Comment*, 154, 166; Dumitrescu, *Jurnal*, 32; Argetoianu, *Pentru cei de mîine*, 3:35; Kirițescu, *Istoria războiului*, 1:383; *RRM*, 1 (D), no. 340; Nicolae Ionescu, *Generalul Eremia Grigorescu* (Bucharest: Editura Militară, 1967), 29.

30. Cholpanov, "Atakata," 120–121; KA (Vienna), AOK, VO, Fasz. 6270, VO/

OKM, 6 September; Negrescu, *Rolul*, 31; Dabija, *Armata română*, 1:240; *RRM*, 1:548–550; *RRM*, 1 (D), nos. 359, 360; Rosetti, *Mărturisiri*, 110; Negrescu, *Comment*, 173–174.

31. *RRM*, 1:551; Dabija, *Armata română*, 1:244; Negrescu, *Rolul*, 35; Argetoianu, *Pentru cei de mîine*, 3:34; Cholpanov, "Atakata," 122; Negrescu, *Comment*, 173–176; KA (Vienna), AOK, VO, Fasz. 6270, VO/OKM, 7 September.

32. Kirițescu, *Istoria războiului*, 1:393–394; Boichev, "Purvata svetovna," 160; *RRM*, 1:552. No complete accounting of casualties exists. The Bulgarians admit that 1,500 were killed in action at Turtucaia. Among the Romanians, the 79th Infantry Regiment alone suffered over 1,500 dead; their total must have been twice that. The best estimate is that each side counted 8,000 to 9,000 men and officers dead, wounded, and missing, and for the Romanians, 25,000 prisoners, totaling 40 percent of their forces in Dobrogea. Cholpanov, "Atakata," 126; Dabija, *Armata română*, 1:245–247.

33. Tarnowski to Vienna, 11 September, HHStA, PA I, Karton 995. Romanian prisoners taken at Turtucaia and later detailed for manual labor: 12,000 for Bulgarian roadwork, 8,000 for military railroad construction, 5,000 for work in Germany, 10,000 for the Austrians. KA (Vienna), AOK, VO, Fasz. 6480, VO/BGK, 18, 24 October.

34. Friedrich von Rabenau, ed., *Hans von Seeckt. Aus meinem Leben, 1866–1917* (Leipzig: Hase und Koehler, 1938), 451; Georg Alexander von Müller, *The Kaiser and His Court*, trans. and ed. Walter Görlitz (New York: Harcourt, Brace and World, 1961), 201–202. Austro-Hungarian troops celebrated with music. Moșoiu, *Memorial*, 86; KA (Vienna), AOK, VO, Fasz. 6270, 6277, VO/OKM, 8, 9, 17 September.

35. Rădulescu-Zoner and Marinescu, *Bucureștii*, 51, 60; Marghiloman, *Note politice*, 2:171, 173; Duca, *Amintiri*, 2:18; Argetoianu, *Pentru cei de mîine*, 3:34–36, 46; D. Iancovici, *Take Ionescu* (Paris: Payot, 1919), 129; Saint-Aulaire to Paris, 8 September, AD, Guerre, Roumanie, vol. 99; *Universul* (Bucharest), 8 September; Cancicov, *Impresiuni*, 1:44, 47, 182.

6. THE FLĂMÂNDA MANEUVER

1. *RRM*, 2:3–4; Rosetti, *Mărturisiri*, 112; Averescu, *NZ*, 2:16–17; Alexandru Averescu, *Răspunderile de Generalul Alexandru Averescu* (Iași: Editura "Ligei Poporului," 1918), 32; Dumitrescu, *Jurnal*, 34; Alexandru Iarca, *Memorialul meu* (Brăila: Liberia și Tipografia "Ion Călinescu," 1922), 157–158; AMR, Fond MCG, 1st Army, Biroul de operații, Instrucțiuni secrete, 11 September.

2. Cancicov, *Impresiuni*, 1:63; Averescu, *NZ*, 2:20–23, 24–28, 115, 119; Averescu to Ferdinand, 9 September, AN (Bucharest), Fond Casa Regală, 1/1916.

3. BCS, Fond St. Georges, Arhiva Coandă; *RRM*, 2:8–13; Torrey, *Romania and World War I*, 160–161; Saint-Aulaire to Paris, 8 September, AD, Guerre, Roumanie, vol. 99, 2; Joffre to Iliescu, 11 September, BCS, Fond St. Georges, Arhiva Iliescu; Military Attaché (London) to Joffre, 12, 16 September, SHAT, 16N3168.

4. AN (Bucharest), Fond Casa Regală, 53/1916, "Părere asupra situaţiunea armatei nostre şi soluţiunile ce propun," 12 September; "Dosarul Prezan," in Ion Pavelescu, Adrian Pandea, and Eftimie Ardeleanu, *Proba focului: ultima treaptă spre marea unire* (Bucharest: Editura Globus, 1991), 44–45; RRM, 2:15–17.

5. No official account of the discussion was made. For Averescu's version of the meeting, see Averescu, *Răspunderile*, 33–34, and *Operaţiile de la Flămânda* (Bucharest: "Cultura Naţională," n.d.), 25. For Prezan's version, see Ardeleanu, *MCG . . . Documente*, no. 22. For secondhand versions of Iliescu's account, see Rosetti, *Mărturisiri*, 115, and Dumitrescu, *Jurnal*, 42. The best analyses of the meeting are in Pavelescu et al., *Proba focului*, 46–54, and Otu, *Averescu*, 140–143.

6. RRM, 2:18–19.

7. RRM, 1:604–607; Dabija, *Armata română*, 1:323–327; Lupaşcu-Stejar, *Din războiul*, 124–126; Dumitrescu, *Jurnal*, 39. The Bode Brigade combined the Hammerstein detachment with some units of the German 101st ID and four Austro-Hungarian mortar batteries. Foerster, *Mackensen*, 228; *Letzter Krieg*, 5:292; KA (Vienna), AOK, VO, Fasz. 6270, VO/OKM, 10, 15 September.

8. Costescu, *Carnetul*, 54–57; Scărişoreanu, *Fragmente*, 63–64. A Bulgarian official confessed to the Austrian minister in Sofia that "only three [Romanian] prisoners were taken and indeed one because he was of Bulgarian origin and a second because he was of Turkish origin. Although such a slaughter was horrible from a humane standpoint, it was payback for all the dreadful, indescribable atrocities which the Romanian troops have committed." A Romanian prefect in Bazargic told his father that "we have committed excesses against our Bulgarians in the Quadrilateral [Southern Dobrogea] which certainly legitimized reprisals." Mittag (Sofia) to Vienna, 21 September, HHStA, PA I, Karton 995; Marghiloman, *Note politice*, 2:193; Scărişoreanu, *Fragmente*, 52–53; Porumbaru to Minister at The Hague, 20 September, AMAER (Bucharest), Fond 71/1914/E2.

9. KA (Vienna), AOK, VO, Fasz. 6277, VO/OKM, 21 September, Fasz. 6270, VO/OKM, 20 September; Foerster, *Mackensen*, 287; Henning, "Erinnerungen," 54–55.

10. Henning, "Erinnerungen," 56–57; Reichsarchiv, *Der Weltkrieg*, 11:207–208; *Letzter Krieg*, 5:293. The Bulgarians were not happy about the presence of Turkish troops, especially in a region with a substantial Turkish minority. Henning, "Erinnerungen," 30.

11. Foerster, *Mackensen*, 288–289; Henning, "Erinnerungen," 28, 58, 66.

12. RRM, 1:627–640; Dabija, *Armata română*, 1:337; Milin, "Operaţiile," 107–108; Henning, "Erinnerungen," 40, 63. The Serbs resisted capture, fearing they might be treated as traitors by Austria-Hungary.

13. Henning, "Erinnerungen," 62; Dabija, *Armata română*, 1:343–349; Costescu, *Carnetul*, 67–78; Scărişoreanu, *Fragmente*, 68–75.

14. RRM, 2: 41–45; Dumitrescu, *Jurnal*, 47–48; Rosetti, *Mărturisiri*, 116; Averescu, *NZ*, 2:31, 34, 37; Averescu, *Operaţiile*, 32–35; Zaionchkovskii, "Dobrudzha," 6, 15. Zaionchkovskii noted that Averescu, born in Bessarabia, spoke good Russian.

15. The village of Flămânda, which no longer exists, was located five kilometers south of present-day Prundu. The commission's summary of its work is in *RRM*, 2 (D), no. 11, and Averescu, *Operațiile*, 53–54. It has been suggested that a site downstream would have been better. At least it would have been farther from the threat of the Austro-Hungarian Danube flotilla. Negrescu, *Comment*, 69–70.

16. Niculescu-Rizea, "Memoriu"; Negrescu, *Rolul*, 86; Negrescu, *Comment*, 245–246; *RRM*, 2:58–59; Averescu, *Operațiile*, 58–59.

17. *RRM*, 2:52–63, 71–72; *Letzter Krieg*, 5:330. When assembled, there were 16 divisions (including Zaionchkovskii's Russo-Romanian Army of the Dobrogea, as it was now called) under Averescu's command, versus 11 divisions total for the three northern armies. Averescu took great pride in this fact. Averescu, *NZ*, 2:35–36.

18. *RRM*, 2:73–74; Reichsarchiv, *Der Weltkrieg*, 11:109; Regele, *Kampf*, 65. The Romanians relied on information supplied by the Allies from Salonika. Averescu, *Operațiile*, 40. These figures vary slightly from source to source.

19. "Jurnal de operațiile al divizie 21," 30 September, AN (Bucharest), Fond Amza Stefanescu; *RRM*, 2:71.

20. Averescu, *Operațiile*, 73–74; Negrescu, *Comment*, 56; Dumitrescu, *Jurnal*, 70–71. Averescu later reproached MCG for allowing him to go ahead in light of the worsening situation in Transylvania, of which he claims he had incomplete information.

21. "Jurnal . . . divizie 21," 1 October; Ordin de operații no. 78, 10th ID, quoted in Dabija, *Armata română*, 1:379–380; Averescu, *Operațiile*, 74, 82–83.

22. Toshev, quoted in Ioanițiu, *Războiul româniei*, 78. Regele, *Kampf*, 71; *Letzter Krieg*, 5:328; Averescu, *Operațiile*, Annex 6.

23. Henning, "Erinnerungen," 66, 68; Toshev, quoted in *RRM*, 2:188; Foerster, *Mackensen*, 291; Reichsarchiv, *Der Weltkrieg*, 11:209; Regele, *Kampf*, 83–84.

24. *Letzter Krieg*, 5:352–353; Reichsarchiv, *Der Weltkrieg*, 11:210; KA (Vienna), AOK, VO, Fasz. 6270, VO/OKM, 1 October.

25. N. Tătăranu, *Acum un sfert de veac. Amintiri din război* (Bucharest: Cartea Românească, 1940), 22; "Jurnal . . . divizie 21," 1 October; Averescu, *Operațiile*, 85; Negrescu, *Comment*, 58; Dabija, *Armata română*, 1:385; *RRM*, 2:91; *RRM*, 2 (D), no. 19; Bălotescu et al., *Istoria aviației*, 96–97; AN (Bucharest), Fond A. Văitoianu, "Flămânda." Văitoianu (1864–1956), a native of Bessarabia like Averescu, served under him throughout the war. AN (Bucharest), Fond A. Văitoianu, "Biografie."

26. "Jurnal . . . divizie 21," 1 October; Averescu, *Operațiile*, 94, 130; Regele, *Kampf*, 78; Niculescu-Rizea, "Memoriu"; Bîrdeanu and Nicolaescu, *Contribuții*, 2:288–289; Negrescu, *Rolul*, 90; Negrescu, *Comment*, 63.

27. Wulff, *Donauflottille*, 88–90; *Letzter Krieg*, 5:330; Negrescu, *Comment*, 55–56; KA (Vienna), AOK, VO, Fasz. 6270, VO/OKM, 2, 3 October; Bîrdeanu and Nicolaescu, *Contribuții*, 2:289.

28. "Jurnal . . . divizie 21," 2 October; *RRM*, 2:99–101; Negrescu, *Rolul*, 87; *RRM*, 2 (D), no. 24; Averescu, *Operațiile*, 95–96; Rosetti, *Mărturisiri*, 121.

29. Averescu, *NZ*, 2:42; Averescu, *Operațiile*, 102; *RRM*, 2:105–106; *RRM*, 2 (D),

nos. 30, 31; Văitoianu, "Flămânda"; "Jurnal . . . divizie 21," 5 October; Wulff, *Donau-flottille*, 91–92; Negrescu, *Comment*, 61; Bălescu to Negrescu, 3 October, AMR, Fond MCG; Negrescu, *Rolul*, 88; Regele, *Kampf*, 84. Few of the missing survived. The Austrian liaison at OKM reported, "Most of the prisoners were killed in order to revenge the cruelties which the Romanians had committed against the population of the [Bulgarian] villages." KA (Vienna), AOK, VO, Fasz. 6270, VO/OKM, 4 October.

30. Foerster, *Mackensen*, 292; Reichsarchiv, *Der Weltkrieg*, 11:210, 212; KA (Vienna), AOK, VO, Fasz. 6277, VO/OKM, 4 October; Toshev, as quoted in *RRM*, 2:188.

31. Dumitrescu, *Jurnal*, 74–75, 77, 79; Duca, *Amintiri*, 2:33; *Universul*, 3, 4, 5 October; Rădulescu-Zoner and Marinescu, *Bucureştii*, 71; Cancicov, *Impresiuni*, 1:84–85, 87, 89, 98.

32. Regele, *Kampf*, 61; R. J. Crampton, "The Balkans, 1914–1918," in *World War I: A History*, ed. Hew Strachan (New York: Oxford University Press, 1998), 74; Nicolae Ciobanu, "Manevra de la Flămânda şi implicaţiile ei asupra planului de campanie al marelui cartier general român," in Prodan and Preda, *ACTA*, 3:90; Protopopescu, *Arta militară*, 39. Otu (*Averescu*, 146–147) offers a balanced assessment.

33. Ciobanu, "Manevra," 91–92; George Protopopescu, "Mari comandanţi români în primul război mondial," *Acta musei napocensis* 7 (1970): 387–388. Some units, early in the war, were entrained four or more times, and more than one fought on four different fronts. E. Ionescu, *Pe Neajlov*, 11.

34. Marie, "Memorii," 10 October; Rosetti, *Mărturisiri*, 125.

7. THE AUSTRO-GERMAN COUNTEROFFENSIVE IN TRANSYLVANIA

1. *Letzter Krieg*, 5:258. More than 60 trains were required to transport one division. Details of the origin, itinerary, and destination of all Austro-German troop movements can be found, together with a map of Transylvanian railroads, in *Letzter Krieg*, vol. 5 Beilage, no. 8. See also Reichsarchiv, *Der Weltkrieg*, 11:216, 219, and Kiszling, "Feldzug," 8–9.

2. Although part of the Bavarian army, the Alpine Corps incorporated men from other regions of Germany. Organized in 1915 and trained and equipped for mountain warfare, it fought in Italy, Serbia, and most recently at Verdun. The majority of the men were young, many officers were of the nobility, and esprit de corps was high. Günther Hebert, *Das Alpenkorps* (Boppard: Harald Boldt Verlag, 1988), 37–77.

3. KA (Munich), Alpenkorps, 1a, Bund 35, "Betrachungen über die Fechtweise auf dem rumänischen Kriegsschauplätze," 13 November 1916. Captain Josef Wild, "Vortrag über die Operationen in Südost Siebenbürgen und die Schlacht bei Brassó an 7–8 X 1916," in AMR, Fond Comandamentul Trupelor din Transilvania; Falkenhayn, *Campania*, 91; Max Osborn, *Gegen die Rumänen. Mit der Falkenhayn Armee bis zum Sereth* (Berlin: Ulstein, 1917), 26.

4. Arz von Straussenburg, *Geschichte*, 112; *Letzter Krieg*, 5:258–259; Reichsarchiv, *Der Weltkrieg*, 11:217.

5. Hebert, *Alpenkorps*, 98. As he discussed his new assignment later with an

American reporter, Falkenhayn "wore a cat-about-to-eat-the-canary smile." Holger Afflerbach, *Falkenhayn: Politisches Denken und Handeln im Kaiserreich* (Munich: Oldenbourg, 1994), 466.

6. Alexandru Baboş, "Bătălia de la Sibiu (13/26–16/29 Septembrie 1916)," in Prodan and Preda, *ACTA*, 3:93; Falkenhayn, *Campania*, 29; *RRM*, 2:284; Atanasiu, *Bătălia*, 67, 114; Dabija, *Armata română*, 2:67. The ineffectiveness of Romanian artillery at Sibiu was noted by opponents. KA (Munich), Alpenkorps, 1a, Bund 35, 51st ID Kmdo to XXXIX Res Corps, 19 September.

7. Duca, *Amintiri*, 2:33; Ion Popovici, "Memoriu asupra conducerii Corpul I Armată în operaţiunile dela Olt," *RRM*, 2 (D), no. 126; Bălotescu et al., *Istoria aviaţiei*, 95; *RRM*, 2:324–325.

8. *RRM*, 2:298, 308–309, 320; *RRM*, 2 (D), no. 127; Falkenhayn, *Campania*, 44–45.

9. Reichsarchiv, *Der Weltkrieg*, 11:232; Dabija, *Armata română*, 2:66–67. Konrad Krafft von Dellmensingen (1862–1953), chief of the Bavarian General Staff, at the outbreak of war passed under the Prussian army. He became commander of the Alpine Corps in 1915. Quite in character, he was an enthusiastic mountain climber. Holger H. Herwig and Neil M. Heyman, *Biographical Dictionary of World War I* (Westport, Conn.: Greenwood Press, 1982), 212–213; Seeckt Papers, NARA, M-132/27, Seeckt to wife, 11 November 1916.

10. Falkenhayn, *Campania*, 29; Falkenhayn to Dellmensingen, 19 September, Falkenhayn to Staabs, Dellmensingen, and Schmettow, 21 September, Falkenhayn to AOK/OHL, 23 September, *RRM*, 2 (D), nos. 100, 106, 109.

11. Franz Ritter von Epp (1868–1946). In 1919 Epp founded Freikorps Epp. Later he was a Gruppenführer in the SA, a NSDAP Reichstag deputy (1928), and premier of Bavaria (1934). Josef Krumbach, ed., *Franz Ritter von Epp. Ein Leben für Deutschland* (Munich: Zentralverlag der NSDAP, Franz Eher Nachf., 1939); *Neue Deutsche Biographie* (Berlin: Duncker and Humblot, 1953–).

12. Friedrich Wilhelm Ernst Paulus (1890–1957). Paulus served as a general staff officer after the war, major general and chief of staff of the Panzer Korps (1939), then field marshal and commander of the 6th Army at Stalingrad. *Neue Deutsche Biographie*.

13. Roland Kaltenegger, *Das Deutsche Alpenkorps im Ersten Weltkrieg* (Graz-Stuttgart: Leopold Stocker Verlag, 1995), 135–140; Ernst Kabisch, *Der Rumänienkrieg, 1916* (Berlin: Vorhut-Verlag Otto Schlegel, 1938), 55–56; Popovici to 1st Army, 23 September, *RRM*, 2 (D), nos. 123, 124, 129, 130; *RRM*, 2:320–322; Moşoiu, *Memorial*, 89–90; Rosetti, *Mărturisiri*, 119.

14. Kaltenegger, *Alpenkorps*, 138–142; Reichsarchiv, *Der Weltkrieg*, 11:227–228; *RRM*, 2:384; Dabija, *Armata română*, 2:98, 108–109; Kabisch, *Rumänienkrieg*, 57–61; Falkenhayn, *Campania*, 54–55. The quantities of explosives that could be carried by hand were insufficient to create a complete blockage of the defile.

15. Falkenhayn, *Campania*, 50; Cupşa, *Armata*, 97; Atanasiu, *Bătălia*, 118–119; Moşoiu, *Memorial*, 36, 98–99.

16. Popovici to 23rd Division, 27 September, Falkenhayn to 9th Army, 26 Sep-

tember, *RRM*, 2 (D), nos. 147–149; Kiszling, "Feldzug," 15; Falkenhayn, *Campania*, 47, 52–53; Reichsarchiv, *Der Weltkrieg*, 11:228–229; Dabija, *Armata română*, 2:105–106; Atanasiu, *Bătălia*, 132–133, 135, 137–138.

17. Kiszling, "Feldzug," 17; Reichsarchiv, *Der Weltkrieg*, 11:230; Falkenhayn, *Campania*, 56–57.

18. Popovici, "Memoriu," *RRM*, 2 (D), no. 126; Atanasiu, *Bătălia*, 141–148; A. Niculescu, *Jiu*, 36–37.

19. Culcer to MCG, 23 September, Crăiniceanu to MCG, 24 September, Popovici to 2nd Army, 27 September, Culcer to MCG, 27 September, Iliescu to 2nd Army, 25, 27 September, *RRM*, 2 (D), nos. 151, 161–163, 167–168. See also the account of Dabija (*Armata română*, 2:77–78), who was on the staff of the 2nd Army at that time.

20. Reichsarchiv, *Der Weltkrieg*, 11:230–231; Falkenhayn, *Campania*, 47, 56–59, 61; *Letzter Krieg*, 5:308. Walter von Lüttwitz (1859–1942), called the "father of the Freikorps," was involved in the Kapp Putsch in Berlin in 1920. *Neue Deutsche Biographie*.

21. Popovici to 2nd Army, 27 September, Popovici to Crăiniceanu, 27 September, *RRM*, 2 (D), nos. 175, 180. Atanasiu, *Bătălia*, 149; *RRM*, 2:409.

22. Kaltenegger, *Alpenkorps*, 142–146; Kirițescu, *Istoria războiului*, 1:296–298; Atanasiu, *Bătălia*, 159, 161, 163; Moşoiu, *Memorial*, 111–112; Popovici, "Memoriu," MCG to 2nd Army, 29 September, *RRM*, 2 (D), nos. 126, 208. Romanian prisoners expressed a sense of helplessness and a desire for the war to end. KA (Munich), Alpenkorps, 1a, Bund 34, "Einsatz in Rumänien," 2 October.

23. Krumbach, *Epp*, 36; Kabisch, *Rumänienkrieg*, 66.

24. Falkenhayn to Staabs and Krafft, 29 September, *RRM*, 2 (D), no. 182; Kirițescu, *Istoria războiului*, 1:299; *Letzter Krieg*, 5:311; Rosetti, *Mărturisiri*, 120–121; Dumitrescu, *Jurnal*, 67–69, 72–74. Popovici was accused of letting himself be "surprised," of retreating prematurely, and then not organizing the retreat. Reportedly Culcer threatened to shoot himself if MCG did not sack Popovici. For Romanian critiques of the Battle of Sibiu, see Atanasiu, *Bătălia*, 186–188; Cupşa, *Armata*, 104–105; and Dabija, *Armata română*, 2:139–147.

25. Falkenhayn, *Campania*, 63, 66–68; *RRM*, 2 (D), nos. 224, 225, 233, 234.

26. *RRM*, 2 (D), no. 238; Reichsarchiv, *Der Weltkrieg*, 11:237; Falkenhayn, *Campania*, 65–67. Falkenhayn was not comfortable turning over the defense of the pass to the Hungarian 51st ID, which lacked mountain equipment. *Letzter Krieg*, 5:315.

27. Morgen, *Meiner Truppen*, 107; Reichsarchiv, *Der Weltkrieg*, 11:237; *Letzter Krieg*, 5:321–322; *RRM*, 2 (D), nos. 240, 241, 242, 246; Dabija, *Armata română*, 2:214–216; Ioanițiu, *Războiul româniei*, 104; *RRM*, 2:592–596.

28. *Letzter Krieg*, 5:326; Reichsarchiv, *Der Weltkrieg*, 11:239–240; Kabisch, *Rumänienkrieg*, 75–76; *RRM*, 2:611–617.

29. Dabija, *Armata română*, 12:228–229, 233–235; Falkenhayn, *Campania*, 82; Kabisch, *Rumänienkrieg*, 77.

30. AMR, Fond MCG, Ordin de operații, no. 40, 7 October; Dumitrescu, *Jurnal*, 78–79, 82; Rosetti, *Mărturisiri*, 124–125.

31. Falkenhayn, *Campania*, 87, 91–95; Kirițescu, *Istoria războiului*, 1:334, 336–339;

RRM, 2:619–620, 623, 627, 639–643; Dabija, *Armata română,* 2:230–231, 240–241; Wild, "Vortrag über die Operationen."

32. *RRM,* 2:644–645; Dabija, *Armata română,* 2:255.

33. Averescu, *NZ,* 2:45; *RRM,* 2:656–657. Averescu also asked for a Russian division, but STAVKA refused. Otu, *Averescu,* 150.

34. *Letzter Krieg,* 5:344–345, 350–351; Ioanițiu, *Războiul româniei,* 113–116; Otu, *Prezan,* 73–76.

35. Osborn, *Gegen die Rumänen,* 26; Kabisch, *Rumänienkrieg,* 72.

36. Ioan Moșoiu, "Note din pribegie, 1916–1919," BA (Bucharest), Fond Kirileanu; KA (Munich), Alpenkorps, 1b, Bund 67, AOK Ops. no. 11795, 1 November; Maior, *Habsburgi și români,* 134–135; Mircea Păcuraru, *Politica statului ungar față de biserica românească din Transilvania din perioad dualismului, 1867–1918* (Sibiu: Editura Institutul Biblic și de Misiune de Bisericii Ortodoxe Române, 1986), 184–185, 190–191; Constantin Voicu, *Biserica strămoseasca din Transilvania în lupta pentru unitatea spirituală și națională a poporului român* (Sibiu: Tiparul Tipografei Eparhiale, 1989), 160–161; Ion Ardeleanu et al., *1918 la români,* 2:892–893.

37. Rădulescu-Zoner and Marinescu, *Bucureștii,* 72; Cancicov, *Impresiuni,* 1:79, 93, 96, 98; "Proces verbal," Prefet de poliție de București, 6 October, Dr. Babeș, Institut de Patologie și Bacteriologie (Laboratory Report), 18 October, AMAER, Fond 72/1914/ E 2, vol. 81; Erhard Geissler, "Anwendung von Seuchenmitteln gegen Menschen nicht erwünscht: Dokumente zum Einsatz biologischen Kampfmittel im Ersten Weltkrieg," *Militärgeschichtliche Mitteilungen* 56, no. 1 (1997): 129–131; BA (Bucharest), Fond Negruzzi, Constantin Negruzzi to Virgil Arion, 15 October; Barclay to London, 13, 16 October, PRO/FO 371/2613; Cancicov, *Impresiuni,* 1:101–103.

38. Larisch (chargé, Berlin) to Vienna, 9, 13 October, memo by Alexander Hoyos (Vienna), 16 October, HHStA, PA I, Karton 954. A copy of Averescu's response is in BA (Bucharest), Fond Rosetti. The letter, intercepted by the government censor, was not made public at the time, but Brătianu used it privately to discredit Averescu. Otu, *Averescu,* 173–174. See also, Duca, *Amintiri,* 2:26, 37–38; Rosetti, *Mărturisiri,* 125, 127, 131, 151.

39. Berthelot, *Mémoires,* 16 October; Glenn E. Torrey, *Henri Mathias Berthelot: Soldier of France, Defender of Romania* (Iași: Center for Romanian Studies, 2001), 155; Dumitrescu, *Jurnal,* 78, 81, 87; Rosetti, *Mărturisiri,* 120.

8. BATTLES ON THE FRONTIERS

1. Falls, *Military Operations,* 1:201.

2. Berthelot, *Mémoires,* 12 October; Torrey, *Romania and World War I,* 242–244. See also the account of General Constantin Coandă, the Romanian liaison at STAVKA: "Memoriu asupra tratativelor cu guvernul și comandamentul suprem Rus în cursul 1916–1918 relativ la cereri de ajutoare, efecte, armament, etc.," BCS, Fond St. Georges, Arhiva Coandă.

3. Foerster, *Mackensen,* 292–293; Reichsarchiv, *Der Weltkrieg,* 11:212–213.

4. Rosetti, *Mărturisiri*, 137; *RRM*, 2:124–125, 128, 134, 144, 149, 161, 178–179, 181–183, annex no. 6; Costescu, *Carnetul*, 91–94, 99; Dabija, *Armata română*, 1:401–411, 421.

5. Foerster, *Mackensen*, 293.

6. KA (Vienna), AOK, VO, Fasz. 6277, VO/OKM, 21 September, 22 October; Henning, "Erinnerungen," 40, 62, 72, 75; Scărişoreanu, *Fragmente*, 92–95; Costescu, *Carnetul*, 126; *RRM*, 3 (pt. 2): 514, 520, 523, 542; Dabija, *Armata română*, 1:433; Foerster, *Mackensen*, 293.

7. *RRM*, 3 (pt. 2): 522, 532, 541; Dabija, *Armata română*, 1:432–435; KA (Vienna), AOK, VO, Fasz. 6270, VO/OKM, 24, 25 October; Ioaniţiu, *Războiul româniei*, 147; Henning, "Erinnerungen," 72.

8. Azmanov, "Kolev," 90; *RRM*, 3 (pt. 2): 551–553, 555–556, 567; Scărişoreanu, *Fragmente*, 92; Costescu, *Carnetul*, 127; Dabija, *Armata română*, 1:436–442; AMR, Fond MCG, de Renty to Berthelot, 8 November; Foerster, *Mackensen*, 294.

9. Reports of Consul Adams, 24, 25 October, Report of the French Consul, 24 October, all in PRO/FO 371/2629; Imperial War Museum (London), Papers of Vice-Admiral J. R. P. Hawksley, letter of L. Joy Brown, 14 December; Scărişoreanu, *Fragmente*, 95–96, 106–107.

10. Dabija, *Armata română*, 1:439, 442; *RRM*, 3 (pt. 2): 522–523, 532–538, 553–554, 562–565; KA (Vienna), AOK, VO, Fasz. 6270, VO/OKM, 25 October.

11. *RRM*, 3 (pt. 2): 588–589; Rosetti, *Mărturisiri*, 141; Negrescu, *Comment*, 277–283; Foerster, *Mackensen*, 295; Henning, "Erinnerungen," 83–84.

12. KA (Vienna), AOK, VO, Fasz. 6270, VO/OKM, 29 October, 28 November; Henning, "Erinnerungen," 78–79, 84; AOK (von Hötzendorf) to Kabinett des Ministers, "Präsidialsektion," 12 December, HHStA, KM Präs. 83–26–7.

13. KA (Vienna), AOK, VO, Fasz. 6270, VO/OKM, 28 November, Fasz. 6408, VO/BGK, 25 October, 24 March; Kiriţescu, *Istoria războiului*, 1:464. Constanţa, the Roman city of Tomis, had been Ovid's place of exile in the reign of Emperor Augustus.

14. KA (Vienna), AOK, VO, Fasz. 6270, VO/OKM, AOK, 29 October, 2 November, 13 November; Azmanov, "Kolev," 91–93; *RRM*, 3 (pt. 2): 666–667; Dabija, *Armata română*, 1:450, 458; Torrey, *Romania and World War I*, 240.

15. *Letzter Krieg*, 5:501; Milin, "Operaţiile," 110. Troop strengths of these divisions at the conclusion of the Dobrogean campaign were: 2nd ID 1,505, 5th ID 2,944, 9th ID 1,800, and 19th ID 3,004. *RRM*, 3 (pt. 2): 738–739.

16. Quoted in Dabija, *Armata română*, 2:348.

17. *RRM*, 3 (pt. 1): 19–31, 37–41; *RAPRM*, 1:391, 463. Prewar fortifications had been limited for financial reasons and to avoid "implications of aggressive intentions" toward Austria-Hungary. However, in 1915 limited projects were initiated. *RRM*, 1 (D), nos. 55, 56; Moşoiu, *Memorial*, 90–91.

18. Falkenhayn, *Campania*, 105–107, 113–115; *Letzter Krieg*, 5:467; Reichsarchiv, *Der Weltkrieg*, 11:244–245; Hans Meier-Welcher, *Seeckt* (Frankfurt: Bernard und Graefe, 1967), 91–103; Rabenau, *Seeckt*, 438.

19. Reichsarchiv, *Der Weltkrieg*, 11:250–251; *Letzter Krieg*, 5:468–471; N. Ionescu, *Grigorescu*, 35; Report of Major Sancery, 22 October, AMR, Fond Grigorescu; *RRM*, 3 (pt. 1): 347–374. Grigorescu's 15th ID suffered 420 killed, 2,175 wounded, and 880 disappeared (*RAPRM*, 1:426). Hans Carossa, later a well-known German writer but then a military doctor, movingly describes the human side of the war on the Oituz front: *Rumänisches Tagebuch* (Leipzig: Insel Verlag, 1934), 80–99. For a recent English translation of Carossa, see Robert S. Carver, *Tagebuch im Weltkriege: A Diary of WWI Rumania* (Claremont, Calif.: Regina Books, 2005).

20. Falkenhayn, *Campania*, 132.

21. Reichsarchiv, *Der Weltkrieg*, 11:248–253; *Letzter Krieg*, 5:450–452; Falkenhayn, *Campania*, 117, 131–132; Rabenau, *Seeckt*, 478–485; Seeckt to his wife, 6 October, Seeckt Papers, NARA, M-132/27.

22. Falkenhayn, *Campania*, 116, 130; Kirițescu, *Istoria războiului*, 2:56–59; *RRM*, 3 (pt. 1): 529; Dabija, *Armata română*, 2:487–492.

23. *Letzter Krieg*, 5:482; *RRM*, 3 (pt. 1): 538–541, 546; Dabija, *Armata română*, 2: 492–494.

24. Morgen, *Meiner Truppen*, 110; Dabija, *Armata română*, 2:465–468; Victor Atanasiu, *Bătălia din zona Bran-Cîmpulung* (Bucharest: Editura Militară, 1976), 52, 65; Falkenhayn, *Campania*, 118; *RRM*, 3 (pt. 1): 424–425.

25. *RRM*, 3 (pt. 1): 431–434; Kabisch, *Rumänienkrieg*, 87; Morgen, *Meiner Truppen*, 112 ; J. Weis, *Mit einer bayerischen Infanterie Division durch Rumänien. Ein Kriegstagebuch* (Munich: Verlag Jos. C. Huber, 1917), 13–14, 18; Averescu, *NZ*, 2:47; Atanasiu, *Bătălia . . . Bran*, 92.

26. Atanasiu, *Bătălia . . . Bran*, 65, 71–74, 98; Kirițescu, *Istoria războiului*, 2:51–53; Averescu, *NZ*, 2:47, 52, 64; *Letzter Krieg*, 5:484; *RRM*, 3 (pt. 1): 455; Dabija, *Armata română*, 2:478–483; Weis, *Mit einer bayerischen Infanterie Division*, 22–23, 32, 36–39; Falkenhayn, *Campania*, 149–150; Reichsarchiv, *Der Weltkrieg*, 11:271.

27. Otu, *Averescu*, 2:152, 154; Torrey, *Berthelot*, 157–158.

28. *Letzter Krieg*, 5:485; Martin Breitenacher, *Das Alpenkorps, 1914–1918* (Berlin: Verhut Verlag Otto Schlegel, 1939), 108–109. His new command was designated Gruppe Krafft, and General Ludwig von Tutschek succeeded him as commander of the Alpine Corps. Albert Reich, *Durch Siebenbürgen und Rumänien* (Munich: A. Reich, 1917), 2, 23.

29. *RRM*, 3 (pt. 1): 712–713; *RAPRM*, 1:429–430; Vasile Isopescu and Gheorghe Preda, *General David Praporgescu* (Bucharest: Editura Militară, 1967), 80–81, 84–86. Praporgescu was a graduate of the French Cavalry School at Saumur with a year of service each in the French and Austrian armies.

30. Kaltenegger, *Alpenkorps*, 148; Falkenhayn, *Campania*, 117–120.

31. *RRM*, 3 (pt. 1): 734, 743–747, 777–779, 966, 1010; *RRM*, 3 (pt. 1) (D), no. 25; AMR, Fond MCG, 1st Army, Colonel Cihoski, "Memoriu asupra operațiunilor detașament Argeșul dela 19–26 Octombrie 1916"; Moșoiu, *Memorial*, 39–40, 121–123.

32. Breitenacher, *Alpenkorps*, 109–111; Kaltenegger, *Alpenkorps*, 148–149; Holger Herwig, *The First World War: Germany and Austria-Hungary, 1914–1918* (London:

Arnold, 1997), 221. In one battalion, almost 50 percent of the men were incapacitated by frostbite. *Letzter Krieg*, 5:487.

33. Kaltenegger, *Alpenkorps*, 150; Kabisch, *Rumänienkrieg*, 118–119; *Letzter Krieg*, 5:487–488; Cihoski, "Memoriu"; *RRM*, 3 (pt. 1): 968, 1031; *RRM*, 3 (pt. 2): 6, 58, 91; Falkenhayn, *Campania*, 136–137.

34. *RRM*, 3 (pt. 2): 43, 106–107, 124–125; *RRM*, 3 (pt. 2) (D), no. 711; *Letzter Krieg*, 5:503. Krafft is quoted in *Letzter Krieg*, 5:529.

35. AMR, Fond MCG, 1st Army, Dare de seamă, 10, 11, 12 November; Dabija, *Armata română*, 2:448–449; *RRM*, 3 (pt. 2): 149–150, 172; *RRM*, 3 (pt. 2) (D), nos. 705, 714, 720, 738.

36. Rosetti, *Mărturisiri*, 147; Marie, "Memorii," 21 November; Lupaşcu-Stejar, *Din războiul*, 156. A detailed report by a French liaison officer told of similar confusion and disorganization in the command of the I Army Corps. AMR, Fond MCG, 1st Army, I Army Corps, 4 November; *RRM*, 3 (pt. 2) (D), nos. 712, 736. Carol II, King of Romania, *Între datorie şi pasiune: Însemării zilnice* (Bucharest: Editura Silex, 1995), 1:40.

37. AMR, Fond MCG, 1st Army, Dare de seamă, 11, 12 November; *Letzter Krieg*, 5:529–531; Breitenacher, *Alpenkorps*, 117, 119, 123, 126; Kaltenegger, *Alpenkorps*, 153; Falkenhayn, *Campania*, 137; KA (Munich), Alpenkorps, 1a, Bund 35, "Betrachtungen," 13 November.

38. *RRM*, 3 (pt. 2): 197, 224; Dabija, *Armata română*, 2:456–459; KA (Munich), Alpenkorps, 1a, Bund 35, "Betrachtungen," 13 November; *Letzter Krieg*, 5:540–542; Ioaniţiu, *Războiul româniei*, 158; Morgen, *Meiner Truppen*, 112.

39. Falkenhayn, *Campania*, 134; *RRM*, 3 (pt. 1): 786–787, 793–794, 805; Dabija, *Armata română*, 2:372; *Letzter Krieg*, 5:491; AMR, Fond MCG, 1st Army, Raport no. 63, 27–29 October.

40. *Letzter Krieg*, 5:492–494; Reichsarchiv, *Der Weltkrieg*, 11:253; Kabisch, *Rumänienkrieg*, 81–82; *RRM*, 3 (pt. 1): 817–821, 824, 848; Niculescu, *Jiu*, 52; Căzănişteanu and Rusu, *Pe aci nu se trece!*, 111–112; Ioaniţiu, *Războiul româniei*, 138; Anastasiu, *Răsboiul*, 354–355; V. Dragalina, *Dragalina*, 414–415; Dabija, *Armata română*, 2:388.

41. *RRM*, 3 (pt. 1): 849, 856, 878. Queen Marie journaled: "Sat for a while with the Dragalina son. . . . We cried and cried." "Memorii," 10 November 1916; V. Dragalina, *Dragalina*, 428–460, recounts the general's death in great detail.

42. *RRM*, 3 (pt. 1): 847, 852, 860; Dabija, *Armata română*, 2:394; Falkenhayn, *Campania*, 125; *Letzter Krieg*, 5:459; Kiriţescu, *Istoria războiului*, 2:92–93; Anastasiu, *Răsboiul*, 368–372. "Only half [the prisoners] were dressed in the newer grey-green uniforms. Most wore black lambswool caps, an impossible combination of all kinds of dirty, torn clothing, unraveling foot cloths and peasant shoes. Many were even barefoot. That certainly does not look much like heroism. Without self-respect, they beg for bread and cigarettes." Württembergisches Hauptstaatsarchiv, Kriegsarchiv [KA (Stuttgart)], Württembergisches Gebirgs-Bataillon [WGB], M-130/9, Kriegstagebuch, 20 October, 1/Lt. Zluhan and Sgt. Petzold, "Das Württembergisches Gebirgs-Bataillon in Rumänien," 1:11.

43. AMR, Fond MCG, 1st Army, Raport no. 63, 27–29 October; Niculescu, *Jiu*, 58, 62–72; Kabisch, *Rumänienkrieg*, 120; *RRM*, 3 (pt. 1): 894, 925.

44. Falkenhayn, *Campania*, 127, 137; *Letzter Krieg*, 5:497–498; Rommel, *Attacks*, 100–101.

45. Falkenhayn, *Campania*, 135; *Letzter Krieg*, 5:499; Niculescu, *Jiu*, 76; Rabenau, *Seeckt*, 490; Anastasiu, *Răsboiul*, 381.

46. Berthelot, *Mémoires*, 9 November; Falkenhayn, *Campania*, 141; *Letzter Krieg*, 5:524–525; Dabija, *Armata română*, 3:13; Niculescu, *Jiu*, 103; AMR, Fond Grigorescu, Ferdinand to 1st, 2nd, North Armies, 14 November, Fond MCG, MCG to 2nd Army, 29 November; *RRM*, 3 (pt. 2): 232–234, 247; Kirițescu, *Istoria războiului*, 2:140–141; Ioanițiu, *Războiul româniei*, 159.

47. KA (Stuttgart), WGB, M-130/9, Kriegstagebuch, 9–13 November; H. Lanz, *Die Württembergischen Gebirgs- u. Sturmtruppen im Weltkriege, 1914–1918* (Stuttgart: Bergers, 1929), 60, 65; Rommel, *Attacks*, 102–106, 109, 113–114; KA (Stuttgart), WGB, M-130, Erwin Rommel, "Gefechtsberichte," 18 November, M-130/9, Zluhan and Petzold, "WGB in Rumänien," 2:14–18, 3:2; *Letzter Krieg*, 5:526, 531.

48. *RRM*, 3 (pt. 2): 256–258, 269, 283, 288; Ioanițiu, *Războiul româniei*, 159; WGB, M-130/9, Zluhan and Petzold, "WGB in Rumänien," 2:14–18, 3:2; *Letzter Krieg*, 5:526, 531.

49. Reichsarchiv, *Der Weltkrieg*, 11:267–268; Falkenhayn, *Campania*, 146–147. Falkenhayn complained to OHL that Seeckt had visited the front without his knowledge. Rabenau, *Seeckt*, 499.

50. AMR, Fond MCG, 1st Army, Raport nos. 83, 85, 19, 20 November; *RRM*, 3 (pt. 2): 298–306; Niculescu, *Jiu*, 108; *Letzter Krieg*, 5:534–535; Kirițescu, *Istoria războiului*, 2:144–152.

9. THE BATTLE FOR WALLACHIA

1. Oltenia is the traditional term applied to the region of Wallachia west of the Olt river, while the eastern region of Wallachia is referred to as Muntenia. See Ian M. Matley, "The Geographical Background," in *Romania. A Profile* (New York: Praeger: 1970), 9–77.

2. Lanz, *Sturmtruppen*, 67; Adrian-Silvan Ionescu, "Amintiriile de front și de prizonierat ale unii ofițer român 1916–1917," *Revista istorică* 11, no. 5–6 (2000): 467–468; AMR, Fond MCG, 1st Army, 1st ID, Raport, 18, 20 November; Zluhan and Petzold, "WGB in Rumänien," 3:6.

3. AMR, Fond MCG, 1st ID to 1st Army, 20 November; Rosetti, *Mărturisiri*, 150; Dumitrescu, *Jurnal*, 140; *RRM*, 3 (pt. 2): 463–464; Dabija, *Armata română*, 3:74–75; Defleury, *Divizia*, 43; *Letzter Krieg*, 5:573–574; *RAPRM*, 2:470.

4. *RRM*, 4 (pt. 1): 28; Berthelot, *Mémoires*, 20 November; Victor Pétin, *Le drame roumain, 1916–1919* (Paris: Payot, 1932), 54–62.

5. *RRM*, 4 (pt. 1): 28–29; Rosetti, *Mărturisiri*, 152. The three men detailed to destroy the bridge had only 100 kilograms of explosives and insufficient time. Tătăranu, *Acum un sfert de veac*, 35.

6. AMR, Fond MCG, 1st Army, 1st ID to 1st Army, 24, 25 November; Reichsarchiv, *Der Weltkrieg*, 11:274–275; Falkenhayn, *Campania*, 158.

7. Regele, *Kampf,* 110–112; KA (Vienna), AOK, VO, Fasz. 6277, VO/OKM, 19 August. Other sites mentioned, Rusé and Turtucaia, were rejected either because they did not have the necessary land communications to assemble the assault troops or because they were out of the operational range of the Austrian Danube flotilla.

8. Reichsarchiv, *Der Weltkrieg*, 11:277; Regele, *Kampf,* 113–115, 117; Wulff, *Donauflottille*, 100–101. Originally it was planned that the Turkish 15th ID would join the assault force, but it was retained in eastern Dobrogea to support the faltering Bulgarian 3rd Army. The 217th ID lacked one regiment that had been sent to Macedonia. KA (Vienna), AOK, VO, Fasz. 6277, VO/OKM, 13 November, Fasz. 6408, VO/BGK, 1 December.

9. KA (Vienna), AOK, VO, Fasz. 6277, VO/OKM, 4, 23, 29 October, 2 November, Fasz. 6408, VO/BGK, 8, 14 November.

10. *RRM*, 4 (pt. 1): 39; Regele, *Kampf,* 154–155; Kiriţescu, *Istoria războiului*, 2:181–182; *RAPRM*, 1:482.

11. *RRM*, 4 (pt. 1): 43, 46–47; Dumitrescu, *Jurnal*, 145; Dabija, *Armata română*, 3:88.

12. Wulff, *Donauflottille*, 101–102; Foerster, *Mackensen*, 300; Regele, *Kampf,* 132, 142, 148, 150–152. Only every fifth man had a life preserver.

13. Mercier to Pétin, 24 November, *RRM*, 4 (pt. 1): 66–67, 72, 98, 126; Berthelot, *Mémoires*, 25 November; Dumitrescu, *Jurnal*, 149.

14. *RRM*, 4 (pt. 1): 72. Colonel Tappen, Mackensen's chief of staff, considered the "inferior" resistance of the Romanians in the first days of the crossing as the key to the success of the operation. KA (Vienna), AOK, VO, Fasz. 6270, VO/OKM, 2 December.

15. Falkenhayn, *Campania*, 165; Reichsarchiv, *Der Weltkrieg*, 11:285; Regele, *Kampf,* 151–152; Dabija, *Armata română*, 3:285. OKM later regretted that Goltz and Schmettow merely "bumped" and did not establish firm contact, a mistake that led to serious consequences. KA (Vienna), AOK, VO, Fasz. 6270, VO/OKM, 2 December.

16. Falkenhayn, *Campania*, 160–163, 167, 169; Rabenau, *Seeckt*, 511–514; Foerster, *Mackensen*, 301; Reichsarchiv, *Der Weltkrieg,* 11:273, 276, 289; Kabisch, *Rumänienkrieg,* 137. This shift did not resolve the command issue. When Falkenhayn requested control over Kosch's forces, Mackensen refused. When Mackensen asked for operational control of Kühne's 11th ID from Falkenhayn's army, OHL initially refused. Offended, Mackensen sent a personal telegram to Hindenburg asking whether he still had confidence in him as a commander. Foerster, *Mackensen*, 304.

17. Berthelot, *Mémoires*, 24 November; Berthelot to Guerre, 26 November, SHAT, 17N573; Rosetti, *Mărturisiri*, 153–154; *RRM*, 4 (pt. 1): 125.

18. Duca, *Amintiri*, 2:71–72; Berthelot, *Mémoires*, 26 November. Prezan's plan was reminiscent of the maneuver used by the Germans to defeat the Russians in East Prussia in August–September 1914.

19. Berthelot, Rapport no. 3, 29 November, SHAT, 16N3168; Duca, *Amintiri*, 2:71–72, 74–75; Averescu, *NZ*, 2:86; Dabija, *Armata română*, 3:102.

20. *RRM*, 4 (pt. 1): 113, 132, 157.

21. KA (Munich), Alpenkorps, 1a, Bund 34, Nachrichten Offizier [NO], Berichte, 8 November; *RRM*, 4 (pt. 1): 15, 120; Socec, *Zile de restriste*, 28–31; E. Ionescu, *Pe Neajlov*, 153; Dabija, *Armata română*, 3:102. Otu summarizes the weaknesses of the Romanian plan of operations in *Prezan*, 96.

22. Coandă, "Memoriu," BCS, Fond St. Georges, Arhiva Coandă; *RRM*, 1:653–661; *RRM*, 2:851–854; Berthelot, *Mémoires*, 19, 23 November; Pétin, *Drame roumain*, 93; *RRM*, 4 (pt. 1): 128–130.

23. Berthelot, *Mémoires*, 26 November; Dabija, *Armata română*, 3:112, 160, 164, 222, 225, 254, 262, 280, 291; Rosetti, *Mărturisiri*, 155–157, 181–182, 184; Socec, *Zile de restrişte*, 33, 37.

24. E. Ionescu, *Pe Neajlov*, 55; *RRM*, 4 (pt. 1): 172–173, 179–182, 200, 202, 239, 275–276.

25. Socec, *Zile de restriste*, 34, 41; Kiriţescu, *Istoria războiului*, 2:204–205; *RRM*, 4 (pt. 1): 195–198, 208–209, 228–229, 261; KA (Vienna), AOK, VO, Fasz. 6270, VO/OKM, 2 December.

26. *RRM*, 4 (pt. 1): 260, 265n1, 278; Socec, *Zile de restriste*, 40–43; Falkenhayn, *Campania*, 173; Reichsarchiv, *Der Weltkrieg*, 11:294; Kiszling, "Feldzug," 32; KA (Vienna), AOK, VO, Fasz. 6270, VO/OKM, 4 December.

27. Dabija, *Armata română*, 3:267, 271; *RRM*, 4 (pt. 1): 330; Dumitrescu, *Jurnal*, 159.

28. *RRM*, 4 (pt. 1): 260. Copies of these documents (in German translation) are preserved in the KA (Vienna), AOK, NA, Fasz. 6281.

29. Falkenhayn, *Campania*, 172–176; Kiszling, "Feldzug," 33–34; KA (Vienna), AOK, VO, Fasz. 6270, VO/OKM, 2 December.

30. E. Ionescu, *Pe Neajlov*, 118; Dabija, *Armata română*, 3:287–288, 293; Socec, *Zile de restriste*, 51–53. BA (Bucharest), Fond Kirileanu contains a dossier prepared for Socec's trial with a deposition by the French liaison attached to Socec's headquarters that gives some support to Socec's contention that he had no choice but to flee enemy fire. Socec was charged with desertion, degraded, and sentenced to five years' forced labor. In 1918, the Marghiloman government acquitted him. Lucian Predescu, *Enciclopedia Cugetarea* (Bucharest: Georgescu Delafras, 1939), 791.

31. *RRM*, 4 (pt. 1): 357–359; *RRM*, 4 (pt. 2): 6; E. Ionescu, *Pe Neajlov*, 126–127; Dabija, *Armata română*, 3:298.

32. *Letzter Krieg*, 5:577–583; Rabenau, *Seeckt*, 515–516; Dabija, *Armata română*, 3:453; *RRM*, 4 (pt. 1): 426–433.

33. Sturdza, "Jurnal," 26, 28, 30 November, 3 December; Dabija, *Armata română*, 3:128–129; *RRM*, 4 (pt. 1): 436–440; KA (Stuttgart), Nachlass General Friedrich von Gerok, "Kämpfe der Armee Gruppe Gerok in den rumänisch-siebenbürgischen Grenzkarparten 1916–1917," 8; KA (Vienna), AOK, VO, Fasz. 6270, VO/OKM, 9 December; *Letzter Krieg*, 5:581–585.

34. *Letzter Krieg*, 5:567; *RRM*, 4 (pt. 1): 342, 373, 378, 380; Coandă, "Memoriu"; Foerster, *Mackensen*, 302–304; *RRM*, 4 (no. 2): 8; KA (Vienna), AOK, VO, Fasz. 6270, VO/OKM, 4 December.

35. *Letzter Krieg*, 5:564–565; Dabija, *Armata română*, 3:137–138, 189; Kaltenegger, *Alpenkorps*, 159; Reichsarchiv, *Der Weltkrieg*, 11:288; Morgen, *Meiner Truppen*, 112; *RRM*, 4 (pt. 1): 296.

36. Dabija, *Armata română*, 3:378–379; Morgen, *Meiner Truppen*, 113; Weis, *Mit einer bayerischen Infanterie Division*, 61.

37. Dabija, *Armata română*, 3:194, 248–249; *RRM*, 4 (pt. 1): 223, 255, 298, 323.

38. Anastasiu, *Războiul*, 421–422; Dabija, *Armata română*, 3:196–197, 216, 281, 283–287; AMR, Fond MCG, 1st Army, 1st ID, Raport no. 98, 3 December; *RRM*, 4 (pt. 1): 298–299; Major Georgescu to 69th IR, 30 November, KA (Vienna), AOK, VO, Fasz. 6281, VO/OKM.

39. Anastasiu, *Războiul*, 420–423; *RRM*, 4 (pt. 1): 285, 295–296; *RRM*, 4 (no. 2): 5, 39–41, 54, 59–62; Dabija, *Armata română*, 3:307; A.-S. Ionescu, "Amintiriile," 468.

40. *RRM*, 4 (no. 2): 23, 57–58; Dumitrescu, *Jurnal*, 161–162; Berthelot, *Mémoires*, 4 December; Ioanițiu, *Războiul româniei*, 265–266.

41. Lupu Kostache, "Memorii," 175ff, BA (Bucharest), Fond Kostache; Reichsarchiv, *Der Weltkrieg*, 11:303–304; Emil Petrescu, "Lucrare dedicată în memoriu lui I. C. Brătianu," 32–37, AN (Bucharest), Fond Berceanu; Foerster, *Mackensen*, 309–312; Bianu, *Însemnări*, 1:51.

42. The occupation authority, Militärverwaltung in Rumänien, was under Mackensen's personal command with an all-encompassing administrative apparatus. Although ostensibly a coalition regime, the Germans controlled political affairs and only allowed their allies, even Austria-Hungary, a restricted role in the economic exploitation of the country. For a description of the organization and functions of the Militärverwaltung in Rumänien, see Kirițescu, *Istoria războiului*, 3:136–141. For its interaction with the populace, see Lisa Mayerhofer, "Making Friends and Foes: Occupiers and Occupied in First World War Romania, 1916–1918," in *Untold War: New Perspectives in First World War Studies*, ed. Heather Jones, Jennifer O'Brien, and Christoph Schmidt-Supprian (Leiden: Brill, 2008), 119–149.

43. Krafft, reacting to reports of "senseless and wanton destruction," had earlier issued a harsh warning to his men against such behavior. He ordered them, "Wherever you stay maintain the quarters in proper condition and leave them as you yourselves would like to find them." KA (Munich), Alpenkorps, 1a, Bund 34, Korpsbefehl, 25 November; Rădulescu-Zoner and Marinescu, *Bucureștii*, 118–120; Petrescu, "Lucrare," 38.

44. KA (Vienna), AOK, VO, Fasz. 6270, VO/OKM, 2, 3, 9 December, Fasz. 6293 6408, VO/BGK, 24, 26 December; Mittag (Sofia) to Vienna, 7 December, HHStA (Vienna), PA I, Karton 995; Petrescu, "Lucrare," 39.

45. Breitenacher, *Alpenkorps*, 133; Dabija, *Armata română*, 3:412; Weis, *Mit einer bayerischen Infanterie Division*, 66–76; Reich, *Durch Siebenbürgen*, 57–59.

46. Robertson to Grey, 30 October, FO to Barclay, 4 November, PRO/FO 371/2629; Keith Middlemas, *The Master Builders* (London: Hutchinson, 1963), 274, 280; Dimitri D. Dimancescu, "A Challenge to Destiny" (unpublished memoirs, copyright 2008, Dan Dimancescu, Concord, Mass.), 10–12; Breitenacher, *Alpenkorps*,

133. The Germans were able to begin pumping oil again in February 1917 and after five months were able to achieve a reasonable output. It was almost five years after the war before the Romanians restored prewar production levels. Storch to Czernin, 20 March, HHStA, PA I, Karton 1044; KA (Vienna) AOK, VO, Fasz. 6272, VO/OKM. 9 February 1917; Maurice Pearton, *Oil and the Romanian State* (New York: Oxford University Press, 1971), 82.

47. Brătianu to Ferdinand, 16 December, AN (Bucharest), Fond Casa Regală, 4/1916; Berthelot, *Mémoires*, 4 January. A short account by Norton-Griffiths of his activities is in the PRO, Cabinet Papers, 17/163. His longer report is in FO 371/2689. Norton-Griffiths later continued his activity in Russia, using his demolition tactics to unsnarl Russian railroads.

10. RETREAT TO MOLDAVIA

1. Falkenhayn, *Campania*, 183, 186–188; Reichsarchiv, *Der Weltkrieg*, 11:309–310. Dabija, *Armata română*, 3:317.

2. KA (Stuttgart), WGB, M-130/9, "Bericht über die Zeit vom, 10 Dezember 1916 bis 16 Februar 1917," 1; KA (Vienna), AOK, VO, Fasz. 6270, VO/OKM, Tagesbericht, 10 December; Falkenhayn, *Campania*, 183; *RRM*, 4 (no. 2): 64–68, 88; Reichsarchiv, *Der Weltkrieg*, 11:305; Reich, *Durch Siebenbürgen*, 61; Weis, *Mit einer bayerischen Infanterie Division*, 71.

3. *RRM*, 4 (no. 2): 82–83; Dabija, *Armata română*, 3:333; Kabisch, *Rumänienkrieg*, 163. This camaraderie between captor and captured was not unique, among officers at least. "A Bavarian major," Captain A.-S. Ionescu relates, "asked me if I had eaten, . . . placed me at the table with them and I ate with everyone from a tureen of beef soup with beans and vegetables. And then they gave me coffee without sugar . . . and a cigarette." Ionescu slept that night alongside the German officers in their quarters. Later, while in Craiova en route to confinement in Germany, he was released for two hours to have a conjugal visit with his wife at a hotel. A.-S. Ionescu, "Amintiriile," 470–471.

4. *RRM*, 4 (no. 2): 64–65, 102; Dabija, *Armata română*, 3:411, 415–419; Reichsarchiv, *Der Weltkrieg*, 11:306; Kabisch, *Rumänienkrieg*, 163; AMR, Fond MCG, Ferdinand to Averescu, 10 December.

5. KA (Vienna), AOK, VO, Fasz. 6270, VO/OKM, Tagesbericht, 9 December; *Letzter Krieg*, 5:572; Reichsarchiv, *Der Weltkrieg*, 11:306; *RRM*, 4 (no. 2): 120; Dabija, *Armata română*, 3:411, 450–451. Regiment 2 "Vâlcea," which had been replenished by fillers on 5 December, lost 873 men and officers on 6 December and another 524 the next day. "Jurnal de operații al regimentului 2 infantrie 'Vâlcea,'" *Revista istorică* 11, no. 5–6 (2000): 484.

6. Otu, *Averescu*, 157; AMR, Fond MCG, Averescu to Ferdinand, 6 December, Prezan to MCG, 12 December; *RRM*, 4 (no. 2): 109, 158.

7. AMR, Fond MCG, MCG to 1st Army, 7 December, Iliescu to Prezan, Averescu, 12 December.

8. AMR, Fond MCG, MCG, Ordin de operații no. 26, 14 December. The 7th Mixed Brigade would soon be designated the 8th ID.

9. Janin (STAVKA) to Berthelot, 30 November, SHAT, 17N1457; *RRM*, 4 (pt. 1): 379–380; *RRM*, 4 (no. 2): 120–121, 158; Dabija, *Armata română*, 3:321, 451–452, 507, 526, 636–637; Ioanițiu, *Războiul româniei*, 269–272.

10. For a fuller discussion of the command issue, see Torrey, *Romania and World War I*, 252–257.

11. Christescu was named assistant chief of staff. Dumitrescu, *Jurnal*, 179; Rosetti, *Mărturisiri*, 164. In Paris, Iliescu established a reputation for corruption in regard to military procurement. "Dossier Iliescu," SHAT, 6N218.

12. Otu, *Prezan*, 102–106; Berthelot, *Mémoires*, 21 December, letter to Louise Berthelot, 22 December; Berthelot to Guerre, 23 December, SHAT, 16N2994; Marie "Memorii," 11 December; Averescu, *NZ*, 1:xxvi, 2:99–100; Duca, *Amintiri*, 2:105; Otu, *Averescu*, 160–161.

13. Morgen, *Meiner Truppen*, 114–115; Dabija, *Armata română*, 3:530, 534–535; Falkenhayn, *Campania*, 193–198; Reichsarchiv, *Der Weltkrieg*, 11:312; KA (Munich), Alpenkorps, 1a, Bund 34, Bericht (Krafft), 20 December; Kabisch, *Rumänienkrieg*, 165–166.

14. Falkenhayn, *Campania*, 193; Berthelot to Guerre, Rapport no. 6, 10 January, SHAT, 16N2994; Berthelot, *Mémoires*, 13, 15, 17 December. After World War II, Soviet occupation troops removed the statue to the USSR. I. Constantinescu, *România de la A la Z* (Bucharest: Editura Stadion, 1970), 295–296; KA (Munich), Alpenkorps, 1a, Bund 34, Bericht (Krafft), 20 December.

15. Falkenhayn, *Campania*, 195; *Letzter Krieg*, 5:609–610; KA (Stuttgart), WGB, M-130/9, "Bericht . . . 10 Dezember 1916 bis 16 Februar 1917," 5; Breitenacher, *Alpenkorps*, 138, 140–141; Kaltenegger, *Alpenkorps*, 171–173; Rommel, *Attacks*, 115; Dabija, *Armata română*, 3:569, 574, 579.

16. Morgen, *Meiner Truppen*, 115–116; Reichsarchiv, *Der Weltkrieg*, 11:318–320; Dabija, *Armata română*, 3:458–459, 566, 570, 574; *RAPRM*, 1:539; Weis, *Mit einer bayerischen Infanterie Division*, 93–104; *Letzter Krieg*, 5:618.

17. BCS, Fond St. Georges, letter of Captain S. C. Lahovary, approximately January 1917; Berthelot to Guerre, Rapport no. 6, 10 January, SHAT, 16N2994; Berthelot, *Mémoires*, 31 December, letter to Louise Berthelot, 30 December.

18. Falkenhayn, *Campania*, 204–205, 212; Reichsarchiv, *Der Weltkrieg*, 11:323; *Letzter Krieg*, 5:615.

19. The five years of construction on these fortifications and a related one at Galați consumed 50 percent of the budget of the ministry of war. The last gun was removed in November 1916. *IMPR*, 5:218–223, 351.

20. Falkenhayn, *Campania*, 208–209; Rommel, *Attacks*, 115; Breitenacher, *Alpenkorps*, 141–144; KA (Stuttgart), WGB, M-130/9, "Bericht . . . 10 Dezember 1916 bis 16 Februar 1917," 3.

21. Dabija, *Armata română*, 3:615; Kaltenegger, *Alpenkorps*, 176–177; KA (Stuttgart), WGB, M-130/9, "Bericht . . . 10 Dezember 1916 bis 16 Februar 1917," 10–13; Rommel, *Attacks*, 117–118.

22. Breitenacher, *Alpenkorps*, 149–149; *RAPRM*, 1:545; Kaltenegger, *Alpenkorps*, 177; Rommel, *Attacks*, 121.

23. Rommel, *Attacks*, 124–125, 129–130; Dabija, *Armata română*, 3:615 ; Kaltenegger, *Alpenkorps*, 176; KA (Stuttgart), WGB, M-130/9, "Bericht . . . 10 Dezember 1916 bis 16 Februar 1917," 4.

24. Dabija, *Armata română*, 3:616–617, 621; Kaltenegger, *Alpenkorps*, 179; Breitenacher, *Alpenkorps*, 150; Falkenhayn, *Campania*, 213–216; Reichsarchiv, *Der Weltkrieg*, 11:325–326; *Letzter Krieg*, 5:619; Morgen, *Meiner Truppen*, 116; Kirițescu, *Istoria războiului*, 2:438; Weis, *Mit einer bayerischen Infanterie Division*, 109–111.

25. Reichsarchiv, *Der Weltkrieg*, 11:328; Falkenhayn, *Campania*, 217; KA (Munich), Alpenkorps, 1a, Bund 34, Tagesbefehl, 8 January.

26. KA (Vienna), B 1892, Nachlass Seeckt, "Allgemeines"; *Letzter Krieg*, 5:606, 612–613; Dabija, *Armata română*, 3:557, 561, 567, 572. The 7th Mixed Brigade had been formed and trained by Sturdza and had not yet seen heavy action. Torrey, *Treason*, 16, 18.

27. KA (Stuttgart), Nachlass Gerok, "Kämpfe der Armee Gruppe Gerok," 29, 30 December; Scărișoreanu, *Fragmente*, 150–152, 182; Dabija, *Armata română*, 3:563–564, 566, 572, 582–583, 585–586; KA (Vienna), NFA, 1st Armeekmdo, 1st Cavalry Division, Fasz. 60, Gerok to 1st CD, 218th ID, 1 January; Berthelot, Rapport no. 6, 10 January, SHAT, 16N2994.

28. KA (Vienna), NFA, 1st Armeekmdo, 1st Cavalry Division, Fasz. 60, 1917 Ops., 3 January; Dabija, *Armata română*, 3:596, 600, 603, 607–808; Averescu, *NZ*, 2:103–104; Scărișoreanu, *Fragmente*, 165; Torrey, *Treason*, 26–27.

29. *Letzter Krieg*, 5:614, 622–623; Ioanițiu, *Războiul româniei*, 277; Scărișoreanu, *Fragmente*, 179–189; Dabija, *Armata română*, 3:629–633.

30. Dabija, *Armata română*, 3:638; KA (Vienna), AOK, NA, Fasz. 6281, "Situation der rumänisches Streitkräfte," 9 February 1917. Counting support units as well as men and formations in training, the 2nd Army totaled about 90,000.

31. Müller, *Kaiser*, 222; Torrey, *Romania and World War I*, 182.

32. Alexander Kontz de Körpenyes, *Österreichisch-Ungarischer Tätigkeitsberichte des Wirtschaftsstabs der Militärverwaltungen in Rumänien* (Vienna: K. K. Hof- und Staats Druckerei, 1918), 13, 23; G. Ionesco-Sisesti, *L'Agriculture de la roumanie pendant la Guerre* (New Haven, Conn.: Yale University Press, 1929), 59.

33. Ritter, *Staatskunst und Kriegshandwerk*, 3:348–349; Torrey, *Romania and World War I*, 181–182.

34. Herwig, *First World War*, 278; Torrey, *Romania and World War I*, 184; Reichsarchiv, *Der Weltkrieg*, 11:335.

35. I have elaborated and documented these issues in Torrey, *Romania and World War I*, 185–191.

36. Ibid., 214–218.

11. RECONSTRUCTING THE ROMANIAN ARMY

1. Berthelot, Rapport nos. 4–5, 13, 23 December, SHAT, 16N2994.

2. Dabija, *Armata română*, 3:642, 4:20; Ioanițiu, *Războiul româniei*, 282; Ion Giurcă, *1917. Reorganizarea armatei române* (Bucharest: Editura Academiei de Înalte Studii Militare, 1999), 106–107; Căzănișteanu and Rusu, *Pe aci nu se trece!*, 177; St. Petrovici to A. C. Cuza, 3 March, BA (Bucharest), Fond A. C. Cuza.

3. Giurcă, *1917*, 108; Ioanițiu, *Războiul româniei*, 283; Dabija, *Armata română*, 3:643. KA (Vienna), NFA, 1st Armeekmdo, NA, Fasz. 123, Nachrichten, 7 February. Prisoners taken by the Alpine Corps included civilian trench workers as young as 15 who said they had been taken from Wallachia by gendarmes. KA (Munich), Alpenkorps, 1a, Bund 39, NO, Gefangene Vernehmungen, 30 January. Exact statistics do not exist, so sources vary. Enemy intelligence estimates largely correspond with the above figures that follow Dabija.

4. Giurcă, *1917*, 74–78; Averescu, *NZ*, 2:113–114; Kirițescu, *Istoria războiului*, 2:362–363; G. Brătescu, ed., *Din istoria luptei antiepidemice în România. Studii și note* (Bucharest: Editura Medicală, 1972), 481–482; Dabija, *Armata română*, 3:642; Lupașcu-Stejar, *Din războiul*, 288. Temperatures dropped as low as –40°C, "a winter as in Siberia."

5. Berthelot, Rapport no. 5, 23 December, SHAT, 16N2994; Giurcă, *1917*, 103–105, 111; Prodan and Preda, *Romanian Army*, 74–75; Ioanițiu, *Războiul româniei*, 284.

6. Berthelot to Guerre, 26 December (plus marginalia), SHAT, 5N143; Guerre to Berthelot and Janin, 28 December, SHAT, 16N3017; Giurcă, *1917*, 80–98. For discussions of the issue, see Torrey, *Romania and World War I*, 260–267 and Otu, *Prezan*, 128–137.

7. Berthelot, Rapport no. 10, 11 March, SHAT, 16N2994; Brătescu, *Din istoria luptei antiepidemice*, 480, 482; Colonel Steghens to Berthelot, 31 January, AMR, Fond MCG.

8. Berthelot, Rapport no. 11 (annexe), 28 March, SHAT, 16N2994. Conditions in other cantonments were similar. George Mavrodi, "Notes et souvenirs de ma vie," 2 March (manuscript in the possession of Mihai Sturdza).

9. Brătescu, *Din istoria luptei antiepidemice*, 483; Major Neilson, 24 February, PRO/FO 371/2880; Berthelot, *Mémoires*, 9, 15 March, letters to Georges Berthelot and Louise Berthelot, 8, 16 March. Berthelot, aghast at the lack of underwear, personally located 30 wagons of fabric in Odessa and ordered them made into "shirts and drawers."

10. Brătescu, *Din istoria luptei antiepidemice*, 484; Rosetti, *Mărturisiri*, 187–188; KA (Vienna), NFA, 1st Armeekmdo, NA, Fasz. 123, Nachrichten, 24 March, 3, 4, 23 April.

11. Barclay to FO, 5 March, PRO/FO 371/2883; Berthelot, *Mémoires*, letter to Louise Berthelot, 16 March; Berthelot, Rapport no. 11, 28 March, Berthelot to Guerre, 8, 9 April, SHAT, 16N2994. The Russians began to replace some of the food they had taken, but of 43,579 wagons drawn from Romanian sources, only 258 had been returned by 28 March.

12. Averescu, *NZ,* 2:115; Rosetti, *Mărturisiri,* 188.

13. Mavrodi, "Notes," 7, 22 January; Lt. Colonel Landrot, Rapport, 26 January, Landrot to Caput, 27 January, Intendant Henry, Rapport, 15 February, AMR, Fond MCG; KA (Vienna), NFA, 1st Armeekmdo, Gruppe Gerok, NO, Fasz. 255, Rumänische Armee, 8, 24 April.

14. Brătescu, *Din istoria luptei antiepidemice,* 487.

15. Ibid., 484–485; Lt. Colonel Letellier, Rapport, 24 March, 14 April, AMR, Fond MCG; Prodan and Preda, *Romanian Army,* 72; Berthelot, Rapport no. 12, 13 May, SHAT, 16N2994.

16. Rosetti, *Mărturisiri,* 186; Brătescu, *Din istoria luptei antiepidemice,* 487; Lt. Colonel Hucher to Pétin, Compte rendu, 15 March, AMR, Fond MCG; Argetoianu, *Pentru cei de mîine,* 3:89; KA (Munich), Alpenkorps, Arzt, Bund 176, Sanitätsdienst "Rumänien," 15 February; Alpenkorps, 1a, Bund 35, Tagesbefehl, 8 January.

17. Brătescu, *Din istoria luptei antiepidemice,* 485; Duca, *Amintiri,* 2:126; Rosetti, *Mărturisiri,* 17, 117; Major de Vassoigne, Rapport, 15 March, AMR, Fond MCG; Michel Roussin, "La mission française en Roumanie pendant la première guerre mondiale," 2 vols. (thesis, University of Paris, 1972), 2:125; Argetoianu, *Pentru cei de mîine,* 3:88, 91, 166–167.

18. E. Ionescu, *Pe Neajlov,* 134; Brătescu, *Din istoria luptei antiepidemice,* 497–498; Argetoianu, *Pentru cei de mîine,* 3:90–91, 166, 188; Marie, "Memorii," 4 February; Barclay to FO, 23 February, PRO/FO, 371/2880.

19. Berthelot, *Mémoires,* 24 March; Ilie Schipor, "Pierderi umane ale misiunii militare franceze în România," in *General H. M. Berthelot 80 ans après la mission française en Roumanie* (Bucharest: Editura Universității din Bucureşti, 1997), 73, 75; Gheorghe Sandu and Mihai Neagu, "Date privind misiunea medicală franceză în România în 1916–1918," in *Momente din trecutul medecinii. Studii, note şi documente,* ed. G. Brătescu (Bucharest: Editura Medicală, 1987), 621–625; Kirițescu, *Istoria războiului,* 2:391–392; Duca, *Amintiri,* 2:125. For details on all aspects of French medical assistance, including Catholic medical missions, see Jean-Noel Grandhomme, "Le général Berthelot et l'action Française en Roumanie et en Russie Méridionale 1916–1918" (thesis, University of Paris, 1998), 506–565.

20. Constantin Căzănişteanu, ed., *Mărăşti, Mărăşeşti, Oituz. Documente militare* [*MMO*] (Bucharest: Editura Militară, 1977), no. 6; Kirițescu, *Istoria războiului,* 2:374; Duca, *Amintiri,* 2:125; Dr. Vasile Bianu recorded almost daily in his journal the names of colleagues who perished. Bianu, *Însemnări,* 2:81, 101, 106–108, 118.

21. Roussin, "Mission française," 2:125; Rosetti, *Mărturisiri,* 186–187. Newly assigned doctors were often late if they did appear. Lt. Colonel de Vassoigne to Antonescu, 15 March, AMR, Fond MCG.

22. KA (Vienna), AOK, NA, Fasz. 6281, Nachrichten, 9 February; NFA, 1st Armeekmdo, NA, Fasz. 123, Nachrichten, 27, 28 February; Constantin Antip, *Publicistica militară în serviciul apărării naționale* (Bucharest: Editura Militară, 1983), 70–71; Oşca et al., *Istoria Statului,* no. 28; Octavian Ungureanu, "George Enescu în visită la spitalul de campanile din Dorohoi," in *Revista de istorie militară* 16, no. 5 (1992): 28–29.

23. Marie, "Memorii," 9 May; Maria Bucur, "Between the Mother of the Wounded and the Virgin of Jiu: Romanian Women and the Gender of Heroism during the Great War," *Journal of Women's History* 12, no. 2 (2000): 41–45; Constantin Nicolau, "Serviciul religios al armatei române în desfășurarea campaniei din 1916," in Prodan and Preda, *ACTA*, 3:102; Ilie Manole, "Assistanța religioasă în anii războiului de întregirea 1916–1918," in Dobrinescu and Dumitrescu, *1917*, 247–266; KA (Vienna), NFA, 1st Armeekmdo, NA, Fasz. 123, Nachrichten, 24 February; Rosetti, *Mărturisiri*, 186; Roussin, "Mission française," 2:134.

24. Letellier, Rapport, 10 February, Major Legros, Rapport, 13 April, Marchal to Berthelot, 7 February, AMR , Fond MCG; Berthelot, Rapport no. 7, 25 January, no. 8, 7 February, SHAT, 16N2994; Berthelot, *Mémoires*, letter to Louise Berthelot, 31 January; Rosetti, *Mărturisiri*, 175–176; Petrovici to Cuza, 3 March, BA (Bucharest), Fond A. C. Cuza.

25. KA (Vienna), NFA, 1st Armeekmdo, 1st Cavalry Division, Fasz. 60, 218th ID to Gruppe Ruiz de Roxas, 7, 22 February, 1st Armeekmdo, NA, Fasz. 123, Nachrichten, 19 February; Torrey, *Treason*, 26, 39–40; Marchal to Berthelot, 7 February, AMR, Fond MCG.

26. Janin to Guerre, 10 March, Théâtre d'opérations extérieurs, "Note sur la réorganisation de l'armée romaine," 13 March, Berthelot to Guerre, 1 April, SHAT, 16N2994, 6N3059, 5N143.

27. *România*, 9, 10, 25, 26 April; Duca, *Amintiri*, 2:178–179.

28. Lt. Colonel de Roice, Rapport, 14, 26 March, 15, 30 April, Lt. Colonel Capitrel, Rapport, 5 May, Lt. Colonel Letellier, Rapport, 24, 31 March, AMR, Fond MCG; Berthelot, Rapport, no. 8, 7 February, SHAT, 16N2994; Giurcă, *1917*, 240–241. For the technical details of French instruction, see Grandhomme, "Berthelot," 375–403.

29. Constantin Oprița, ed., *Contribuții la învățămîntului militar în România* (Bucharest: Editura Militară, 1978), 109; Giurcă, *1917*, 237–239; Berthelot, *Mémoires*, 3 April; *România*, 5 April; Lt. Colonel de Menditte, Rapport, 15 March, Legros, Rapport, 13, Letellier, Rapport, 14 April, AMR, Fond MCG; Ioanițiu, *Războiul româniei*, 287; N. Cerbulescu, *Generalul Henri Berthelot* (Sibiu: "Tipografia Scolii Militare," 1931), 59.

30. Letellier, Rapport, 6 May, Legros, Rapport, 9 May, AMR, Fond MCG; Berthelot, Rapport no. 13, 28 May, SHAT, 16N2994.

31. Lt. Colonel Sancery, Rapport, 14 March; Legros, Rapport, 13 April, Letellier, Rapport, 6 May, AMR, Fond MCG.

32. Roussin, "Mission française," 2:130; Intendant Henry, Rapport, 15 February, AMR, Fond MCG; Giurcă, *1917*, 169–172; Ioanițiu, *Războiul româniei*, 199; Scărișoreanu, *Fragmente*, 211–213, 233.

33. Pétin, Rapport no. 7, 25 January, Berthelot, Rapport nos. 12–14, 24, 29 May, 13 June, SHAT, 16N2994; Prodan and Preda, *Romanian Army*, 74.

34. Otu, *Averescu*, 164–165; Averescu, *NZ*, 2:271; Argetoianu, *Pentru cei de mîine*, 3:182–183; Dragu and Dumitriu, *Istoria infanteriei române*, 107; *MMO*, no. 20; AMR, Fond MCG, Marchal to Berthelot, 7 February, 2nd Army, Jurnal de operații, 10–20

March. Austrian intelligence carefully tracked the rotations. KA (Vienna), NFA, 1st Armeekmdo, NA, Fasz. 133, 255, Nachrichten, 9, 19, 24 March.

35. Dabija, *Armata română*, 4:21; KA (Vienna), NFA, 1st Armeekmdo, NA, Fasz. 255, Rumänische Armee, 24 March, AOK, VO, Fasz. 6280, VO/OKM, 24 April; Legros, "Note sur l'encadrement des unités de la 12th division," 13 April, AMR, Fond MCG.

36. The German 9th Army suffered 3,000 cases of severe frostbite, some of which resulted in amputations and even death. The best shelter was in the wine cellars of occupied estates. Reichsarchiv, *Der Weltkrieg*, 11:395; Foerster, *Mackensen*, 333.

37. Dabija, *Armata română*, 3:644; Pétin, "Envoi de matériel et munitions de France en Roumanie," 17 April, AMR, Fond MCG; Torrey, *Berthelot*, 185.

38. Jean Delmas, "Les problèmes logistiques de l'armée roumaine et l'aide française 1916–1917," in *Berthelot 80 ans après*, 32–33; Berthelot, Rapport, no. 11, 28 March, SHAT, 16N2994; FO to Barclay, 9 March, Barclay to FO, 18, 29 March, 24 April, 3 May, PRO/FO 371/2880.

39. *RAPRM*, 2:105–108; Giurcă, *1917*, 241–242, 256–257.

40. Bîrdeanu and Dan Nicolaescu, *Contribuţii*, 2:302–305; Negrescu, *Rolul*, 100–103, 113–121; Jean-Noel Grandhomme, "La mission navale française en Roumanie 1916–1918," *Revue historique des armée* 29, no. 1 (2002): 86; Vasile Scodrea, "Memoriu"; Roussin, "Mission française," 2:136.

41. Torrey, *Berthelot*, 42–43; "La mission aéronautique française en Roumanie pendant la grande guerre 1916–1918," in *Berthelot 80 ans après*, 41–42, 44; Simone Presquies-Courbier, "Ajutorul acordat României de către Franţa cu personal şi material aeronautic, 1916–1917," in *File din istoria militară a poporului român* 12 (1984): 175–179; Grandhomme, "Berthelot," 428, 436–437, 1408. Hall claims he was responsible for downing two enemy planes on 20 February. Bert Hall, *One Man's War: The Story of the Lafayette Escadrille* (London: J. Hamilton, 1929), 236.

42. Bălotescu et al., *Istoria aviaţiei*, 103, 114; Roussin, "Mission française," 2:147–148; Grandhomme, "La vie quotidienne les officers française en Roumanie," in *La présence française en Roumanie pendant la Grande Guerre, 1914–1918,* ed. G. Cipăianu and V. Vesa (Cluj: Presa Universitară Clujiană, 1997), 111.

43. Roussin, "Mission française," 2:10; Berthelot, *Mémoires*, 2 January; Ardeleanu, *MCG . . . Documente*, no. 58; KA (Vienna), NFA, 1st Armeekmdo, NA, Fasz. 123, Nachrichten, 28–30 July, 25 August.

44. Grandhomme, "Berthelot," 363–366; Grandhomme, "La vie quotidienne," 112–114; George Cipăianu, "Roumains et Français sur le front de roumanie (1917–1918), in Cipăianu and Vesa, *La présence française*, 81–104; Costescu, *Carnetul*, 209; Mavrodi, "Notes," 7 January; Constantin Turtureanu, *În vâltoarea războiului, 1914–1919* (Cernăuţi: "Litera Romanească," 1938), 32–33; N. Costachescu, "Jurnal de campanie," *Magazin istoric* 21, no. 8 (1987): 13–14.

45. Antonescu to Pétin, 17 March, AMR, Fond MCG; Roussin, "Mission française," 2:131–132; Grandhomme, "Berthelot," 376; Marie, "Memorii," 14 June.

46. Marie, "Memorii," 17 June; Janin to Guerre, 31 March, SHAT, 16N2994;

Rosetti, *Mărturisiri*, 133–134; Dumitrescu, *Jurnal*, 160; Ion Antonescu, *Epistolarul in-fernului* (Bucharest: Editura Viitorul Românesc, 1993), 310. See also Gheorghe Nico-lescu, "Ion Antonescu și misiunea Berthelot," in Dobrinescu and Dumitrescu, *1917*, 109–116.

47. Averescu, *NZ*, 2:271–273; Berthelot, *Mémoires*, 19, 26, 28 June; Roussin, "Mis-sion française," 2:137; Berthelot to Prezan, 9, 12 June, AMR, Fond MCG.

48. Argetoianu, *Pentru cei de mîine*, 4:12. Duca's eulogy to Berthelot on his death, quoted in Cerbulescu, *Berthelot*, 58.

12. THE RUSSO-ROMANIAN OFFENSIVE

1. Costica Prodan, "Planuri de campanie ale beligeranților pe frontul român," in Dobrinescu and Dumitrescu, *1917*, 37; Louise Heenan, *Russian Democracy's Fatal Blunder: The Summer Offensive of 1917* (New York: Praeger, 1987), 44.

2. Averescu, *NZ*, 2:120; Prodan, "Planuri," 37–38; Otu, *Averescu*, 176; Mircea Vul-canescu, *Războiul pentru întregirea neamului* (Bucharest: Saeculum, 1999), 106.

3. Glenn E. Torrey, *The Revolutionary Russian Army and Romania, 1917* (Pittsburgh: University of Pittsburgh, Center for Russian and Eastern European Studies, 1995), 3–7; Hoover Institution Archives (Stanford, Calif.), Collection Heroys, D. G. Shcherbachev, "Situation politique et stratégique au printemps 1917 durant les pré-paratifs de l'offensive sur le front roumain"; Robert G. Feldman, "The Russian Gen-eral Staff and the June 1917 Offensive," *Soviet Studies* 19 (1968): 532; Berthelot, *Mé-moires*, 27 April; SHAT, 16N2994, Berthelot, Rapport no. 12, 14 May.

4. Alan K. Wildman, *The End of the Russian Imperial Army* (Princeton, N.J.: Prince-ton University Press, 1980), 2:18–19; Feldman, "Russian General Staff," 534, 537–541.

5. Shcherbachev, "Situation politique"; Dabija, *Armata română*, 4:41; AMR (Bucharest), MCG, 2nd Army, Ordin de operații. no. 29, 1 June; Berthelot, "Opéra-tions offensives du front Roumain en juin 1917," 29 August, SHAT, 16N2994; *MMO*, no. 23.

6. Shcherbachev, "Situation politique"; Averescu, *NZ*, 2:133, 136–139; Berthelot, *Mémoires*, 13 June; Prodan, "Planuri," 41–42; Prezan, quoted in Mihail Ionescu, *Zile epopeice* (Bucharest: Editura Militară, 1989), 80.

7. AMR, Fond MCG, MCG to Shcherbachev, 30 May, 2nd Army "Istoricul acțiu-nii Mărăști 9–18 July (23–31 July) 1917"; Berthelot, Rapport nos. 14–15, 13, 21 June, SHAT, 16N2994; *MMO*, no. 30; Scărișoreanu, *Fragmente*, 215; Kirițescu, *Istoria războiului*, 2:438.

8. Berthelot to Guerre, 7 July, SHAT, 16N2994; *MMO*, no. 32; Cupșa, *Armata*, 212–213; Kirițescu, *Istoria războiului*, 2:439–440.

9. Roussin, "Mission française," 2:141; Dabija, *Armata română*, 4:76; Kirițescu, *Istoria războiului*, 2:449–451; Gheorghe Bichicean, "Fortificațiile, și războiul de pozi-ție. Campania românească din vara anului 1917," in Dobrinescu and Dumitrescu, *1917*, 39; KA (Vienna), *Österreich-Ungarns Letzter Krieg, 1914–1918*, vol. 6, *Das Kriegs-jahr, 1917*, 349.

10. AMR, Fond MCG, 2 Army, Ordin de operaţii, no. 1638, 3 July; Dabija, *Armata română*, 4:44–48, 66–67, 89; *MMO*, nos. 34, 35.

11. Otu, *Averescu*, 179–180; Dabija, *Armata română*, 4:76–77; Averescu, *NZ*, 2:142–143; Berthelot's representative at 2nd Army headquarters reported that Averescu was "telling anyone who would listen that he has no confidence in the outcome of his attack." Berthelot, *Mémoires*, 17 July. See also Adrian Pandea, "Campania anului 1917 în visiunea doi mareşali: Constantin Prezan şi Ion Antonescu," and Constantin Hlibar, "Mareşal Ion Antonescu şi războiul de reîntregirea naţională," both in Dobrinescu and Dumitrescu, *1917*, 95–100, 101–108.

12. Berthelot, "Opérations offensives du front roumain," SHAT, 16N2994; Cassian Munteanu, *Bătălia de la Mărăşeşti* (Bucharest: Editura Facla, 1977), 82; KA (Vienna), NFA, 1st Armeekmdo, NA, Fasz. 123, Nachrichten, 17 July; Cupşa, *Armata*, 204; Berthelot, *Mémoires*, letter to Louise Berthelot, 15 July.

13. Torrey, *Russian Army*, 30–33; AMR, Fond Grigorescu, Mavrocordat Raport, 18, 20 July.

14. Berthelot, *Mémoires*, 22–24 July; *Letzter Krieg*, 6:244–252.

15. Morgen, *Meiner Truppen*, 118–119; Foerster, *Mackensen*, 333; *Letzter Krieg*, 5:621, 6:76; Rabenau, *Seeckt*, 577; Torrey, *Russian Army*, 4.

16. Gerhard Wettig, "Die Role der Russischen Armee im Revolutionären Machtkampf 1917," in *Forschungen zur Osteuropäischen Geschichte* 12 (1967): 254, 256, 264–267, 270, 274; Rabenau, *Seeckt*, 563–564; BA (Koblenz), Reichskanzlei, R43/ F2732, Lersner to Reichskanzler, 3 July; *Letzter Krieg*, 6:341, 343; Reichsarchiv, *Der Weltkrieg*, 12:502–505.

17. KA (Vienna), NFA, 1st Armeekmdo, NA, Fasz. 123, Nachrichten, 12, 18 June, 13, 21 July, Fasz. 117, 15 July, Fasz. 118, 2 July, Fasz. 145, 10 June, Fasz. 255, Rumänische Armee, 25 June; *Letzter Krieg*, 6:343–345; Rabenau, *Seeckt*, 577, 583.

18. KA (Vienna), NFA, 1st Armeekmdo, NA, Fasz. 123, Nachrichten, 11, 17 July; *Letzter Krieg*, 6:341; AMR, Fond MCG, 2nd Army, IV Corps, Raport, 14–21 July; Reichsarchiv, *Der Weltkrieg*, 13:180; Rabenau, *Seeckt*, 590; KA (Stuttgart), Nachlass Gerok, "Kämpfe," 14 July; KA (Vienna), AOK, VO, Fasz. 6275, VO/OKM, 15, 23 July.

19. Dabija, *Armata română*, 4:332–333; Reichsarchiv, *Der Weltkrieg*, 13:180–182; AMR, Fond MCG, "Auszüge aus des wichtiges Situationsmeldungen des beim OKM eingeteilen bevollmächtigen Gstb Offiziere an das k u k AOK während der Zeit der Schlacht bei Mărăşeşti 1917" [hereafter "Auszüge"] 28, 29 July; Foerster, *Mackensen*, 334.

20. Rabenau, *Seeckt*, 589–590; *Letzter Krieg*, 6:343–344, 346, 348; Ioaniţiu, *Războiul româniei*, 303–304; AMR, Fond MCG, 2nd Army, Birol de Informaţii, "Memoria" (approximately 15 May). Seeckt's comments are revealing: 1st CD "especially good," 8th MB "strong nationality mixture, unfavorably composed . . . no good troops, many desertions," KA (Vienna), B 892, Seeckt Nachlass, "Allgemeines"; Cupşa, *Armata*, 218; *MMO*, no. 34.

21. AMR, Fond MCG, 2nd Army, Dare de seamă, 22–23 July, Fond Grigorescu,

MCG to 1st, 2nd Armies, 23 July; Ioanițiu, *Războiul româniei*, 301–302; Averescu, *NZ*, 2:144; Kirițescu, *Istoria războiului*, 2:461–462; Hauptmann Seeger, *Die Württembergische Gebirgs-Artillerie im Weltkrieg, 1915–1918* (Stuttgart: Belsersche Verlag, 1920), 125, 126; *Letzter Krieg*, 6:348, 350.

22. AMR, Fond MCG, 2nd Army, "Istoricul acțiunii Mărăști," 24 July; KA (Vienna), NFA, 1st Armeekmdo, NA, Fasz. 123, Nachrichten, 24, 26, 30 July; *MMO*, nos. 49, 50, 51; *Letzter Krieg*, 6:350, 351.

23. Berthelot, "Opérations offensives du front roumain"; AMR, Fond MCG, Shcherbachev, Order no. 0163, 25 July; Dabija, *Armata română*, 4:94; Kirițescu, *Istoria războiului*, 2:174; *RAPRM*, 2:171–172; Meier-Welcher, *Seeckt*, 121; *Letzter Krieg*, 6:350–351.

24. AMR, Fond MCG, 2nd Army, Dare de seamă, 24 July; *MMO*, nos. 54, 60; Dabija, *Armata română*, 4:91–92; Prodan and Preda, *Romanian Army*, 88; Roussin, "Mission française," 2:149; *Letzter Krieg*, 6:352; KA (Vienna), NFA, 1st Armeekmdo, NA, Fasz. 123, Nachrichten, 24, 26 July.

25. KA (Stuttgart), Nachlass Gerok, "Kämpfe," 24 July, 21 August; *Letzter Krieg*, 6:351, 352, 355; Dabija, *Armata română*, 4:94, 96, 100, 106–108, 114, 129–130; Rabenau, *Seeckt*, 593–596.

26. AMR, Fond MCG, 2nd Army, Dare de seamă, 25 July; *MMO*, no. 57; Berthelot, "Opérations offensives du front roumain"; Scărișoreanu, *Fragmente*, 221, 223; Dabija, *Armata română*, 4:100, 106.

27. Argetoianu, *Pentru cei de mîine*, 4:13; Shcherbachev, "Situation politique"; AMR, Fond Grigorescu, Shcherbachev to 4th, 6th, 9th Armies, 25 July, Fond MCG, MCG to 1st, 2nd Armies, 25 July; *MMO*, no. 61; Berthelot to Guerre, 26 July, SHAT, 16N2994; Duca, *Amintiri*, 2:216.

28. Averescu, *NZ*, 2:146–148; Seeger, *Gebirgs-Artillerie*, 126; AMR, Fond MCG, 2nd Army, Dare de seamă, 26 July, "Istoricul acțiunii Mărăști," 26 July; Scărișoreanu, *Fragmente*, 227–228; Dabija, *Armata română*, 4:112–113; *MMO*, no. 65. Gerok later affirmed the contribution of Romanian civilians. KA (Stuttgart), Nachlass Gerok, "Kämpfe," 21 August.

29. *MMO*, no. 68; Cupșa, *Armata*, 225; Dabija, *Armata română*, 4:116–117; M. Ionescu, *Zile epopeice*, 130.

30. AMR, Fond MCG, 2nd Army, Dare de seamă, 27, 28, 29 July; *MMO*, nos. 68, 71, 73; KA (Vienna), NFA, 1st Armeekmdo, NA, Fasz. 124, Nachrichten, 29 July; *Letzter Krieg*, 6:357; Dabija, *Armata română*, 4:118–119, 125–126.

31. Berthelot, "Opérations offensives du front roumain"; Ardeleanu, *MCG . . . Documente*, no. 74; Dabija, *Armata română*, 4:120, 122, 135–135, 140; Averescu, *NZ*, 2:149; M. Ionescu, *Zile epopeice*, 130.

32. Berthelot to Guerre, 28 July, 4 August, SHAT, 16N2994; Ardeleanu, *MCG . . . Documente*, no. 76; Averescu, *NZ*, 2:153; Otu, *Averescu*, 182–183.

33. KA (Vienna), AOK, VO, Fasz. 6273, VO/OKM, 28, 29 July; Rabenau, *Seeckt*, 596; *Letzter Krieg*, 6:354, 355, 358, 360; Reichsarchiv, *Der Weltkrieg*, 13:182; Dabija, *Armata română*, 4:129, 135.

34. *MMO*, nos. 68, 71–73; Kirițescu, *Istoria războiului*, 2:124–125, 132; AMR, Fond MCG, 2nd Army, Dare de seamă, 27 July; Dabija, *Armata română*, 4:123–125, 132; KA (Vienna), NFA, 1st Armeekmdo, NA, Fasz. 124, Nachrichten, 23, 24, 29 July.

35. AMR, Fond MCG, 2nd Army, Dare de seamă, 28, 30 July; Dabija, *Armata română*, 4:132; *Letzter Krieg*, 6:356; *MMO*, nos. 74–76, 80.

36. *MMO*, nos. 81, 85, 87; M. Ionescu, *Zile epopeice*, 160; *Letzter Krieg*, 6:363; Dabija, *Armata română*, 4:141–143.

37. Reichsarchiv, *Der Weltkrieg*, 13:182; Ioanițiu, *Războiul româniei*, 314; Seeger, *Gebirgs-Artillerie*, 126; Dabija, *Armata română*, 4:145, 147, 151.

38. BCS, Fond St. Georges, Averescu to (wife?), n.d.; Otu, *Averescu*, 181–182.

13. THE AUSTRO-GERMAN OFFENSIVE: MĂRĂȘEȘTI

1. KA (Vienna), AOK, VO, Fasz. 6273, VO/OKM, 28, 29 July; KA (Stuttgart), Nachlass Gerok, "Kämpfe," 3 August; Reichsarchiv, *Der Weltkrieg*, 13:182; *Letzter Krieg*, 6:359–360; Rabenau, *Seeckt*, 597, 599. The Germans wanted simply to extend Mackensen's military government from Wallachia into Moldavia. The Austrians were prepared to allow the Germans control only in southern Moldavia. They intended to establish their control north of the line Ghimes Pass–Adjud Nou–Bacău–Pașcani–Iași. BA (Koblenz), Reichskanzlei, R43/F2735, Lersner to Reichskanzler [RK], 4 August; HHStA (Vienna), PA I, Karton 1056, Arz to Czernin, 5 August.

2. Morgen, *Meiner Truppen*, 122–123; *Letzter Krieg*, 6:362; KA (Vienna), AOK, VO, Fasz. 6273, VO/OKM, 4 August.

3. KA (Vienna), AOK, VO, Fasz. 6273, VO/OKM, 4, 7 August; *Letzter Krieg*, 6:368; Dabija, *Armata română*, 4:356. On the general staff of the German 89th Division was Captain Günther von Kluge, the future field marshal. BA/MA (Freiburg), RA 7/704.

4. Ardeleanu, *MCG . . . Documente*, nos. 93, 95; Dabija, *Armata română*, 4:355–356, 371–372; Berthelot, *Mémoires*, 3 August; Berthelot Rapport no. 17, 7 August, SHAT, 16N2994; L. Hetzer, "Acești români s-au bătut ca niște lei," *Magazin istoric* 21, no. 9 (1987): 17; AMR, Fond MCG, "Auszüge," 29 July, 4 August. Berthelot (*Mémoires*, 9 August) quotes a captured German officer: "We wanted to attack Russians and we have found French" (i.e., Romanian troops outfitted and fighting like French soldiers).

5. *MMO*, no. 97; Dabija, *Armata română*, 4:360–361.

6. Morgen, *Meiner Truppen*, 123–124; AMR, Fond MCG, "Auszüge," 6–7 August; BA (Koblenz), Reichskanzlei, R43/F2735, Lersner to RK, 4 August; *Letzter Krieg*, 6:367–368; AMR, Fond MCG, 1st Army, Jurnal de operații, 6 August; *MMO*, no. 99. Gas, which both sides utilized regularly, was ineffective against troops, who wore gas masks, but it was deadly to animals and civilians. KA (Munich), Alpenkorps, 1a, Bund 44, Kriegstagebuch, 24 August, 3 September.

7. KA (Vienna), AOK, VO, Fasz. 6273, VO/OKM, 6 August; Dabija, *Armata română*, 4:384.

8. Mihai Macuc, "Considerații cu privire la criză de comandament de pe fron-

376 NOTES TO PAGES 214–221

tul din Moldova din vara anului 1917," in Dobrinescu and Dumitrescu, *1917*, 70; AMR, Fond MCG, 1st Army, Jurnal de operații, 7 August, Christescu to MCG, 6 August; *MMO*, nos. 99, 100; Dabija, *Armata română*, 4:382, 386–387; Kirițescu, *Istoria războiului*, 2:506.

9. Reichsarchiv, *Der Weltkrieg*, 13:184; Hetzer, "Acești români," 18; Căzănișteanu and Rusu, *Pe aci nu se trece!*, 215; AMR, Fond MCG, 1st Army, Jurnal de operații, 5, 7 August, "Auszüge," 7 August; Kirițescu, *Istoria războiului*, 2:510; Ardeleanu, *MCG . . . Documente*, no. 78; *MMO*, no. 102.

10. Dabija, *Armata română*, 4:391–392, 395, 399; *MMO*, no. 103; AMR, Fond Grigorescu, Christescu to MCG, 7 August, Caput to Pétin, 9 August; Ioanițiu, *Războiul româniei*, 324; KA (Vienna), AOK, VO, Fasz. 6273, VO/OKM, 7 August; Reichsarchiv, *Der Weltkrieg*, 13:184; *Letzter Krieg*, 6:368.

11. *MMO*, nos. 106–108; *Letzter Krieg*, 6:368; Dabija, *Armata română*, 4:412–413; Hetzer, "Acești români," 18; Reichsarchiv, *Der Weltkrieg*, 13:184.

12. BA (Koblenz), Reichskanzlei, R43/F2735, Lersner to RK, 8 August; KA (Vienna), AOK, VO, Fasz. 6273, VO/OKM, 8, 9 August; *Letzter Krieg*, 6:369–371; Berthelot, *Mémoires*, 95; AMR, Fond MCG, "Auszüge," 8 August; Dabija, *Armata română*, 4:415; Rabenau, *Seeckt*, 599; Reichsarchiv, *Der Weltkrieg*, 13:185.

13. KA (Vienna), AOK, VO, Fasz. 6273, VO/OKM, 9, 10, 12 August; *Letzter Krieg*, 6:175, 216, 370; AMR, Fond MCG, 1st Army, Dare de seamă, 9–10 August; *MMO*, nos. 109, 110, 113; Ioanițiu, *Războiul româniei*, 326–328; Dabija, *Armata română*, 4:420–436.

14. *MMO*, no. 114; AMR, MCG, 1st Army, Dare de seamă, 10–11 August; Dabija, *Armata română*, 4:440, 444–446, 448.

15. AMR, Fond MCG, 1st Army, Dare de seamă, 11–12 August, Caput to Berthelot, 11 August; KA (Vienna), AOK, VO, Fasz. 6273, VO/OKM, 11 August; *MMO*, nos. 116–117; Dabija, *Armata română*, 4:446–447.

16. AMR, Fond MCG, Christescu to MCG, 11 August; *MMO*, nos. 119, 122; Dabija, *Armata română*, 4:459–461; Kirițescu, *Istoria războiului*, 2:536–537.

17. AMR, Fond MCG, "Auszüge," 13 August; Ioanițiu, *Războiul româniei*, 328. Dabija gives a periodic tabulation of Romanian losses (*Armata română*, 4:393, 415, 436, 447, 465).

18. KA (Vienna), AOK, VO, Fasz. 6273, VO/OKM, 12 August; *Letzter Krieg*, 6:272; *MMO*, no. 128; Berthelot Rapport, no. 18, 18 August, SHAT, 16N2994: Dabija, *Armata română*, 4:481–482.

19. Breitenacher, *Alpenkorps*, 137–138; AMR, Fond MCG, "Auszüge," 12 August.

20. Breitenacher, *Alpenkorps*, 159–161; AMR, Fond MCG, 2nd Army, Jurnal de operații, 9, 10 August, "Auszüge," 12 August; Dabija, *Armata română*, 4:486–487. Units of Averescu's II Corps had relieved the Russian VIII Corps of some of its positions.

21. KA (Munich), Alpenkorps, 1a, Bund 44, Kriegstagebuch, 12 August; Breitenacher, *Alpenkorps*, 162–164; *Letzter Krieg*, 6:373; Reichsarchiv, *Der Weltkrieg*, 13:185–186; BA (Koblenz), Reichskanzlei, R43/F2735, Lersner to RK, 13 August.

22. Ardeleanu, *MCG . . . Documente*, no. 88; Berthelot Rapport no. 18, 18 August, SHAT, 16N2994; Berthelot, *Mémoires*, 12 August; Berthelot, "Sur le front roumain en 1917," *Revue de France*, 1 September 1927, 111; AMR, Fond MCG, Christescu to MCG, 8, 9, 11 August, Ragoza to Shcherbachev, 8 August, Caput to Petin, 9 August; Macuc, "Considerații," 75. The French liaison at 1st Army headquarters had substantiated, in essence, Christescu's version of events and had recommended that he be given command of the Russian and Romanian forces.

23. Shcherbachev, "Situation politique"; AMR, Fond MCG, Antonescu to Christescu, 9, 14 August, Antonescu, "Referate," 10 August; Macuc, "Considerații," 75. Although Christescu was later rehabilitated and served as chief of the general staff (1918, 1920–1922), he never really recovered from this devastating experience. For a full analysis of the sacking of Christescu, see Otu, *Prezan*, 184–194.

24. N. Ionescu, *Grigorescu*, 64–65, 72; AMR, Fond MCG, Shcherbachev to 4th, 6th and 1st Armies, 12 August, Grigorescu to MCG, 12 August, Prezan to 1st, 2nd Armies, 12 August; Ardeleanu, *MCG . . . Documente*, no. 89; Dabija, *Armata română*, 4:494–495, 499.

25. AMR, Fond Grigorescu, telex Prezan/Grigorescu, 13 August, telex Shcherbachev/Grigorescu, 13 August, Grigorescu to V Army Corps, 13 August; Dabija, *Armata română*, 4:500.

26. *Letzter Krieg*, 6:374, 383; AMR, Fond MCG, 2nd Army, Dare de seamă, 12, 13 August, "Auszüge," 13 August; Ardeleanu, *MCG . . . Documente*, nos. 90, 91.

27. KA (Munich), Alpenkorps, 1a, Bund 44, Kriegstagebuch, 11, 12, 16 August; AMR, Fond MCG, "Auszüge," 14 August; Kaltenegger, *Alpenkorps*, 196–198; *Letzter Krieg*, 6:384; Berthelot to Guerre, 14 August, SHAT, 16N2994; *MMO*, nos. 137, 140; Dabija, *Armata română*, 4:519–521; BA (Koblenz), Reichskanzlei, R43/F2735, Lersner to RK, 16 August.

28. AMR, Fond MCG, 2nd Army, 3rd ID, Col. Alexiu Raport, 16 August, "Auszüge," 14 August; Dabija, *Armata română*, 4:522; Foerster, *Mackensen*, 336.

29. Morgen, *Meiner Truppen*, 124–125; KA (Vienna), AOK, VO, Fasz. 6274, VO/OKM, 13 August; BA (Koblenz), Reichskanzlei, R43/F2735, Lersner to RK, 15 August; Dabija, *Armata română*, 4:523–527, 533, 537; Kirițescu, *Istoria războiului*, 2:550; AMR, Fond MCG, 1st Army, Jurnal de operații, 15 August, Razu to 5th ID, 14th ID.

30. AMR, Fond Grigorescu, telex Antonescu/Samsonovici, 15 August, telex Prezan/Grigorescu, 15 August; N. Ionescu, *Grigorescu*, 84; Dabija, *Armata română*, 4:543.

31. KA (Vienna), AOK, VO, Fasz. 6274, VO/OKM, 19, 21 August, AMR, Fond MCG, "Auszüge," 16–18 August; *Letzter Krieg*, 6:388; Dabija, *Armata română*, 4:553.

32. KA (Munich), Alpenkorps, 1a, Bund 44, Kriegstagebuch, 1 September; Dabija, *Armata română*, 4:552; *Letzter Krieg*, 6:522; *MMO*, no. 155; Kirițescu, *Istoria războiului*, 2:570–574.

33. *MMO*, nos. 153, 155, 157; Munteanu, *Bătălia*, 88; Kirițescu, *Istoria războiului*, 2:572–573; Dabija, *Armata română*, 4:565; Vasile Mocanu, *Capitanul Grigore Ignat* (Bucharest: Editura Militară, 1967), 89–104.

34. AMR, Fond MCG, 13th ID, Dare de seamă, 19 August; *MMO*, nos. 151, 153, 157; Rosetti, *Mărturisiri*, 215–217; "Din Memoriile General Colonel Constantin Popescu," *Magazin istoric* 27, no. 5–6 (1993): 21.

35. *MMO*, nos. 156, 157, 163; Dabija, *Armata română*, 4:566–567, 570; *RAPRM*, 2:260–263; Munteanu, *Bătălia*, 88; *Letzter Krieg*, 6:388; KA (Vienna), AOK, VO, Fasz. 6282, VO/OKM, 23 August; Kirițescu, *Istoria războiului*, 2:580.

36. AMR, Fond MCG, 13th ID, Dare de seamă, 21 August; *MMO*, no. 163; Dabija, *Armata română*, 4:567, 571, 576; KA (Munich), Alpenkorps, 1a, Bund 44, Kriegstagebuch, 1 September; AMR, Fond Grigorescu, telex Antonescu/Samsonovici, 21 August. Grigorescu's decision not to try to exploit the success of 19 August immediately has been both criticized and praised. Cupşa, *Armata*, 249; Dabija, *Armata română*, 4:576.

37. KA (Vienna), AOK, VO, Fasz. 6274, VO/OKM, 21 August; AMR, Fond MCG, "Auszüge," 29 August; *Letzter Krieg*, 6:390; N. Ionescu, *Grigorescu*, 98; BA (Koblenz), Reichskanzlei, R43/F2735, Lersner to RK, 20 August; Reichsarchiv, *Der Weltkrieg*, 13:186–187; Dabija, *Armata română*, 4:271–273.

38. KA (Vienna), AOK, VO, Fasz. 6274, VO/OKM, 20, 27 August; *Letzter Krieg*, 6:392–393; Dabija, *Armata română*, 4:591; Foerster, *Mackensen*, 336–337. The "political consequences" Mackensen had in mind was the replacement of the Romanian government with one under German influence, which the defeat of the Romanian army would make possible.

39. Breitenacher, *Alpenkorps*, 167–169; KA (Vienna), AOK, VO, Fasz. 6282, VO/OKM, 1 September; AMR, Fond Grigorescu, telex Grigorescu/Văleanu, 1 September, Fond MCG, 1st Army, Jurnal de operații, 29 August; *MMO*, nos. 179, 180; Dabija, *Armata română*, 4:598–600.

40. Breitenacher, *Alpenkorps*, 172; Berthelot, Rapport no. 19, 31 August, SHAT, 16N2994; Dabija, *Armata română*, 4:605; AMR, Fond Grigorescu, telex Prezan/Grigorescu, 30 August.

41. *MMO*, no. 185; Dabija, *Armata română*, 4:612, 618; Breitenacher, *Alpenkorps*, 172. See the critical comments on the battle by a French observer. AMR, Fond MCG, Capt. Cherel to Colonel Rosetti, 6 September.

42. AMR, Fond Grigorescu, telex Sansonovici/Antonescu, 4 September; *MMO*, nos. 189, 191; *RAPRM*, 2:275; Bucur, "Between the Mother," 45–50.

43. Breitenacher, *Alpenkorps*, 171–173; Reichsarchiv, *Der Weltkrieg*, 13:187; *Letzter Krieg*, 6:394; Dabija, *Armata română*, 4:611, 614.

44. Dabija, *Armata română*, 4:641–642. Reichsarchiv, *Der Weltkrieg*, 13:187. A Red Cross accounting of Romanian prisoners dated 1 October 1917 listed 67,240 in Germany and 38,376 in Austria-Hungary plus 63,000 in Bulgaria, Turkey, and occupied Romania. AN (Bucharest), Fond Comitetul . . . Crucii Roşii, 52/1916.

45. KA (Munich), Alpenkorps, 1a, Bund 44, Armeebefehl, 20 August; Morgen, *Meiner Truppen*, 125–126; Reichsarchiv, *Der Weltkrieg*, 13:187; Dabija, *Armata română*, 4:629–631, 635–636. See also Wenninger's long retrospective report in Dabija, *Armata română*, 4:631–635.

46. AMR, Fond Grigorescu, Prezan to 1st, 2nd Armies, 25 August; Berthelot, *Mémoires*, 4 September.

47. Dabija, *Armata română*, 4:641; Morgen, *Meiner Truppen*, 126; KA (Vienna), NFA, 1st Armeekmdo, NA, Fasz. 255, NO Gruppe Gerok, 25 September, Fasz. 118, Halbmonatsberichte, 15 August; *Letzter Krieg*, 6:394.

48. Pétin to Niessel, 27 September, in Roussin, "Mission française," 2:169; Florian Tuca, *Triunghul Eroic: Mărăşti, Mărăşeşti, Oituz* (Iaşi: Editura Juminea, 1973), 115; *RAPRM*, 2:287; N. Ionescu, *Grigorescu*, 120; Maria Mihăilescu, "6 August 1917—Semnificaţii şi comemorări," in Dobrinescu and Dumitrescu, *1917*, 219–226; Maria Bucur, *Remembering War in Twentieth Century Romania* (Bloomington: Indiana University Press, 2009), chaps. 3, 4.

14. THE AUSTRO-GERMAN OFFENSIVE: OITUZ

1. KA (Vienna), AOK, VO, Fasz. 6273, VO/OKM, 29 July; Rabenau, *Seeckt*, 597–599; Dabija, *Armata română*, 4:161–162.

2. KA (Stuttgart), Nachlass Gerok, "Kämpfe," 3 August; *Letzter Krieg*, 6:360.

3. AMR, Fond MCG, 2nd Army, Jurnal de operaţii, 2 August, MCG, Ordin de operaţii, nos. 37, 39, 2, 5 August; *MMO*, no. 89; KA (Vienna), NFA, 1st Armeekmdo, NA, Fasz. 124, Nachrichten, 9 August.

4. AMR, Fond MCG, Ordin de operaţii, nos. 40, 42, 7, 8 August; Cupşa, *Armata*, 255, 257–258.

5. *Letzter Krieg*, 6:365–366, 374; Seeckt rated the 71st ID as "good," especially its Szekler 82nd IR. In the 70th ID, he rated the "spirit" of the Hungarians and Croats as "good," but he had concern that division replacements were "now 40 percent Romanian, 20 percent of the overall total." KA (Vienna), B 892, Nachlass Seeckt, "Allgemeines."

6. *Letzter Krieg*, 6:375; Dabija, *Armata română*, 4:172–173.

7. KA (Stuttgart), Nachlass Gerok, "Kämpfe," 5 August; *Letzter Krieg*, 6:374–375; AMR, Fond MCG, 2nd Army, Jurnal de operaţii, 8 August.

8. AMR, Fond MCG, 2nd Army, Jurnal de operaţii, 8 August; *Letzter Krieg*, 6:376; Ioaniţiu, *Războiul româniei*, 350; Kiriţescu, *Istoria războiului*, 2:599; Averescu, *NZ*, 2:159; "1917: Rudolf Hess în România," *Magazin istoric* 17, no. 9 (1983): 33. During his convalescence leave, Hess, who had prewar experience in flying, transferred to the air service. Wolf Rüdiger Hess, ed., *Rudolf Hess. Briefe 1908–1933* (Munich: Langen Müller, 1987), 205.

9. AMR, Fond MCG, 2nd Army, Jurnal de operaţii, 8 August; Cupşa, *Armata*, 263; KA (Stuttgart), Nachlass Gerok, "Kämpfe," 8 August.

10. AMR, Fond MCG, 2nd Army, Jurnal de operaţii, 9 August; *Letzter Krieg*, 6:377; Averescu, *NZ*, 2:170; KA (Stuttgart), WGB, M-130/9, Kriegstagebuch, 7–18 August; Rommel, *Attacks*, 137–146; Lanz, *Sturmtruppen*, 74.

11. KA (Vienna), NFA, 1st Armeekmdo, NA, Fasz. 123, Nachrichten, 9 August; Dabija, *Armata română*, 4:189; Scărişoreanu, *Fragmente*, 234.

12. AMR, Fond MCG, 2nd Army, Jurnal de operaţii, 10 August; Ardeleanu, *MCG* ... *Documente*, no. 84; Ioaniţiu, *Războiul româniei*, 350; Duca, *Amintiri*, 2:219–220. See Otu, *Averescu*, 183, for a balanced assessment of this incident.

13. *Letzter Krieg*, 6:377–378; AMR, Fond MCG, 2nd Army, Jurnal de operaţii, 10 August; Dabija, *Armata română*, 4:195–196, 198–199.

14. Rommel, *Attacks*, 148–153; Lanz, *Sturmtruppen*, 74; Dabija, *Armata română*, 4:198. The Germans identified him as "Lt. Berge." Most certainly it was Captain Paul Berge who, on his own initiative, had led a company in a vigorous counterattack. KA (Stuttgart), WGB, Kriegstagebuch, 7–18 August; *RAPRM*, 2:305.

15. AMR, Fond MCG, 2nd Army, Jurnal de operaţii, 11 August; *MMO*, no. 120; *Letzter Krieg*, 6:379; Dabija, *Armata română*, 4:205–206, Kiriţescu, *Istoria războiului*, 2:696–697; Seeger, *Gebirgs-Artillerie*, 121.

16. KA (Stuttgart), WGB, Kriegstagebuch, 11 August; ibid., Nachlass Gerok, "Kämpfe," 11 August; Rommel, *Attacks*, 156, 162–163; AMR, Fond MCG, 2nd Army, Jurnal de operaţii, 11 August.

17. *RAPRM*, 2:308; Dimancescu, "Challenge to Destiny," 16–17; Rommel, *Attacks*, 166–167; Dabija, *Armata română*, 4:207.

18. KA (Stuttgart), WGB, Kriegstagebuch, 12, 13 August; Rommel, *Attacks*, 169–172; Lanz, *Sturmtruppen*, 76; AMR, Fond MCG, 2nd Army, Jurnal de operaţii, 12 August; *MMO*, no. 124; Dabija, *Armata română*, 4:212–213.

19. AMR, Fond MCG, 2nd Army, Jurnal de operaţii, 13 August; KA (Stuttgart), Nachlass Gerok, "Kämpfe," 13 August; *Letzter Krieg*, 6:381; *MMO*, no. 129; Dabija, *Armata română*, 4:220–221; Cupşa, *Armata*, 266.

20. KA (Stuttgart), WGB, Kriegstagebuch, 13 August; Lanz, *Sturmtruppen*, 76; Rommel, *Attacks*, 181–183.

21. *MMO*, nos. 129, 130; *Letzter Krieg*, 6:381; Ioaniţiu, *Războiul româniei*, 353; Scări-şoreanu, *Fragmente*, 243–247; Dabija, *Armata română*, 4:224; Cupşa, *Armata*, 267–268.

22. AMR, Fond MCG, Averescu to MCG, 16 August, Prezan to Averescu, 19 August.

23. Dabija, *Armata română*, 4:226, 228–230, 233; *Letzter Krieg*, 6:384; KA (Vienna), NFA, 1st Armeekmdo, NA, Fasz. 255, NO Gruppe Gerok, 25 September.

24. *Letzter Krieg*, 6:382, 386–387; Dabija, *Armata română*, 4:228; KA (Stuttgart), Nachlass Gerok, "Kämpfe," 16 August; Scărişoreanu, *Fragmente*, 253–257.

25. *Letzter Krieg*, 6:388–389; *MMO*, no. 152; Dabija, *Armata română*, 4:258–261. The range of the Austro-German heavy artillery enabled it to support both points of attack, north and south of the Oituz river.

26. KA (Stuttgart), WGB, Kriegstagebuch, 17 August; Rommel, *Attacks*, 187–193.

27. Dabija, *Armata română*, 4:259; Rommel, *Attacks*, 194–196; Lanz, *Sturmtruppen*, 77. The WMB Kriegstagebuch echoes Rommel's opinion: "If we had yet one regiment in reserve, we could have broken through to Târgu Ocna" (Überblick, 19–25 August).

28. Dabija, *Armata română*, 4:262–264; Rommel, *Attacks*, 198–199; *Letzter Krieg*, 6:389; KA (Stuttgart), WGB, Kriegstagebuch, 20 August.

29. KA (Stuttgart), WGB, Kriegstagebuch, 21, 22 August; Dabija, *Armata română*, 4:266ff; *Letzter Krieg*, 6:391.

30. Ioanițiu, *Războiul româniei*, 355; Rommel, *Attacks*, 200; Lanz, *Sturmtruppen*, 78; KA (Stuttgart), WGB, Kriegstagebuch, Überblick, 19–25 August.

31. KA (Stuttgart), Nachlass Gerok, "Kämpfe," 25, 27 August; *Letzter Krieg*, 6:403; Averescu, *NZ*, 2:163, 168, 170; Ioanițiu, *Războiul româniei*, 355–357; Dabija, *Armata română*, 4:305–308.

32. *Letzter Krieg*, 6:403–404; Dabija, *Armata română*, 4:309–318, 321–324, 326; Ioanițiu, *Războiul româniei*, 357–359; *RAPRM*, 2:330.

33. KA (Vienna), NFA, 1st Armeekmdo, NA, Fasz. 255, NO Gruppe Gerok, 25 September; *Letzter Krieg*, 6:391–392; Reichsarchiv, *Der Weltkrieg*, 13:188.

34. Grandhomme, *Triplice*, 147; Ştefan Pâslaru, "Mărăşti–Mărăşeşti–Oituz: Ecouri şi impact strategic," in Dobrinescu and Dumitrescu, *1917*, 217; Torrey, *Romania and World War I*, 288–289.

35. Konradsheim to Czernin, 29 August, HHStA, PA I, Karton 1044.

36. Torrey, *Romania and World War I*, 218, 349–350, 356; Kalvero Hovi, *Cordon Sanitaire or Barrière de l'Est: The Emergence of the New French Eastern European Alliance Policy, 1917–1919* (Turku: Turun yliopisto, 1975), 176–180; Grandhomme, *Triplice*, 236–238.

37. Ioan Scurtu, "Consecințele marea unire din 1918. Viața politică din România în anii 1918–1923," in Ioan Scurtu, ed., *Marea unire din 1918 în context European* (Bucharest: Editura Encyclopedică, 2003), 298; Argetoianu, *Pentru cei de mîine*, 4:18. Argetoianu continues: "Until Mărăşti and Mărăşeşti, when we met French officers we preferred not to speak about our war. After the battles of July and August, things changed and we also entered into the ranks of men" (i.e., gained self-respect).

38. Kirițescu, *O viață, o lume, o epocă*, 13. See also the introduction by Mircea Popa to the 1989 edition of Kirițescu, *Istoria războiului pentru întregirea României, 1916–1919*, 2 vols. (Bucharest: Editura Ştiințifică şi Enciclopedică, 1989), 1:1–2, 19.

15. BETWEEN WAR AND PEACE

1. Rabenau, *Seeckt*, 603–605; Reichsarchiv, *Der Weltkrieg*, 13:341–342; AMR, Fond MCG, Prezan to 1st Army, 24 September, Secție de operații, Dosar 356, "Aprecieri generale asupra situație inamicului," 13 October, Shcherbachev to 4th, 6th, 8th, 9th Armies, Prezan to 2nd Army, 31 October; Berthelot to Guerre, 7 November, SHAT, 16N2994.

2. AMR, Fond MCG, 1st Army, Jurnal de operații, 24 September; Dabija, *Armata română*, 4:65; *Letzter Krieg*, 6:408, 412, 721–723, 737–738, Beilage 21; Ioanițiu, *Războiul româniei*, 360–361; *RAPRM*, 2:410. Although the 8th Army was not on Romanian soil, it was attached to the Romanian front command and faced the Austrian 1st Army.

3. KA (Vienna), NFA, 1st Armeekmdo, NA, Fasz. 118, Halbmonatsberichte, 1, 16 September, 1 October; AMR, Fond MCG, Secție de operații, Buletin de informații, 8 September.

4. KA (Vienna), NFA, 1st Armeekmdo, NA, Fasz. 145, OHL to 1st Armeekmdo, 10 June, Fasz. 255, Rumänische Armee, 1, 14 September.

5. KA (Vienna), NFA, 1st Armeekmdo, NA, Fasz. 255, Rumänische Armee, 1, 15, 26 September, Referate über Rumänien, 8–14 September, Fasz. 123, 124, Nachrichten, 7, 11, 13, 15, 22, 24 September, 5, 6, 9, 10 October.

6. KA (Vienna), AOK, VO, Fasz. 6283, VO/OKM, 22 September, NFA, 1st Armeekmdo, NA, Fasz. 255, Rumänische Armee, 26 September, 30 November; SHAT, 17N542, Compte Rendu . . . 2nd Army, 19 September, Compte Rendu . . . 9, 22 September, Colonel Letellier, Rapport, 22 September, 14 October; Berthelot, Rapport no. 22, 22 October, SHAT, 17N545.

7. KA (Vienna), NFA, 1st Armeekmdo, NA, Fasz. 255, Rumänische Armee, 16, 26 September, Fasz. 123–124, Nachrichten, 5, 6, 28, 29, 30, 23 October, AOK, VO, Fasz. 6283, VO/OKM, 1 September, 19 November; AMR, Fond MCG, 1st Army, Jurnal de operaţii, 25 September.

8. KA (Vienna), NFA, 1st Armeekmdo, NA, Fasz. 123, 124, Nachrichten, 7, 15, 20, 22, 27, 28 September; 1, 5, 27, 28, 29 October; 8, 20, 25, 26, 27, 28, 30 November.

9. KA (Vienna), AOK, VO, Fasz. 6283, VO/OKM, 26 November, NFA, 1st Armeekmdo, NA, Fasz. 123, 124, Nachrichten, 28 October, 8, 16 November, Fasz. 255, Rumänische Armee, 31 December, 15, 28 February, 15 March.

10. KA (Vienna), AOK, VO, Fasz. 6282, VO/OKM, 19 November, NFA, 1st Armeekmdo, NA, Fasz. 255, Rumänische Armee, 30 November, 31 December. On the Transylvanian legion, see Marin Stănescu, *Armata română şi unirea Basarabiei şi Bucovinei cu România, 1917–1919* (Constanţa: Ex Ponto, 1999), 129–148.

11. AMR, Fond MCG, Mission Militaire Française [MMF] to MCG, Lt. Colonel Letellier, Rapport 10, 14, 21 October, 15 November; Berthelot to Guerre, 24 October, SHAT, 17N545; KA (Vienna), NFA, 1st Armeekmdo, NA, Fasz. 124, Nachrichten, 27 October, AOK, VO, Fasz. 6280, VO/OKM, 29 November, Fasz. 6283, Wochenberichte, 18–24 November.

12. Torrey, *Russian Army*, 49–53; Berthelot to Guerre, 22 October, SHAT, 17N545; AMR, Fond Grigorescu, Prezan to Grigorescu, Antonescu to Samsonovici, 9 October.

13. AMR, Fond MCG, 1st Army, Jurnal de operaţii, 4 November, MCG to 1st Army, 15 November, Grigorescu to MCG, 17, 19 November; Torrey, *Russian Army*, 53–54; Berthelot to Guerre, 23 October, SHAT, 17N545; PRO/FO, 371/2895, "Serbo-Czech Army for the Romanian Front," 13 November; Ioan Saizu, "Repere noi în relaţiile român-cehe octombrie 1917: T. G. Masaryk la Mărăşeşti," in Dobrinescu and Dumitrescu, *1917*, 275–292.

14. AMR, Fond MCG, Secţie de operaţii, Dosar 34, Shcherbachev to Mackensen and Archduke Josef, 3 December, Mackensen to Shcherbachev, 4 December; KA (Vienna), AOK, VO, VO/OKM, Fasz. 6283, Berichte Russland no. 355, AOK, OpAbt, Ops. Geheime no. 494, 4 December, Manuskripte Weltkrieg, Rudolf Kiszling, "Unterlagen über die Österreich-Ungarns Mitwirkung bei den Friedenverhandlungen mit Rumänien," 1, 2.

15. Torrey, *Romania and World War I*, 291–300; Ardeleanu, *MCG . . . Documente*, no. 37; Pavelescu et al., *Proba Focului*, 244–249; AMR, Fond Grigorescu, Antonescu (MCG), "Chestiunea armistițiului," 28 March 1918, Fond MCG, Secție de operații, Dosar 34, Președenția Consiliului de Miniștri, no. 234, 4 December, 2nd Army, Prezan to 1st, 2nd Armies, 4 December; Averescu, *NZ*, 2:211–212; Otu, *Averescu*, 194–195; KA (Vienna), AOK, Ops. Geheime no. 510, 5 December.

16. Morgen, *Meiner Truppen*, 127–128; *Letzter Krieg*, 6:735–737; Torrey, *Romania and World War I*, 304, 307–308; KA (Vienna), AOK, VO, VO/OKM, Fasz. 6275, "Verhandlungen in Focșani . . . Tagebuch," 4, 6, 7 December, Ops. Geheime, nos. 513, 525, 531, 5, 6 December.

17. Kiszling, "Unterlagen," 3–5; KA (Vienna), AOK, VO, VO/OKM, Fasz. 6275, Hranilovici to AOK, 7, 8, 9 December, Ops. Geheime nos. 536, 543, 8, 9 December; AMR, Fond MCG, Secție de operații, Dosar 34, Kelchevskii to Shcherbachev, 7 December, Lupescu to Prezan, 9, 10 December, Antonescu to Lupescu, 9 December.

18. AMR, Fond MCG, Lupescu to Prezan, 10 December; KA (Vienna), AOK, VO, VO/OKM, Fasz. 6275, Hranilovici to AOK, 9 December, Fasz. 6276, 6277, VO/OKM, 13, 14, 20 December, 4 January; BA/MA (Freiburg), N 326/35, "Sitzung Protocol . . . Brălia," 14 January. The Romanian *proces-verbal* with comments is in Pavelescu et al., *Proba Focului*, 275–284.

19. KA (Vienna), AOK, VO, Fasz. 6275, VO/OKM, 8 December, Ops Geheime no. 823, Hranilovici, "Gang der Verhandlungen in Focșani 7 December," 12 December; Morgen, *Meiner Truppen*, 129; Kiszling, "Unterlagen," 6, 7; Torrey, *Romania and World War I*, 307. A mixed military commission to monitor the armistice agreement continued to function at Focșani.

20. AMR, Fond MCG, Secție de operații, Dosar 34, 1st Army to MCG, 11 December, 1st Army, Jurnal de operații, 5–6 December, Buletin de informații, 6 December.

21. AMR, Fond MCG, 1st Army, Buletin de informații, 19 December, Dare de seamă, 5–11, 11–18 January; AA, PA, Weltkrieg, WK no. 2f, no. 2, Horstmann (OKM) to AA, 25 December.

22. AMR, Fond MCG, 1st Army, Moșoiu to 12th ID, 7, 12 December, 2nd Army, Margineanu to 3rd ID, 7 December, IV AC, Ordin Circular, 8, 9, 11 December, Fond Grigorescu, Prezan to 1st, 2nd Armies, 14 December; KA (Vienna), NFA, 1st Armeekmdo, NA, Fasz. 255, Rumänische Armee, 25, 31 December.

23. KA (Vienna), NFA, 1st Armeekmdo, NA, Fasz. 255, Rumänische Armee, 29, 31 December, 15 January; Brătianu, *File rupte*, 146–148; AA, PA, Weltkrieg, WK no. 2f, no. 2, Horstmann (OKM) to AA, 19, 21, 25 December, Lersner (OHL) to Hertling, 21 December.

24. KA (Vienna), NFA, 1st Armeekmdo, NA, Fasz. 255, Beilage, Ops. no. 7228, Major Kirsch to 1st Armeekmdo, 8 December, Rumänische Armee, 31 January, 15 February; AMAER, Fond 71/1914/E2, vol. 31, Diamandy to Brătianu, 22 December; Torrey, *Russian Army*, 61.

25. Torrey, *Russian Army*, 61–66.

26. AMR, Fond MCG, 2nd Army, "Evenimente 1–10 [14–23] December," Raport, 26, 28 December, 1 January, Mărdărescu to 2nd Army, 19 December, Fond Grigorescu, 1st Army to MCG, 12 December, Prezan, Ordin circular, 15 December; KA (Vienna), AOK, NA, Fasz. 6284, Nachrichten, 23–28 December. The death penalty was enforced under Romanian military law.

27. M. S. Frenkin, *Russkaia armiia i revoliutsiia, 1917–1918* (Munich: Logos, 1978), 721; AMR, Fond MCG, 2nd Army, Raport sumar, 21–31 December, 1st Army, Jurnal de operaţii, 20, 21, 22 January; KA (Vienna), NFA, 1st Armeekmdo, NA, Fasz. 255, Rumänische Armee, 12, 26 January; Torrey, *Russian Army*, 68–72. Mackensen was flabbergasted at the Russo-Romanian imbroglio. Foerster, *Mackensen*, 344.

28. KA (Vienna), NFA, 1st Armeekmdo, NA, Fasz. 255, Rumänische Armee, 2 February.

29. AMR, Fond MCG, 2nd Army, Jurnal de operaţii, 17 January, 2 February, "Instrucţii operative," 3 February; M. S. Fremkin, *Revoliutsionnoe dvzhenie n rumynskom fronte 1917g–mart 1918* (Moscow: Nauka, 1965), 244.

30. AMR, Fond MCG, 2nd Army, Jurnal de operaţii, 2, 13 February, 21 March; *Letzter Krieg*, 7:107; Ion Antonescu, *Românii. Origina, trecutul, sacrificiile, şi drepturile lor* (Bucharest: n.p., 1919).

16. BESSARABIA AND THE PEACE OF BUFTEA

1. Torrey, *Berthelot*, 207–208; Grandhomme, "Berthelot," 756–757; BCS, Fond St. Georges, Arhiva Coandă, Brătianu to Coandă, 2 January.

2. For a survey of events in Bessarabia 1917–1918, see Harald Heppner, "Zwischenspiel in Bessarabien: Die Moldauische Republik, 1917–1918," *Südost-Forschungen* 56 (1997): 279–289.

3. Wim P. Van Meurs, *The Bessarabian Question in Communist Historiography* (Boulder, Colo.: Eastern European Monographs, 1994), 55–61, 354, 360; Ion Ţurcanu, *Unirea Basarabiei cu România. Preludii, premise, realizări 1918* (Chişinău: Tipografia Centrală, 1998), 124–125; Izeaslav Levit, *An de răspîntie. De la proclamarea Republicii Moldovaneşti pînă la desfiinţarea autonomiei Basarabiei (noiembrie 1917–noiembrie 1918)* (Chişinău: Universul, 2003), 52–54.

4. BCS, Fond St. Georges, Erhan (Chişinău) to Iancovescu (Iaşi), 4 January; Torrey, *Romania and World War I*, 313–316.

5. SHAT, 17543, "Réponse du Colonel Antonescu au sujet de l'envoi des troupes roumaines en Bessarabie," approximately 14–15 January; V. F. Dobrinescu and D. Tompea, "Ion Antonescu şi Basarabia," in *1917*, 299–304; Ţurcanu, *Unirea Basarabiei*, 132; Torrey, *Romania and World War I*, 317–318, 323, 329–330; HHStA, PA I, Karton 1044, Abwehr Berichte (Bucharest), 7 December; Marghiloman, *Note politice*, 3:239, 269, 282; Argetoianu, *Pentru cei de mîine*, 4:99–100.

6. Dumitru Seserman, *Acţiunile armatei române în spaţiul dintre Carpaţii Orientali şi Nistru, 1917–1920* (Bucharest: Editura Universităţii Naţionale de Apărare, 2004),

100; Kirițescu, *Istoria războiului,* 3:84–85; Levit, *An de răspîntie,* 170–173; Berthelot to Guerre, 22 January.

7. SHAT, 17N543, Prezan to 11th ID, 21, 22 January, Prezan, "Instructions concernant les troupes envoyées en Bessarabie," 19 January; AMR, Fond Grigorescu, Grigorescu to 1st Army, 21 January, 1st Army to 11th ID, 23 January; Stănescu, *Armata română,* 72, 74–75, 109–110; AD, Europe 1918–1929, Roumanie, vol. 48, "Proclamation . . . citoyens de la république Moldave," 25 January.

8. KA (Vienna), NFA, 1st Armeekmdo, NA, Fasz. 255, Rumänische Armee, 26 January; Seserman, *Acțiunile armatei române,* 102; Kirițescu, *Istoria războiului,* 3:89–90; Stănescu, *Armata română,* 68, 73, 75–76; Levit, *An de răspîntie,* 192–193.

9. Otu, *Averescu,* 212–225; Levit, *An de răspîntie,* 224–226; Kirițescu, *Istoria războiului,* 3:52–56; Stănescu, *Armata română,* 152ff; William Rodney, *Joe Boyle, King of the Klondike* (Toronto: McGraw Hill-Ryerson, 1974), chap. 23, "The Odessa Affair."

10. Seserman, *Acțiunile armatei române,* 103–106; Levit, *An de răspîntie,* 205; Kirițescu, *Istoria războiului,* 3:91–93. There were an estimated 20,000 deserters from the Romanian army and navy in South Russia. About 600, along with some workers, formed two battalions of Red Guards in Odessa. AMR, Fond MCG, Secție de operații, Dosar 34, Vivescu (Odessa) to MCG, 10 February.

11. AMR, Fond MCG, 1st Army, Jurnal de operații, 23 January, 13th ID, Dare de seamă, 26, 27, 28 January; Levit, *An de răspîntie,* 10.

12. KA (Vienna), NFA, 1st Armeekmdo, NA, Fasz. 255, NA to AOK 4, 5, 9 February; Seserman, *Acțiunile armatei române,* 107; Levit, *An de răspîntie,* 113, 225; AMR, Fond MCG, Secție de operați, Dosar 356, Buletin de informațiunii, 12 February; Kirițescu, *Istoria războiului,* 2:107; Virgil A. Dragalina, "Carnet de campanie," 2:214–222 (manuscript in possession of Opry Popa); AN (Bucharest), Fond Casa Regală, 7/1918, "Raport asupra situațiunea trupelor române din Basarabiei . . . ," 25 February; Stănescu, *Armata română,* 122–123.

13. AMR, Fond Grigorescu, MCG Ops. 23, 30 January; Seserman, *Acțiunile armatei române,* 111–112.

14. Seserman, *Acțiunile armatei române,* 113–114; AMR, Fond MCG, Secție de operații, Dosar 356, "Informațiunii: nota," 10 February; Levit, *An de răspîntie,* 177, 194, 202, 221–222; Dimancescu, "Challenge to Destiny," 29–30; AN (Bucharest), Fond Casa Regala, 7/1918, "Raport asupra situațiunea trupelor," 25 February; KA (Vienna), AOK, OpAbt, Ops. Geheime no. 1391, 6 April; AMR, Fond Grigorescu, MCG to VI AC, 1st CD, 5 May.

15. KA (Vienna), AOK, OpAbt, Ops. Geheime nos. 1391, 1697, 12, 17 March; HHStA, PA X, Karton 154, "Bessarabien 1918," 18 April; AMAER, Fond 71/1914/E2, vol. 50, Prezan to Ministerului Afacerilor Externe, 9 March, Averescu to MCG, 9 March; Stănescu, *Armata română,* 125. Sources differ on these figures.

16. AMAER, Fond 71/1914/E2, vol. 34, Prezan to Miniștri de Război, 15 February; Țurcanu, *Unirea Basarabiei,* 126; Levit, *An de răspîntie,* 191, 193–194, 199–200, 220.

17. Berthelot, *Mémoires,* 11 February; AD, Guerre 1914–1918, Russie, Bessarabie,

vol. 48, Sarret to Saint-Aulaire, 29 January, 5, 11 February; Berthelot to Vouillemin, 29 January, 11 February, SHAT, 17N543; Levit, *An de răspîntie*, 191, 200–201.

18. AMR, Fond MCG, Secţie de operaţie, Dosar 356, Buletin de informaţiunii, 6 February, 12 February; Levit, *An de răspîntie*, 204, 221, 298, 302–303; AMAER, Fond 71/1914/E2, vol. 34, Colonel Anastasiu, "Note din Basarabiei," 12 February, Colonel Racuila, "Stare spirit a locuitorilor din Basarabiei, 18 February, "Sumar la raporturi asupra situaţiunea din Basarabiei," 20 February, Lupescu to VI AC, 12 February; Ţurcanu, *Unirea Basarabiei*, 133, 247–248.

19. AMAER, Fond 71/1914/E2, vol. 34, Anastasiu, "Note în Basarabiei," 12 February; Levit, *An de răspîntie*, 201–202, 300.

20. Hoover Institution Archives (Stanford, Calif.), A. N. Krupensky Archive, Krupensky to Istrate, 14 April; Ţurcanu, *Unirea Basarabiei*, 247–248; AD, Guerre, Russie, Bessarabie, vol. 48, Sarret to Saint-Aulaire, "La République Moldave: Tableau de la situation politique," 27 February, AMAER, Fond 71/1914/E2, vol. 34, "Nota," 2 March.

21. Meurs, *Bessarabian Question*, 68–69; Heppner, "Zwischenspiel in Bessarabien," 287–289; Mitru Ghitiu, "Sfatul Ţării şi processul de unire a Basarabiei cu România în 1918," *Destin Românesc* 1 (1994): 6–7; Ion Ţurcanu, "Unire condiţionată a Basarabiei cu România la 28 March (9 April) 1918," *Revista de Istorie a Moldavie* 4, no. 17 (1994): 1–19; Stelian Stoian, "Viaţa politică din Basarabia în perioada de autonomie provizorie (27 Martie–27 Noiembrie 1918). Activitatea Sfatului Ţării," *Revista de Istorie a Moldave* 2, no. 10 (1992): 49–55; Levit, *An de răspîntie*, 298–314; Seserman, *Acţiunile armatei române*, 172–177; Pavel Moraru, *La Hotarul românesc al Europei. Din istoria siguranţei generale în Basarabia, 1918–1940* (Bucharest: Institutul Naţional Pentru Studiul Totalitarismului, 2008), 39–40, 61.

22. AA, PA, Deutschland 130, Horstmann to AA, 1 January; BA (Koblenz), Nachlass Schwertfeger, Mackensen to Hindenburg, 31 December, Hindenburg to Wilhelm II, 8 January; Mühlmann, *Oberste Heeresleitung*, 242; Elka Bornemann, *Der Frieden von Bukarest, 1918* (Frankfurt: Peter Lang, 1978), 20–26; KA (Vienna), AOK, OpAbt, Ops. Geheime nos. 819, 831, 897, 14, 18, 21, 29 January; KA (Vienna), *Österreich-Ungarns Letzter Krieg, 1914–1918*, vol. 7, *Das Kriegsjahr, 1918*, 109.

23. KA (Vienna), AOK, VO, Fasz. 6409, VO/BGK, 1 January.

24. AA, PA, Weltkrieg no. 2f no. 2, Lersner (OHL) to AA, 24 January; (Vienna), AOK, OpAbt, Ops. Geheime no. 893, 25 January, Ops. no. 49406; Ludendorff to Arz, 26 January, Ops. no. 49755, AOK to Kövess, 6 January, Kövess to OKM, 9 February; *Letzter Krieg*, 7:109; Reichsarchiv, *Der Weltkrieg*, 13:359; Kövess intended to concentrate on the quick capture of Târgu Ocna.

25. AA, PA, Weltkrieg no. 2f no. 2, Rosenberg (Brest-Litovsk) to AA, 24 January; KA (Vienna), AOK, OpAbt, Ops. Geheime no. 899, 28 January; Berthelot to Guerre, 1 February, SHAT, 17N545; Bornemann, *Frieden*, 27.

26. Bornemann, *Frieden*, 29–32; KA (Vienna), AOK, OpAbt, Ops. Geheime no. 1031, Hranilovici to AOK, 14 February.

27. AMAER, Fond 71/1914/E2, vol. 34, Bratianu to Mişu, 31 January; Berthelot

to Guerre, 2 February, SHAT, 17N545; Argetoianu, *Pentru cei de mîine*, 4:114; AMR, Fond MCG, 2nd Army, Jurnal de operaţii, MCG Ops. no. 7533, Instrucţiunii operative, 3, 9 February.

28. AMR, Fond MCG, Secţie de operaţi, Dosar 39, telex Lupescu / Prezan, 4 February; SHAT, Fonds Privés (Berthelot), 1K77, "Dare de seamă asupra discuţiilor urmate la Focşani . . . 4, 5 Februarie"; KA (Vienna), AOK, VO, Fasz. 6303, Hranilovici to AOK, 4, 5, 6 February, Arz to Kövess, 6 February.

29. Otu, Averescu, 202–206; Averescu, *NZ*, 2:243; Argetoianu, *Pentru cei de mîine*, 4:151.

30. KA (Vienna), AOK, OpAbt, Ops. Geheime nos. 989, 1031, 1041, Arz to Hranilovici, 9 February, Hranilovici to AOK, 9, 12, 13, 15 February, Hempl to AOK, 16 February.

31. Averescu, *NZ*, 2:249–251; Argetoianu, *Pentru cei de mîine*, 4:152–153; Foerster, *Mackensen*, 345–346; KA (Vienna), AOK, VO Fasz. 6303, Hempl to AOK, 19 February, Hranilovici to AOK, 18 February; Bornemann, *Frieden*, 37–38. For background on Bulgaria's position, see Bornemann, *Frieden*, 89–96.

32. KA (Vienna), AOK, OpAbt, Ops. Geheime nos. 1045, 1065, Ludendorff to Arz, 19 February, Arz to Czernin, 20 February; BA (Koblenz), Reichskanzlei, R43 / F2458, Kühlmann to Reichskanzler, 23 February; Bornemann, *Frieden*, 38–39.

33. AA, PA, Kommissionakten Brest/Litovsk, Bukarest, Bukarestenakten, Rumänien, pol. no. 1, Kühlmann to Reichskanzler, 24 February; KA (Vienna), AOK, OpAbt, Ops. Geheime no. 1076, Ops. nos. 73, 76, 24 February; AMAER, Fond 71 / 1914 / E2, vol. 50, Averescu to Ferdinand, 24 February.

34. AMAER, Fond 71 / 1914 / E2, vol. 50, Averescu to Czernin, 24 February; HHStA, PA I, Karton 1089, Czernin to wife, 28 February; AA, PA, Bukaresterakten, Rumänien, pol. no. 1, Kühlmann to Reichskanzler, 28 February; Bornemann, *Frieden*, 44. "Ferdinand whimpered like a lap dog," Kaiser Wilhelm commented with obvious delight. Müller, *Kaiser*, 339.

35. Otu, *Averescu*, 212–225, gives a full and insightful analysis of this agreement.

36. KA (Vienna), AOK, OpAbt, Ops. Geheime nos. 1114, 1115, 1116, Hranilovici to AOK, Ludendorff to Arz, Hranilovici to AOK, all 28 February; Reichsarchiv, *Der Weltkrieg*, 13:359; HHStA, PA I, Karton 1085, Karl to Czernin, 26 February; AA, PA, Bukaresterakten, Rumänien, pol. no. 1, Kühlmann to Reichskanzler, 28 February.

37. Reichsarchiv, *Der Weltkrieg*, 13:360; AA, PA, Bukaresterakten, Rumänien, pol. no. 1, Kühlmann to Reichskanzler, 26 February, Bussche to Kühlmann, 28 February, 2 March; Bornemann, Frieden, 42.

38. AMAER, Fond 71 / 1914 / E2, vol. 50, Averescu to Kühlmann / Czernin, Kühlmann / Czernin to Averescu, 1 March; KA (Vienna), AOK, OpAbt, Ops. Geheime nos. 1122, 1125, 1128, Mackensen to Averescu, 1 March, Hranilovici to AOK, 2 March; Argetoianu, *Pentru cei de mîine*, 4:171–174.

39. Averescu, *NZ*, 2:254–256; Otu, *Averescu*, 210.

40. AMR, Fond MCG, 2nd Army, Jurnal de operaţi, 2, 3 March; SHAT, 17N543, MCG "Instrucţiunii opertiv," 3 March; Berthelot to Guerre, 2 March, SHAT, 17545.

41. AMAER, Fond 71/1914/E2, vol. 50, Averescu to Kühlmann/Czernin, 2 March; Averescu, *NZ,* 2 254–255; Argetoianu, *Pentru cei de mîine,* 4:179–183; KA (Vienna), OpAbt, Ops. Geheime no. 1117, Hranilovici to AOK, 2 March.

42. Argetoianu, *Pentru cei de mîine,* 4:184–191; AA, PA, Bukaresterakten, Rumanien, pol. no. 1, Kühlmann to AA, 4 March; KA (Vienna), AOK, OpAbt, Ops. Geheime nos. 1143, 1156, Hranilovici to AOK, 4 March, Arz to Kövess, 4 March; *Letzter Krieg,* 7:116.

43. Argetoianu, *Pentru cei de mîine,* 4:196–198, 232, 5:198; KA (Vienna), AOK, OpAbt, Ops. Geheime nos. 1160, 1168, Hranilovici to AOK, 5 March; Foerster, *Mackensen,* 348.

44. Bornemann, Frieden, 45, gives the text of the short, eight-point document. An original German copy, with seals, is in AA, PA, Bukaresterakten, Rumänien, pol. no. 1.

45. AA, PA, Bukaresterakten, Rumänien, pol. no. 1, "Protocol," 6, 8 March; HHStA, PA I, Karton 1088, Czernin to AMR, 6, 9 March; Bornemann, *Frieden,* 220–229.

17. PEACE, DEMOBILIZATION, REENTRY

1. AMR Fond MCG, Secţie de Operaţii, Dosar 34, Averescu to MCG, 6 March, Hranilovici to Misiunea Română, 10 March, Mircescu to Averescu, 10 March; Argetoianu, *Pentru cei de mîine,* 5:249–250; Kiszling, "Der Österreich-Ungarns Vormarsch in der Ukraine 1918," KA (Vienna), Manuskripte Weltkrieg; SHAT, 17N543, Berthelot to Prezan, 3 March; AMAER, Fond 71/1914/E2, vol. 50, Argetoianu to Averescu, 6, 8 March; Torrey, *Berthelot,* 231–233.

2. AMAER, Fond 71/1914/E2, vol. 50, Averescu to Argetoianu, 8, 9 March, Samsonovici to MCG, 8 March, OKM to Mircescu, 9 March, Averescu to Mircescu, 10 March, Ressel to Argetoianu, 15 March; Berthelot, *Mémoires,* 11 March; Otu, *Averescu,* 239–240; Reichsarchiv, *Der Weltkrieg,* 13:378–379.

3. KA (Vienna), AOK, OpAbt, Ops. Geheime nos. 1036, 1086, 1170, Arz to Ludendorff, 15 February, 6 March, Ops. no. 431/8, Lupescu to Hranilovici, 21 April; AN (Bucharest), Fond Casa Regală, 7/1918, MCG, Secţie de operaţii, Raport, 28 March; Reichsarchiv, *Der Weltkrieg,* 13:361; Bornemann, *Frieden,* 64–65.

4. Argetoianu, *Pentru cei de mîine,* 5:240 (Col. Eliad to MCG, 8 March); AMAER, Fond 71/1914/E2, vol. 50, Argetoianu to Averescu, 6 March, Averescu to Mircescu, 10, 12, 13 March; Fond MCG, 2nd Army, Jurnal de operaţii, 13 March; KA (Vienna), OpAbt, Ops. Geheime no. 1223, Hranilovici to AOK, 15 March; Seserman, *Acţiunile armatei române,* 127–128; Bornemann, *Frieden,* 66.

5. AN (Bucharest), Fond Casa Regală, 12/1918, MCG, Ordin circular, 27 March; Argetoianu, *Pentru cei de mîine,* 5:264; Marghiloman, *Note politice,* 3:417; Cancicov, *Impresiuni,* 2:352–353; Rădulescu-Zoner and Marinescu, *Bucureştii,* 275–276; Kiriţescu, *Istoria războiului,* 3:265–266, 289.

6. HHStA, PA I, Karton 1044, Consul Reports, 30 March (Brăila), 3 April (Cra-

iova); KA (Vienna), AOK, OpAbt, Ops. no. 140971, Forester to AOK, 17 April, Hranilovici to Mackensen, 17 April.

7. Otu, *Averescu*, 242, 244; AMAER, Fond 71/1914/E2, vol. 50, Averescu to Argetoianu, 9 March; Argetoianu, *Pentru cei de mîine*, 5:239; Marghiloman, *Note politice*, 3:399; Torrey, *Romania and World War I*, 338–339; Bornemann, *Frieden*, 46–47.

8. KA (Vienna), AOK, OpAbt, Ops. Geheime nos. 1227, 1294, 1309, Hranilovici to AOK, 15, 21, 25 March; AA, PA, Bukaresterakten, Rumänien pol. no. 1, Bussche to Kühlmann, 23, 25 March, Hindenburg to Hell, n.d., Kühlmann to Marghiloman, 25 March, Kühlmann to Reichskanzler, 26 March, Ludendorff to OKM, 27 March; Marghiloman, *Note politice*, 3:431–432.

9. Reichsarchiv, *Der Weltkrieg*, 13:361; *Letzter Krieg*, 7, Beilage 12; Jean Delmas, "L'État major française et la front oriental après la révolution bolshévique 9 novembre 1917–11 novembre 1918," (thesis, University of Paris, 1965), 170.

10. Torrey, *Romania and World War I*, 340; Kirițescu, *Istoria războiului*, 3:277; AN (Bucharest), Fond Casa Regală, 1918/21, Marghiloman to Ferdinand, 17 April; AA, PA, Rumänien 11a no. 2, Horstmann to AA, 24 April; Marghiloman, *Note politice*, 3:451–453, 472–474, 516; Duca, *Amintiri*, 3:134; Ardeleanu, *MCG . . . Documente*, nos. 25–28; *IMPR*, 5:680.

11. SHAT, 7N1455, Lafont to Guerre, 14 June, État-Major de l'Armée, 2e Bureau, "La situation actuelle de la Roumanie" (Rosetti), 11 July.

12. For details, see Bornemann, *Frieden*, pt. 2, for chapters on each of these concessions.ă

13. AMAER, Fond 71/1914/E2, Lt. Colonel Foerster-Straffleur to Ministerului Afacerilor Externe, 13 May; HHStA, PA I Karton 1057, "Entsendung der Oberst Randa nach Jassy, Mai 1918"; KA (Vienna), AOK, OpAbt, Ops. no. 148464, Randa to AOK, 10 October; AOK, VO, VO/R (Verbindungsoffizier . . . beim Rumänisches Oberbefehlshaber), Colonel von Brandenstein, "Berichte," 14 May. Ironically, the German mission occupied the former quarters of the MMF.

14. AMR, Fond MCG, 2nd Army, Jurnal de operații, 11, 18, 28 May, Fond Grigorescu, 1st Army, MCG to 1st Army, 13 May; Brandenstein, "Berichte," 28, 30 May, 6 June; KA (Vienna), NFA, 1st Armeekmdo, NA, Fasz. 255, Rumänische Armee, 17 June. For details, see Seserman, *Acțiunile armatei române*, 130–134.

15. Brandenstein, "Berichte," 14 May, 6 June; KA (Vienna), NFA, 1st Armeekmdo, NA, Fasz. 255. Rumänische Armee, 31 August; AMR, Fond MCG, 1st Army, Jurnal de operații, 23 April.

16. AA, PA, Rumänien 6, OHL, NA to AA, 22 June; KA (Vienna), NFA, 1st Armeekmdo, NA, Fasz. 255, Rumänische Armee, 5, 15 July; BA (Koblenz), Sammlung Ersten Weltkrieg, Balkan, "Wochenberichte der Politisches Polizei OKM über der Lage in Rumänien," 3–10 August, 2–6 September, Brandenstein, "Berichte," 6 June. In May 1917, King Ferdinand had promised land reform after the war. This undoubtedly increased the urgency to return home. Vasile Liveanu, *1918. Din istoria luptelor revoluționare din România* (Bucharest: Editura Politică, 1960), 330–334.

17. KA (Vienna), AOK, VO, Fasz. 6287, VO/OKM, 5, 9 September, NFA, 1st

Armeekmdo, NA, Fasz. 255, Rumänische Armee, 17 June, 15, 31 July, 25, 26, 29, 31 August.

18. AN (Bucharest), Fond Preşedenţia Consiliului de Miniştri, 1918/2, 16 August; KA (Vienna), NFA, 1st Armeekmdo, NA, Fasz. 255, Rumänische Armee, 15, 31 July; BA (Koblenz), "Wochenberichte . . . Polizei OKM," 23–29 June; Brandenstein, "Berichte," 23 May, 1 June, 29 July.

19. Dumitru Preda, Vasile Alexandrescu, and Costica Prodan, *La roumanie et sa guerre pour l'unité nationale. Campagnes de 1918–1919* (Bucharest: Éditions Encyclopédiques, 1995), 89–92; KA (Vienna), NFA, 1st Armeekmdo, NA, Fasz. 255, Rumänische Armee, 25 July; Seserman, *Acţiunile armatei române*, 130.

20. SHAT, 7N1455, Lafont to Guerre, 14 June, État Major de l'Armée, 2e Bureau, "Le situation actuelle de la Roumanie" (Rosetti), 11 July; Torrey, *Berthelot*, 253ff; Argetoianu, *Pentru cei de mîine*, 5:131; Cancicov, *Impresiuni*, 2:509–510; Rădulescu-Zoner and Marinescu, *Bucureştii*, 294–295. Berthelot was commander of the French 5th Army July–September 1918.

21. AA, PA, Deutschland 130, Horstmann to AA, 8 August; Marghiloman, *Note politice*, 3:567–568, 569, 574, 4:12; KA (Vienna), AOK, VO, Fasz. 6287, VO/OKM, 25 July, 5, 7 August, NFA, 1st Armeekmdo, NA, Fasz. 255, Rumänische Armee, 25, 31 July, 15, 31 August.

22. AA, PA, Deutschland 130, Horstmann to AA, 13, 17 August, Bussche to Horstmann, 15 August; KA (Vienna), AOK, NA, Fasz. 6286, 6287, NA/OHL (NO/OKM) 25 July, 7, 23, 30 August; Argetoianu, *Pentru cei de mîine*, 5:133–135; Grandhomme, "Berthelot," 967–969.

23. BA (Koblenz), "Wochenberichte . . . Polizei OKM," 3–10, 11–18, 17–24 August, 1–7, 7–14, 14–21 September; KA (Vienna), NFA, 1st Armeekmdo, NA, "Verordnungsblatt für die Zivilbevölkerung in Besetzten Gebiet Rumänien," 10 September; Marghiloman, *Note politice*, 4:8, 12, 30, 32.

24. AA, PA, Deutschland 130, Schwarzkoppen to AA, 6 August, Horstmann to AA, 8 August, Bussche, Memorandum, 10 August; Foerster, *Mackensen*, 358; *Letzter Krieg*, 7:415; KA (Vienna), AOK, OpAbt, Ops. Geheime nos. 1876, 1878, 1880, 8, 13, 14 September; AA, PA, Rumänien 11 no. 1, Hintze to AA, 5 September. Army Group Kövess encompassed the Austrian 1st and 7th Armies.

25. KA (Vienna), AOK, OpAbt, Ops. Geheime nos. 1880, 1889, Arz to Hindenburg, 16 September, Hindenburg to Arz, 18 September, Burian to Trautmansdorff, 22 September; AA, PA, Deutschland 130, Lersner to AA, 17 September; *Letzter Krieg*, 7:535. The German foreign ministry was also convinced that "an armed intervention against Romania was to be avoided at any cost" (Hindenburg to Arz, 18 September).

26. Reichsarchiv, *Der Weltkrieg*, 13:400–403, 407–412; *Letzter Krieg*, 7:401–406, 501–512; Mühlmann, *Oberste Heeresleitung*, 228–240; Falls, *Military Operations*, 2:147ff; Richard Hall, *Balkan Breakthrough: The Battle of Dobro Pole, 1918* (Bloomington: University of Indiana Press, 2010), chap. 8.

27. SHAT, 7N1455, Attaché Berne, 15 October; Marghiloman, *Note politice*, 4:32, 35,

37, 42, 46, 47; Rădulescu-Zoner and Marinescu, *Bucureştii*, 302–306; Duca, *Amintiri*, 3:135; Saint-Aulaire to Paris, 7 November, AD, Europe 1918–1929, Roumanie, vol. 31.

28. Seserman, *Acţiunile armatei române*, 135–138, 142, 145–146; Argetoianu, *Pentru cei de mîine*, 5:123; *RAPRM*, 2:533–534; AA, PA, Deutschland 130, "Rumänische Armee in August 1918," 22 August; Ardeleanu, *MCG . . . Documente*, no. 113; Pavelescu et al., *Proba Focului*, 335–336; Bornemann, *Frieden*, 67.

29. *IMPR*, 5:682; Preda et al., *La roumanie*, 92; Seserman, *Acţiunile armatei române*, 140–141, 143.

30. SHAT, 7N1455, Grande quartier général, 2e Bureau, 3, 15 October; KA (Vienna), AOK, NA, Fasz. 6287, NO/OKM 22, 24, 27 September, 3 October; BA (Koblenz), "Wochenberichte . . . Polizei OKM," 4, 5, 7–10, 15 October; Seserman, *Acţiunile armatei române*, 138; *RAPRM*, 2:535; HHStA, PA I, Karton 1057, Burian to Trautmansdorf, 24 October; Marghiloman, *Note politice*, 4:59, 76; AA, PA, Deutschland, 130, Bussche to OHL, 13 October.

31. AA, PA, Deutschland, 130, Mackensen to Hindenburg, 4 October; Foerster, *Mackensen*, 358; Reichsarchiv, *Der Weltkrieg*, 13:395; *Letzter Krieg*, 7:538–539; Ioan Chiper, "Atitudinea Germaniei faţă de problema unirii Transilvania cu România (1918–1929)," *Revista de istorie* 31, no. 11 (1978): 2066; Marghiloman, *Note politice*, 4:56–57; KA (Vienna), AOK, OpAbt, Ops. Geheime nos. 1893, 2035, Demblen to Burian, 4 October, Kontz to AOK, 10 October.

32. AN (Bucharest), Fond Marghiloman, Dosar 326, notes of 5, 7, 8, 9, 10 October, Fond Casa Regală, 47/1918, Marghiloman to Ferdinand, "Memoriu," 13 October; Saint-Aulaire to Paris, 7 October, AD, Europe 1918–1929, Roumanie, vol. 31; Duca, *Amintiri*, 3:138.

33. Torrey, *Berthelot*, 265; Torrey, *Romania and World War I*, 349–350; AD, Europe, 1918–1929, Roumanie, vol. 31, Berthelot, Rapport no. 1, 20 November, annexes nos. 1, 2.

34. Victor Antonescu, "Un courier de guerre," in *Hommage à Monsieur de Saint Aulaire* (Bucharest: Socec, 1930), 18–19; G. I. Brătianu, *Acţiunei politică şi militară a României în 1919* (Bucharest: Cartea Românească, 1939), 18; AN (Bucharest), Fond Casa Regală, 52/1918, Averescu to Ferdinand, 22 October; Argetoianu, *Pentru cei de mîine*, 5:159–161; Otu, *Prezan*, 268; Marghiloman, *Note politice*, 4:81, 94.

35. BCS, Fond St. Georges, Arhiva V. Antonescu, "Aprecierii generale asupra posibilităţii şi oportunităţii reintrara noastre acţiune contra Puterile Centrale," dated 22 October; *Letzter Krieg*, 7:536–537, 757–761; 796–797; Max Luyken, *General Feldmarschall von Mackensen. Von Bukarest bis Salonika* (Munich: J. F. Lehmanns, 1920), 7; Foerster, *Mackensen*, 359.

36. Jean Bernachot, *Les armées françaises en Orient après l'armistice de 1918*, 2 vols. (Paris: Imprimerie Nationale, 1970), 1:35; AN (Bucharest), Fond Casa Regală, 103/1918, Arion to Marghiloman, 5 November; Ardeleanu, *MCG . . . Documente*, nos. 107, 108, 109; Marghiloman, *Note politice*, 4:116; Seserman, *Acţiunile armatei române*, 53ff. Erich Protokowitsch, *Die Ende der Österreichisches Herrschaft in der Bukovina* (Munich: Oldenbourg, 1959), 48–65, tells the story in detail.

37. *IMPR*, 5:680; AN (Bucharest), Fond Casa Regală, 101/1918, Marghiloman to Ferdinand, 6 November; AD, Europe 1918–1929, Roumanie, vol. 31, Saint-Aulaire to Paris, 6 November; Brătianu, *Acţiunea*, 21–22; Duca, *Amintiri*, 3:140–141. Grigorescu replaced Hârjeu and Prezan replaced Christescu on 11 November.

38. AD, Europe, 1918–1929, Roumanie, vol. 31, Berthelot, Rapport no. 1, 20 November, annex no. 4; Rosetti, *Mărturisiri*, 277–278; Bernachot, *Les armées françaises*, 2:27, 29, 30–32; Brătianu, *Acţuinea*, 22–23; Preda et al., *La roumanie*, 69–70.

39. Berthelot, *Mémoires*, 8, 10, 11 November; SHAT, Fonds Privés, 1K77 (Berthelot), "Extraits du journal de guerre du General Berthelot," 11 November.

EPILOGUE

1. Foerster, *Mackensen*, 358–359, 360; *Letzter Krieg*, 7:706ff; Chiper, "Atitudinea Germaniei," 2068–2070; Marghiloman, *Note politice*, 4:116, 122; Luykens, *Mackensen*, 25.

2. SHAT, 20N718, Brătianu to Rosetti, 25 November; Berthelot, "Extraits," 12, 17 November; Emil Răcilă, *Contribuţii privind lupta românilor pentru apăraria patrie în primul război mondial 1916–1918* (Bucharest: Editura Ştiinţifică şi Enciclopedică, 1981), 337–339, 342; Berthelot to Mackensen, 18 November; SHAT, Fonds Privés, 1K77; Luyken, *Mackensen*, 34–35.

3. V. Varga, "Retragerea armatei germaniei din România la sfîrşit anulul 1918," *Studii. Revista de istorie* 14, no. 4 (1961): 881, 883; Foerster, *Mackensen*, 355–356; Grigoire Antipa, *L'occupation enemie de la Roumanie et ses conséquences économiques et socials* (New Haven, Conn.: Yale University Press, 1929), 158. Marghiloman's automobile was among vehicles taken. Even the oil fields did not escape the vandalism of the looters. Cancicov, *Impresiuni*, 2:633; Pearton, *Oil*, 95.

4. Luyken, *Mackensen*, 28, 32, 34–35, 37–40; Varga, "Retragerea," 884; Berthelot, "Extraits," 17 November; Berthelot to Clemenceau, 17 November, Berthelot to Guerre, 24 November, SHAT Fonds Privées, 1K77; Berthelot, *Mémoires*, Berthelot to Georges, 24 November; Bernachot, *Les armées françaises*, 2:38–39; Foerster, *Mackensen*, 368–369.

5. Berthelot to Guerre, 21 November, SHAT, 20N218, Fonds Privés, 1K77, Major Mablais, "Compte-rendu de mission. Relations avec les délégués du Commandement Allemand," 24–26 November; Bernachot, *Les armées françaises*, 2:40–41; Berthelot, *Mémoires*, 24 November; Luyken, *Mackensen*, 56; Foerster, *Mackensen*, 368–371.

6. Bernachot, *Les armées françaises*, 1:37–38; Luyken, *Mackensen*, 63–66; Foerster, *Mackensen*, 373–374.

7. Luyken, *Mackensen*, 67; Varga, "Retragerea," 893; Bernachot, *Les armées françaises*, 1:39–41; Foerster, *Mackensen*, 375–389. Luyken (*Mackensen*, 69–90) contains a full account of Mackensen's internment.

8. Brătianu, *Acţiunea*, 23–24; Preda et al., *La roumanie*, 93–95.

9. Berthelot, *Mémoires*, 16–23, 26 November; Rosetti, *Mărturisiri*, 280, 284–288; Otu, *Prezan*, 259–264; Prezan (Antonescu) to Coandă, AN (Bucharest), Fond Preşedenţia Consiliului de Miniştri, 16/1918, 4 December (marginalia, 7 December, "Col-

laboration approved"). On Berthelot's plans for Romanian troops, see Torrey, *Berthelot*, 293–294.

10. Cancicov, *Impresiuni*, 2:675; Marie, "Memorii," 1 December; Duca, *Amintiri*, 3:147–148; Berthelot, *Mémoires*, 1 December, letter to Louise Berthelot, 2 December.

11. Jorg K. Hoensch, *A History of Modern Hungary, 1867–1986*, trans. Kim Traynor (London: Longman, 1984), 80–82, 84, 86–89; György Litván, "The Home Front during the Károlyi Regime," in *Revolutions and Interventions in Hungary and Its Neighbor States, 1918–1919*, ed. Peter Pastor (Boulder, Colo.: Atlantic Research and Publications, 1988), 124–125.

12. Hoensch, *Hungary*, 84–85; Torrey, *Romania and World War I*, 349–350, 367–369.

13. Preda et al., *La roumanie*, 169–185; Peter Pastor, "Hungarian Territorial Losses during the Liberal–Democratic Revolution, 1918–1919," in *Trianon and East Central Europe: Antecedents and Repercussions*, ed. Béla Király and László Veszprémy (Boulder, Colo.: Atlantic Research and Publications, 1995), 173–175; Mária Ormos, "The Military Convention of Belgrade," in Király and Veszprémy, *Trianon*, 55–91. Banat, which was also allotted to Romania, was already occupied by Serbian troops and was not the objective of the Romanian advance.

14. Torrey, *Berthelot*, 275–277, 293; Torrey, *Romania and World War I*, 228; Sherman David Spector, *Rumania at the Paris Peace Conference: A Study in the Diplomacy of Ioan I. C. Brătianu* (New York: Bookman Associates, 1962), 102–108.

15. Hoensch, *Hungary*, 85, 90–92; Pastor, "Hungarian Territorial Losses," 177; Spector, *Rumania*, 109, 113–114.

16. György Borsányi, "Béla Kun and His Views on Strategy and Defense," 61–62; Ervin Liptai, "War and Home Defense, October 31, 1918 to November 3, 1918," 26–28; László Forgarassy, "The Eastern Campaign of the Hungarian Red Army, April 1919," 35, all in Pastor, *Revolutions and Interventions*.

17. Tibor Hajdu, "Plans of Strategic Cooperation between the Russian and Hungarian Red Armies" in Pastor, *Revolutions and Interventions*, 367–372; Torrey, *Romania and World War I*, 376–377, 382; Preda et al., *La roumanie*, 281–282, 310–312; Mária Ormos, "The Hungarian Soviet Republic and Intervention by the Entente," in Király and Veszprémy, *Trianon*, 97–98; Forgarassy, "Eastern Campaign," 36.

18. Forgarassy, "Eastern Campaign," 40–44; Preda et al., *La roumanie*, 316–318.

19. Preda et al., *La roumanie*, 320–324; Forgarassy, "Eastern Campaign," 45.

20. Torrey, *Romania and World War I*, 378; Preda et al., *La roumanie*, 329–333; Hajdu, "Plans," 368–369.

21. Tibor Hetés, "The Northern Campaign of the Hungarian Red Army, 1919," 55–59; Peter Gosztony, "The Collapse of the Hungarian Red Army," 69–73; Jean Nouzille, "The July Campaign of the Hungarian Red Army against Romania as Seen by France," 82–84, all in Pastor, *Revolutions and Interventions*; Preda et al., *La roumanie*, 355–383; Torrey, *Romania and World War I*, 381–383.

22. Spector, *Rumania*, 227; Preda et al., *La roumanie*, 405–484; Torrey, *Romania and World War I*, 383–386.

23. Hitchins, *Rumania*, 290–291.

IN CONCLUSION

1. Brătianu, *File rupte*, 21.

2. Marthe Bibesco, *Lord Thomson of Cardington: A Memoir and Some Letters* (London: J. Cape, 1932), 119.

3. Ritter, *Staatskunst und Kriegshandwerk*, 3:249.

4. Stone, *Eastern Front*, 265.

5. I have elaborated and documented this paragraph in Torrey, *Romania and World War I*, 186–191.

6. Hitchins, *Rumania*, 445–450; Hoensch, *Hungary*, 102.

Selected List of Sources

Only the most important sources for this study are mentioned here. Consult the notes for additional references. Acronyms or abbreviations used in the text or notes for these sources appear in brackets.

ARCHIVES

In Romania

Arhivele Militare Române [AMR]
    Fond Marele Cartier Generale [MCG]
    Fond Grigorescu
    Fond Comandamentul Trupelor din Transilvania [CTT]

Arhivele Ministerului Afacerilor Externe Române [AMAER]
    Fond 71/1914/E2

Arhivele Naţionale Istoric Centrale [AN]
    Fond Casa Regală, Fond Regina Maria, Fond Marghiloman, Fond Sturdza, Fond Rosetti, Fond Preşidenţia Consiliului de Miniştri

Biblioteca Centrală de Stat [BCS]
    Fond St. Georges (Arhive Filodor, Coandă, V. Antonescu, Maiorescu, Iliescu)
    Manuscrise
    Corespondenţa

Biblioteca Academiei [BA (Bucharest)]
    Fond Palatului, Fond Sturdza, Fond Kirileanu, Fond Rosetti, Fond Brătianu, Fond Berthelot, Fond A.C. Cuza, Fond Maiorescu
    Manuscrise
    Corespondenţa

In Austria

Österreichisches Staatsarchiv, Haus-, Hof-, und Staatsarchiv [HHStA]
Politisches Archiv [PA], Abteilungen I, X, XVIII, XXXVIII, XL

Österreichisches Staatsarchiv, Kriegsarchiv [KA (Vienna)]
Armeeoberkommando [AOK]
AOK Ops. Geheime nos. 494–2035 (1917–1918)
Verbindungsoffiziere [VO], Fasz. 6270–6480
VO/OKM (Bucharest)
VO/BGK (Bulgaria)
VO/R (Iaşi, 1918)
Neue Feldakten [NFA]
1. Op. Armee [1st Armeekmdo]
Nachrichten Abteilungen [NA] Fasz. 33, 118, 123, 124, 145, 255
Manuskripte Weltkrieg
Rudolf Kiszling, "Der Feldzug in Siebenbürgen und Rumänien,"
"Unterlagen über die Österrich-Ungarns Mitwirkung bei den
Friedenverhandlungen mit Rumänien," "Der Österreich-Ungarns
Vormarsch in die Ukraine 1918"
Nachlässe
B892, Nachlass Seeckt

In Germany

Archiv des Auswärtigen Amts (Berlin) [AA], Politisches Archiv [PA]
Deutschland 128 no. 2, Deutschland 130, Rumänien 11, Weltkrieg 2f no. 2
Kommissionakten Brest-Litovsk/Bukarest, Bukaresterakten

Bundesarchiv [BA (Koblenz)]
Sammlungen Ersten Weltkrieg Balkan
Akten des Reichskanzlei
Various Nachlässe

Bundesarchiv/Militärarchiv [BA/MA (Freiburg)]
Bestand: N 326, N 440, PH 5, PH 51, RA 7/704, RM 40, RM 401

Bayerisches Hauptstaatsarchiv, Kriegsarchiv [KA (Munich)]
Bestand Weltkrieg 1914–1918
Alpenkorps, Abteilung 1a, 1b

Württembergisches Hauptstaatsarchiv, Kriegsarchiv [KA (Stuttgart)]
Württembergisches Gebirgs Bataillon [WGB]
M-130 Tagebücher, Gefechtsberichte, Skizzen
M-130/9 "Das Württembergisches Gebirgs-Bataillon in Rumänien"

M-1/11 "Tagebuch des Oberleutnant Rommel . . . August 1917"
Nachlass Friedrich Gerok

In France

Service historique de l'armée de terre (Vincennes) [SHAT]
Various series especially 6N, 7N, 16N, 17N, 20N, 1K77

Archives Diplomatiques, Ministère des Affaires Étrangères (Paris) [AD]
Série Guerre 1914–1918, Balkans/Roumanie, Russie/Bessarabie
Série Europe 1918–1929, Roumanie

Elsewhere

Moscow, *Tsentral'nyi Gosudarstvennyi Voenno-Istoricheskii Arkhiv [TsGVIA]*
Fond 69

Rome, *Archivio Storico Diplomatico del Ministero degli Affari Esteri [AS (Rome)]*
1914–1918, Romania, Telegrammi di Gabinetto in Arrivo

London, *Public Record Office [PRO]*
Foreign Office [FO] especially classes 371, 608, 800

Stanford, CA, *Hoover Institution Archives*
Collections Heroys, Krupensky

Washington, DC, *National Archives and Records Administration [NARA]*
War Department, Reports of the Military Attaché in Romania
Papers of General Hans von Seeckt, Microcopy M-132
Wilhelm Groener, "Memoirs," Microcopy M-137

PUBLISHED DOCUMENTS

Eftimie Ardeleanu, Alexandru Oşca, and Dumitru Preda, eds., *Istoria Statului Major General Român. Documente 1859–1947*. Bucharest: Editura Militară, 1994.

Eftimie Ardeleanu, ed., *Marele Cartier General al armatei române. Documente 1916–1920*. Bucharest: Editura Machiavelli, 1996. [*MCG . . . Documente*]

Eftimie Ardeleanu, Adrian Pandea, and Ion Pavelescu, eds., *Proba focului. Ultima treaptă spre mare unire. Dosare ale participării României în primul război mondial*. Bucharest: Editura Globus, 1991.

Constantin Căzănişteanu, ed., *Mărăşti, Mărăşeşti, Oituz. Documente militare*. Bucharest: Editura Militară, 1977. [*MMO*]

Jean-Noel Grandhomme and Thiery Sarmant, eds., *La Roumanie dans la grand guerre et l'effondrement de l'armée russe. Édition critique des rapports du Général Berthelot, chef de la mission française en Roumanie, 1916–1918*. Paris: L'Harmattan, 2001.

Alexandru Oşca, Dumitru Preda, Eftimie Ardeleanu, eds., *Proiecte şi planuri de operaţii al marele stat-major român (pîna în 1916)*. Bucharest: Arhivele Militare Române, 1992.

ACCOUNTS OF MILITARY OPERATIONS

Romanian

Ministerul de Războiu, Marele Stat Major, Serviciul Istoric, *România în război mondial, 1916–1919*, 4 vols. + 4 vols. Documente-anexe. Bucharest: Imprimerea Naţională, 1934–1946. [*RRM*]

The official history prepared by the Historical Service of the Romanian General Staff. Based not only on access to Romanian military archives but on additional documentation provided by the German Reichsarchiv and the Austrian Kriegsarchiv. *RRM* contains an extremely detailed, chronological account of military operations without comment or interpretation. Unfortunately, its publication ceased in 1946 during the political upheaval after World War II and is unlikely to be completed. Its 5,000 total pages of text and documents have been a gold mine for subsequent researchers, but they cover only the period August 1916 to January 1917. Some Romanian critics claim that the tone of the earliest volumes favors the German army and its command.

Gheorghe A. Dabija, *Armata română în războiul mondial 1916–1918*. 4 vols. Bucharest: Editura IG Hertz, 1936.

During the war, Dabija served on the general staff of two Romanian armies and later as a brigade and division commander. After the war, he joined the Army Historical Service, where he used its Romanian and foreign documentation for this detailed (2,300 pages) account. Dabija uses his extensive linguistic abilities to access a wide variety of sources. He freely expresses his opinions, which are generally favorable to Averescu and critical of Prezan and the High Command. Given the incompleteness of the official history, his 700-page volume 4 provides indispensable detail on the crucial battles of 1917. It includes liberal reproduction not only of Romanian operational orders and reports, but those of the German and Austrian forces as well.

Alexandru Ioaniţiu, *Războiul româniei, 1916–1918*. Bucharest: Tipografia Geniului, n.d.

Ioaniţiu likewise served in the war and in the Historical Service, where he also used its resources for this 400-page survey of military operations. He concentrates on 1916, reserving a mere 80 pages for the 1917 campaign. His account is concise, factual, and largely free of comment or interpretation. Of special value are its annexes, which list the orders of battle for Romanian, Russian, German, Austro-Hungarian, Bulgarian, and Turkish units, including their commanders and chiefs of staff. Incidentally, Ioaniţiu rose to become chief of staff of the Romanian army in 1940 and died in an airplane accident while visiting the Russian Front in 1941.

Constantin Kirițescu, *Istoria războiului pentru întregirea României, 1916–1919*. 2nd ed. 3 vols. Bucharest: Editura Casei Scoalelor, 1925.

A modified second edition has been republished in two volumes (Bucharest: Editura, Ştiințifică şi Enciclopedică, 1989). There is also an abbreviated single-volume French translation.

Constantin Kirițescu, *La Roumanie dans la guerre mondiale* (1916–1919), trans. L. Barral. Paris: Payot, 1934. The citations in this study are from the 1925 second edition.

Deeply affected by the experience of the war, Kirițescu, an educator and self-taught historian, determined to make available to a "wide public . . . especially young people" the story of "those millions of heroes, dead in order to make us a great and free nation." His is the classical nationalist history of the war, which had an enormous influence on the postwar generation. Despite its limitations, it contains a useful, comprehensive account of military operations, including the Hungarian campaign of 1919. In addition, he movingly describes the nation's experience on the home front.

Victor Atanasiu et al., *România în anii primului război mondial*. 2 vols. Bucharest: Editura Militară, 1987. [*RAPRM*]

A quasiofficial history by a team of authors that covers the home front as well. It contains more than a dozen well-organized, comprehensive chapters on military operations with accompanying maps and sketches. It maintains a nationalist point of view and emphasizes the valor and sacrifice of Romanian soldiers.

Ion Cupşa, *Armata română în campaniile din anii 1916, 1917*. Bucharest: Editura Militară, 1967.

A short, balanced, thoughtful account of military operations based on the most important Romanian printed sources plus a fresh look at some of the relevant archival material. Cupşa comes to sensible conclusions on disputed issues. Includes a helpful bibliographical essay and maps.

Costica Prodan and Dumitru Preda, *The Romanian Army during the First World War*. Bucharest: Univers Enciclopedic, 1998.

Authored by two well-published members of the Romanian Commission on Military History, it provides a concise, factually reliable survey for the English reader with excellent maps. The narrative continues through the Hungarian campaign of 1919. It is written from a Romanian perspective but takes note of secondary literature from abroad. Its text is not documented but its detail, including helpful statistics, demonstrates that the authors utilized archival information and relevant printed sources.

Non-Romanian

Austria, Kriegsarchiv, *Österreich-Ungarns Letzter Krieg, 1914–1918*. 7 vols. + 7 vols. Beilagen. Vienna: Verlag der Militärwissenschaft Mitteilungen, 1930–1938.

This official history devotes extensive coverage to operations on the Romanian

Front, which is largely the work of the noted historian Rudolf Kiszling. He was the chief of staff of the Austrian 71st ID on the Romanian Front during the war and later the chief of the Historical Section of the Kriegsarchiv. The Beilagen (annexes) include many elaborate maps as well as helpful charts that detail all AustroHungarian and German troop movements to and from Romania.

Germany, Reichsarchiv, *Der Weltkrieg 1914 bis 1918*. 14 vols. Berlin: Mittler, 1925–1954.

This official history contains less detail on the Romanian Front than the Austrian account but is essential in following the interplay within the German command and its relations with its allies, especially the Bulgarians. It is candid about the mistakes made during the failed offensive to subdue the Romanian army in the 1917 campaign.

Erich von Falkenhayn, *Campania armatei 9-a împotriva românilor și rușilor 1916–1917*. Translated from the German by Al. Budiș and C. Franc. Bucharest: Socec, 1937. Original German edition: *Der Feldzug der 9. Armee gegen die Rumänien und Russen 1916/1917*. Berlin: Mittler, 1921. The citations in this study are from the Romanian edition.

"Written for the most part at the time the events developed," Falkenhayn tells us, this is both a memoir and an account of operations under Falkenhayn's command. Of special interest is his personal reaction to developments on the battlefield as well as explanations of the reasoning behind his tactical decisions. The general left his Romanian command before the 1917 campaign.

Ernst Kabisch, *Der Rumänienkrieg, 1916*. Berlin: Vorhut-Verlag Otto Schegel, 1938. This short but informed account by General Kabisch is based on the most important German and Austrian published sources, but no Romanian ones. It is aimed at a general audience and covers only the 1916 operations. Kabisch admires Falkenhayn and considers the Romanian campaign a validation of the general's military ability.

Victor Pétin, *Le drame roumain 1916–1918*. Paris: Payot, 1932. Pétin served as chief of staff on Berthelot's mission in 1916–1917. His book is both a memoir and an account of the operations of the Romanian army after the arrival of the French mission in October. Pétin had access to the archives of that mission and to unpublished accounts of its members. His emphasis is on the Battle of Bucharest (November–December 1916), in whose conception and implementation he was intimately involved. Unfortunately, the book devotes only a brief epilogue to the year 1917, a weakness of almost all non-Romanian accounts.

Jean Leopold Èmile Bujac, *Campagnes de l'armée roumaine 1916–1919*. Paris: Charles-Lavauzelle, 1933. Bujac, a French interwar military critic and writer, utilized a variety of published sources available in 1933. He gives a comprehensive account of military operations in the campaign of 1916, but the narrative is less successful in clarifying the overall course of operations and what was going on behind the front, especially at the command level. A more serious omission is his cursory treatment of the campaign of 1917, which devotes only 21 pages to the critical battles of Mărăşti, Mărăşeşti, and Oituz, with only a single page on the latter. Nevertheless, he adds a third section on the Hungarian campaign of 1919.

Norman Stone, *The Eastern Front, 1914–1917.* New York: Charles Scribner's Sons, 1975.

Stone devotes only one chapter to the Romanian Front. However, his survey of developments on the Eastern Front, 1914–1916, provides a helpful context for Romania's two years of negotiation with the Entente. His chapter on the Brusilov Offensive takes a critical look at the attitude of the Russian command toward Romania's intervention and its reluctance to aid it immediately. His coverage of Romania's campaign of 1916 is based on Russian and Austrian sources but not Romanian ones. Stone does not cover the campaign of 1917.

MEMOIRS/BIOGRAPHIES

Alexander Averescu, *Notiţe zilnice din război*, vol. 1, 1914–1916, and vol. 2, 1916–1918. Edited by Eftimie Ardeleanu and Adrian Pandea. Bucharest: Editura Militară, 1992. [NZ]

Publication of the first edition of General Averescu's journal (1937) created a sensation because of its vitriolic and often unfair comments directed at King Ferdinand, Brătianu, Berthelot, Prezan, and the High Command. Averescu assumes his own ideas to be correct, and his failures are blamed on others. Nevertheless, he was a major actor in over 30 years of Romanian history. His account is essential for understanding many events and command decisions during the war.

Petre Otu, *Mareşalul Alexandru Averescu: militarul, omul politic, legenda.* Bucharest: Editura Militară, 2005.

Military historian Otu has written an excellent, critical, and balanced assessment of Averescu's career. The general's wrongheaded attitudes and mistakes are prominently discussed, as are those that were wise and correct. Averescu comes across as a flawed personality but a great military leader in Romania's time of crisis. A much-needed book.

Petre Otu, *Mareşalul Constantin Prezan. Vocaţia datoriei.* Bucharest: Editura Militară, 2009.

Prezan left little personal source material for a biographer, with no journal or memoirs other than a short memorandum. Even his official dispatches and memoranda during the war were, for the most part, written by Antonescu. Otu has gleaned enough information from official documents and the testimony of contemporaries as well as from printed media to present a believable, nuanced portrait. He acknowledges the general's limitations but argues that he should be judged on his life of character and service, especially his steady leadership of the Romanian High Command during the war.

Radu R. Rosetti, *Mărturisiri 1914–1919.* Edited by Maria Georgescu. Bucharest: Editura Modelism, 1997.

Rosetti, Brătianu's brother-in-law, was an insider at the Romanian Command in 1914–1916, later a field commander, and a member of Berthelot's staff in 1918–1919. His memoirs are supplemented with reference to the journals of other officers and documents from the Romanian army archives. His account is valuable for gaining insight into the functioning of the Romanian High Command in 1916, for an account of his role as a regimental commander in the heavy combat of 1917, and documentation of Berthelot's return to Romania in October 1918.

Ion Gheorghe Duca, *Amintiri politice*. 3 vols. Munich: Jon Dumitru-Verlag, 1982.
As the cabinet minister closest to Brătianu, Duca participated in many crucial meetings and decisions during the war. As might be expected, his memoir is partisan, especially in its anti-Averescu tone. But it is essential in understanding what was going on behind the scenes in Romanian political and military life, especially since Brătianu left no personal account.

Constantin Argetoianu, *Pentru cei de mîine. Amintiri din vremea celor de ieri*. 5 vols. Edited by Stelian Neagoe. Bucharest: Humanitas-Machiavelli, 1991–1995.
Composed in the 1930s, Argetoianu's memoirs are valuable as he was a well-informed figure in the political elite, a member of Averescu's cabinet, and the Romanian signatory of the Peace of Buftea. They are full of colorful and quotable phrases, but as his editor points out, Argetoianu sometimes does not clearly delineate the line between history and literature. After the war, Argetoianu gained a reputation as an unprincipled politician.

Alexandru Marghiloman, *Note politice, 1897–1924*. 5 vols. Bucharest: Eminescu, 1927.
These detailed journal entries are invaluable for understanding not only Marghiloman's premiership in 1918, but also the course of events in occupied Romania, including the thinking of Mackensen's command. Marghiloman still awaits a proper evaluation of the unpopular and self-sacrificing role he played when accommodation with the Central Powers became necessary.

Non-Romanian

Glenn E. Torrey, ed., *General Henri Berthelot and Romania. Mémoires et Correspondance 1916–1919*. Boulder, Colo.: East European Monographs, 1987.
Berthelot's testimony, based on his journal entries and letters to his family, provide insight into the work of the French Mission, the role of France and the Entente, and the functioning of the Romanian command. Berthelot had enormous influence on King Ferdinand, Brătianu, and Prezan. He fostered a spirit of resistance and hope among the population as well as among their leaders. His anti-Averescu bias is proverbial.

Glenn E. Torrey, *Henri Mathias Berthelot. Soldier of France, Defender of Romania*. Iaşi: Center for Romanian Studies, 2001.
Approximately half of this biography is devoted to the general's involvement

with Romania. It is based on his memoirs, letters to his family, and his personal papers, as well as documents in the French military archives. It explains why Berthelot became a hero in Romania and is counted as one of the principal founders of Greater Romania.

Wolfgang Foerster, ed., *Mackensen. Briefe and Aufzeichnungen des Generalfeld-marschalls aus Krieg und Frieden*. Leipzig: Bibliographisches Institut AG, 1938.

Mackensen's key role in every aspect of the war against Romania renders his memoirs indispensable for understanding the military operations and the occupation policy of the Central Powers. Personally, he gained great satisfaction from his experience in Romania and even developed a fondness for the country.

Curt von Morgen, *Meiner Truppen Heldenkämpfe*. Berlin: Mittler, 1920.

Only a portion of Morgen's memoirs covers the Romanian Front, but they are important because of his command of the German I Reserve Corps in both the 1916 and 1917 campaigns as well as his role in the armistice and peace negotiations.

Erwin Rommel, *Attacks*. Vienna, Va.: Athena Press, 1979. Original German edition: *Infantrie greift an*. Potsdam: Voggenreiter, 1937. First English edition: *Infantry Attacks*, translated by G. E. Kidde. Washington, D.C.: Infantry Journal, 1944. Citations in this study are from the 1979 edition.

Rommel, as a first lieutenant in the Württemberg Mountain Battalion in the Romanian campaigns of 1916 and 1917, demonstrated the brilliant and aggressive combat leadership that later made him world famous. His original German account was translated by the American military during World War II and reportedly had a great influence on General George C. Patton. Rommel's detailed combat account provides insight into the Romanian army's failure in the first year of the war and its strong resistance in the second, which draws his repeated praise.

SPECIALIZED STUDIES

Timothy C. Dowling, *The Brusilov Offensive*. Bloomington: Indiana University Press, 2008.

This study, based on archival research in the Austrian Kriegsarchiv, carefully traces the background, course, and consequences of the last successful Russian offensive. Dowling's account is helpful in clarifying the context in which the Romanians carried out their final negotiations with the Entente in July and August 1916. He considers Romanian intervention to be the most significant accomplishment of the Brusilov Offensive.

Oskar Regele, *Kampf um die Donau 1916*. Potsdam: Ludwig Voggenreiter Verlag, 1940.

Regele, a noted Austrian historian, utilized a wide variety of German, Austrian, and Romanian printed sources for this detailed study of both the Romanian assault crossing of the Danube in October and that of the Central Powers in November. Accompanied by excellent maps and diagrams, this is the definitive study from the perspective of the Central Powers.

Elke Bornemann, *Der Frieden von Bukarest 1918*. Frankfurt: Peter Lang, 1978.

Based on German and Austrian archival material (but not Romanian), this detailed study is easily the best account of the negotiation of the Romanian peace written from the perspective of the Central Powers. The author analyzes at length each of the major clauses of the peace treaty. A strong point is its description of the interplay among the various echelons of the political and military authorities of the Central Powers.

Ion Giurcă, *1917. Reorganizarea armatei române*. Bucharest: Editura Academiei de Înalte Studii Militare, 1999.

Giurcă uses documents from the Romanian military archives to detail the rebuilding of the Romanian army during the period December 1916–July 1917. Much statistical information is included.

Dumitru Seserman, *Acţiunile armatei române în spaţiul dintre Carpaţii Orientali şi Nistru* (1917–1920). Bucharest: Editura Universităţii Naţionale de Apărare, 2004.

Seserman documents the efforts of the Romanian army to control the revolutionary disorder of the Russian army, first in Moldavia and then in Bessarabia. He provides details of the Romanian occupation of Bessarabia in 1918 and the immediate postwar period. Based on Romanian military archives.

Dumitru Preda, Vasile Alexandrescu, and Costica Prodan, *La roumanie et sa guerre pour l'unité nationale. Campagne de 1918–1919*. Bucharest: Éditions Encyclopédiques, 1995.

This is the definitive Romanian account of the entry of the Romanian army into Transylvania and its occupation of Hungary in 1919. Based on archival sources, it covers military operations in great detail. Romanian action in Hungary is explained and defended. It contains helpful information on the condition and remobilization of the Romanian army in October–November 1918.

Glenn E. Torrey, *The Revolutionary Russian Army and Romania, 1917*. Pittsburgh, Pa.: University of Pittsburgh, Carl Beck Papers, 1995. In Romanian translation: *Armata revolutionară rusă şi România 1917*. Bucharest: Editura Militară, 2005.

This text traces the rise of revolutionary disorder among Russian soldiers on the Romanian Front after the March revolution and its effect on both the Russian and Romanian armies. Based on Romanian, Russian, French, and Austrian archival material.

Ion Ţurcanu, *Unirea Basarabiei cu România. Preludii, premise, realizări. 1918*. Chişinău: Tipografia Centrală, 1998.

Ţurcanu, a contemporary historian in the Republic of Moldova, brings together several of his studies to explain the development of the Moldavian National Movement in 1917, the proclamation of the Independent Moldavian Republic, the intervention of the Romanian army, and the union of Bessarabia with Romania in 1918. His account is balanced, and his conclusions, as a whole, stake out middle ground between supporters and critics of Romanian intervention.

Izeaslav Levit, *An de răspîntie. De la proclamarea Republicii Moldoveneşti pînă la desfi-inţarea autonomiei Basarabiei (noiembrie 1917–noiembrie 1918)*. Chişinău: Univer-sul, 2003.

Levit covers some of the same ground as Ţurcanu but from the Russian point of view. He goes into detail on the Romanian occupation, and understandably, he is highly critical. Levit is also critical of the Sfatul Ţării and the union with Romania. Although Levit is arguing a thesis, his account is good balance to many traditional Romanian accounts.

Jean-Noel Grandhomme, "Le Général Berthelot et l'action de la France en Roumanie et en Russie Méridionale (1916–1918)." Thesis, University of Paris, 1998.

A detailed history of French military missions headed by General Berthelot in Romania and South Russia. It provides background on the composition, func-tioning, and life of the personnel of the missions as well as on their attitudes to-ward the Romanians. Based on a wide variety of material from French military archives and from private accounts of individual members of the mission. This is an exhaustive and authoritative survey.

Şerban Rădulescu-Zoner and Beatrice Marinescu, *Bucureştii în anii primul război mondial, 1914–1918*. Bucharest: Albatros, 1993.

This book captures the atmosphere in Romania's capital during the period of neutrality when entry into the war was being debated in the press and on the street. During the campaign of 1916, it follows the swing of public opinion from hope to fear as a defeat emerged. It also provides an informative and interesting account of life under enemy occupation.

Background Studies

Keith Hitchins, *Rumania 1866–1947*. Oxford: Oxford University Press, 1994.

This book, which is by far the most informed and reliable guide to the history of modern Romania, provides the larger historical context to the subject of the pres-ent study. It couples the author's long familiarity with a full range of primary and secondary sources with balanced analysis. Of special interest for the pres-ent study is Hitchins's discussion of Romanians outside of Romania, particu-larly in the Austro-Hungarian and Russian empires. His analysis of these mi-norities and their status, a subject enmeshed in controversy, is dispassionate and fair.

Charles King, *The Moldovans: Romania, Russia, and the Politics of Culture*. Stanford, Calif.: Hoover Institution Press, 2000.

King provides an excellent survey of the history of the new Republic of Moldova, which occupies the territory between the Prut and Dniester rivers, at one time known as Bessarabia. His account of its transition from the eastern sec-tion of the medieval Romanian principality of Moldova (known in English as Moldavia) through its years under Russian rule from 1812 to 1918 is a helpful background to understanding events during the war. His description of Bessarabia under Romanian administration in the interwar period, as Soviet Moldova (1940–1991), and as contemporary independent Moldova is a reliable guide in controversial territory.

Jean-Noel Grandhomme, *La Roumanie de la Triplice a l'Entente, 1914–1919.* Paris: Éditions Soteca, 2009.

Grandhomme provides an informed survey of Romania's shift from the prewar German alliance to her postwar role in the French alliance system. In addition to two short chapters on the military operations in 1916–1917, others cover the pre-1914 background, the period of neutrality in 1914–1916, the Romanian experience of enemy occupation, the consolidation of Greater Romania in 1919, and the nation's role in postwar Europe. His conclusions on controversial issues are balanced.

Sherman David Spector, *Rumania at the Paris Peace Conference.* New York: Bookman Associates, 1962.

A pioneering study of the diplomacy of Premier Ion Brătianu. After surveying the periods of neutrality and war, Spector gives detailed attention to his role in the postwar negotiations at Paris. Although based on sources available in 1962, it is still extremely helpful, especially in following the response of the Great Powers to Brătianu's impassioned and inflexible arguments for Romania's desiderata.

Collections of Studies

Costica Prodan and Dumitru Preda, eds., *ACTA III al III-lea colcviu internaţional de istorie militară.* Bucharest: Comisia Română de Istorie Militară, 1996.

Communications presented on the eightieth anniversary of Romania's entry into the war and the operations of 1916 by historians from Romania, England, France, Bulgaria, Serbia, and Portugal. Of special interest are articles on the Serb division fighting in Dobrogea, the Romanian Aviation Service, local reaction to the entry of the Romanian army into Transylvania, and the reconstruction of the Romanian army.

V. F. Dobrinescu and Horia Dumitrescu, eds., *1917 pe frontal de est.* Focşani: Editura Vantrop, 1997.

A substantial volume of papers presented at Focşani on the eightieth anniversary of the Battles of Mărăşti, Mărăşeşti, and Oituz by Romanian historians. Several were of particular interest for this study, including two that analyze the role of Ion Antonescu, the differences between the plans of Averescu and Prezan for the 1917 offensive of the Romanian army, the functioning of Orthodox chaplains during the war, and the commemoration of the Battle of Mărăşeşti as a national holiday.

Glenn E. Torrey, *Romania and World War I: A Collection of Studies.* Iaşi: Center for Romanian Studies, 1999.

A reprint of 19 articles first published in American, Canadian, English, German, Australian, and Romanian historical journals covering specific aspects of Romania's neutrality, belligerence, and the occupation of Hungary in 1919.

Kurt Treptow, ed., *Romania in the World War I Era*. Iaşi: Center for Romanian Studies, 1999.

A collection of articles by American, Romanian, and British historians on various aspects of Romania before, during, and after the war. It includes contributions on personalities such as Professor Nicolae Iorga, Queen Marie, and Ion Antonescu. The one on the latter, authored by Larry Watts, provides a detailed analysis of his role as the Romanian army's operations officer. The volume also contains several contributions on the influence of the war on Romanian culture.

Index